Morals and Markets

Morals and Markets

An Evolutionary Account of the Modern World

Daniel Friedman

palgrave
macmillan

MORALS AND MARKETS
Copyright © Daniel Friedman, 2008.

First published in 2008 by PALGRAVE MACMILLAN® in the US—a division
of St. Martin's Press LLC, 175 Fifth Avenue, New York, NY 10010.

Where this book is distributed in the UK, Europe and the rest of the world,
this is by Palgrave Macmillan, a division of Macmillan Publishers Limited,
registered in England, company number 785998, of Houndmills,
Basingstoke, Hampshire RG21 6XS.

Palgrave Macmillan is the global academic imprint of the above companies and has
companies and representatives throughout the world.

Palgrave® and Macmillan® are registered trademarks in the United States, the United
Kingdom, Europe and other countries.

ISBN-13: 978-0-230-60097-3
ISBN-10: 0-230-60097-2

Library of Congress Cataloging-in-Publication Data

Friedman, Daniel, 1947–
   Morals and markets : an evolutionary account of the modern world / by Daniel
Friedman.
      p. cm.
   Includes bibliographical references and index.
   ISBN 0-230-60097-2
   1. Economics—Moral and ethical aspects. 2. Free enterprise—Moral and ethical
aspects. 3. Capitalism—Moral and ethical aspects. 4. Business ethics. I. Title.

HB72.F75 2008
174'.4—dc22   2008004018

A catalogue record of the book is available from the British Library.

Design by Scribe Inc.

First edition: September 2008

10 9 8 7 6 5 4 3 2 1

Printed in the United States of America.

Transferred to Digital Printing in 2011

Contents

Prologue

This book is about the modern world. We have acquired deep knowledge of stars and atoms, and increasingly, of our human selves. Networks of cooperation and friendship span the globe. Yet at the same time, we have ugly politics, recurrent genocides, a deteriorating environment, and more than a billion people living in desperate poverty. How did our world become a crazy quilt of such magnificence and squalor?

The book has a thesis about how human morals and markets shape our world. Once grasped, the idea is rather simple. But it goes against ideologies of both the Left and the Right, and so it takes a while to explain. I'll spell it out later in this prologue.

The book is based on science. It is my personal summary of insights recently gained by an amazing collection of economists, anthropologists, psychologists, biologists, political scientists, and mathematicians.

But the book is not a scientific monograph. It doesn't delve deep into technicalities, or sort out all controversies, or try to give the final word. It aims to enlighten, entertain, and inspire the reader to learn more.

I try to convey the main ideas by telling true stories. Most of them are quite short, just a paragraph or so, and they run the gamut from amoebas and William Blake to Boris Yeltsin and Zorro. Each story helps explain something about morals or markets or the connections between the two.

Let's begin with the tangled tale of the Crooked E.

Anatomy of a Scandal

In the late 1990s, the Enron Corporation was a corporate superstar. Ambitious MBAs flocked to Houston, each hoping to be the next Rebecca Mark—she built Azurix, a (supposedly) visionary trading platform plus international water utility, and pocketed more than $100 million. Enron topped Fortune magazine's list of the most innovative companies for five straight years, put its name on the Houston Astros' baseball stadium, and enjoyed direct access to the White House and Congress. Enron's rise seemed unstoppable.

But Enron stalled out in 2001, and then cratered. In January, California's governor Gray Davis blamed Enron and other "out-of-state profiteers" for his state's energy crisis. In February, Enron CEO Kenneth Lay stepped down in favor of Jeffrey Skilling. Rumors of questionable profits began to surface, but the accountants at Arthur Andersen continued to give Enron clean reports. By May, the stock price had started to drop and, during the summer and fall, top executives quietly sold off large chunks of their own shares. Mr. Skilling shocked analysts when he resigned in July, and by October, the *Wall Street Journal* reported a brewing scandal. The Securities and Exchange Commission (SEC) began to investigate. In December, Enron filed for bankruptcy. Investor losses eventually reached about $60 billion, and Skilling, Lay, and more than a dozen other Enron officials were sentenced for fraud, conspiracy, and other crimes.

In 2002, WorldCom admitted falsifying its income statements and became the biggest bankrupt company ever. The scandal wave soon swept away other corporate giants such as HealthSouth, Tyco, and Arthur Andersen, and brought jail terms to many, even homemaking icon Martha Stewart. The firm managing my own pension lost over $140 million on Enron alone, but I am much luckier than the many thousands of people who lost their jobs or their life savings.

The 2001–3 scandals were spectacular, but they were not the first to hit our markets, nor the last. As I write this paragraph in late 2007, the subprime mortgage mess threatens millions of homeowners, and CEOs at several of the world's most powerful banks are being fired as they report losses in the billions or tens of billions. Apparently, loan officers pushed many homeowners into inappropriate mortgages and, partly due to complex financial engineering, the banks misled themselves and everyone else about who would be responsible for delinquencies.

What caused these epidemics of immoral behavior? And why did they devastate our financial markets? The answers reveal much about the modern world, but at the same time, they raise deeper questions. Like peeling an onion, we'll take it one layer at a time.

Markets were devastated because they are built on trust. You don't put your hard-earned money into banks or pension funds (or stocks) unless you are confident that they will honor their promises and return your money with interest (or your share of the earnings). Enron, WorldCom, and the others violated that trust. They lied about what they were doing and hid behind accounting gimmicks.

But surely, the top officials knew that the gimmicks and lies might be discovered and ultimately lead to bankruptcy, disgrace, and jail. Why would they take the risk? The answer is high power incentives. Top managers at Enron were already at risk of losing their jobs if they failed to meet short-run earnings targets. By the same token, they could get huge rewards if reported earnings grew quickly. Azurix projected impressive earnings and Rebecca Mark got her monster bonuses, even though Azurix ended up losing money after she moved on. Jeffrey Skilling pushed special purpose entities (SPEs) that hid big losses and turned red ink into black, and he got even bigger bonuses and the top job. Less aggressive executives were left in the dust, or even out of work.

It wasn't just Enron. Over the last decade or two, top American company managers who met earnings goals took home on average about ten times as much money as their predecessors of the previous generation—enough to support dozens, or hundreds, of middle-class families. But those who don't meet the goals are more likely than ever to be fired. Given such a choice, you might choose to bend the rules. Or, if you had unusually strong moral principles, you might look for a different line of work.

Of course, this answer begs a deeper question: why did companies choose such high power incentives? The answer lies in the next layer down: market imperatives for rapid change.

More than ever before, in the 1990s, businesses had to adjust quickly to the changing world, as globalization and information technology opened new opportunities and new competitive threats. Rapid response could easily hurt some people, like the company's traditional suppliers or customers, or longtime local workers who couldn't match the flexibility and low cost of young workers in Mexico or Korea or China. Old-fashioned managers often delayed action to reduce the pain. The new high power incentives were supposed to encourage ruthless efficiency and quick response to the new threats and opportunities.

Corporate policy makers realized that the high power incentives required safeguards. Auditors, corporate boards of directors, independent stock analysts, and government agencies—they all are there to monitor top executives and to keep them honest. But in several industries, the safeguards all failed. Why?

The details vary, but the basic theme is the same: the high power market incentives corroded the moral infrastructure and shrank the safeguards. Take auditors, for example. Arthur Andersen and the other big accounting firms developed a new, very profitable line of business: consulting. Leveraging the detailed knowledge gained from auditing a company's books, they began selling advice on how to reduce taxes and other costs, and also on how to respond to new opportunities and threats. Even when they only state the obvious, consultants can be useful change agents. Managers can blame the most painful decisions on their high-priced consultants.

But consulting compromises the auditors—a bad audit report might derail the consulting gravy train. Conflicts of interest also increased for Boards of Directors and outside stock analysts. For example, back in 1998, stock analyst John Olson raised questions about Enron's earnings prospects. He was forced out by his employer, Merrill Lynch, which hoped to earn millions of dollars underwriting new Enron securities.

The official government watchdogs—the regulatory agencies—were compromised by politics and corporate donations. For example, the SEC chairman Arthur Levitt tried to crack down on misleading accounting for the biggest slice of top executives' pay—special stock options—but pressure from Congress forced him to back off.

Elected representatives, of course, are supposed to look after the interests of their constituents, including investors, workers, and taxpayers who are hurt when the economy malfunctions. But election campaigns rely on donations and have become quite expensive. The biggest donors often are corporations with the most to gain from favorable government decisions, notably Enron and the large accounting firms in the 1990s.

Voters are the last line of defense in a democracy. Scandals can trigger their sense of moral outrage, and that helps keep officials honest and reform-minded.

Congress created the SEC after corporate scandals in the 1920s helped precipitate the Great Depression in the 1930s. Both presidential candidates played the morality card in the 2000 presidential election, but the Republicans did so more successfully. The new administration gave the top SEC job to Harvey Pitt, who initially promised to give managers and auditors an easier time than Levitt. As the scandal intensified, Pitt backtracked and eventually was forced out. In 2002, Congress passed the Sarbanes-Oxley Act, which increases corporate accounting and reporting requirements. It's not yet clear whether the extra protection justifies the extra cost.

A Marital Spat

The corporate scandals have a unifying theme. At each layer—top managers, auditors, analysts, boards of directors, regulators, Congress, voters—market imperatives trumped moral imperatives. Yet, the result was that markets (and the public!) took a terrible beating.

The story raises deeper questions: what, really, are market imperatives, and why do they matter so much? And what are the real moral imperatives? Where do they come from? What drives the conflict between markets and morals, and how might it be resolved?

This book will work on these questions. Its premise is that the modern world is a troubled marriage of morals and markets. The scandals are but one example of marital discord, where markets sabotaged morals, and morals hurt markets. We will see that many of the world's worst problems—environmental disasters, criminal gangs, terrorism, and war—also come from struggles between markets and morals. Yet, sometimes, the marriage works well, and brings health, wealth, and new friends to billions of people across the planet.

Here is the thesis in a nutshell. All social creatures face a fundamental dilemma—what's good for the individual is not always what's good for the group. Humans evolved two distinctive new ways to cope with this dilemma. Morals go back to our human origins, and work best in small groups. Markets work best at large scale, and their rise 200 years ago ushered in the modern world. With 6.6 billion mouths to feed, divorce is not an option. Prospects for the future will brighten when reformers, and the general public, better understand the marriage of morals and markets, and work to improve it.

Where We are Going

Chapter 1 tells stories about amoebas, vampire bats, bonobos, and chimps in order to spotlight the fundamental social dilemma, and prehuman devices for coping with it. Our own species grew up with a moral system built on those earlier devices.

The chapter defines morals in terms of a group's shared understanding of what's right and what's wrong, and how people are supposed to behave. Morals are the linchpin of human culture, and they enable groups of humans to cooperate. They are anchored in powerful feelings, such as gratitude, guilt, and vengeance, and rely on our ability to read each other's emotions and intentions. Stories about mirror neurons and about games played in remote tribes show how morals work and point to the role of gossip and the in-group effect.

The second chapter traces the emergence of civilization and the moral origins of markets. Stories about the very ancient city of Uruk, and about nearby shepherds, illustrate how morals changed from egalitarian to hierarchical. The black glass called obsidian, Joseph in Egypt, and several other tales show how one aspect of morals—gift exchange—gradually gave rise to money, prices, and the marketplace—the bazaar. The chapter explains the unrivalled power of markets to organize masses of people, and also lists markets' many weaknesses.

Chapter 3 recounts a great transformation two centuries ago. The economy, once subordinate to rigid custom and ties of vassalage, slipped its bonds in Western Europe and began to reshape nations. China's treasure ships and the stories of two Henrys—Portugal's Navigator and Champaign's Count—illustrate the process. Markets catalyzed political and legal changes and technological advances, and these, in turn, catalyzed further market advances. These runaway feedback loops brought us modernity.

Why Western Europe? Why not earlier than two hundred years ago, or never? The chapter finds a plausible explanation.

Right from the beginning, lots of people hated modernity. Chapter 4 begins with William Blake's dark satanic mills, the enclosure movement, and Charles Fourier's utopian visions. These and other stories reveal disruption and disorientation when modern markets opened for land and labor. Dissidents of all stripes vied for attention. How did one particular band—the Communists—manage to grab so much power? Why did scorn for markets doom their creation, the world's last great empire? The chapter finds answers to these questions and more.

Chapter 5 continues the saga. Pundits predicted a bright economic future for Russia when it renounced Communism in 1990, yet it soon became a pillaging ground. New tycoons like Boris Berezovsky, and their partners in government and the Russian mob, destroyed about as much Russian wealth as Hitler's invasion fifty years earlier. The transition from Communism was among the twentieth century's worst disasters.

Why? The chapter shows that the new markets lacked a moral foundation. In the 1990s, Russian companies didn't compete by trying to give the consumer better value, but instead by bribing officials, by sabotaging or murdering rivals, and by stealing more and faster.

Japan's experience after 1990 shows the flip side of the same coin. Chapter 6 explains why, by the late 1980s, Japan had the world's second largest economy and one of the fastest growing. That island nation seemed to have overcome the conflict between morals and markets by stressing social harmony (*wa*) and tradition. Firms enjoyed friendly ties with regulators, as management did with labor, while bosses made decisions by consensus with their underlings. Karl Marx would scarcely have believed it.

But Japan's growth collapsed in 1990, and its financial system stopped functioning. For fifteen years the economy stagnated and endured deflation reminiscent of the Great Depression. Zombie companies, like giant retailer Sogo, paralyzed entire industries, and stocks lost more than two-thirds of their peak value. Why? The chapter argues that the problem was too much *wa*. The moral ties that had helped Japan for so long immobilized the economy when it needed to change direction.

Chapter 7 tells tales of financial market meltdowns. The great South Sea Bubble of 1720 was a traumatic experience for Sir Isaac Newton, as it was for thousands of other English investors. Most citizens of a small European nation, Albania, lost their life savings in a 1997 financial fiasco. Other episodes include the recent U.S. dot-com and telecom bubbles, and Japan's bubbles in real estate and stocks in the 1980s. The U.S. stock market crash in October 1929 triggered the worldwide Great Depression.

Why are financial markets so vulnerable to crises? And why do advanced economies tolerate them when they can cause such misery? Stories going back to ancient Athens and medieval Florence shine light on these mysteries, and reveal finance's long and tangled relationship with morals.

Chapter 8 recounts two business transformations. In the first, a century ago, impersonal companies displaced homey partnerships and family firms. How did they morph into multidivisional corporations, and dominate the twentieth-century economic landscape? The second transformation is gaining speed today. Why is the corporate world fracturing, and how do new fission-fusion groups—like Linux developers and eBay—expand in the cracks? Stories from Silicon Valley, from academia, and from Prato in Italy show how our savanna instincts drive the process.

Why do modern societies spend so much on fighting crime, and why don't we get better results? The first part of Chapter 9 looks at crime prevention in premodern societies. It traces the rise of the legal system and the long fall in crime until the twentieth century. How does the market system in the United States amplify vice, together with dubious policies for fighting vice and crime? The second part of the chapter explains, using stories of the eccentric moral philosopher Jeremy Bentham, the California prison guards union and the War on Drugs.

Chapter 10 tells tales of the Symbionese Liberation Army, Chicano youth gangs, and the Assassins in order to answer questions such as: what are the moral codes of gangs, cults, and terrorist cells? What are their market plans? How do they evolve with mainstream society, and how do they coevolve with anti-terror tactics?

Markets have battered nature. Commerce has led us to burn the ozone hole, strip forests with acid rain, fish out the oceans, warm the globe, and cause extinction rates unseen since the Cretaceous. Chapter 11 shows that the underlying problem is the Tragedy of the Commons.

How can we cope? Our natural reaction is to appeal to moral instincts. Stories of Bali's rice terraces and of Rachel Carson show that that tactic can sometimes work well. But it's not enough in the modern world, as illustrated in stories of cod fishermen, the Dust Bowl, and Exxon-funded researchers. Can markets become the solution instead of the problem? The chapter finds some hopeful hints.

The final chapter ties some loose ends, with stories of a Saudi princess, Southern honor codes, China's cultural revolution, the Battle of Seattle, Belgium's woes, California's disastrous electric power markets, and many more. What sort of markets do we really want? And what sort of morals? The chapter concludes with a few modest proposals.

...And Beyond

Following Chapter 12 is an appendix that collects technical details not readily found in the literature. Some sections are accessible to general readers; for example, the first two briskly summarize evolutionary concepts such as fitness and coevolution, while section A7 lists classical and newly discovered facts about markets' strengths and weaknesses. Other sections require some math. A good high school class in analytic geometry is enough for A3 and A4 on social dilemmas, while calculus is used in A8, which formally analyzes the Duke-Serf game. The Appendix is entirely optional, intended only for readers curious about technical details.

Each chapter has an extensive set of endnotes. These are meant for all readers who, after finishing a chapter, want to learn more. The notes point to sources of the key facts and stories. Some notes are tangential comments, of possible interest but outside the narrative flow. When it is not clear from the text, the endnotes should indicate which statements are known fact, which reflect current consensus belief, and which are minority opinions.

The endnotes for this prologue begin with acknowledgements. My intellectual and practical debts are huge, and it is a pleasure to acknowledge the people who helped me understand the material I present in this book, and the people who helped me put the book together.

1

The Savanna Code
What Good Are Morals?

Being both systematically more brutal than chimps and more empathic than bonobos, we are by far the most bipolar ape. Our societies are never completely peaceful, never completely competitive, never ruled by sheer selfishness, and never perfectly moral.

—*Frans de Waal,* Our Inner Ape

As animals go, humans are not very impressive. We think we are smart, but few valedictorians would last long if left alone on the African savanna. We are slower than top predators and their prey, like lions and antelopes. Our strength is no match against our cousins, the chimpanzees, much less against elephants or rhinos. We can't swim as well as otters, or fly like birds or even squirrels. We don't have scary claws or fangs, or paws to dig, or good enough molars to grind leaves and grass. Our skin is delicate and so is our digestion.

Yet, somehow, our species has survived. Indeed, we have grabbed the top spot on just about every food chain on the planet, from jungle to tundra, from alpine pastures down to the sea.

How did we do it? This chapter argues that, of all things, it was our moral system that made the difference. Other hallmarks of humanity—intelligence, tools, language—were acquired along the way, just to help out. Morals are what made us human and allowed us to cooperate.

Cooperation is our specialty. Thinking and working together, we now build cars and computers, hopeless tasks for a solo individual. We often cooperate without effort or thought, yet cooperation is a delicate enterprise. It is fraught with risks of free-riding and betrayal, and we see dramatic examples every day in the headlines and courtrooms. Cooperation raises the I-versus-we social dilemma—what's good for the group may not be what's good for me.

A Slimy Social Dilemma

To understand the power and the perils of cooperation, consider the amoeba *Dictyostelium discoideum*. Commonly called "slime mold," these microbes spend most of their lives in forest soil as separate individuals, eating bacteria, growing and dividing. It is a rather monotonous and solitary existence.

Things get interesting when the food runs out and the amoebas begin to starve. Nearby individuals then ooze closer together. In slow motion over several hours, up to a million amoebas in the neighborhood (a few cubic inches of soil) stream together into a central mound. The mound begins to resemble a small slug, moves to the soil surface, and sprouts a stalk. Most of the amoebas cluster near the top, in the bulbous "fruiting body." They dehydrate and become spores that scatter in the breeze, to find a better life in far away places. The colony is saved!

How can hundreds of thousands of brainless, competing individuals cooperate to build such an elaborate escape platform? Biologists have discovered the basic mechanics. Starving amoebas produce pulses of the ancient biological chemical cAMP (cyclic adenosine monophosphate) and respond to its concentration gradient. They automatically move toward the highest concentrations of cAMP, cling to their fellows, and begin slug and stalk construction. This process is now fairly well understood.

The deeper question, however, is how the process could ever have evolved. The genes for producing and synchronizing cAMP pulses, for moving up the gradient, and so forth, must somehow bring greater fitness. That is, they must eventually, and on average, produce more amoebas than genes that favor a solitary life.

The fitness benefit of these prosocial genes is that the amoeba may become a spore high up the stalk, with good prospects for finding a rich new patch of forest floor. The fitness cost is that the amoeba has to use its scarce nutrients to generate and respond to the chemical signal, and it still may end up starving at the bottom of the stalk. The benefit must exceed the cost if the social behavior is to endure.

Actually, the problem is even more vexing. There is a mutant gene that helps an amoeba reach the top of the stalk by slowing down its neighbors. This strategy benefits the individual, but at a cost to the colony. If the strategy became widespread, then the stalk wouldn't form properly and the colony would die out.

Thus, the amoebas face a social dilemma: what is good for the individual conflicts with what is good for the colony. To succeed as social creatures, amoebas must somehow suppress selfish strategies that increase personal benefits while shifting costs on to other individuals.

Of course, some forms of cooperation are win-win, with no dilemma. Anchovies swim together in tight schools that confuse predators. Pelicans fly in V-formation, saving energy by riding their neighbors' bow waves. Packs of wild African dogs are far more successful than loners at bringing down a gazelle. In these examples, individual self-interest and the group interest are served simultaneously—no sacrifice is necessary. Biologists call it mutualism.

Nepotism to the Rescue

The most interesting and important cases, though, are the social dilemmas. Individual slime mold amoebas, and a vast variety of other social creatures, incur a personal cost when they cooperate for the good of the group. Less cooperative individuals can reap the group benefits, yet save on costs, and seemingly, would gain greater fitness. By the basic principle of evolution, then, the selfish strategies would become more prevalent and cooperation would break down.

Yet, somehow, cooperation thrives among amoebas and many other creatures, including ourselves. Why? How do social creatures resolve their dilemmas?

Darwin himself struggled with the problem, and by the mid-twentieth century, it obsessed several top biologists, including William Hamilton (1936–2000). A rather shy individual with a striking mane of hair and a quiet voice that sometimes lulled students to sleep, Hamilton had more than his share of originality and courage. Even past his sixtieth birthday, he braved the Rwanda genocide to search for ants, and he died from an infection while conducting field research in the Congo.

After long pondering the puzzle, Hamilton finally cracked it before his thirtieth birthday. He wrote a dense, highly mathematical paper detailing his solution and submitted it to the prestigious journal *Nature*, which rejected it. Eventually, the lesser-known *Journal of Theoretical Biology* published the work in two parts in 1964. For the next ten years, the scientific world ignored it, and Hamilton later wrote that he occasionally doubted his sanity during this time. Finally, in the 1970s, books like Richard Dawkins's *The Selfish Gene* revealed its importance, and now Hamilton's solution is a mainstay of biology textbooks.

Hamilton said that slime molds, bees, and ants have developed a special solution to the I-versus-we dilemma: kin selection. They are hardwired for extraordinary nepotism.

Others had assumed that evolution takes place at the level of individuals. It doesn't. The competition occurs among genes, the instructions for making individuals. It's a copying contest. Genes that pass on plenty of duplicates survive— genes that don't, thin out or vanish. Normally, gene competition looks much like individual competition. When an animal vies successfully for survival and a good mate and has numerous offspring who grow up to do the same, its genes persist through the millennia.

But Hamilton saw that this pattern could take an eerie twist among very closely related individuals, who share a high percentage of genes. Selfish strategies don't work so well then. The genes bear the full cost of greedy strategies that shift costs to other individuals who carry the same genes, and at the same time, these genes capture all the benefits of cooperation. Thus, from the perspective of a "selfish gene," cooperation becomes a win-win proposition. Kinship transforms the social dilemma into mutualism.

Consider, again, the slime mold. Each amoeba is usually a clone of the others. Indeed, a whole colony can arise from a single ancestor, by the asexual growth and division familiar to biology lab students. The cooperating amoebas are about as closely related as is biologically possible. So, even if an individual dies in the stalk, the instructions for making a copy of it survive elsewhere. It can reproduce by proxy, after its own death and because of it. In this contest, it doesn't matter where the template to copy your genes comes from. So the gene for self-sacrifice prospers.

On the other hand, the mutant gene that lets one amoeba scamper to the top of the fruiting body faces a different fate. It might leave a raft of descendants wherever it lands. But if in the next emergency, these aggressive amoebas all try to reach the top, they'll build a poor platform and fewer will escape. The free-rider line will wane.

The most famous examples of cooperation include insects from the order *Hymenoptera*, especially ants and bees. Their unusual genetics produce super-sisters who share up to three-quarters of their genes. As a result, the sister workers are infertile, yet cooperate in amazing ways. You might think, for example, that a worker ant would be better off if she took more breaks and actually ate the food she gathered. But her genes do better if she promptly brings all food back to the nest, because that behavior helps the colony thrive and spread the genes that she shares with the queen and the other workers.

Hamilton's analysis gives insight into cooperation among many other creatures. For example, the trees in a redwood grove are usually very closely related, often sprouting from the same root system. They cooperate by dropping branches and needles that suppress most other plant species and give relatives room to grow, and by precipitating moisture from fog and clouds for the good of all.

Naked mole rats live underground in Africa in hive-like colonies that are very closely related, due to inbreeding. They and their cousin species, Damaraland mole rats, are the only known mammals with social castes reminiscent of bees, including a queen and non-breeding workers and soldiers.

Most mammals specialize in cooperation across generations. Mothers' bodies have special adaptations for nourishing youngsters (especially the placenta before birth, and milk glands for after), and in many species, the mothers teach and protect their kids for a season or more. Although this all comes at a cost to the mom, the benefits to the kids make it worthwhile for a selfish mammalian gene.

Hamilton showed how the proper fitness calculation should include costs and benefits to kin. The more genes we share with others, the more our genes benefit by helping them. Brothers and sisters in most species share 50 percent of their genes. This amount doesn't justify antlike self-sacrifice, but it does mean siblings can help propagate their own genes by aiding each other (not that they always do). Uncles and aunts share one-quarter of their genes with nieces and nephews, and favoritism here, too, can benefit one's genes. For example, a sleepy lioness whose own cub is already full is more likely to let a niece or nephew cub nurse than an unrelated one. The delightful TV show "Meerkat Manor" gets it right. It shows clans of a dozen or so related individuals helping guard the group from predators and other meerkat clans.

Of course, we see kinship effects in ourselves as well. In the famous novel *Les Miserables*, Jean Valjean steals a loaf of bread to feed his hungry family, and readers nod in understanding; if he had pilfered to feed a stranger, the justification would be harder. Nepotism is ancient and has led to dynasties in states and businesses, as the powerful follow inner urges and pass on more of their genes. The Confucian ethical system centers on family obligations, and most religions impose special responsibilities on relatives and encourage a stronger bias toward them. As we'll see, family-run businesses can be more effective than non-family ones, and extended families like Marco Polo's handled much early long-distance trade.

Kinship is the first tier in cooperation. We are now ready to deal with two other, progressively broader tiers: reciprocity and morals.

Reciprocity in Blood and Backscratch

What about cooperating with others who are not kin? In a 1971 paper, brash young Harvard biologist Robert Trivers showed that it is theoretically viable. A streamlined version of his argument runs as follows. One creature, the donor, does a favor for a recipient, expecting that the favor eventually will be returned. If the donor's cost is less than the recipient's benefit, and if the delays and risks of the return favor are not too large, then reciprocity pays: a reciprocator will achieve greater fitness than a non-reciprocator.

Once again, the social dilemma is transformed into mutualism. This transformation comes not from sharing genes, but instead from the symmetric, ongoing relationship between donor and recipient. The algebra turns out to be exactly the same as for kin selection, with the degree of relatedness replaced by a discount factor that takes into account the delays and risks of the return favor. (Mathematically inclined readers will find this spelled out in section A4 of the Appendix.)

Reciprocity has one other necessary condition: that cheaters don't prosper. A recipient who cuts costs on the return favor, or never returns the favor at all, is called a cheater. Reciprocators must be able to identify and avoid cheaters, or else the cheaters will achieve higher fitness and become more prevalent, and cooperation will break down. This parallels Hamilton's condition that cooperators must avoid non-kin when they bestow costly favors.

About ten years after Trivers' paper appeared, field biologist Gerald Wilkinson reported a perfect example. He had been studying vampire bats (*Desmodus rotundus*) in Costa Rica.

Life is tough if you are a vampire bat. Every night you have to search for an unwary cow or other large animal whose blood you can drink without interruption. If you fail to tap a vein two nights in a row, you are in danger of starving to death. Without a social safety net, your life would probably be rather short.

Adult female vampire bats cope by living in colonies of eight to twelve individuals, most of them distant cousins. An unlucky adult will beg by licking the wings of a well-fed potential donor, who will often regurgitate some blood into her mouth. Wilkinson reported that refusals are rare if, on previous nights of success, the current beggar had never refused the current donor. He estimated that the survival benefit to the hungry bat of a gram of blood is at least twice its cost to the well-fed donor. Since the colonies are stable over years of nightly excursions, the chance for a return favor is fairly high. So, reciprocity theory fits the report from the field.

Since Wilkinson's study, very few new examples of reciprocity turned up-except among primates. However, there we see it clearly. Monkeys and apes commonly swap grooming favors: one will scratch another's back, picking out lice and other parasites, and later, the other will return the favor.

Grooming promotes health, but also forges vital social bonds. Grooming partners include unrelated individuals as well as kin. The activity can fill several hours each day, and individuals of similar age and status typically spend about equal time grooming each other. In many primate species, individuals tend to spend more time grooming those of higher status and those who have shared food.

Reciprocity builds on kinship. For example, young vampire bats lick their mothers' wings to signal hunger, and mother primates groom their kids. Reciprocity recycles these habits and puts them to new use, with distant kin or non-kin in daily social contact.

Among the best reciprocators are our closest relatives, the highly social bonobos and chimpanzees, who live in the forests of central Africa. Chimps live in bands of several dozen related males, together with distantly related adult females and their youngsters. The entire band collects when the tree branches are drooping with ripe fruit, but at other times, it splits into subgroups with shifting membership.

Male chimps dominate these fission-fusion bands, which are very territorial and hierarchical. The males patrol the perimeter of the band's territory, and occasionally, a few of them gang up to capture and eat a colobus monkey or other small game. The gang shares the spoils fairly equally. Gangs of males also hunt down, and beat to death, stray males from other groups. More often, though, the males just hang out and groom their buddies.

Adult female chimps outnumber males two to one. Young females migrate to neighboring territories and settle down. After mating and giving birth, they take care of their youngsters until age five or so, when they become fertile again, signaled by swollen pink bottoms. The alpha male does his best to keep other males away from fertile females, and fathers a majority of baby chimps. No alpha reigns forever, though, and when a new alpha (usually in an alliance with friends and brothers) overthrows the old one, he often kills the younger babies. The evolutionary logic is that the mothers will become fertile sooner with no baby to nurse, increasing the new alpha's chances of fatherhood.

Bonobos are just as closely related to us as are chimps, but their social lives are very different: older females rule. They form tight alliances, and adult males' status comes mainly from their moms. Bonobos are less interested than chimps in hierarchy and power plays, but they have much better sex lives. Females have swollen pink bottoms most of the time, whether or not they are actually fertile, and they enjoy quickie sex with lots of unrelated males (and females) in all positions all day long. For bonobos, sex is like grooming: a way to diffuse tension and to build social bonds. Females don't worry about infanticide. Any male that tried would gain nothing but a nasty beating by the ruling clique of females. The males might not get much respect, but constant sex games and the one-to-one adult sex ratio suggest that they lead happier and longer lives than male chimps. Bonobos of both sexes seem especially empathic and communicative.

African Crucible

We humans share much with our primate cousins, but our bodies and our social behavior have diverged from theirs over the last five million years. To understand the divergence, we must piece together evidence from observing bonobos and chimps in the wild and in zoos, from human societies isolated from civilization, from fossils and DNA samples and genetics, from historical linguistics, and from behavioral ecology and evolutionary anthropology. Although controversies still abound, the evidence is beginning to tell a coherent story of human origins.

Here is a quick sketch, beginning with the last common ancestor, a small ape called *Sahelanthropus tchadensis*. It lived near the shores of ancient Mega-Lake Chad, then 155 thousand square miles, larger than the Caspian Sea. Its environment might have resembled today's Okavango Delta in the Kalahari Desert, a maze of reed-lined waterways separating wooded isles filled with palm, fig, and date trees. *Sahelanthropus* shared the forest with snakes and saber-toothed cats, and the lake was home to prehistoric crocodiles, hippos, and turtles.

The lineage split as the African climate cooled. The forest shrank and savanna emerged—grasslands dotted with trees, rather like the parks we create today for our pleasure. Chimp and bonobo ancestors remained in the forest, but by four million years ago, our own ancestors, the *australopithecines*, had ventured into the new habitat. They had softball-sized brains, only slightly larger than chimps', and their best-known representative, Lucy, stood no taller than a yardstick. They saved energy by walking on two legs, and they gathered nutritious tubers that were more plentiful than in the forest.

But the savanna is sensitive to seasonal changes, and it has more dangerous predators and offers less shelter than forest. Our ancestors' bodies evolved in ways that reinforced certain sorts of social behavior and, conversely, our social behavior—especially our emerging moral system—reinforced certain sorts of genetic changes.

By 2.5 million years ago, the first member of our own genus, *Homo habilis*, appeared. About 50 percent larger than *australopithecines*, and with a proportionately larger brain, it added meat to its diet and began to use stone tools routinely. Some were sharp flakes that could have bloodied predators and sliced tough hides, and others could crack open antelope thighbones to get to the nutrient-rich marrow. A top scavenger, *habilis* probably hunted when given the chance.

Habilis faced severe environmental stress. The many layers of volcanic ash in East Africa's Rift Valley tell of zones of destruction and occasional winters lasting years. Climate graphs of the last two million years, based on Greenland ice cores and Atlantic sediment cores, look a bit like a seismograph when an earthquake rumbles through. Our ancestors had to deal with increasingly violent temperature fluctuations around a general cooling trend.

When temperatures rose, the monsoons and trade winds of Africa brought heavier rainfall. Lake Chad again swelled into Mega-Lake Chad, the middle Congo River overflowed its banks and became a vast inland sea, and elsewhere, bodies of water grew larger and commoner. As recently as five thousand years ago—later than the founding of Ur—lakes speckled the central Sahara. On the other hand, when temperatures fell, drought swept Africa. Often, a broad swath of desert stretched from the Sahara along the Rift Valley down to the Namib and Kalahari, dividing and isolating patches of savanna.

Patchy habitats separate the gene pools, which evolve along separate tracks and increase diversity. When the habitats merge again, the genes compete, accelerating evolution. Moreover, rapid climate changes turn an ecological kaleidoscope. They throw together plant and animal species that, in more settled times, would live in the separate biomes of desert, savanna, and forest.

Homo erectus first appeared around 1.7 million years ago, during another major faunal turnover and grassland expansion. It may well have had naked skin and sweat glands, and an external nose, to help it keep cool on the savanna. Its brain ballooned to twice the size of the *australopithecines'*, almost a liter, on average. This is an astonishing event, since brains are greedy for nourishment and therefore costly. (At 1.35 liters, adult human brains consume about 16 percent of our metabolism; for most mammals, the figure is 2 to 5 percent.)

Erectus was bigger than *habilis*, and made far more tools. We know that it was adaptable, since around one million years ago (and possibly much earlier), it spread out of Africa into different habitats in Asia, leaving fossil remains known as Peking Man and Java Man.

Specialized animals thrive for a while, but they often go extinct when the climate turns, while generalists like our ancestors (or like ravens and coyotes in North America) muddle along and adapt to survive the big shifts. *Erectus* descendents evolved agile hands for wielding weapons and tools, a flattened face, a throat capable of speech, and larger brains. About 200 thousand years ago, our own species, *Homo sapiens*, first appeared in northeast Africa.

Moral Capacities

What do we know about our ancestors' social behavior? Bonobos and chimps diverged even though both stuck to the forest. Our savannah ancestors' behavior no doubt changed even more but, of course, the evidence is indirect. One clue is reduced sexual dimorphism since *habilis*: male skeletons are only slightly larger than female skeletons. The implication is that our male ancestors didn't constantly fight, like chimps, over fertile females.

Apparently, our ancestors, perhaps all the way back to *erectus*, formed groups of nuclear families, in which the father helped the mom provide food and raise the kids. This type of pair bond is unknown in other great apes, but is almost universal among human societies. The evolutionary logic works as long as the father can be reasonably sure that the kids are his. Paternal help frees the mom to have kids more often, say every two years instead of every five, and allows a longer childhood so that larger brains can mature.

Among primates, larger brains (relative to body size) are closely associated with larger social groups. The statistics suggest that early human groups reached 150 adults, and some anthropologists suspect the fusion of much larger groups.

How did these groups function? Modern hunter-gatherers offer some clues. In known hunter-gatherer cultures, even very young kids help gather and adolescent boys begin to hunt, but it is not until around age twenty that the average person brings in more food than he or she consumes. At this point (later than in civilized society, until recently!), the kids are ready to marry and raise a family. Women stop bearing children around age forty, but help raise their daughters' kids and other young relatives. People remain productive and influential into their late fifties and sometimes far beyond that. It seems that even in "primitive" societies, experience and guile can match youngsters' strength and quickness.

The !Kung San people of Africa's Kalahari Desert go back, according to linguistic and genetic studies, to a branching of the human race about fifty thousand years ago. Many !Kung lived in traditional hunter-gatherer groups late into the twentieth century, and anthropologists had the opportunity to carefully study them. During the dry season, people would gather at the best oases in groups as large as two hundred to swap stories and goods, initiate the youngsters, find marriage partners for the adolescents, and generally socialize. But week by week, people would have to go farther to find food, and it became increasingly difficult to maintain a cooperative attitude. Conflicts would arise between hunting parties over who spotted the antelope first, and so forth. At some point, usually well before the local food disappeared, people would run out of patience and, a few households at a time, the big camp would fission. Small groups, typically comprised of two to six nuclear families, friends, and, sometimes, distant kin, would then go their separate ways.

Shoshone tribes thrived for many centuries in the variable habitat of American Great Basin—that is, Nevada plus sizeable chunks of neighboring states. When big game was scarce, they would fission down to the level of nuclear families, subsisting on small game like rabbits and fish and local vegetation. Rich hunting opportunities, such as a large buffalo herd occupying a valley, could temporarily fuse up to a thousand individuals into a single band. Western observers, from Lewis and Clark onward, remarked on their fluid, egalitarian marriages and organizations, and their ability to keep the peace internally and with most neighboring tribes.

Did our ancestors' societies resemble those of the Shoshone or the !Kung? The climate in the last eleven thousand years has been remarkably stable and warm, so we must be cautious in projecting modern day hunter-gatherer behavior back to the Paleolithic. However, it is safe to say that, like other social creatures, our hunter-gatherer ancestors faced social dilemmas. For example, a man might personally be better off disappearing at the first sign of danger, but that would increase the vulnerability of young children and their moms, and the group would suffer. Of course, food sharing is as much an issue with humans as it is with ants. How did our ancestors cope?

Kinship is not enough because it works well only when group members are very closely related. In a group of one hundred or more humans, average relatedness, at best, would be like first or second cousins. Anthropologists find about the same degree of relatedness even in small fission bands of hunter-gatherers. It's not enough to get very far.

Reciprocity helps. It works well among friends who see each other every day, and when the favors are simple and repetitive, like grooming. But reciprocity breaks down when the favors involve once-off opportunities, and when the group is likely to fission. Our ancestors lived in large complex groups operating in erratic situations. They needed more than direct reciprocity.

All known hunter-gatherer groups manage their social dilemmas pretty much the same way, relying on an egalitarian moral system. It builds on kinship and reciprocity, but takes them in a new direction. It enables cooperation in complex groups facing novel opportunities, and is extremely flexible and adaptable. The next section explains how it works.

The moral system turns out to be very demanding. It could emerge only as our ancestors refined their capacities beyond those of *Sahelanthropus* and the *australopithecines*. Its imperatives must have shaped the emotional, cognitive, and linguistic capacities of *habilis*, *erectus*, and our more recent ancestors.

"Human morality is firmly anchored in the social emotions, with empathy at its core," writes primatologist Frans de Waal, echoing Adam Smith and Charles Darwin. We share some of our emotional repertoire with other social mammals. Dogs, elephants, and monkeys appear to love some specific individuals and hate others. They also may experience the temporary versions of those emotions, gratitude and anger, in response to specific actions. Capuchin monkeys can become envious and outraged at not getting their share, and bonobos and chimps fear arousing envy in others. The human sense of fairness is a next step. Dogs seem to experience pride and shame, but only humans seem to experience guilt. Self-righteousness, generalized disgust, and righteous wrath also seem distinctively human.

Fossil skulls show the increasing brain size of our nearer ancestors, especially in the neocortex, suggesting increased cognitive powers. The fossils can't show when distinctively human brain structures first emerged—our greatly increased numbers of mirror neurons and spindle cells, and our huge posterior ventromedial nucleus and insulas. Recent research ties these brain structures to humans' unrivaled capacity for putting themselves in another's shoes ("theory of mind") and self-awareness, and with the more complex social emotions. For instance, if you see someone pick up a cup of coffee, your mirror neurons will tell you at once whether the person intends to drink it or simply clear off the table. Moreover, if you see the person take a sip of coffee and wrinkle her nose in disgust, your mirror neurons will simulate that disgust. You literally feel what she feels.

Language is perhaps our species' greatest social talent, and mirror neurons may also have played a role in its development. The same front-brain circuits used to make complex hand gestures for sign language are also used to make spoken sentences using tongue and lip movements. Although other social animals communicate, they can't share their experiences as we do. Language was probably the last ingredient in our ancestors' powerful new solution to the social dilemma.

The Moral System

Morals are a shared understanding, within a group of people, of how to live and work together. The understanding can be summarized in a code or set of rules, some explicit and others implicit. The specifics of the code, sometimes called social norms, differ across cultures. However, the moral system itself is universal, used in the same way by humans everywhere.

Like the air we breathe, the moral system is so much a part of our everyday experience that it is hard to see clearly. A thought experiment may help bring it into focus. Imagine that you are a hunter-gatherer, or, if you prefer, on a wilderness trip with Outward Bound. One morning, you see a member of your group trapped by floodwaters. You alert the other members, and a rescue party forms: someone finds strong vines and stands guard, another wades out and brings the victim back, while you anchor the vine. Everyone celebrates, and that evening around the campfire, people tell jokes and stories about the exploit.

How did your group cooperate so effectively in a new and urgent situation? You all reacted emotionally, empathized with the victim's distress, and became eager to help, even though it put some of you at personal risk and distracted everyone from more personally advantageous activities. Cognition and memory were needed to plan the rescue. It took communication skills to implement the plan, and to congratulate everyone afterward.

But what brought it all together were morals—the group's shared understanding of how people should behave. In your group, it was understood that everyone should be willing to sacrifice their time and take risks to help out, that ideas should be pooled to make the most effective plan, that roles should be assigned according to capabilities, and that, afterward, everyone's contribution should be recognized and appreciated.

Emotions guide all actions—social or otherwise. They respond quickly to new developments (much more quickly than our conscious reasoning) and tell us what to attend to, and what to value. Unless you are a sociopath, you love your friends and most members of your family. It is a true pleasure to work with trusted colleagues on a project of mutual benefit, be it a hunting party or a startup company.

We know about emotions from introspection and personal experience, but recently, social scientists and biologists have gathered evidence in the laboratory. One popular experiment asks a college student to propose a division of, say, $10 between himself and another student whose identity he will never know. That other person responds either by accepting the proposal (so both go home with the proposed cash) or else by rejecting it (so both go home with nothing).

Economists don't traditionally think about social emotions, so they had expected that responders would accept any positive offer—after all, getting something is better than nothing. In that case, the proposer's most advantageous move is to offer the responder a minimal amount, say $1, and to keep the rest. But that isn't what happened. Responders often rejected the smaller amounts. Most proposers, fearing rejection (or out of a sense of fairness), offered something close to an even split, say $5, which was usually accepted.

The puzzle here is responders' rejection of small positive offers. Recent studies using brain scans and measuring physiological reactions conclude that the main reason is anger, or moral outrage. The satisfaction of punishing a greedy proposer (so he loses the $9 and takes home nothing) is worth more to many proposers than keeping the chump change.

Roughly similar behavior is reported with college students on every continent. However, anthropologists have recently tried the same game with people in dozens of isolated societies, and have found a wide range of behavior. Machiguenga tribesmen in the Amazon rainforest played the game much closer to the way the economists expected than did the students. At the other extreme, very generous offers (above $5 in the example) were often rejected in Au and Gnau bands in New Guinea. The data reinforce the idea that the contents of moral codes greatly differ in these remote societies, but that the emotional responses to the code are universal. For example, the Machiguenga code doesn't call for sharing outside the family, while a Gnau responder accepting a very generous offer would feel obliged to track down his benefactor and return the favor with interest.

Social emotions help overcome social dilemmas. When it makes you happy to see others benefit from your actions, you are more likely to act in the interest of the whole group. Moreover, the recipients of your affection then have a material incentive to help you. The other side of the coin is anger at slackers and swindlers. You may try to punish them if your moral code endorses it, and sometimes even if it doesn't. Such vengeful emotions deter anti-social behavior, and help keep cheaters from prospering. When people who uphold the code do better than those who do not, the code transforms social dilemmas into win-win mutualism.

The moral system is anchored in the social emotions, but it draws on other human capacities. Arriving at a shared understanding requires communication, and speech is invaluable. As in the floodwater rescue story, we routinely use speech and gestures to offer and request help, and to point out opportunities. Speech helps us to coordinate our actions in novel situations, to assign roles, to promise rewards, and to convey threats. It widens the application of a moral code and makes it more flexible.

Idle chatter and gossip are just as important. They are the traditional way of sharing information (reliable or not) about the character and current status of other people in the group. Gossip extends memory beyond direct personal experience, and affects our future choices on whom to work with and whom to avoid.

The moral code itself is communicated partly through story, myth, and song. Young people (or recent arrivals to an existing group) learn what sort of behavior is expected by seeing what group members do, and also by hearing about the deeds of heroes and villains.

The behavior prescribed in any moral code depends on status and circumstance. In most traditional codes, the healthy are supposed to help sick or injured family and group members; women are supposed to be faithful to their husbands (but in some codes, not necessarily the other way around); grandmothers are supposed to help watch the kids when the mom is out gathering food; and hunters are supposed to share large game with other families in the group, while gatherers share mainly within the nuclear family.

Of course, not everyone follows the moral code perfectly, and the code typically prescribes sanctions. For example, it may call for shunning a petty thief until he returns the goods with interest. Equally important, those who fall short of the code's prescriptions are subject to gossip, and their reputation and status may suffer. Maintaining good standing in a well functioning group is a powerful human motive, and it obviously strengthens morals.

Sanctions and reputation effects deter serious cheating. Of course, in some situations, the code is ambiguous and leaves too much wiggle room. Sometimes the code is clear but is ignored because the prescribed behavior is onerous and enforcement is weak. The group can still muddle along if the matter is minor. But when it affects the group's survival, then the code must tighten up and stop the cheating.

The code must ensure that cheaters don't prosper. If they do, then more and more people will cheat and, at some point, the code will collapse. For example, herdsmen all over the world enforce severe punishments on rustlers, sometimes death even for first time offenders; gentler codes evidently don't do as good a job at preserving the herding lifestyle.

Us and Them

Morals are shared understandings among members of a group. What about people outside the group?

Traditional moral codes make a sharp distinction between in-group and out-group, between *us* and *them*. The underlying logic is compelling: you know the members of your own group personally, and you know the code they are supposed to follow. But it is different with *them*. You probably don't know much about the status, personality, and history of particular individuals. You may only have a foggy idea of the moral codes they are supposed to follow, and you have little social leverage if they misbehave. So you have good reason to be wary. Most moral codes tell us to trust *them* less than *us*, and many tell us to regard strangers as less than fully human.

In thinking about members of other groups, we tend to fall back on some sort of group reputation. One consequence is that many moral codes demand that we be tough with outsiders, to uphold the reputation of our own group as people not to be trifled with. Some moral codes go further, and encourage stereotyping, racism, and xenophobia.

A recent field experiment in Papua New Guinea spotlights several issues. The Ngenika and the Wolimbka tribes live about a day's journey apart from each other and enjoy generally good relations. The experimenters ran lots of three-player games in which player A (the dictator, we'll say) decided how to divide ten Kina—a substantial sum of local money—between himself and player B (the recipient). Player C was given five Kina and told about A's decision. If he wished, player C could spend his own money to punish player A: each one Kina spent would reduce player A's take home pay by three Kina. When all three players were from the same tribe, player C typically did punish greedy dictators—even though it was personally costly, he usually enforced the norm that player A should divide the money about equally. Player C's were even harsher on greedy dictators from the other tribe when the recipient was in their own tribe, but were much easier on greedy dictators when the recipient was from the other tribe. Dictators were less likely to be greedy with members of their own tribe than with outsiders.

Another team found similar results with Swiss Army recruits. The experiments cleanly demonstrate that egalitarian norms are usually obeyed within the group and, even in an unusual and rather artificial situation, people are willing to sacrifice their own self-interest to ensure that nobody (especially outsiders) takes advantage of fellow group members.

Of course, some parts of the moral code vary greatly from one group to another. The majority of cultures catalogued by anthropologists allow polygamy, for example. Many, like our own, demand monogamy, and a few (notably in Tibet) encourage polyandry, two or three husbands sharing one wife. The Bari women of northwestern Venezuela take it a step further and seek multiple "fathers" for each of their children.

A major source of the variation is the environment: the code adapts to local conditions. For example, the harsh climate in Tibet requires very labor-intensive subsistence farming on fields that can't be efficiently subdivided. The combined efforts of several brothers are necessary to support a woman and young children. The local custom of polyandry among brothers goes back several centuries and, over time, it became increasingly compatible with other elements of the moral code. Until the 1950s, when China annexed Tibet, the custom spread among Nyinba farming families because those who adhered to it did better than their monogamous neighbors.

Underneath the variation lies unity. The moral system, whatever its specific content, has the same function: it enables groups of families to work together and make a living. Its sanctions and rewards make cooperation more attractive than shirking or cheating.

African Exodus

Our human ancestors remained in Africa until about fifty thousand years ago. Slowly, over many millennia, their hunter-gather lifestyle had become increasingly sophisticated. They started to make fitted clothing about seventy-five thousand years ago, according to evidence from the genes of body lice. They developed better techniques for constructing shelter and tending fire. Weapons improved, especially slings and atlatls, spear-throwing devices that allowed our ancestors to kill top predators and big game.

The real breakthrough, though, was not technological. It was the moral system itself, and its cultural extensions. (Among hunter-gatherers, technology and production and art blend seamlessly with the moral system—they are not separate spheres, as in the modern world.) Once the system took root, human progress accelerated and our ancestors became "behaviorally modern." Cave art became common around forty-five thousand years ago and, at about the same time, complex tools of ivory, antler, and bone suddenly appeared, as well as bird-bone flutes and personal ornaments of shell and ivory beads. Archaeologists call it the Upper Paleolithic cultural explosion.

The detonator was cultural evolution. Social behavior became adaptive and cumulative: our ancestors could transmit the best practices and best ideas from one generation to the next, and they could quickly adapt behavior when new conditions arose. Ties loosened between human behavior and the slow processes of biological evolution. Different groups tried different codes of behavior, and different ways to make things. Groups grew faster when their way turned out to be better adapted to local circumstances. Other groups imitated or shrank.

The Nuer and Dinka are a textbook example from more recent times. For many centuries, the Dinka people maintained a pastoral lifestyle in the upper Nile basin. Beginning sometime in the early 1700s, a single mutation occurred in their moral system. One local group, who called itself the Nuer, slightly changed marriage customs in a way that created stronger bonds between the in-laws' families. Although the Nuer were otherwise culturally (and genetically) identical to the Dinka, the intergroup bonds enabled the Nuer to form larger raiding parties than their neighbors. That gave them an unbeatable military edge and, decade by decade, the Nuer took territory away from their Dinka neighbors. Men either joined voluntarily, or were driven away or killed. Women willingly or unwillingly took new Nuer husbands and raised their children as Nuer. The Nuer were poised to take over the remaining Dinka territory when the British intervened around 1880.

Cultural mutations can also spread peacefully. Suppose, for example, that one local band's moral code is more welcoming to newcomers. Then, if there is a steady supply of productive newcomers, that band will grow more quickly than other local bands, and will fission more often. The other bands may or may not emulate its success. Either way, unless conditions change, the more hospitable moral code will prevail in the region.

What sort of moral codes did our ancestors follow? There are notable differences in the moral codes prevailing in different hunter-gatherer groups observed by anthropologists, but even more remarkable are the common features. All evidence suggests that our Upper Paleolithic ancestors lived mostly in egalitarian bands consisting of dozens of individuals, with language ties among dozens (or possibly more) of neighboring bands in the same tribe. Most bands moved with the seasons or moved when local food resources became depleted. Permanent settlements were rare to nonexistent.

Known hunter-gatherers' moral codes still enforce egalitarian behavior, in sharp contrast to our chimpanzee cousins. Although some men are stronger or better hunters than others, they don't get to boss others around. If some guy tried to monopolize access to women, or to grab a disproportionate share of the best food, he would face escalating sanctions. The others in the group would gossip about his bad behavior, and word would get back to the bully. If he didn't mend his ways, he would be subject to ridicule and hostile looks and words. Eventually, he'd face physical threats by a coalition of the other males, and ultimately would face exile, injury, or death. If the bully had too many allies, the other folks would simply leave.

Egalitarianism spread among our ancestors because it worked. Hunting parties (mostly male) needed only casual, temporary leadership, and informal peer organization (mostly female) worked well for gathering edible plants. Class structure was unnecessary and, indeed, was not viable. Food sharing and mutual aid almost eliminated the genetic selection pressure within an egalitarian group, while selection pressures intensified across groups. The moral code, and culture more generally, evolved faster.

By fifty thousand years ago, then, our African ancestors had modern human bodies and an advanced hunter-gatherer behavioral toolkit. A few of these people—perhaps a single band of just 150—then left Africa. Their descendants spread out. When things got crowded, a few groups moved into new territory and adapted to the local conditions.

Our ancestors first spread along the coast to India. Then to Australia and the East Asian coast. Then inland into central Asia and Europe, where they encountered other *erectus* descendents. Those others eventually disappeared (the Neanderthals, thirty thousand years ago) and left no detectable DNA trace in today's people.

Descendents of the African emigrants eventually moved over the Bering land bridge to the New World and, most recently, using canoes and sophisticated navigation, reached most of Polynesia. Thanks to their adaptive culture, centered on the moral system, they inherited the earth.

2

Bazaar and Empire

How Did We Become Civilized and Why Did We Start Shopping?

Imagine yourself waking up in the Sumerian city of Uruk six thousand years ago. You find the water jug and splash your face, then wolf down some wheat-barley mush, cooked yesterday, plus a couple of figs, grab your bronze-bladed hoe, and, along with two thousand others, head off to work. As you pass the city gates, the crowd splits up. You head north to the garbanzo bean fields, where the overseer has you start clearing an irrigation ditch from the great river, the Euphrates. Later, you help dry the harvest and prepare the next planting.

Late that afternoon, work stops an hour earlier than usual. Your crew fills big baskets with dried garbanzos and marches to the city center, Inanna's temple. The priests take the beans and hand out treats in honor of tomorrow's big holiday. That evening, you feast on roast duck with lentils and leeks and coriander, and wash them down with a jar of dark beer. You fall asleep and dream of a lissome young priestess (or, if you prefer, a young priest) who might cavort with you at tomorrow's celebration.

As this little fantasy suggests, Uruk's residents must have considered themselves blessed by the gods. They lived in the world's largest city, created (they believed) at the dawn of time by the goddess Inanna and her servants. The residents only had to obey her current human servants, the king and the temple's high priest, and their life was secure. Compared to their neighbors outside the walls, the city folk seldom had to worry about famine or raiders. They thought the gods had always favored Uruk, and always would.

With the benefit of six thousand years' hindsight, we know better. Uruk then was a rather recent human creation, one of the first in a long string of imperial capitals. Favorably situated in the fertile delta above modern-day Basra, ancient Uruk grew to over fifty thousand people before it was supplanted by Ur and later cities. Records written in baked clay begin about five thousand years ago, and from them, we know of Uruk's later prosperity, and occasional calamities. We see no evidence that gods created Uruk, nor protected it long from plague and bloody war.

But if not god-given, how did civilization get started? How did people leap the deep chasm that separates wandering tribes from city life?

This chapter tells the tale. In the prelude, some tribes settle down and exchange gifts. The story continues with major mutations in moral codes, which eventually gave us hierarchy and empire. Another series of mutations took longer, and eventually gave us the marketplace—the bazaar.

Settling Down

The Americas were almost the final frontier for our hunter-gatherer ancestors. They crossed the Bering land bridge and spilled through a gap in the ice sheet into North and then South America about twelve thousand years ago. Within a few centuries, their descendants became diverse tribes living in virtually all the fertile New World habitats. Humans already covered Eurasia, Africa, and Australia. Except for remote Pacific islands, the planet was fully occupied, by perhaps three or four million people.

Until then, the evolutionary imperative was to find expansive new lifestyles for the new land. Tribes thrived that first discovered how to kill the big animals, like New World horses and woolly mammoths, and cook or dry the meat, tan the hides, and work the bones into tools and decorations. When food got scarce in one river valley, the tribe simply moved on to the next valley.

Things changed when there were no more frontiers. With neighbors in every habitable direction, the recipe for success was to find more efficient ways to make a living, ways that sustained more people on a single piece of land.

My home territory, the central California coast, is a relatively recent example. Until historical times, it was one of Earth's more isolated regions. Rugged mountains and broad deserts cut California off from the rest of North America. Isolation and recurrent droughts, some of which lasted for decades or even centuries, kept the population mobile and relatively small, perhaps ten thousand people, until about three thousand years ago. Growth rings from the oldest redwood trees indicate a millennium of mostly good rainy seasons after that, and archaeological digs suggest a growing population to perhaps 100 thousand people by the year 1 CE.

Archaeologists detect a different lifestyle emerging around then: more and more tribes stuck to the same seasonal routes year after year, or even stayed in one compact territory. Tribes prospered when they figured out how to burn the undergrowth around tan oaks each year to increase acorn yields, how to build varmint-proof storage facilities, how to grind and leach more efficiently, and how to bake flatbreads and boil up acorn mush.

Some tribes found special local resources. Several sites had obsidian, the beautiful black volcanic glass that can be fashioned into top quality knives and arrow points. California's Mono Lake always produced tons of alkali fly larvae that could be harvested each August, dried, and pressed into storable and highly nutritious cakes called *kutsavi*. More appealing to the modern palate, many North Coast rivers had huge salmon runs every fall. Yields increased when the local tribes built specialized equipment like fishing nets and rock dams that the fish have to jump, and smoking and drying racks.

Nets and dams were serious investments, and so were well-tended oak groves. Such investments paid dividends if the group could maintain access, and the dividends allowed the group to grow larger. More and more people lived for longer periods on their resource investments.

The dynamic goes back to the Old World, tens of thousands of years ago. Once a tribe discovered a very useful trick, the neighbors with similar habitat had to imitate or improve it. Otherwise, the neighbors would, sooner or later, be pushed aside. Thus, the tricks spread, increasing productivity and, ultimately, the population. Better ways to gather and safely prepare shellfish and seaweed must have spread rapidly along a coastline, and that might have helped fuel our ancestors' initial expansion out of Africa. Techniques for netting fish near ocean and lakeshore spread even further, and, in some places, local tribes found ways to sustain the yield year after year.

Herding is an especially effective trick, or bag of tricks. Instead of waiting for caribou (or wild cattle or sheep or llamas) to wander by, your band could follow the herd. The more your band depended on the herd for meat, the greater your interest in protecting it from other predators and disease, and in helping it find good pasture. Each new trick—tying up and harnessing the herd leader, milking the mothers after their calves are weaned, domesticating dogs to help guard, and many more—boosted the tribe that introduced it, and other tribes soon imitated. The human population grew.

With a denser population, the pace of change picked up. Innovations were more common when there were more people to think of them. Imitation became easier and, at the same time, more important. When a neighboring band developed better rules—whether for processing acorns or sharpening obsidian knives or bonding with in-laws—the local band would be left behind if it didn't imitate. With more and closer neighbors, the new ideas spread more quickly to the neighbors' neighbors and beyond. For example, bow and arrow technology first appeared in one of the world's more densely populated and diverse regions, the Caucasus, about twenty thousand years ago and, with a few centuries, it diffused west into Europe, east into Asia and then into Africa (but not to Australia, which had been cut off by the rising sea).

Jared Diamond's wonderful book *Guns, Germs, and Steel* explains how geography shapes the process. Eurasia stands out because of its seven thousand-mile east-west axis. A good idea could eventually spread from China to Spain, and not be stopped by an ocean or desert or impassable mountains. Equally important, it didn't have to pass through completely different climates. The process went slower in the Americas, partly because of its north-south axis. A good idea in Alaska might also work well in Patagonia, but to get there, it would have to pass through the tropics, where it might not work so well.

Giving Gifts

Hunter-gatherer people exchange ideas occasionally, but they exchange goods every day. Within the nuclear family, the mom typically gathers with the other women and the younger kids, and the dad hunts with the other men in the band, sometimes including the adolescent boys. The family shares food around the camp-fire, and works together to provide shelter and other essentials. Such exchange seems universal.

Sharing across families within a hunter-gatherer band varies somewhat, but typically includes meat from larger game. This sort of sharing is humanity's original social safety net, and is regulated by our moral system. The evolutionary logic is the same as with vampire bats: sharing reduces the risk of an activity that some-times brings a bonanza but often comes up empty.

Human moral systems often encourage the exchange of gifts across group boundaries and even across tribal boundaries. For example, a thousand years ago, after a good salmon run, the local Costanoan band might have invited their inland neighbors over for a three-day feast. After lots of good eating, schmoozing, drum-ming, and dancing, the neighbors might have returned home with lots of dried salmon and strings of fiery pearl beads made from abalone shells. The neighbors may have brought some favors, or invited the local tribe for a feast later, and so the locals could have ended up with obsidian and good bows and acorn cakes.

Such gift exchange brought many benefits, especially once tribes settled down. Your band would be more productive, healthier, and happier if you didn't have to worry about raids from neighboring bands, and if you could get their assistance in emergencies. In patchy environments like California's, a bad year for harvest-ing acorns or seeds, or for hunting, could easily have been a fair to good year in one of the neighboring territories. Both bands would be better off if they helped each other in hard times. Also, intruders might have moved in along the territorial boundary, and tried to raid or take over. Your band's chances of driving them off would be far better if the neighbors helped out. For all these reasons, you wanted the neighboring bands to be part of your broader social safety net, so generous gifts paid off.

Gift exchange brought economic benefits even in good years, and even when the neighbors didn't have any resources different from yours. The point was first explained by economist David Ricardo (1772–1823), but the logic is prehistoric. Suppose that, on average, it takes your tribe about two hours to prepare a pound of smoked salmon and four hours to prepare a pound of acorn cakes. You and your neighbors can both benefit from trade to the extent that their necessary efforts have different proportions. Say that the poor upstream neighbors take five hours for prepare the cake and five hours for the salmon. Your band has the absolute advantage in both products, but Ricardo would say that they have a comparative advantage in acorn cakes. Both bands will be able to eat more (and still enjoy more leisure time!) after exchanging some of your salmon for some of their cakes. It's a win-win proposition: if everyone does what they do comparatively well and par-ticipates in suitable exchanges, then everyone will be better off.

Mutual gains are especially large in patchy environments. Anthropologists recently discovered a startling example a few miles down the coast from my home: the remains of industrial-scale processing of the northern fur seal fifteen hundred years ago. The local Costanoan tribe killed large numbers of seals, more than they could eat themselves, and the cut patterns on the bones are consistent with commercial products: furs and smoked delicacies, like fat chunks, marbled meat, and roast fins. The Costanoans evidently traded with inland valley tribes to get chia seeds (now enjoying a vogue for their high concentration of omega-3 oils) and elk. They also got lots of obsidian quarried further east, on the far side of the Sierra.

The local Costanoans were among the wealthiest Californians of their day, but their lifestyle was not sustainable. Within a century or so, they had hunted the fur seal to extinction in their part of the world, perhaps marking America's first commercially driven ecological disaster. However, later generations found sustainable ways to harvest abalone and other seafood products, and the east-west exchange continued. It allowed more people to live a better life.

Moral codes of hospitality and obligation, not the impersonal forces of supply and demand, governed early exchange between settled tribes. But civilization changed everything. It brought a new moral order. It also intensified the need for exchange, and gave it a separate space—the bazaar—partly detached from the moral sphere. The rest of the chapter sorts it all out.

Building Empires

Civilization as we know it began about twelve thousand years ago in what is now a Kurdish-speaking region near the border of Turkey and Syria. People there invented agriculture.

Even the earliest hunter-gatherers were doubtless aware that they could increase grass seed yields by planting seeds and watering. But doing so is pointless if your group is always on the move. For sedentary groups with plentiful game and wild plants, it still seems not worth the trouble. So what was different in Kurdistan twelve thousand years ago? Some historians think that climate change tipped the balance.

Following several millennia of warm, wet weather, that part of the world suddenly entered an era of cooler, dryer weather called the Lesser Dryas. It lasted several centuries and forced tribes to gather more densely in the remaining good territories. With more people going after the local game and plants, almost anything that broadened the food supply became worthwhile. Very likely women took the lead in finding tricks that improved yields of the wild grasses now called emmer and einkorn: deliberately sowing seeds, using digging sticks and, later, hoes to give the seeds and seedlings a better chance, sowing the best varieties, and so on.

Each new trick was natural, and spread among the local people. They developed better scythes for cutting the grass stems, better techniques for separating the edible grains from the stems and husks, better storage and grinding techniques, and better recipes for cooking and baking. Yields kept increasing, century after century. At some point, some tribes got so good at growing their own food that hunting and gathering wild plants became only a sideline.

Then the transition accelerated. Each increase in yield increased the population density, and that tended to boost innovation and further boost the population. Some of the major innovations: better grains, especially a hybrid called wheat; new sorts of cultivated plants, especially legumes like lentils and garbanzos, whose complementary amino acids hugely boost nutrition; and more domesticated animals. The new tricks started to cross-fertilize, as, for example, when animals domesticated for their meat were harnessed to provide muscle power and milk.

Yields really took off in river valleys with rich soils washed down from the surrounding hills. Yields climbed still higher when farmers learned how to use oxen and plows, and when they developed specialized skills and built specialized structures—dams and irrigation ditches, grain storage bins, plows and hoes and scythes. Economists refer to the process as capital accumulation.

Inhabitants of one village in a river valley would find a better way to encourage ducks to stick around and lay eggs, or better ways to irrigate. The ideas might not be what we consider scientific—for example, egg gathering might involve stories about pleasing the duck spirits—but what matters is whether they work. If so, they are copied by neighboring villagers, and perhaps young men and women will found a new village when things get too crowded. Some of the capital is transportable: you can carry seeds and drive livestock. The trick will spread throughout the river valley, and from one river valley to the next. Nomadic herders don't accumulate as much fixed capital as villagers, but their geographic mobility helps spread ideas widely and rapidly.

Could anything have stopped this runaway process? Much later, something similar fizzled out in North America. Beginning about 700 CE, the Anasazi people developed ways to plant and irrigate corn (maize) and other crops along the tributaries of the Colorado River. They built defensible towns called pueblos and stored their harvests in underground pits called kivas. In decades of good weather, the towns grew quite rapidly. The largest, at Chaco Canyon, housed about five thousand people at its peak. Using big logs dragged from as much as fifty miles away, its residents built the largest structures seen in North America until the late 1800s. But Chaco collapsed around 1150 or 1200 CE and, over the next century or two, so did the other major towns. The reason? Apparently, the dense population at the center required unsustainable irrigation techniques and logging. A drought cycle then pushed the system into collapse, and the population never recovered.

In the Mideast, however, nothing stopped the transformation. Intensive irrigation eventually made the soil too salty in spots, but the Tigris and Euphrates river system was vast and diverse, and no barriers separated it from the rest of Eurasia. The new ideas kept spreading.

Agriculture and herding displace hunter-gatherer lifestyles wherever the climate, water, and soil permit. It is not necessarily progress, however, in the sense of bringing better, happier lives. Twentieth-century anthropologists estimated that !Kung adults worked only twenty-five to forty hours per week, even though they had been pushed out of the best parts of their traditional range in the last couple of centuries. Costanoans probably worked even shorter hours. By contrast, for most of the year, subsistence farmers work from dawn to dusk every day. Comparing skeletons, archaeologists conclude that hunter-gatherers generally enjoyed better nutrition and health than most civilized farmers. We will soon see that the hunter-gatherers probably also enjoyed a better social life.

Settled lifestyles prevailed not by their appeal, but instead by simple arithmetic. They allowed much greater population density, and that was decisive when conflicts arose. If lifestyle A supports one thousand people in a small valley while lifestyle H supports only one hundred, then H will be crowded out. Slowly, over centuries and millennia, hunter-gatherers retreated to marginal habitats unsuitable for agriculture and herding.

For hunter-gatherers, a group of a few dozen or less is usually the efficient size. Larger groups deplete the local resources too quickly and they soon fission. By contrast, raising crops (especially irrigated crops) and livestock and fending off raids is done more efficiently by larger groups, hundreds or even thousands of people living together in the same town for decades at a time. Larger numbers and lower turnover rates help build the infrastructure and help harvest and protect crops.

Thus, the big river valleys filled up. By nine thousand years ago, pretty much all the land along the Tigris and Euphrates rivers suitable for irrigation was intensively farmed. Soon, the same was true of the Nile, and then the other great rivers of temperate and subtropical Eurasia. Their populations exploded, from tens of thousands of people to tens of millions, the majority living in agricultural villages and towns, and then in cities like Eridu, Uruk, and Ur. The age of empires was about to begin.

Imperial Morals

The agricultural revolution didn't just change what our ancestors ate. It turned their moral codes upside down and ushered in alien new lifestyles. For better and for worse, our ancestors became civilized.

But how can we know how it happened? Ancient moral codes don't leave as clear evidence as ancient food technologies. Archaeologists dig up objects like butchered ox bones and millstones that tell us rather plainly how people got their daily bread and meat. To understand the evolution of moral codes, however, we must rely on historical accounts and on twentieth-century anthropologists' descriptions of isolated villagers and herders, and try to fill in the gaps using abstract logic.

One of the cleanest historical accounts comes from the Hawaiian Islands, before Captain Cook put them on the map in 1778. The islands' long isolation makes their experience almost like a controlled experiment on how population density coevolves with agriculture and the moral system.

Hawaii's first human inhabitants, Polynesian navigators and colonists, arrived about 300CE. The population doubled every century, reaching about fourteen thousand by 1350 CE. Up to that point, the people lived in small, egalitarian groups along the coast, gathering seafood supplemented by crops that the original colonists brought with them, like coconuts and taro. But by 1400 CE, all suitable habitats for the simple coastal lifestyle were filled. A new pattern took hold, with large inland settlements supported by labor-intensive agriculture, featuring irrigation systems and pond fields. Field managers, called *konohiki*, supervised the commoners on behalf of the *ali'i*, a hereditary chiefly class. The *kahuna*, a priestly and professional class, emerged about the same time.

As the population expanded further (reaching 225 thousand by the time Cook arrived), the inland habitats also filled and the *ali'i* came into territorial conflict with their neighbors. More successful chiefs (those who could extract more wealth from their people and therefore afford more warriors and gifts to allied chiefs) expanded their domains, occasionally encompassing an entire island. In 1810, with some help from British and American traders, King Kamehameha gained control over all the islands, but unified rule might well have been on the way even without Western contact.

Thousands of years earlier, Eurasia's river valley civilizations had followed the same social trajectory. On the Tigris and Euphrates and the Nile, and a bit later on the Indus and Yellow and Yangtze, villages became more numerous and larger as new agricultural techniques spread. Semi-egalitarian "big man" organizations in smaller villages gave way to hierarchies in the larger towns, which eventually grew into cities like Uruk.

At the top of the hierarchy sat a military and religious elite. They fought their counterparts upstream and downstream, and the winners were those with the most effective military, often because they controlled the most efficient agriculture. Over the centuries, the top guy controlled larger and larger collections of cities and villages, and started to call himself king. Eventually, one of these guys would conquer the whole region, as the Scorpion King seems to have done for the upper and lower kingdoms of the Nile around 3450 BCE.

This course of events has an evolutionary logic. Agricultural populations depend on storable harvests and livestock herds—without them, most people would starve. These forms of wealth are transferable—they can be given from one person to another and, by the same token, can also be taken by force. They are tempting targets for hunter bands that are down on their luck, and for unfriendly neighboring villagers. Indeed, raiders and rustlers owe their existence to stored harvests and herds of livestock—they can't make a living off the meager stored wealth of hunter-gatherers.

Agriculture thus multiplies the need for efficient defense at the same time that it multiplies the population size. Unfortunately, egalitarian moral codes can't cope. They can work quite well for small groups where eye contact is enough to organize a counterattack on raiders. But they break down when the group size gets too large.

Part of the problem is simply coordination. For example, I once worked in downtown San Francisco and often met friends near the Banker's Heart to choose a lunch spot. There were hundreds of options. Would it be something quick at North Beach? Maybe a Sichuan restaurant in Chinatown? When there were only about four of us, we usually made a decision in less than a minute, but it often took more than five minutes to decide when there were eight or more friends. Section A6 of the Appendix lays out the unpleasant arithmetic of egalitarianism: the probability of reaching timely consensus on a plan of action falls rapidly as the group size increases. When a large village has to react immediately to invaders, there is no time to seek consensus. Someone has to be in charge and give orders.

Hierarchy is the inevitable result. Moral codes that give authority to a single individual or small subgroup tend to do better once the permanent population size exceeds a few hundred. They displace the traditional egalitarian code because they work better. Over hundreds of years, moral codes compete, and the codes that spread are those that are most effective in maintaining internal cohesion and productivity and building military strength.

The greatest good for the greatest number has nothing to do with it. The new moral codes in the early agricultural societies often brought misery to those at the bottom, the 90 percent who tilled the soil. Unlike hunter-gatherers, who can punish would-be tyrants or leave if they don't get their fair share, people at the bottom of the civilized order have little recourse. They can't just leave (unless they happen to know of unclaimed and defensible fertile land elsewhere, and this usually doesn't last long), and it is hard to oppose professional soldiers. The ruler needs to allow people at the bottom sufficient resources to survive, reproduce, and work, but often finds it in his interest to take everything else.

Some primates are naturally hierarchical, for example, chimps and baboons. Others are not, including orangutans and bonobos. Humans go either way, but seem to prefer egalitarian lifestyles. Civilization, therefore, is a mixed blessing, and to the people at the bottom rung of the hierarchy, life might seem like a fall from the Garden of Eden.

Civilization and hierarchy reshaped morality. As mentioned in Chapter 1, hunter-gatherers have unified moral codes. The proper way to behave seamlessly covers all activities—raising kids, sharing food, finding a spouse, working with neighboring tribes and with the spirits of Nature, and dealing with death. In sharp contrast, civilized morals are fragmented and hierarchical. Ordinary adults are encouraged to take a subservient, childlike role in dealings with the religious and political elite. And the elite groups have their own special in-group codes justifying their privileged positions, sometimes including paternalistic obligations toward their inferiors. In many cases, the ruling elite descended from conquerors from a different ethnic group. Such elites find it easier to maintain a separate in-group identity but harder to maintain the loyalty of commoners.

The larger and more diverse the kingdom by ethnicity and class, the more problematic is maintaining order using only implicit moral codes. People often deal with strangers who may not share the same understanding of proper way to behave and who might not be sanctioned by peers if they misbehave.

Every civilization responded to the problem by externalizing morals: the rulers announced explicit rules and appointed professional enforcers. The people then knew what to expect and could get on with their business. Some of the earliest known writing, in Babylonia and beyond, was to announce rules. And, as we will see in later chapters, most empires had a state-sanctioned religion that bolstered the rulers.

But externalized morals were not enough to keep everyone fed and on task. Civilization needed another device for coping with social dilemmas: markets.

Bazaar Logic

> The propensity to truck, barter and exchange one thing for another . . . is common to all men, and to be found in no other race of animals. . . . . Man is an animal that makes bargains: no other animal does this—no dog exchanges bones with another.
>
> —*Adam Smith, Wealth of Nations*

Civilization might not bring the good life to everyone, but it does open up new possibilities. The class structure becomes far more complex. The ruling families, including the military and religious authorities, take the top positions, and subsistence farmers or farm workers or slaves are at the bottom. In between are a few specialized classes such as soldiers, craftsmen, scribes, and eventually, traders and merchants.

The larger the city, the greater the scope for specialized work, say in making pottery or weapons, or in managing irrigated fields. Specialists generally are more efficient, perhaps because their talents lead them to their line of work, and surely because they get to refine their skills and equipment. And more efficient production means that the total wealth grows faster than the total population.

But people will specialize only when they know they can get the necessities (and hopefully some luxuries) that they don't make themselves. They must be able to exchange the fruits of their labor for the other items. As noted by Ricardo and his followers, the potential gains are larger when the people involved have greater differences in preferences, technology, and endowments. Patchy environments create such diversity for sedentary tribes. The class structure itself creates very diverse endowments and preferences, and therefore enlarges the mutual gains.

Of course, there is no guarantee that the gains will be shared equally. Indeed, the ancient upper classes almost always took the lion's share.

How does the exchange take place? One way is to alter gift exchange by making the "gifts" mandatory. This is called redistribution. For example, in a famous Bible story, Joseph foresaw seven good years in Egypt followed by seven years of failed harvest, and the Pharaoh asked him to deal with it. Nowadays, Joseph probably would have bought grain in the open market during the seven fat years, but markets on that scale did not yet exist in Egypt, or anywhere else. Instead, Joseph collected grain as a 20 percent in-kind royal tax on the farmers, and then rationed it out to the Pharaoh's subjects during the seven lean years.

Some historians believe that redistribution dominated the economies of the world's first cities. According to a recent account, the central temple at Uruk directed the efforts of tens of thousands of city dwellers beginning around 4500 BCE. The temple staff collected mandatory contributions (in-kind taxes) from everyone in the city, and then gave everyone rations throughout the year. The first writing in the world, now called cuneiform, evolved from the marks used to keep accounts.

Around 2500 BCE, after a resurgent Ur had replaced Uruk as Sumeria's cultural capital, the city's ruler took over the temple's role in coordinating redistribution. In part due to climate change and accumulated salt in the fields, the whole system began to break down after 2000 BCE.

Redistribution has its limits. It works best when the authorities proceed according to a well-understood plan. But such plans can't accommodate special circumstances. For example, one family might not need their entire oil ration that month, and might need fish for a sick child, while a fisherman might have a large catch that day. It's almost impossible for redistribution to deal with such once-off situations, yet they occur all the time.

Could true, voluntary gift exchange fill the gap? After all, reciprocity is one of the building blocks of the moral system: I do something for you at some personal expense, but I expect you eventually to return the favor so that we both come out ahead. As we saw in Chapter 1, this works wonderfully for symmetric favors that are low cost to the donor and high value to the recipient, if they expect to interact often into the indefinite future.

But gift exchange also has its limits. Self-serving bias creates problems, even within a family or tribe, when the favors are not symmetric. For example, when I do my sister a favor, she may underestimate the time and trouble I took. Over time, she may forget how much my favor helped her and so undervalue her debt to me. Despite my own exceptional resistance to bias, I, likewise, may overvalue the debt.

Gift exchange becomes increasingly problematic as we move from family and close neighbors to more distant neighbors and strangers. The favors become more asymmetric and future interaction becomes increasingly doubtful. At the same time, the potential gains from exchange are much larger with strangers, since there is greater diversity in productive capacity, resources, and preferences. The conclusion is clear: the larger and more diverse a human society is, the more it needs something beyond gift exchange.

Thousands of years ago, humans developed just such a device, called *spot exchange*. The return favor is not expected sometime in the indefinite future, but rather, right now, on the spot. In spot exchange, we may "truck and bargain," but nobody does anyone any favors until we reach agreement. Then we simultaneously exchange the favors (or goods or services). For example, I give you three bushels of corn at the same time you give me an axe blade.

As Adam Smith said, spot exchange is unknown in other species, but is widespread among humans. It is simpler than gift exchange in that you don't have to worry so much about past and future behavior since it is less tightly tied to ongoing social obligations. But it is more complex in that explicit agreements must be negotiated and executed.

Spot exchange transforms the basic social dilemma—the divergence between self-interest and group interest—but does not make it disappear. Tough bargainers tend to do better personally, but they also tend to shrink the pie. For example, if you won't accept less than four bushels of corn for the axe blade, I might give in, but I will trade less often. Or I might not give in and we both lose the opportunity for gains from trade. The transformed dilemma is that everyone has a personal incentive to get better terms by understating her willingness to trade, and such understatements block some of the mutual gains.

As spot exchange becomes more frequent and routine, several things happen spontaneously that make it work better. First, people find a customary time and place to trade. A new seller will find more buyers near existing sellers during their business hours, so he'll open his shop next door at the same times. More sellers attract more buyers, and vice versa, so the process feeds on itself. The upshot is a central marketplace—a bazaar.

Bazaars might have originated in prehistoric harvest festivals. As population densities increased, festivals became monthly affairs, then more frequent. (Weeks are a later invention!) Some people then found it worthwhile to become part-time specialized sellers or middlemen, and eventually (when the bazaar operated daily), full-time. Bazaars survive today in cities on every continent, for example, as souks in the Arab world, as night markets in large East Asian cities, as weekly street markets in many European cities, and as farmers' markets and crafts fairs in the United States. Shopping malls are a modern U.S. mutation that has spread around the world.

Sellers in most modern bazaars, and perhaps in all ancient bazaars, expect to bargain with buyers. The bargaining process itself can be costly, as illustrated by a scene in *Life of Brian*, a Monty Python film. Brian hopes to quickly purchase a disguise before his pursuers catch up, and pays the seller, Harry, the asking price of twenty shekels. But Harry refuses the money and insists on teaching Brian how to haggle properly. In his anxiety, Brian is a slow learner, but Harry finally gets Brian to haggle and, in the end, happily accepts sixteen shekels. Brian dons the disguise, barely in time to escape.

Haggling survives where most traders' time is less valuable, and where there are some impatient buyers (e.g., tourists with high time costs). Impatient buyers are weak bargainers, and the local Harrys may extract so much extra profit from them that posting realistic prices is not worthwhile. That's how twentieth century U.S. car dealers worked: customers who were weak bargainers would pay the list price and patient hagglers would get a better deal.

Market Magic

The bazaar takes exchange to the edge of the moral sphere. Its moral code is rudimentary, and anybody can participate. No group membership or ongoing personal relationship is required.

It might seem that bazaars would choke on their own success. They attract new participants and increase the number of different goods on offer. Potentially, that is a severe problem—it becomes harder to find a direct trade as the variety of goods increases. For example, you might have fish to sell and want to buy a shirt. There may be several people willing to sell shirts, and many others willing to buy fish, but it might be impossible for you to find someone willing to do both. You need something beyond direct trade—something like money.

Economists Robert Clower and Peter Howitt recently ran a computer simulation to see how the problem plays out. Starting from a completely unorganized state with no trade, their simulated traders followed very simple rules. At random times, some trader would open a shop for a random pair of commodities, trading one directly for the other in both directions. Other traders just looked for shops at which they could trade to personal advantage. Shops went out of business when they couldn't cover costs, and they expanded when profitable.

Clower and Howitt found that money and organized markets emerged spontaneously after a few simulated centuries of weekly activity. That is, if you joined their simulation, you'd have trouble trading in early decades, but after markets matured, you could solve your shirt-fish problem by making two trades at two different shops. All shops would trade one particular good, call it money, for some other good. You could just sell your fish at one shop for money, and use it to buy a shirt at another shop. Toward the end of their simulations, everyone could buy and sell the goods they wanted, and enjoy the gains from trade.

In the simulations, the good that emerged as money usually was the one that was cheapest to transport. The same thing seems to happen in the real world: goods that are widely accepted in transactions are those whose value (per unit volume) is high and easy to verify. Gold and silver coins are classic examples, but other possibilities range from strings of shells (a specialty of Chumash villagers living off the southern California coast a thousand years ago) to today's printed paper and secure electronic records. When money is used, trades are defined by prices: so much money per unit of the traded good.

Another spontaneous improvement is that prices unify as markets thicken. That is, as more buyers and more sellers transact more often, the sellers will tend to charge the same price for equivalent goods and services. This reduces guesswork and haggling.

Even more important, thick markets vaporize the transformed dilemma, because nobody gets better terms by understating willingness to trade. For example, consider a farmers' market, where the going price today for a standard bunch of carrots is $1.00. As a shopper, you'd walk by a booth that asked $1.25 for a standard bunch, or asked $1.00 for a substandard bunch. The booth manager will usually pass up your offer of 75 cents for a standard bunch. Market competition is the key. When there are lots of alternative buyers and sellers, tough bargaining hurts only the tough guy. An exception that proves the rule: at the end of the day, there are few alternative buyers, and, at that point, a booth manager with lots of unsold carrots might accept your tough offer.

But what determines the going price? This is a favorite topic of economics textbooks, which show how the intersection of the supply curve and the demand curve sets the competitive equilibrium price. Here is a less abstract example of the argument. Sellers at the farmer's market use their experience and the costs of acquiring produce to decide how much to bring that day and what prices to post. They adjust prices that are out of line with other sellers, or on items that sell very fast or very slow. These trade specialists thus choose prices to keep inventories in line, that is, to balance the quantity produced (supply) with the quantity consumed (demand). Prices change from one week to the next so as to reflect changes in production costs (e.g., due to a bumper crop or to a blight or drought) and changes in consumers' willingness to pay (e.g., due to a carrot juice craze or a warning against too much carotene).

The centerpiece of economic theory is the proposition that trade at competitive equilibrium (CE) prices is efficient. The basic argument is simple. All carrot consumers who value a bunch at more than the CE price of $1.00 will pay just $1.00 and keep the surplus value. Likewise, all carrot growers who can produce (and bring to market) at unit cost less than $1.00 will do so and keep the difference as profit. In this way, all potential gains from carrots are realized, and are split in a particular way between producers and consumers.

The argument applies, of course, not just to carrots and other produce, but to everything sold in organized markets. CE price is an efficient filter, satisfying all customers who value the thing most highly and turning away those who value it less, and encouraging all low cost producers and discouraging higher cost producers. The kicker is that the CE price filter adjusts to meet changing conditions, so that all potential gains are always realized.

It all sounds rather mundane, but the result is magical. The social dilemma is completely solved! Thick markets command complete cooperation among all participants, even when they are total strangers.

This seems too good to be true. What's the catch? Do prices really unify under realistic conditions? As conditions change, do prices really adjust and track competitive equilibrium? Textbooks traditionally couldn't answer these questions because supply and demand are not observable in the farmer's market or in any other ongoing market. As a seller, you might know your own cost but probably not that of other sellers, so you don't know the actual supply curve. Likewise, buyers are unlikely to reveal their true willingness to pay, so demand, too, is unknown. Until fairly recently, the magic of markets always seemed a bit hypothetical.

Vernon Smith won the 2002 Nobel Prize in economics largely for his laboratory dissection of market performance. In a typical experiment, Smith gave one token each to four sellers, and privately told each its cost, say $2.00 or $2.50. So he knew the exact supply curve. Likewise, he induced a demand curve by privately telling four other traders the values at which he would repurchase units they acquired, say $2.25 or $3.25. Smith ran a continuous double auction market, in which each seller could call out an offer price ("ask") at any time and, likewise, buyers could call out bids. Smith kept track of accepted prices, and paid the profits in cash. For instance, if a buyer with value $3.25 accepted a $2.75 ask from a seller whose cost was $2.00, then the gains on this transaction would be the value in excess of cost, $3.25 − $2.00 = $1.25. The buyer would take home his value less price, $3.25 − $2.75 = $0.50, while the seller's take home profit would be price less cost, $2.75 − $2.00 = $0.75.

Amazingly, within a few repetitions of the market, transaction prices clustered very near the CE price. Even better, when Smith shifted supply or demand by privately changing the costs for some sellers or the values of some buyers, the actual prices tracked the CE price pretty well. And almost all potential gains from trade were actually realized. When I heard about these results as a graduate student I was very skeptical, but later I got the chance to try it myself. It really does work.

If markets are so wonderful, though, why do we still have severe economic problems? Indeed, why has the world always had such problems?

Markets do have their limitations. For example, they don't work so well when there is no competition among sellers to offer buyers the best deal. Markets freeze up when sellers (or buyers) fear being cheated or robbed. Other problems crop up when one side has better information than the other does, or when benefits or costs leak out to nonparticipants.

Later chapters will examine all these limitations. For now, we'll just look at the first one, because it loomed large in the ancient world. It is nicely illustrated in a legend about the renowned Greek philosopher Thales of Miletus (624–546 BCE). He decided to demonstrate the practical value of philosophy by quietly purchasing all the olive presses on his island. When the crop arrived, he didn't have to compete with anyone, and was able to charge olive growers very high prices. This trick (now called cornering and squeezing the market!) no doubt earned him a juicy profit, but it must have bankrupted many olive growers and raised the price that local people paid for olive oil. Overall, the harm to the local economy surely exceeded Thales' economic benefits.

Mercantile Empires

The ancient river valley empires based their economies on intensive agriculture. Long-distance trade—to India and Egypt and beyond—was quite useful in Uruk and the other leading Sumerian cities. Sometimes, it was controlled by networks of merchant families from another city, notably the ancient Assyrians, but often, the long distance trade was conducted by high-ranking servants of the king or the temple.

Political forces normally trumped market forces in the ancient empires. The rulers' priority was not protecting traders from cheaters and thieves but rather in protecting their own entrenched monopolies. To illustrate, suppose that salt is much in demand in the kingdom's inland capital city, and can be obtained cheaply at a coastal province. By monopolizing the salt trade, the king (or a loyal retainer) can charge a high price and get a steady income for the royal treasury. If just any-one were allowed to import salt, its price would fall dramatically, essentially to the cost of producing it at the coast plus transportation. The lower price would greatly benefit the people as a whole, and boost the economy, but would reduce the king's income and power. So the royal choice is clear.

The problem is not just with salt, but also with silk and slaves, and pretty much any good that could provide a lucrative royal monopoly. The ruling elite would typically make sure nobody but their own inner circle could deal in those goods, and thereby earn what economists call "monopoly rents." These rents fed the royal treasury, but stifled innovation and stunted ancient markets.

This "rent seeking" problem prevailed even in empires based on trade. At their peak, from 1200–800 BCE, the Phoenicians dominated trade from Turkey to Spain, and monopolized several distinctive commodities, including royal purple dye, transparent glass, and cedar. The Bible mentions King Solomon's Phoenician ally, King Hiram of Tyre, and his gifts of cedar and skilled artisans in building the Temple. From their home base on the coast of Lebanon, the Phoenicians founded numerous colonies in North Africa, Cyprus, Sicily, and Spain, and reportedly sailed far into the North Atlantic and down the West African coast. Phoenicia had one of the first alphabetical scripts, a precursor of the Greek alphabet and our own.

Trade expeditions—the lifeblood of the Phoenician empire—were led by princes and priests, especially those serving the god Melqart, the "protector of trade" who, according to hostile accounts, required human child sacrifices. To maintain rents for the priestly cartels, the Phoenicians launched numerous wars against foreign rivals and won most of them. As usual, the cartels shrunk the economic pie but steered the lion's share to the temple and palace. Eventually, Phoenicia faced competition from its colonies. Carthage, in North Africa, was the most prominent by the time the Phoenician homeland faded around 600 BCE.

By then, much of the northern Mediterranean and Black sea coast was dominated by Greek colonies. In contrast to the Phoenicians, Greek upper classes scorned commerce—to them, plunder, and even humble farming and crafts production, seemed morally superior. However, Greece is a land of islands and peninsulas, and maritime trade was what brought wealth and power to her cities. Greek city-states that lowered class barriers and opened to commerce pulled ahead of their rivals.

Athens is a prime example. It became the first among equals, and Athenian silver coins help monetize trade throughout the Greek world and beyond. Later, Athens became an imperial power. Her golden age faded as the political base narrowed and the cartels gained power. Alexander the Great opened new and very lucrative trade routes, but after his early death, his vast empire broke into three pieces and again tended toward royal cartels.

Rome, founded by tribesmen influenced by local Greek colonies, dominated the Mediterranean, and far beyond, after finally wiping out Carthage in 146 BCE. In the days of the Republic, Romans maintained a very practical attitude toward trade. Roman laws were quite favorable to commerce, as they protected property rights and enforced contracts. Rome's central gathering place, the Forum, was a bazaar as well as a platform for public speech. The Republic's many innovations include the world's first stock market and what we now call English auctions.

Some economists argue that Rome's rise was largely due to the world's most open market economy prior to sixteenth-century Europe. Surely, the empire generated more wealth than any of its predecessors. However, the usual rent-seeking forces grew stronger over time, especially after the emperors seized control from the senate. Many historians note that innovation virtually disappeared then. The main cause, I suspect, was the centralization of political power and cartelization of the economy.

The fall of the (Western) Roman Empire is discussed in hundreds of books that offer many conflicting interpretations. I am not qualified to compare their merits, but do want to mention an economic episode. In 301 CE, Emperor Diocletian imposed price and wage controls after issuing more coins, and imposed the death penalty on speculators and merchants who tried to evade the controls. The results, of course, were disastrous. With more money in circulation, buyers bid up prices of goods, and sellers' costs also rose. The price controls prevented markets from adjusting. Sellers couldn't recover their costs, so they stopped selling and markets stopped functioning.

Many Roman citizens by then were accustomed to producing for the market and buying what they needed, and they were devastated. Entire towns went bankrupt, especially those producing cloth or wine for trade. Imperial tax revenues plummeted.

Diocletian and his successors tried ever more desperate measures—in-kind taxes, permanent tax exemptions for political and financial supporters, and minting more and more coins with lower contents of gold or silver or copper. Trade dried up across the Mediterranean, and Europe entered an economic Dark Age.

3

The Great Transformation
Why Is the Modern World So Rich?

About two hundred years ago, a new system took root in Western Europe. That system then spread across the globe, bringing down the last of the great empires and setting humanity on a new course. Markets are the core of the new system, but it reaches far beyond the economic sphere and pervades all aspects of our social life, including governance, technology, education, and even religion.

As in all evolutionary transitions, the new system used preexisting components. It combined them in a new way, gained critical mass at an edge of the existing order, and then swept the world, creating new niches and destroying old ones.

What was the new combination? Economic historian Karl Polanyi (1886–1964) put it this way: "Instead of economy being embedded in social relations, social relations are embedded in the economic system." He added that the "great transformation" to the self-regulating market system "resembles more the metamorphosis of the caterpillar than any alteration that can be expressed in terms of continuous growth and development."

Economist Axel Leijonhufvud describes the transformation by comparing the life of a hypothetical modern Frenchman, M. Baudot, to the surprisingly well-documented life of an actual tenth-century French serf named Bodo. "Bodo had short life expectancy, was unfree and uneducated, and lived a life of unceasing hard physical labor," writes Leijonhufvud. Almost all of Bodo's consumption was produced by his own household, and a handful of others he knew personally, while, by contrast, a vast and ever-changing network of producers sustains M. Baudot. It includes people halfway around the world, "whom he has never met, and of whose existence he is hardly aware. On the other hand, he may or may not know his immediate neighbors, nor is he economically dependent on them in any significant way."

This chapter studies the metamorphosis. We begin with the caterpillar.

1000 CE

A thousand years ago, things were looking good for Basil II, Emperor of Constantinople. He had consolidated control of the empire's core, now modern-day Turkey and Greece. He had also recaptured much of the Empire's southern and eastern lands, now Lebanon, Syria, and northern Iraq, for the first time since Muslim armies swept through centuries before. In 1000 CE, Armenia had rejoined the empire as a tributary. Basil's treasury was getting stronger by the day, and his alliance with the Rus gave him confidence that he could finally take on his most dangerous enemy, Samuil, King of the Bulgars.

Basil had navigated treacherous currents. Born to Emperor Romanos II and his beautiful young Armenian wife, Theophano, young Basil saw his father die of poison and his mother keep power by marrying a top general. But, conspiring with her new lover John, his mother poisoned Basil's unpopular stepfather a few years later. The Church Patriarch allowed John to be crowned emperor, but only after he agreed to exile Theophano. In her rage, she denounced John, and when Basil stood with him, she screamed that her son was conceived illegitimately. A few years later, in 976 CE, John died of—you guessed it—poison, and eighteen-year-old Basil inherited the crown.

Basil moved cautiously at first. He honed his military skills, and learned administration (a weak point of his predecessors) from the wily eunuch Lekapenos. In 988 CE, he made a deal with Prince Vladimir of Kiev, leader of the Rus barbarians. The Prince married Basil's young sister Anna, and in exchange, he and his subjects converted to Christianity. Vladimir also sent six thousand shock troops, giving Basil the muscle he needed to capture and kill the powerful landholders who presumably had poisoned his predecessor. With internal threats finally neutralized, Basil was able to fill the depleted treasury while reducing farmers' taxes.

Basil eventually did beat the Bulgars. At the time of his death in 1026 CE, his Byzantine (or Eastern Roman) Empire was stronger than since the days of Justinian, five centuries earlier.

But Basil never was able to revive the western part of the Roman Empire, and his successors frittered away his gains. His exploits had no lasting effect. Nor did those of his contemporaries, the great Muslim rulers Al-Mansur of Cordoba (Spain), Mahmud of Ghazni (Pakistan and Afghanistan), Tenkaminen of Ghana, and Al-Hakim of North Africa. Indeed, since the dawn of the age of empires six thousand years earlier, nothing fundamental had changed.

Imperial Economics

According to the *Wall Street Journal*'s millennium edition, Basil and his peers were the richest men of their era. Like their predecessors, each owed his wealth to some combination of plunder, taxing peasants and miners, and control of long distance trade.

In those days, plunder and long distance trade were close substitutes. Basil might have been able to increase his wealth and power by sacking Cairo, Al-Hakim's capital, but that was a risky proposition. Basil would have to cover the up-front costs of assembling and moving a large enough army. He'd have to worry about how the soldiers, many of them farm boys from Thrace and Armenia, would perform on the road, and about what might happen meanwhile back in Byzantium. All things considered, Basil instead found it more prudent to send Al-Hakim furs and slaves (coming into his empire from the Rus) and silk (from Song China via Afghanistan), and to encourage Al-Hakim to send gold and ivory (from Ghana) in return.

Such long distance trade is more like gift exchange than like a market transaction. Often using polite diplomatic language (or, sometimes, rude ultimatums), the rulers bargained and made long-term deals, and delegated the details and the logistics to favored subjects. The terms of trade often had more to do with military capabilities than with impersonal forces of supply and demand.

A few traders enjoyed a degree of independence, especially those in a network that spanned the Muslim Mediterranean a thousand years ago. The region included about a dozen major trade centers between Cairo and Cordoba, each with a large bazaar and specialized traders, warehouses, and swarms of retailers. The Maghribi network shipped goods from a center with lower prices to centers with higher prices, say wheat and pepper from Cairo and wool and wine from Cordoba.

Economic historian Avner Greif points out that long distance traders faced a severe social dilemma. Agents at remote centers could siphon off a lot of money and not face questioning for many months, and then could plausibly tell their master that bandits (or local officials) had taken the goods, or that prices were low because the goods had deteriorated or because other cargoes had arrived earlier. The veil of risk and delay made it difficult to prove that the agent had cheated.

Greif argues that the Maghribi network thrived due to a unique moral system. Most of the traders descended from Jewish émigrés from Baghdad, and their minority status and ethnic ties made the network very difficult for outsiders to enter. With many network members in each trade center, there were ample opportunities for cross-monitoring and gossip, as in hunter-gatherer bands. High levels of literacy and the exchange of personal and commercial letters extended monitors' reach. Any would-be cheater risked the loss of reputation, and that would be a professional and personal disaster. Network members could cheat a disgraced trader with impunity, or just shun him, and, at the same time, his marriage prospects (or those of his children) would suffer. Cheaters, therefore, were very few and, once identified, they usually returned their ill-gotten gains quickly. The network thus enjoyed a high degree of honesty, and that enabled profitable long distance trade.

In 1000 CE, the vast majority of the planet's quarter of a billion people hardly noticed the long distance trade. Most were peasants, paying taxes to local authorities. Market exchange was quite limited—perhaps a few times each year, a peasant might take a spare duck or pig or extra grain to the local market and come back with farm tools or furniture constructed locally, or perhaps a little pepper from far away.

People, in those days, worked and lived in a thicket of social obligations. European peasants, for example, owed local authorities and neighbors various sorts of unpaid weekly and annual labor called weekwork, boonwork, corvée, and banalities. In return, the peasant could grow certain crops on particular strips of land, share the communal grain fields, and get limited access to the lord's pastures, flour mills, and ovens. He and his family seldom had much choice in how to spend their time, but they did receive a small degree of social security. Polanyi summarizes as follows:

> Though the institution of the market was fairly common since the later Stone Age, its role was no more than incidental to economic life . . . man's economy, as a rule, is submerged in his social relationships. He does not act so as to safeguard his individual interest in the possession of material goods; he acts so as to safeguard his social standing, his social claims, his social assets. He values material goods only insofar as they serve this end. (43, 46)

Taxation and plunder, in those days, also were closely related, and bound up in the social web. To understand the connections, it may be helpful to consider a simple and stylized two-person game. Player 1, the serf, let us say, chooses, during the growing season, how much to plant and how much effort to invest in raising the crop. At harvest time, Player 2, the landlord or duke, chooses how much of the crop to grab for himself, leaving the rest to Player 1.

The solution to this game depends on whether the two players think that the game is one-shot or, alternatively, that they will play it every year into the indefinite future. In the one-shot case, Player 2 may be thought of as a "roving bandit," and the equilibrium is very unfortunate. It then is rational for Player 2 to take virtually everything, and Player 1, anticipating this, will invest virtually nothing in raising the crop. Both players receive a minimal payoff. The lesson is that when plunder is expected, everyone suffers, even the bandit. The situation breeds extreme poverty and a low population.

Things turn out better when Player 2 is a "stationary bandit." In this case, it is in his interest to encourage Player 1 to invest more next year. The more patient Player 2 is, the more he will let Player 1 keep, so the more Player 1 will invest. A game theoretic analysis shows that the result is larger crops and higher payoffs for both players. This solution to the game would be implemented via social customs and obligations, sometimes reinforced by emotional ties of loyalty and trust.

That is, when the local authority is confident that he will remain in control into the indefinite future, he will tax serfs at a lower rate, and the serfs will increase the harvest, benefiting everyone. This may help explain why, after he killed the evil landlords, Basil was able to reduce farm taxes and strengthen his treasury at the same time.

Imperial Politics

Although details varied, the basic plan for civilized life was the same everywhere, millennium after millennium. Peasants formed the base of the political pyramid. The local authorities took some of their crop as taxes, and some of their boys to serve as soldiers. (Slaves often anchored the base, doing the worst tasks in farming, mining, or rowing.) The pyramid quickly narrowed as you moved higher. Junior officers and artisans and merchants occupied the middle tier. Above them, stood small elite groups such as generals, nobles, high officials, and religious leaders. One man—the emperor, we'll say, though his title might be caliph or king or khan—sat at the apex and held the reins of power.

The emperor always faced threats, both internal and external. Always, some ambitious nephew or duke or neighboring emperor was ready to grab the pyramid's top spot whenever he thought his soldiers could beat the incumbent's. Therefore, the emperor's first priority was military might. Young Basil learned horsemanship, sword fighting, and military tactics before anything else.

But how do you build a loyal and strong military? You need a coalition of elite groups. Basil, for example, received the blessings of the Patriarch, the highest official in the Eastern Christian Church, and (despite complaints about its increased taxes) the church enjoyed support and protection throughout Basil's empire. Unlike his predecessors, Basil adopted the children of fallen officers, and spent years with the troops in the field, earning their personal loyalty.

Personal ties help, but they are not enough to sustain a medium or large empire—the elite groups are just too numerous and diverse to bind together into a single in-group. To maintain control, every imperial dynasty needed steady streams of revenue. Take the silk trade, for example. Mahmud of Ghazni would allow traders to buy bolts of fine cloth in Western China and (after paying him a hefty tax) sell them at Basil's eastern border. But Basil wouldn't let just anyone buy. Silk was a royal monopoly, a crucial source of revenue and power. He'd allow only favored merchants to buy the silk and to sell it to the Maghribi traders and other customers in the west. The merchants would return a large chunk of the revenue to Basil's treasury, and offer him political support. If they didn't, Basil could exile or execute them and find someone more pliable.

It wasn't just Basil, and it wasn't just silk. Monopoly profits from key commodities were the economic lifeblood of traditional empires. Merchants could not obtain the goods (say sesame oil or salt) without royal permission. That came at a price—high taxes or license fees—but in return, the merchant didn't have to worry about new rivals entering and cutting price, and usually he got some protection from roving bandits. These royal cartels were economically very inefficient, but they provided steady income that glued the top of the pyramid together.

Of course, there were variants of the basic plan. Occasionally, a woman occupied the top position—most notably, Hatshepsut in Egypt (reigned 1479–58 BCE) and Elizabeth I in England (1588–1603). Once in awhile, two or three people shared the top spot. For example, a triumvirate took over Rome after the assassination of Julius Caesar, but that only lasted a few years until Augustus pushed the other two aside and became the first Roman emperor.

The pyramid flattened in the hinterland and in border regions occupied by self-sufficient farmers and herdsmen. The lifestyle there could be more egalitarian and natural, and this has always had an appeal. Indeed, my own generation felt the tug, and many of us went "back to the land" in remote rural areas. We tried, as much as possible, to produce our own food, shelter, and clothing, to trade goods and favors with our neighbors, and to avoid long-distance trade.

Such a life is quite satisfying in many ways, but it is seldom a practical option. To carve out a family homestead takes a pretty good tool set and access to fertile, unpopulated land. Such opportunities are rare and fleeting. When conditions are good enough for the homesteaders to prosper, the population expands rapidly and hierarchy normally returns within a generation or two. This was the story of the Western frontier in nineteenth-century North America, and also the story of the northeastern European plains in medieval times, after the wheeled plow and draft animals made it practical to farm the heavy soil. Where the land is less fertile, say, in remote mountain regions, one might find yeoman farmers for many generations, but the lifestyle never spreads back into the more densely populated areas.

Thus, until a few centuries ago, markets always played a subordinate role in every society. Among hunter-gatherers or herdsmen or self-sufficient farmers, personalized gift exchange is much more important than market exchange. In the great empires, the ruler and his minions monopolized access to the most important commodities. They extracted as much income as possible, and seldom left much for ordinary people. So markets were static and uncompetitive, just one component of the traditional political order.

The European Advantage

How did Western Europe find a new way forward? As late as 1400, it still lagged behind the great empires of China, India, and the Islamic world. For example, the most promising new technologies of that time—the water wheel, eyeglasses (which greatly increased craftsmen's productive years), clockwork, printing, and gunpowder—were all invented elsewhere, mostly in China.

Europeans had the lead in only one significant technology. Leveraging expertise in casting iron church bells, they made bigger and better cannons than anyone else. In 1450, the Ottomans hired Transylvanian Christians to build cannons to help break the previously invulnerable defenses of Constantinople. They did their job, and the Ottomans overran Basil's city three years later—the final fall of the Roman Empire.

Western Europe's real advantage was subtler: in the 1400s, it was more open to the new technologies than anywhere else, and the technologies spread more rapidly. New economic practices also spread more quickly in Europe. For example, about then, the new "putting out" system allowed farm families to earn cash by weaving and sewing at home in seasons when they weren't busy planting and harvesting crops. Equally important, new governance practices started to take root, especially free cities. Europe still lagged, but somehow it was able to move faster.

Why? Two reasons. First, the dark ages had lifted, and once again, Western Europe was in contact with the outside world. In most respects, the Crusades (1096–1272) were disastrous—despite the high cost in blood and treasure, Jerusalem had become less accessible, and many Christian countries, especially Byzantium, were weakened—but they helped reopen connections to the Mediterranean and beyond. By 1400, and ever after, goods and new ideas poured into Europe from the world's most advanced civilizations.

Second, Europe was so fragmented politically that nobody was able to stop disruptive new practices. Suppose, for example, that you were an ambitious young apprentice dyer in Bruges in 1500, and that you just discovered a new and cheaper way of dyeing cloth. Widespread adoption of your idea would threaten the livelihoods of established dyers and their suppliers, so, in a traditional empire, the dyers would work through their patrons in the ruling elite to suppress your idea. But in Bruges, you'd have many options. Your master could profit by adopting your method, and if the local dyers' guild cracked down, then you (or perhaps another apprentice who picked up your idea) could go to Amsterdam or some other city where the dyers' guild wasn't so strong, or where the guilds wanted to grow. Weavers and tailors in your new town would then have an advantage due to their access to cheaper, higher quality dye.

Europe's Markets

Even deep in the Dark Ages, following the collapse of the Western Roman Empire, there were still lots of local spot markets open at least once a month. By 1100 CE, several Italian port cities (especially Genoa and Venice, but also Pisa and Amalfi) had developed personalized trade networks, somewhat like the Maghribis', that reached into the western backwaters as well as eastward across the Mediterranean.

The biggest gains, though, came from impersonal trade between disparate regions. As the centuries went by, the toughest roving bandits of the north—the Vikings and Normans—became more stationary, and a growing population spun a web of new roads. At the same time, more pilgrims and merchants braved the Brenner and Montgenèvre passes and the other old Roman roads through the Alps. Regional trade fairs, like those of St Ives in England, expanded, and some began to go international.

The Champagne fairs are the prime example. Henry the Liberal (ca. 1122–81), recently returned from the Second Crusade, took over as count of the northern French region of Champagne in 1152 CE. His lands lay at a major crossroad, and Henry realized that the local annual fair could attract cloth makers from the Rhine delta, as well as Italian dyers and exporters. Henry quickly made the roads safe from bandits, gave autonomy and protection to the fair organizers, and kept taxes low. Within a few years, and for more than a century after, the merchants swarmed in from France and the Low Countries and Italy, and also from Germany and Spain and beyond. Eventually, there were nine separate fairs each year, each lasting six weeks or so, rotating among Troyes, Provins, and a few other towns of Brie and southwest Champagne.

Markets thicken when many buyers and sellers show up at the same time from many different places, and thick markets catalyze change. The wholesale markets in Champagne reliably funneled income to those Dutch villagers who wove cloth from wool and linen. Their relative prosperity attracted more people to the trade, and sixty northern European towns eventually were dominated by cloth makers who sold their output exclusively through the fairs. They could pay their suppliers well, so more people spent more time raising sheep and growing flax. Likewise, more young people were drawn into the dyeing and tailoring trades, and into industries that made equipment or otherwise catered to the cloth producers and merchants.

For the first time since the zenith of the Roman Empire, a large number of Europeans made their living by producing goods to sell in the marketplace, and bought their necessities. The old regime of rigid social obligations and local self-sufficiency began to melt.

The most interesting part of the story may be the evolution of market formats and practices. Imagine that you are a medieval merchant looking for fine wool cloth for your Italian customers. Your first two problems are finding a seller, and agreeing on price. These are easily solved when you go to Troyes in July: you look over the merchandise in the huge warehouses, find what you want, check the fair's registry for prices for similar goods sold in the last couple of days, and, over a flagon of ale at your inn, you make a deal with two cloth sellers. Thick markets do the trick.

But you still have two other big problems. You have to make sure that you get the goods you bargained for—full measure with no moth eggs or inferior stuff mixed in—and that you can transport them safely back to Italy. Likewise, the sellers have to make sure they get paid on time, and in full, so they can pay their suppliers. Since you don't personally know the sellers and might not transact with them again, everyone needs assurance against cheating. The other problem is financial. You will deliver the goods to your customers in Italy two or three months after they were produced in northern towns, and, in the meantime, someone will have to provide credit. Markets have to deal with these credit and assurance problems, or they will shrivel as surely as if roving bandits took over the roads.

According to Greif, Europe's first widespread solution was the community responsibility system. Here's how it worked. Suppose you were cheated by a merchant from Bremen. Then, the next time you saw any Bremenite, you would get the backing of your fellow townsmen and seize his goods. The Bremenite and his friends would pressure the cheater to compensate you. This system hooks into our ancient moral instincts about group identity. It also gives everyone a direct incentive to monitor and discipline their fellow townsmen: if anyone misbehaves, then everyone from the town is endangered.

But, of course, the system doesn't work perfectly. Sometimes, false accusations are hard to detect, and there can be honest differences of opinion. The matter then can escalate into feuds, disrupting trade and conceivably leading to open warfare. Also, the system didn't scale up very well as trade increased during the 1200s.

When your town has too many merchants to know personally, and when satellite towns spring up, the lines of responsibility begin to blur.

A better system grew from the fairs at Champagne and elsewhere. *Lex mercatoria*, the "law merchant," was administered by a respected, experienced merchant who listened to both sides in a trade dispute and decided who owed what to whom. His decisions stuck, because defiant merchants were shunned by everyone, and thus lost their livelihood. Even today, in dozens of industries—diamonds, independent films, printing, rice, and tea, to name a few—disputes are resolved in such merchant tribunals, and decisions are enforced by the threat of expulsion from the trade association.

Some recent economic historians say that the medieval law merchant was not really autonomous, and was actually subject to local control and local idiosyncrasies. Be that as it may, in Champagne, he had the backing of Count Henry the Liberal and his successors. Several generations of merchants prospered as the law merchant enforced credit agreements and quality assurances.

In 1273, Philip III, King of France, invaded Champagne and brought it into the royal demesne. Over the next several decades, taxes rose, merchant privileges were curtailed, and facilities deteriorated. The Champagne fairs withered. But dozens of other places throughout Western Europe filled in. Nurtured by the law merchant and other new practices, her markets just kept growing. By 1400, Europe had some of the world's most supple and sophisticated markets.

Inside the Chrysalis

Every historian has a favorite way to explain the great transformation. For a long time, the most popular way was to focus on the Industrial Revolution, and tell a heroic tale of brave explorers and brilliant scientists and inventors who discovered a host of new technologies: better sailing ships and looms, then steam engines, trains, sewing machines, the telegraph, open hearth and Bessemer steel production, and so on, up to cars and airplanes. In this explanation, the new technologies naturally opened new markets and transformed the economy.

Why did all these heroes happen to turn up in Western Europe (or, toward the end, also in North America) and not elsewhere? Racist explanations won't wash—other peoples did better in other eras—and simple good luck seems unlikely for such a long string of discoveries. The great sociologist Max Weber (1864–1920) pointed to a moral and cultural advantage—the "Protestant work ethic." Toward the end of the twentieth century, politically correct pundits spotlighted the accomplishments of other cultures and tried (rather unconvincingly) to minimize the uniqueness and importance of the great transformation. Recent historians, such as Landes and Clark, have updated Weber, and argued that Western morals were the root cause.

I will tell the story a different way, centered on markets. The engine driving the great transformation was a dual positive feedback system. One feedback loop runs through markets and technology: advances in one spur advances in the other. The other loop runs through markets and the moral code, broadly construed to include legal and political institutions. Once the engine first turned over, around 1400, its internal dynamics made it run faster. Nobody stopped it for four hundred years, and by 1800, it was unstoppable. It transformed a caterpillar society into the bountiful butterfly we call the modern world.

Enough metaphors. Let's take a closer look at how markets interact with technology, and begin in Sagres, at the southern tip of Portugal, in 1420. There, Prince Henry the Navigator (1394–1460) built a unique enterprise. Its mission: to explore the Atlantic, especially the coast of Africa. Henry recruited the best mapmakers, navigational instrument makers, and boat builders he could find, including Jews and Muslims from North Africa, and Christians from Italy and Scandinavia.

Year by year, Henry's men advanced the state of the art. They drew the first reliable charts of the Atlantic coastline, constructed robust cross-staffs and mathematical tables for accurately measuring latitude, and perfected the caravel, a ship that could tack sharply against the wind and carry a substantial cargo, yet still navigate shallows and survive storms. His men quickly rediscovered and settled the Madeira Islands and, in 1427, they found the Azores. The great breakthrough came in 1434, when his men first passed Cape Bojador, long thought to be the end of the world. The new sea routes gave direct access to the riches of Africa beyond the Sahara desert, and gold, ivory, and slaves started to pour into Portugal.

Commercial success encouraged the Portuguese to continue improving their seafaring technology. In 1498, Vasco de Gama became the first sailor ever to round the Cape of Good Hope and reach India. Portugal dominated overseas trade from 1450 to 1550, operating about 90 percent of the 770 ships that then sailed the high seas. But her pioneering role began to slip after 1497, when Spain and Rome forced her to crack down on heretics. Over the next several decades, Jews and Muslims had to be baptized or leave, and the Inquisition eventually forced out even the less orthodox Christian scholars.

Portugal was just a prelude. After Columbus and de Gama, all sorts of new opportunities and new ideas from the Orient and the Americas streamed into European port cities and trickled into inland towns. For reasons to be discussed shortly, the towns were primed for the new ideas. New markets opened for the resulting products: machine-spun threads and machine-woven cloth, better waterwheels to power better mills, and always, better ships and carts. The new products and cheaper transportation accelerated trade in goods, and that boosted new markets for labor and finance. It's a standard story, but still true: technological innovations spur markets.

The other part of the loop has received less attention: markets spur innovation and new technologies. The cascade of new inventions was not due to the lucky appearance of dozens of brilliant individuals—every generation and every locale has its share. (It is true that from about 1500 onward, more Europeans were educated and exposed to latest developments, and this helped.) In my view, the main reason was the unprecedented rewards that markets in Europe bestowed on innovators.

Innovation is normally suppressed in traditional empires, but increasingly in Europe, it found wealthy supporters. Powerful interests might oppose the innovation, but somewhere, someone stood to benefit. For example, canal owners in the early 1800s might not want to see railroads develop, but owners of ironworks would. Using the emerging financial markets, ironworks owners and other investors would provide resources to build the railroads, and those with a stake in canals (barge builders, toll collectors, etc.) could do little to slow it down.

Indeed, innovation was sometimes subsidized. Wealthy individuals and governments sponsored contests with huge prizes for inventions that would improve their market opportunities. Dava Sobel's recent book *Longitude*, for example, describes the contest to produce a device that would measure east-west position, a key to navigation on the high seas.

More importantly, as markets grew, the incentives increased for new innovation. Maturing markets for land, labor, and capital made it far easier and quicker to roll out a new technology. And the wider goods markets meant more revenue and profit for the first companies to do so. Innovation became a major source of wealth in the more advanced countries, eventually surpassing plunder and the control of long distance trade.

Nowadays, it is obvious that the market drives innovation, and private companies, as well as governments, spend huge sums on research and development. Baumol's recent book *The Free Market Innovation Machine* focuses on the last fifty years in the United States. As I see it, however, the push from markets goes all the way back to Europe hundreds of years ago.

The Moral Transformation

The great transformation is not just of the economy and technology, but also of law, politics, and personal morals. Let's take a closer look at the loop from markets to politics and law.

In traditional empires, towns and cities grew best near the imperial capital, but in medieval Europe, free towns sprang up in spaces between the fiefdoms. Usually dominated by merchant and craft guilds, the towns provided vital tax revenue to the local feudal lords. The local lord therefore found it in his interest to protect the guilds' local monopolies, to defend the town against bandits and invaders, and to grant townsmen privileges, such as exemption from corvée. The medieval German proverb *stadtluft macht frei* translates roughly as: freedom is in the city air.

Changes in military technology increased the towns' leverage. From the 1400s onward, cannon and gunpowder favored offense over defense, and professional soldiers for hire were increasingly effective against local knights and conscripted serfs. Military success, more than ever, required cash.

Impatient (or stupid) lords tried to squeeze neighboring towns harder but, as in Champagne around 1300, this was self-defeating. The local businesses simply moved elsewhere and, soon, the lord's take declined. More enlightened and patient lords kept taxes moderate and offered better privileges than rivals, and that allowed their local towns to grow and prosper. Greater wealth, and greater military success, increasingly went to regions and nations with laws and politics more favorable to merchants and other townsmen.

Britain and the Low Countries led the way. From the 1500s onward, political power there flowed toward elected representatives of the people (at least of wealthy people). At the same time, these countries developed new and efficient commercial law and commercial courts. Private property enjoyed unprecedented protection, and efficient commercial techniques (such as double entry bookkeeping) took root. Commerce and wealth accelerated in these countries, and other countries scrambled to catch up.

There is a paradox here: surrendering royal power to the courts became the best way to maintain royal wealth and power. The simplistic Duke-Serf game described earlier helps clarify an underlying strategic issue. When an impartial, independent court can compel the Duke to obey, the Serf can take the tax rate as given. Such protection from arbitrary seizures gives him greater incentive to increase the crop size, benefiting both Serf and Duke. Indeed, both are better off than in the case where the Duke is a stationary bandit, even a rather patient one. The conclusion holds, with even more force, for relations between the local lord and townsmen whose businesses can go elsewhere.

Thus, markets grew faster in cities and countries with more market-friendly laws and politics, and those places became more wealthy and powerful. To avoid oblivion, other places had to follow, or leapfrog. This ratchet pulled Europe's political and legal systems away from feudalism toward modernity, expanding markets all the while.

Personal moral codes also changed. Historians have noted that the countries leading the industrial revolution were predominantly Protestant, and that Catholic countries like Spain and Italy tended to lag. Weber suggested that the reason might be the "Protestant work ethic." His point was that Calvinist doctrine encouraged wealth accumulation, saving, and investment, and that investment (in new factories, for example) is essential to economic growth and development. By contrast, traditional Catholic teachings like "it is easier for a camel to pass through the eye of a needle than for a rich man to enter heaven" discourage savings and investment in things like new factories. In Catholic southern Europe, most wealthy people gave higher priority to enhancing their social standing by conspicuous consumption—building larger castles, for example—and conspicuous donations to the church and to charities.

Landes points out that the Protestant predilection for savings and investment was part of a whole suite of personal traits—rationality, skepticism of authority, orderliness, diligence, productivity—that helped people succeed in a dynamic market economy. So, too, were the emerging middle class habits of passing moral judgments on neighbors and exerting peer pressure. These traits were more common in Protestant Western Europe than in traditional cultures, and they surely helped boost the economic transformation.

So Weber's thesis is true, as far as it goes, but it misses half of the loop. The "Protestant" virtues became more prevalent precisely because they worked—they gave people a real advantage when new opportunities opened in commerce and industry. These virtues were not the lucky *cause* of the industrial revolution, as claimed by some of Weber's followers, but rather an *effect*, a part of the runaway dynamic. The logic is the same as with the moral transition associated with the spread of river valley civilizations, from unified egalitarian moral codes to fragmented hierarchical codes.

Moral traits conducive to the new market system were bound to appear somewhere. If the Protestant reformation had not already been handy, then very similar traits would have evolved directly from Catholicism or some other religious or philosophical tradition—a later chapter will note that this happened in Japan, for example. Once present, the new morals would spread, boosting and boosted by the new market system.

Rich Caterpillars: Spain and China

The process can also be understood by looking at places it was slow to reach. Two very rich countries, Spain and China, escaped the transformation until late in the twentieth century. Why?

Muslims, Christians, and Jews shared the Iberian Peninsula for eight centuries. Its major cities, especially Cordoba, Seville, and Granada, were the western hub of the civilized world, wealthy in goods and ideas. But everything changed in 1492, when Christian rulers united the Peninsula (except for the western strip, Portugal, already held by allies), and got the inside track to the New World. Spain then had no more border problems and soon enjoyed the richest stream of plunder the world has ever seen. In an average year in the 1500s, Spain's galleons brought home two to four tons of gold, mostly from her New World colonies, and the annual silver haul averaged over two hundred tons toward the end of the century.

Spain's rulers, then, could pretty much do whatever they wanted. So what did they want? As you might expect, they built up their capital, Madrid, and erected huge and luxurious palaces. They also funneled vast sums of money to religious fanatics. The Inquisition smothered dissent and new ideas within Spain's borders and beyond, and well-funded missionaries spread a particularly intolerant version of their faith. Spanish rulers spent even more on military adventures, building a huge armada and hiring vast armies. They enjoyed some success, but never quite were able to conquer England or the Netherlands.

By virtue of its geography and wealth, Spain (with Portugal in tow) was able to isolate itself from the market-driven changes sweeping the rest of Western Europe in the 1600s and 1700s. Landes and other historians point up Spain's *hidalgo* mentality, scorn for people who had to work for a living—sort of a Protestant ethic in reverse. Spain started to fall behind. In the 1800s, their richest colonies broke away and in 1898 the United States snapped up the remaining few. (The United States still holds Puerto Rico and Guam, having spun off Cuba right away and the Philippines after the World War II.) In the twentieth century, a fascist dictatorship delayed Spain's modernization until the late 1970s, but since then she has made up for lost time.

By 1000CE, China clearly had the world's most advanced civilization and more than a quarter of the world's population. Peasants irrigated fields in the vast floodplain of the Yangtze, Hwang He (Yellow), and other east-west rivers. Her infrastructure already included the Great Wall on her northern border and, much more important, the thousand-mile Grand Canal, connecting the five largest rivers as it ran from Beijing and Kaifeng south to Hangzhou. Inland waterways were far cheaper than other transportation modes of the day, so China's national network of watery highways was an unrivalled asset.

For most of the previous 1,500 years, China had enjoyed unified rule, but the exceptions were especially fruitful. The Three Warring States period (403–221 BCE) saw great advances in iron technology, the beginnings of China's civil service, classic treatises on warfare like Sun Tzu's, and the flowering of the Hundred Schools of Thought, including Confucianism and Taoism. The period of Five Dynasties and Ten Kingdoms (907–60) saw the first military application of gunpowder and a new creativity in art and literature.

The Song dynasty ruled from Kaifeng in 1000 CE. They kept order until the Jin dynasty ousted them from the north in 1127, and from Hangzhou, they ruled the south for another century and a half. Then the Mongols took over the entire country, as well as much of Muslim world—for them, most of Europe wasn't worth the trouble.

By 1400, the Ming dynasty had ousted the Mongols. The story of Zheng He (1371–1433, often written Cheng-ho) reveals much about that era. Born to an aristocratic Muslim family in the China's remote southwestern corner, Zheng was captured at age eleven as the Ming consolidated control. He was castrated and taken to the new Ming court in Beijing.

Somehow, a decade or so later, Zheng impressed the third Ming emperor, the great Yongle. Perhaps it was Zheng's stories of his father and grandfather's hajj to exotic Mecca, or maybe the emperor wanted tribute from India. For whatever reason, Yongle ordered the construction of huge treasure ships, dwarfing Prince Henry's caravels and anything the world had ever seen. He put Zheng in charge of a series of naval expeditions, the first with 317 ships carrying 28,000 armed troops. Between 1405 and 1433, the fleet planted colonies of Muslim Chinese in present-day Malaysia, quashed the local pirates, and visited ports in India, Arabia, and the east coast of Africa. Zheng gave out gifts of silk and porcelain, occasionally intervened militarily (as in Ceylon), and brought back wonders like giraffes and zebras.

Back in Beijing, a powerful faction saw the voyages as a threat. Its leaders convinced Yongle's successor that the Middle Kingdom had no need for the trinkets from lesser civilizations, or for their subversive ideas on religion and politics. The new emperor cracked down. On his orders, the great treasure ships were decommissioned and allowed to rot. Zheng's charts and logs were destroyed and the shipyards were torn down, along with the world's greatest ironworks that had helped supply them. Even the shipbuilders were exiled to remote provinces. China never again had a great navy.

The episode is symptomatic. China had a long lead over Portugal in seafaring, but due to internal politics, it threw it away. Centuries earlier, China's powerful and unified government suppressed its advanced gunpowder and cannon technologies, mainly because it was more interested in defending fortifications than in attacking them. It maintained tight monopolies on its key commodities such as silk and porcelain. Unauthorized people who tried to produce these items, or even get an education, were severely punished. China had a rich society, but it was closed to outside stimuli.

Sometime in the 1700s, Europe began to surpass China economically and militarily. Europeans humiliated China in the opium wars of the mid-1800s, and afterward grabbed what they wanted. China finally began to modernize, but it was a slow process until the Japanese invaded in 1937. The communists led the resistance and, not long after the end of World War II, they took over the entire Chinese mainland. They modernized education and health care, but imposed their own political and economic monopolies. Beginning in 1978, China began to liberalize the economy and it has grown since then at an unprecedented rate. The Communist Party recently opened its ranks to businesspeople, but so far has not allowed open political competition.

The Butterfly

In 1000 CE, Western Europe was an unpromising backwater, a patchwork of petty Christian fiefdoms (including a pitiable collection that called itself the Holy Roman Empire) and pagan territories. By 1400, an outsider trying to predict future world powers would have to take Western Europe seriously, although, in the end, he probably would have bet on more established players like the Ottomans in Turkey and Greece, or the Mings in Beijing, or possibly the emerging Sayyid dynasty in Delhi.

By 1800, that contest was over. Western Europe had become the leading edge of the great transformation, and traditional pyramid societies in the rest of the world began to crumble. Still, somehow, it seems a bit mysterious. Why Western Europe, 1400–1800, and not some other time or place?

A short answer is that, for those four centuries, Europe enjoyed two conditions that rarely coexist: access to long-distance trade, and fragmented political control. Throughout most of history, only people living in a capital city are exposed to long-distance trade in goods and ideas. Living in Kaifeng a thousand years ago, for example, you could meet barge operators from South China, and they might have talked with traders or scholars from India and other exotic places. But the Song rulers would never give you the opportunity to try anything that might undermine their rule. On the other hand, if you lived in a remote province where their control was weak, then you probably wouldn't have access to the latest ideas or to markets, or to resources to do new things. Hence, in China, as in all traditional empires, innovation languished at both center and periphery.

Western Europe's political weakness was a crucial asset. The long external coastline, the internal mountain barriers (especially the Alps, Carpathians, and Pyrenees), and the lack of rich resources (not much gold or spice) discouraged the rise of stable empires. The feudal system created fragmented loyalties to kin, to overlord, and to the church, and weak and erratic control of Europe's two thousand free towns and cities.

At the same time, the coastline and extensions of Roman roads encouraged long distance trade. By 1400, Europeans had access to the best ideas in the world, and had the opportunity to try them out. If an idea didn't work in one town, the others didn't suffer. If it did work out, it could spread. In fact, competition among the fragmented authorities virtually guaranteed that an idea would spread if it boosted local wealth.

Normally, what happens is that some fragment gets an advantage and consolidates power. Then it can suppress threats, and things slow back down to normal. Greece had a golden age when its many city-states vied with each other, but that faded when the Macedonians—Philip, then Alexander and his successors—centralized power. Likewise, innovation slowed considerably in Rome after Julius, and then Augustus, wrested power from the fractious Senate.

Something similar almost happened in Europe around 1600. Spain had engulfed Portugal and several other regions, and squelched dissent and innovation. But Europe didn't lose its momentum because people and ideas went elsewhere. Sparked partly by refugees from Iberia, a golden age bloomed in the Low Countries. Britain also blossomed and took the lead in industrial technology. The government tried to hoard industrial secrets, but somehow they always leaked out. Ideas spread to France, Germany, and the rest of the continent, and cross-fertilized.

Later, around 1800, revolutionary ideas spread in the wake of Napoleon's conquests. He tried to impose a unified empire, but it didn't last long enough to slow things down. Europe remained fragmented and open, and the market transformation swept over the entire continent. The butterfly took flight.

4

Utopias of Cooperation
Romantics, Communists, and Other Anti-moderns

Fifty years ago, communism looked like a juggernaut. Small, quarrelsome bands of dissidents had grown over the previous half century into one of the largest and most ambitious empires the world has ever seen. The ideology had engulfed Russia, Eastern Europe, and China, and it seemed to be taking hold in other big countries like India and Indonesia. In the West, many opinion leaders predicted a communist future for the entire world, some (like economist Joseph Schumpeter) sadly, and others gladly.

But by the late 1980s, the communist world was collapsing. Russia and Eastern Europe soon renounced the ideology, and China quietly abandoned it. North Korea's hereditary communist dictators can't feed their own people, and communism is withering, even in Cuba and Vietnam. The scrapheap of history is its final resting place.

Where did this strange creed come from? Why was it so successful for so much of the twentieth century? And why was its fall so sudden and total?

The answers tell us much about today's world. Communism's appeal, and its fatal flaw, was moral outrage at the market system. In attempting a divorce, it bred moral catastrophes and the world's most perverse markets. It's a spectacular story, and it began innocently, with the nineteenth century Romantic reaction against the emerging markets for land and labor.

Markets are Unfair

Not everybody loved the market system as it started to take hold around 1800. Take William Blake (1757–1827). His poems glorified a natural and spontaneous lifestyle ("Bathe in the waters of life") and depicted industrialization with its "dark Satanic mills" as a threat to the environment and to the human soul. The anti-market spirit of Romantic egalitarianism pervades Blake's work, and that of many of his contemporaries.

The talkative, choleric Thomas Carlyle (1795–1881) had little patience with Blake's egalitarianism or mysticism, but he was equally hostile to the market system. This leading British essayist argued that the law of supply and demand destroys social responsibility and the god-given hierarchical order. Forceful "captains of industry" had to bring the market to heel and "reduce [the working class] to order, to just subordination." Otherwise, chaos would prevail, with ceaseless strikes, demonstrations, and general anarchy.

Why did so many eloquent writers of the day hate the market system? Indeed, why do so many people today? My answer is that the market system invaded the moral sphere.

Two aspects are particularly noxious. First, markets turned embedded social relations into commodities. Land and labor, once defining fixtures of life, became saleable like shoes. As Christopher Lasch later put it: "Money, even more than other good things like beauty, eloquence and charm, has a tendency to 'seep across the boundaries' and to buy things that should not be for sale: exemption from military service; love and friendship; political office." The problem continues today—the laws on political campaign contributions and lobbying, for example, seem due for yet another round of reform—but it was especially jarring in the early nineteenth century. At that time, markets for the key resources—land, labor, and capital— were just detaching from the moral sphere, amid great pain and dislocation. I'll discuss this process shortly.

Second, the market system brings quick, unsettling transitions. When faced with a major new opportunity—such as railroads, a new colony, a new form of organization, electricity, or microprocessors—the system grants huge rewards to the first few individuals or organizations lucky and skillful enough to seize the new turf. The winners are people like Cornelius Vanderbilt, Andrew Carnegie, John D. Rockefeller, and Bill Gates—not necessarily the conceptual innovators, but rather, those who got there early, grew fast and didn't let go.

As competitors flock to the new opportunity, the rewards eventually return to normal, but that may take decades. Meanwhile, the new opportunity starves the older ways, and many people lose their livelihoods. Railroads impoverish the canal owners and workers, new agriculture and industry leaves behind the landed aristocrats and their retainers, and innovation displaces skilled craftsmen such as blacksmiths and weavers. Joseph Schumpeter called the process "creative destruction," and even now, business pundits write about "disruptive technologies." A hallmark of the market system in times of rapid change is to bestow enormous wealth on a few lucky or greedy individuals, and to dispossess many good people. It seems extraordinarily unfair.

Moral outrage is natural, so it bears repeating that the market system has greatly improved material conditions for workers as well as capitalists. In virtually every country that has joined the market system in the last two centuries, the population boomed as nutrition and public health improved, and death rates plunged. With free entry into new activities and appropriate transfers (such as social safety nets), any innovation that increases productivity will benefit everyone. Even without appropriate transfers, the great majority of people can expect to come out ahead once things settle down. The problem with the market system is not that it takes from the poor, but rather that it disrupts lives and clashes with established moral codes.

Disruptive New Markets for Land

Let's look first at the emerging market for land. In feudal Europe, as in most other times and places, the local community owned the land and managed it within a web of personal relationships. Often the community was hierarchical—the lord of the manor ruled over his serfs—but sometimes it was egalitarian, as with rights to summer pasture in the Alps. Either way, a complex set of customs, rights, and obligations governed use of the land. For almost a thousand years, this open field system did a pretty good job of supporting Europe's population and maintaining the land's fertility. Markets played little role.

The great transformation broke those traditions, and the town-based rules of private property came to apply to the countryside. The process, called the "enclosure movement," began in economically liberal England and the Low Countries around 1550, and started to accelerate around 1750. Soon, the great open meadows and pastures, where commoners had long grazed livestock, were fenced, hedged, and walled. Only the owners, and their tenants and hired hands, could get access, and many poor villagers were cut off.

The right to own land free and clear—in "fee simple"—spread for several reasons. For one thing, the land yields crops with greater market value when an owner or manager, rather than ancient custom, chooses what to plant and when. Owners also are more likely to make investments and to use new techniques—like fertilizer, mechanical seeders for row crops, and crop rotation instead of letting land lie fallow—that boost production. The new system paid huge dividends as regional produce markets opened up, along with markets for labor and equipment. The price of food fell as productivity rose, and the old ways couldn't compete. Finally, land ownership also helped emerging credit institutions. Fee simple title to land is much better collateral than manorial rights, that is, the right to tax the peasants, who (as we saw in the last chapter) have means of passive resistance.

The French Revolution and Napoleon's conquests spread property rights to farmers in much of Western Europe, greatly accelerating productivity. Land reform seems to be a key to development everywhere, into the twentieth century.

Yet, the new markets for land had a human cost. Enclosure cut off villagers from the fields their parents tilled, and that's just the start. Greater farm productivity and lower food prices meant that the population soared at the same time that the need for peasant labor fell. So masses of people were pushed off the land. Under bad conditions—say, Ireland in the mid-1800s—they starve or emigrate. Under the best of conditions—China in the 1980s and 1990s—the people find booming urban labor markets. Even then, their lives are disrupted, and many of the new urbanites live amid violence and squalor.

...And for Labor

Around 1800, new factories sprouted up everywhere, boosting demand for unskilled workers. Supply increased even more rapidly, thanks to the encloure movement and the population boom, and so labor markets thickened while real wages remained low.

Easy access to cheap labor and new technology encouraged factories to refine the assembly line and other new methods of organization. The factories started to produce an unprecedented variety of goods at unheard-of low prices, displacing traditional craftsmen and guilds. In the Portsmouth dockyard in 1801, for instance, machinery tended by ten unskilled workers replaced 110 skilled block makers.

The human toll was incalculable. For example, in 1824, young Charles Dickens, age twelve, got up early every morning to work at Warren's bootblacking factory, near Charing Cross in London. Every day, it was the same dreary job: paste labels on jars of shoe polish, as fast as possible, for ten hours straight. Still, Charles could still count his blessings. The job was far less dangerous and unhealthful than many, and his wage, six shillings a week, was paid on time. It allowed him to live in a simple boarding house, and to buy a few treats for his family, locked up in Marshalsea debtor's prison. It also allowed him to occasionally think back to happier days in the Kent countryside, and to dream about finding a better life in the big city. (Of course, young Charles' luck did turn. In the next few years, he was able to get an office job, add to the two years of schooling he already had, and hone his writing skills.)

The human moral system is tuned to help us work spontaneously with our peers and family. It grates on us to have our time regulated by the factory whistle, and to take orders from bosses we hardly know. Here is William Blake's perception of urban labor markets:

> There souls of men are bought and sold
> And milk fed infancy for gold
> And youth to slaughter houses led
> And beauty for a bit of bread.

If you peel away the slapstick from Charlie Chaplin's last silent movie, *Modern Times*, you will find the same bleak view.

Factories bred other problems. They typically demanded fifteen hours a day, six days a week, and were often hazardous to life, limb, and health. Most industrial jobs were deadly dull. As Adam Smith observed in *The Wealth of Nations* (1776), in the preindustrial system, "every man has a considerable degree of knowledge, ingenuity, and invention." On the assembly line, by contrast, the typical worker spends his whole life "performing a few simple operations . . . [with] no occasion to exert his understanding or to exercise his invention. . . . He naturally loses, therefore, the habit of such exertion, and generally becomes as stupid and ignorant as it is possible for a human creature to become."

The dumbing down of work made child labor viable. In addition, the factory system thwarted ambition, blocking personal advance as from apprentice to journeyman to master. The dead-end jobs therefore required more external discipline—overseers—increasing their intrinsic unpleasantness. The need for close coordination squelched spontaneity and initiative, and it alienated worker from product. On the assembly line, responsibility was so diffuse that nobody could take personal pride in the quality of the final product.

... And for Anti-market Politics

The emerging market system of the nineteenth century created vast new wealth and, at the same time, sprawling political problems. Among the poor, lower food prices mainly meant more surviving children and thus more poor people. They became more urban and visible, and remained near the Malthusian edge: think of *Oliver Twist*. The rich grew richer than ever, and hundreds of English families accumulated wealth beyond the imaginings of Basil II and his peers. The middle class, the bourgeoisie, expanded as never before. Leisure was now a real possibility for a substantial fraction of the population.

Leisure and dispersed wealth combined with moral outrage to create an unprecedented demand for dissident thought. Romantic philosophers, perhaps taking Jean-Jacques Rousseau too literally, extolled the life of the noble savage, and some individuals (including young Sam Houston, future leader of Texas) found that they preferred tribal life to modern civilization. Thomas Jefferson idealized the yeoman farmer, as did several other fathers of the American and French revolutions. But reality in nineteenth-century Europe (and the eastern United States) was ever-greater urbanization and industrialization. Young people from working class and bourgeois families began to look for practical ways to change the world.

The supply of dissident thought was ample and varied. Romantic poets and philosophers abounded, and so did Christian, as well as secular, writers. Some dissidents were apolitical, or took the passive view that desirable change was either impossible or automatic. Activists believed that only concerted action would usher in a better world, but they differed on the best means. Should one work peacefully within the system, or try to bring it down? Should one begin by rebuilding a small local community, or aim for a national or international organization?

And what was that better world? A return to nature? Or to farming? Or a reorganization of industrial society? Should we try to change human nature or find better ways to accommodate it? Visions appeared, merged, proliferated. A few mixes were rare—apparently, no international Romantic Christian aristocratic movement ever advocated violent return to nature—but most possible combinations had at least one nineteenth-century group as standard-bearer.

Take the liberals, like John Stuart Mill (1806–73). They argued that personal liberty was best served by letting the market system rip. Mill thought laissez-faire would usher in a better world, while some other liberals simply deemed it personally advantageous. They slowly gained the upper hand in Britain and many other places.

Or take the Luddites. According to legend, in Leicestershire, one night around 1780, a man named Ned Ludd smashed machines that had taken jobs from skilled knitters and weavers. Over the next couple of decades, whenever new textile equipment was sabotaged, the locals would say, "Ludd must have been here." Beginning in 1811, large bands of masked men launched nighttime raids and destroyed new machinery in Nottinghamshire. They swore allegiance, not to any British king, but to their own "King Ludd." Supporters included the great Romantic poet Lord Byron (1788–1824), who likened them to American revolutionaries in this little ditty:

As the Liberty lads o'er the sea
Bought their freedom, and cheaply, with blood,
So we, boys, we
Will die fighting, or live free,
And down with all kings but King Ludd!

The movement spread, and the British government responded with massive troop deployments (at one time, more than against Napoleon) and imposed the death penalty for machine breakers. By 1816, the leaders were all executed or transported to Australia or in hiding, but their legend lives on. If you hate a new technology, the people who love it may call you a Luddite.

Then there were the utopian socialists, like Charles Fourier (1772–1837). Born into a French cloth merchant's family, Fourier was a traveling salesman who wrote down his ideas at night. He completely rejected industrialism, advocated total sexual freedom and sexual equality, and saw himself as the Isaac Newton of social science. Unlike the famous mathematician Joseph Fourier (1768–1830), it seems that Charles was clueless about physics, but he was fascinated by numerical combinations. Charles "discovered" the twelve fundamental passions, which included the delightfully named *la Papillone* (the butterfly), or love of variety, and *la Cabaliste*, or love of conspiracy and rivalry. From his list of passions (which also included things like love and ambition and the five senses), he deduced 810 distinct personality types, and concluded that, ideally, people should live in communes of 1620 people, including a man and a woman of each type. These egalitarian, self-sufficient communes, or Phalanxes (named after Alexander the Great's battle formations) would avoid the inefficiencies of private property and fragmented storage and transportation. Work would take place in rival teams spurred by *la Cabaliste* and, appealing to *la Papillone*, people would change tasks every two hours and have different schedules on different days of the week. In the evening, everyone would enjoy good food and drink (prepared by the Phalanx's most talented chefs and winemakers) and have great sex with their favorite partners.

Fourier's writings inspired devoted followers like Victor Considerant, who tried to found a Phalanx in Texas (a nearby town is still called Utopia) and later publicized socialist reform programs. Fourier himself died in obscurity, but some of his ideas trickled down to the late twentieth century. They reappeared in co-ops, Japanese production teams, Israeli kibbutzim, U.S. hippie communes, and in the writings of gurus such as Herbert Marcuse and Abraham Maslow.

Two other utopian socialists actually put their ideas into practice. Claude Henri de Saint-Simon (1760–1825), a freethinking aristocrat, favored industrialization, but under the direction of public minded technocrats. His followers founded a commune in 1730. It failed within two years, but its alumni became some of France's leading reformers. Robert Owen (1771–1858) was a rich industrialist who greatly improved working conditions in his textile factory. He founded New Lanark in 1805 as the first Village of Cooperation. Although New Lanark sustained itself for decades, the idea never really caught on in England. In 1825, Owen founded his New Harmony colony in Indiana, and he and imitators launched fifteen more over the next several years. None of them lasted, partly because they attracted too many people who cared more about singing and dancing than about working hard for the sake of the colony.

The Evolution of Marxism-Leninism

A rich stew of competing dissident groups simmered in Europe during the early 1800s. Things came to a boil in 1848. Early that year, and without much bloodshed, broad alliances of socialists, republicans, and liberal reformers overthrew the post-Napoleon monarchy in France and repressive police states in much of the rest of the continent. They installed legislatures and proclaimed the right for all men to vote. But the alliances soon fractured. The peasants wanted to restore their rights to the commons and cheap credit, while the workers wanted better pay and working conditions, and the reformers wanted to liberalize land, labor, and financial markets—completely incompatible demands. Within two or three years, the idealists were turfed out, and "the generous, conciliatory, humanitarian, romantic" approach to social reform never recovered.

What does it take for a dissident group to survive and grow? Then, as now, helpful tactics include:

- Building tight ingroups. Slogans, songs, and a sense of community all help forge close social bonds.
- Appealing to a high moral sense. An egalitarian style and a compelling picture of a better world help engage people's moral sympathies.
- Reaching out to idealistic young people, especially those with an education and some leisure time.
- Finding interest groups with resources. Dispossessed artisans and unemployed intellectuals had resentments, time, and talent; working people had numbers and muscle; aristocrats had money.
- Maintaining a flexible ideology, able to respond to new opportunities and rapidly changing political and economic conditions.
- Creating an efficient internal organization to spread the word to new groups and in new provinces or countries, and to mobilize for political (or perhaps military) pressure at the right time and place. Groups won style points by seeming egalitarian, but in practice, it helped to be hierarchical.
- Having opportunistic leaders, not too constrained by ideals to seize all available means to achieve their goals.

Marxism, and its later mutant Leninism, turned out to be especially well adapted to the harsher environment after 1848. To see why, let's first take a quick look at the founder and his ideas.

Karl Marx (1818–83) was a brilliant, wide-ranging thinker with a PhD in philosophy, a thundering prose style, and a dismissive attitude toward opponents. The Prussian government shut down his academic career and then his newspaper, so he moved his family to London, where they lived in clutter and poverty as he scribbled away in the British Museum and fended off creditors.

Marx agreed with Adam Smith and William Blake about the urban labor market: "Labor produces wonderful works for the rich, but it produces poverty for the worker. It produces palaces, but hovels for the laborer. It produces beauty, but deformity for the laborer. It replaces labor with machines, but at the same time it throws the laborer into the most barbarous labor and at the same time makes the laborer into a machine. It produces intelligence and culture, but it produces senselessness and cretinism for the laborer."

Marx turned Ricardo's classic economic doctrine, the labor theory of value, into a scathing critique: capitalists were getting rich by stealing the surplus value that the workers created. This idea dovetailed nicely with those of the first anarchist, Pierre-Joseph Proudhon (1809–65) who, referring to landlords and factory owners, famously wrote, "property is theft." Marx described class structure based on economic interests, emphasizing the proletariat (factory workers) versus the bourgeoisie (managers and owners). Above all, Marx told a compelling story about the course of history: an inevitable rise from primitive communism to feudalism to capitalism to scientific socialism. He predicted that workers in industrial nations like England would soon rise up and take charge of the means of production.

(How do Marx's ideas stand up early in the twenty-first century? His labor theory of value is now discredited—it looks like moral outrage in economic dress. The idea that evolution means upward progress toward an inevitable goal is a Victorian fallacy that Darwin never endorsed, and, of course, Marx turned out to be no better than anyone else at predicting the future. However, sociologists still benefit from Marx's economic analysis of class structure and dynamics.)

Together with his friend and patron, Friedrich Engels (1820–95), Karl Marx published *The Communist Manifesto* on the eve of the 1848 uprisings. Compared to his other writings, it was short and to the point, and it had a stirring conclusion: "Proletarians have nothing to lose but their chains. They have a world to win. Workers of the world, unite!"

The new creed attracted idealistic young people, who saw themselves riding the wave of history and science. As with other socialist and anarchist movements, Marxist politics fostered close emotional ties among comrades, brothers, and sisters in the struggle. People worked intensely together in small groups, laughed and sang songs, and met in larger groups for occasional mass demonstrations. These political movements harnessed social emotions going back to hunter-gatherer bands, and filled a psychological void left by the market system.

Marxists didn't sweep the field, however. In the late nineteenth century, they often trailed the anarchists, and the trade unions grew far larger than any of the more radical groups. As the factory system matured, demand for labor rose faster than supply, and real wages rose. Workers achieved higher standards of living, and reformers achieved major goals, like child labor laws, the ten-hour working day, and universal male suffrage. The market system was working better than ever, and Marx's predictions seemed increasingly dubious.

Vladimir Lenin (1870–1924) argued for radical changes in ideology and organization. Standing Marx on his head, Lenin dropped the idea that the working class would spontaneously revolt and install communism. He acknowledged in a famous 1902 text that, left to their own devices, workers would simply join trade unions. So, instead, he called for a "vanguard" of professional revolutionaries to disrupt elected governments and to infiltrate the trade union leadership. Lenin also abandoned the notion that only advanced industrial countries were ready for communism, and instead nominated Czarist Russia, which still was trying to shake off feudalism and join the industrial world, as the first candidate for revolution.

Communism Reaches Russia

World War I spelled disaster for reform-minded socialists and trade unionists. Elected representatives in all European countries had to choose either to fund the war or to maintain solidarity with fellow workers in other countries. Everywhere, the socialist movement splintered into factions, and everywhere, the war faction gained the upper hand, crippling international cooperation. The peaceful socialist movement never recovered.

The Great War also gave Lenin's vanguard its chance. The Russian czar was overthrown in early 1917 and moderate democrats took over. In order to destabilize his enemy to the east, the German Kaiser gave Lenin free passage from his Swiss exile back into Russia. Lenin's Bolsheviks then sprang into action. In November 1918, allied with co-operatives, anarchists, and peasant groups, they swept away the moderate democrats and seized power. Then, one by one, the Bolsheviks picked off their erstwhile allies and consolidated power, and finally, in 1919–20, they beat back a counterattack by the remaining czarists and their foreign supporters. By the time of Lenin's death in 1924, the Bolsheviks controlled all of Russia.

An inside view of the takeover comes from the American writer, Emma Goldman (1869–1940). A four foot ten dynamo with thick glasses, Goldman had emigrated from Russia to the United States as an idealistic sixteen-year-old. After working in a Rochester, NY, factory and studying political tracts at night, she joined the anarchist movement; by 1900, she had become its leading American spokesperson and journalist. Imprisoned in 1917 for anti-war agitation (and for helping women get access to birth control), she was deported to the USSR in late 1919.

The Bolsheviks saw Goldman as a propaganda tool, and gave her interviews with Lenin and other top officials. She, however, was shocked by their cold and manipulative ways, and by the brutal house arrest of her anarchist hero, the saintly Peter Kropotkin. She saw sullen workers, resentful of their clumsy and hypocritical new bosses. Her new friends confided to her about how the secret police, the Tcheka, ran kidnap and extortion rings. Supposedly as an emergency measure, the Tcheka forebade free speech and blocked news from the outside world.

The final straw for Goldman came in March 1921, in the Kronstadt naval base. The sailors had been an advance guard in ousting the czar and the moderate democrats, and now they wanted to elect their own leaders. The Bolsheviks knew the anarchists would win a free election, so they brought in their best troops to crush the Kronstadt sailors. Soldiers who held back were shot, and the sailors were liquidated and called counterrevolutionaries. Goldman wrote: "The Bolsheviki now proved themselves the most pernicious enemies of the Revolution. I could have nothing further to do with them."

Later that year, Goldman was able to sneak out of the country. After stewing for six months, she began to write a book about her experiences. It concludes: "True Communism was never attempted in Russia, unless one considers . . . privileges to some and indifference to the great mass as Communism. . . . [T]he tyranny of the dictatorship has cowed people into slavish submission and all but extinguished the fires of liberty; organized terrorism has depraved and brutalized the masses and stifled every idealistic aspiration; . . . coercion at every step has made effort bitter, labor a punishment, has turned the whole of existence into a scheme of mutual deceit."

Lenin's heir in 1924 was not Leon Trotsky, another ruthless intellectual, but instead was the Bolshevik hatchet man, Joseph Stalin (1879–1953). Stalin was not burdened by the socialist fantasy that, with the greedy capitalist owners driven off, the workers would happily work alongside their comrades and spontaneously increase production. Instead, he made Lenin's emergency measures permanent. The Communist Party and the Tcheka (later renamed the KGB) controlled everything—where you lived, what your children learned in school, all agriculture and industry, radio and newspapers, even grocery prices—and Stalin personally ran the Party and the KGB. To maintain power, he murdered millions, many of them by firing squads, more in the Siberian Gulag. Another ten million or so perished in famines engineered to bring peasants to heel. The survivors lived in fear.

Many Western idealists, focused on the moral deficits of capitalism, had no idea (nor wanted to know) what life was really like in Russia, now called the Soviet Union. Soviet propaganda hijacked the moral high ground, but Soviet reality was exploitation of workers, and everyone else, to serve their masters' imperial ambitions.

The Rise of the Soviet Empire

Marxist ideology was supposed to sweep the world, beginning in the advanced industrialized countries. Inconveniently, workers' lives continued to improve in the United States, England, France, and other countries victorious in World War I. Revolutionary opportunities seemed better among the war's losers—Germany and fragments of the Austro-Hungarian empire. New possibilities arose with the onset of the Great Depression, a huge setback to the market system.

The Soviet Union tried to seize these golden opportunities, but found itself outflanked by an even more opportunistic movement—fascism. Benito Mussolini (1883–1945) and Adolf Hitler (1889–1945) followed a powerful recipe:

- recruit from same pool as the Communists, focusing on World War I veterans, wannabes, and street bullies;
- mix in Romantic nationalist pretensions;
- vow vengeance on globalizers, foreigners, and local minorities who supposedly had betrayed the glorious fatherland; and
- add contempt for bourgeois law and civility. Any action was justified for the noble national cause. Facts didn't matter, just will and unity under the glorious leader.

This recipe improved on the Communists', in substituting raw nationalism for complicated Marxist theory, and in tolerating the market economy and the existing class structure.

Traditional conservatives regarded the fascists as shock troops to counter the Soviet threat. Once in power, the fascists elbowed aside their conservative allies, but didn't try to liquidate them. The fascists recycled Soviet governance techniques: mass demonstrations, propaganda, party hierarchy, sham ideology, and state capitalism. Hitler's party even borrowed part of its name—National Socialists—from the Marxists.

Fascism had no ideological core, but like Communism, it exploited the us-versus-them moral complex. It demonized local minorities and foreign investors, glorified the imperial past and extolled military adventures. The fascist program was expropriation and conquest. It could only lead to war.

Ever the opportunist, Stalin allied himself with the fascists on the eve of World War II. Preoccupied with internal unrest, he barely survived the initial onslaught when Hitler suddenly invaded in 1941. Despite enormous casualties, the war boosted the communist empire from 1942 onward. The Soviet army harnessed loyalty to the motherland and, supported by American and British military aid, it wore down the Nazis on the eastern front. At war's end, the Soviet empire annexed Eastern Europe up to the middle of Germany and strengthened its hold in northern Asia.

World War II was also a godsend for Mao Zedong's communist movement in China. A ragtag group that barely survived the early 1930s, his Red Army became the rallying point for young Chinese who wanted to fight the Japanese invaders. By 1949, riding a wave of patriotic ardor, Mao's forces swept away the corrupt nationalist government and assumed control of all of mainland China. It seemed to Westerners that China had joined the Soviet empire.

In the 1950s, the French colonies in Indochina appeared ready to fall to Communist groups that had fought the Japanese. Local Communist parties seemed to be gaining increasing influence in postcolonial Indonesia. Even in newly independent and democratic India, there seemed to be more sympathy for the Soviets than for the British and their allies. World domination appeared within the Soviet empire's grasp.

World War II and its aftermath gave the Soviet system a tremendous boost at home as well as abroad. The Great Patriotic War, and the subsequent cold war against the United States and its allies, allowed the Soviet leaders to enlist citizens' us-against-them moral emotions and to inspire heroic feats of teamwork. The Soviet system channeled a huge share of resources to military technology, including missile systems and nuclear weapons. The Soviets tested atomic and hydrogen bombs only a few years after the United States. They launched Earth's first artificial satellite, Sputnik I, in 1957, and in 1961, Russian Yuri Gagarin became the first man in space. These triumphs cemented the Soviet Union's image as a superpower.

Decline and Fall

But inside it was all creak and sway. Soviet economic growth slowed to a crawl in the 1960s, and Stalin's heirs, Khrushchev and Brezhnev, were neither able to discipline the workers by terror nor to modernize. The United States got serious about the Space Race and, in 1969, sent several astronauts to the moon and brought them back safely. The Soviets could not keep up.

The problem was fundamental. Marx wrote endlessly about the central role of economic forces, but never quite explained how socialism works. If the market doesn't organize the economy, what does?

Left to their own devices, the Soviets reverted to Uruk's ancient pyramid plan, updated only slightly. Moral outrage at the market system was Marx's core principle, so the Soviets smashed self-regulating markets. Decisions on who got what were instead made by the privileged elite atop the pyramid. Like Inanna's high priests (but without their bawdy myths), the Communist Party bosses decreed what was good and what was bad, and how everyone was supposed to behave, and their underlings tried to keep the common folk in line The Soviet underlings were not mere scribes and soldiers, though—they had been updated as Gosplan technocrats producing five-year plans, together with newspaper and TV propagandists and, of course, the secret police.

This quasi-theocracy worked well enough in wartime and in the postwar chaos, but over time, it tended to wear down. Repetition strengthens market imperatives, but not hypocritical appeals to an official moral code. Incessant calls for worker solidarity lost their impact after the Nazi invaders were defeated, and people found ways to evade the Party's orders.

The practical and moral difficulties of the Soviet economy were myriad. On collective farms, harvests never rose above dismal, and by the 1980s, the Soviet Union was a net importer of food. Huge factories, Stalin's economic hallmark, often turned out to be inefficiently large, even when the plan was on track. But the Gosplan itself became dysfunctional as the economy grew more complex. Partly, it was the perverse incentives: exceeding the plan's quotas just meant higher quotas in the future, so factories tried to get by with minimal effort and substandard quality. To avoid input shortages, managers often had to bribe their suppliers. In light industry and agriculture, employee pilferage became almost universal, to supplement meager wages. Gray and black markets filled some gaps but, of course, they functioned poorly in the absence of enforceable property rights. The list of absurdities rumbles on and on. The system had no oversight for people at the helm, and corruption naturally increased. Aging top officials and their cronies didn't want to risk their sweet positions by innovating, so reform was blocked. Basically, the Soviet economic system was a a nonstarter that looked viable only thanks to smoke and mirrors, and to the vast Russian endowment of natural resources.

As the Soviet economy weakened, so did control of the empire. China started to go her own way in 1960, and by 1970, was clearly on a separate path. The Soviet invasion of Afghanistan in 1979 was the beginning of the end. An ill-advised attempt to shore up an unpopular communist regime, the war soon became a quagmire that devoured resources and morale. The final blow might have been Reagan's Star Wars program. Although its premise was bogus—there was, and still is, no technology capable of stopping a serious ballistic missile attack—the Soviets believed they had to respond, but they had no more resources to put into advanced technology.

It took a long time, but the Soviet decline eventually became obvious to everyone. The last holdouts in the west were the CIA, which gave credence to official Soviet economic statistics until the mid-1980s, and a few true believers, like my friend's dad, Abe. A lifelong devoted Marxist, he had walked away from a bright professional career in the 1940s to organize workers in Buffalo, New York. In the 1960s, Abe confidently told me and my high school friends that, despite flaws, the Soviet Union was mankind's best hope for the future. But by the late 1970s, even he acknowledged its moral and economic bankruptcy. The utopian dream was dead.

5

Russia's Transition to Kleptocracy
When Markets Need Morals

You rob your workplace. You cut in line. You skip out on contracts if it's convenient. Dishonesty is deep-rooted. When a person in business is honest, it is because he has made a conscious, and usually temporary, decision to be honest. There is not a deep-rooted sense of ethics.

—*Vladimir Aleksanyan, Russian import-export executive*

When the Soviet Union fragmented around 1990, most observers predicted a splendid economic future for its core, Russia. With a bonanza of natural resources, advanced technology and a well-educated workforce, Russia no longer had to prop up the more backward parts of the Soviet empire, nor contort itself to satisfy communist ideology.

The transition to a market economy got off to a rocky start. Responding to critics in 1992, Harvard professor Jeffrey Sachs, a top advisor to Boris Yeltsin's government, wrote that reform would yield "very great" benefits, and that data about Russia's progress after a year was "incomplete and misleading, and easily misinterpreted to give an overly bleak account . . . [resulting in] undue pessimism about the reform policies."

As it turned out, the pessimists were way too optimistic. Russia in the 1990s was the sort of place that gives anarchy a bad name. The new tycoons, called "oligarchs," and their partners in government and in the Mafiya, the Russian mob, destroyed almost as much Russian wealth as did Hitler's invasion fifty years earlier. No longer a superpower, Russia, at one point, trailed Peru in per person income, and her GNP ebbed by half. Russian education and health care were husks of their former selves.

What was Russia's problem? This chapter argues that the transition failed due to an inadequate moral infrastructure.

The Soviet Swamp

The Soviet Union was bloated, corrupt, and rudderless in 1990 as it began its crossover to the market system. A vast experiment in central planning, the economy had expanded, especially in wartime, and by the early 1960s, it was the world's second largest. It grew by drawing on its cornucopia of natural resources: free-flowing oil, natural gas, metals (including almost all the world's nickel), diamonds, and vast stands of timber. A rising population and good schools helped as well. State policies more or less forced citizens to put much of their earnings into bank deposits. The government then funneled these deposits into factories and other production facilities. Central planners—bureaucrats headquartered in Moscow—orchestrated everything, and announced healthy economic growth year after year.

The economy looked good from a distance, but up close you could see it was a sham. A common joke was: "They pretend to pay us and we pretend to work." The system generated colossal waste as managers tried to meet their production targets on the cheap. A typical tale: A nail factory has only a few weeks to meet the annual quota. It succeeds by producing twenty tons of 30-centimeter nails—a foot long and useless, but much easier to make than real nails.

Central planning needs shadow markets because a large national economy is ultimately unknowable. Even the best planners see only the broad outline, and miss the filigree detail and ripples. A shortage of bolts in Kiev, for instance, could cause a Leningrad factory to fail to meet its quota, surprising planners and disrupting downstream operations. As in Sumeria thousands of years earlier, unofficial traders filled in the gaps and lubricated the whole process. Soviet managers swapped favors in the gray market ("Ship me a boxcar of seat fabric so I can meet my car production quota, and I'll send you eight new cars"), and they occasionally ventured into the black market, as by selling extra tampons and buying French wine. And, of course, even if planners had been omniscient, they didn't have the final word. The Communist Party did, backed by the secret police organization, the KGB.

Party kingpins had often butted in, as when Nikita Khrushchev ordered corn planted on eighty-five million dry and empty acres (sixty-nine million failed). But by the 1970s, the state was caring less and less. Officials were selling permits and jobs, and growing fat on the cream of the economy. The resemblance of Leonid Brezhnev to a dissolute Roman emperor was no coincidence. He was the greediest and most venal of the Soviet dictators. According to one story, his mother comes to visit him from her drab life in the provinces, and he proudly shows her his diamonds, luxury cars, and opulent homes. "Well, it's good, Leonid," she says, amazed. "But what if the Reds come back?"

Meanwhile, citizens dwelt in a world of ineptitude. Store shelves were vacant, workers cheapened goods to meet impossible quotas, and government spun lies about production. Thefts from the government rose—in 1975, the official newspaper *Izvestia* guessed that a third of drivers were using gas filched from the state.

In fact, the ethical problems were systemic. In-group comradeship was the state myth, endlessly promulgated over the media; in reality, mutual support was hard to find and mutual suspicion was everywhere. People trusted only close friends and relatives, if anyone. They had come to expect short-run selfishness from everyone else, especially from those in authority, and they tended to respond in kind. It was a moral vicious cycle that choked the economy.

Some economists who spent time in the USSR in the late 1970s said privately that the Soviet economy was dysfunctional and heading down. Most Western observers, however, including the CIA, looked mainly at the bountiful resources and the falsified official data, and predicted continued growth.

The Perils of Perestroika

Mikhail Gorbachev took power in 1985 with a mandate to modernize and reinvigorate the economy. Raised in a mud cabin, he had seen his grandfather dragged off to Siberia for nine years on the local informer's accusation of hoarding grain. In his rise through party ranks, Gorbachev stood out for his integrity and, at the top spot, he was a shocking change from the geriatrics who preceded him. He was bright and compelling, and his candor—"Our rockets can find Halley's comet and reach Venus, but our fridges don't work"—boded well.

Yet fortune was unkind. The cost in treasure, lives, and morale of the Soviets' 1979 Afghan invasion was spinning out of control, and by 1989 the troops withdrew. The Soviet empire had become dependent on selling oil to the West at high prices, and in 1986, world oil prices began to plunge. That same year, the Chernobyl meltdown also drained Soviet economic and political resources.

Gorbachev's policies didn't help. Although perestroika (restructuring) and glasnost (openness) were mildly popular at first, they didn't boost the economy. Gorbachev's moral crusade against alcoholism—rampant in Russia then as now—was a multidimensional fiasco. Suppressing vodka sales cost perhaps a quarter of government revenue and may actually have harmed public health, as alcoholics turned to coolant, shoe polish, and eau de cologne. And just as in the United States, this latter-day prohibition was a gift to the mob and a growth hormone for official corruption.

As his popularity sagged in the late 1980s, Gorbachev dropped the anti-vodka campaign and raised wages. But in a planned economy, the wage increase didn't help much. What good is additional cash when prices are fixed and the shops are empty? So people just saved their extra rubles and waited. Economists called this situation "repressed inflation" and "ruble overhang," and it was like magma swelling under a volcano. It grew worse in 1991, when the Soviets printed more money than they had in the previous thirty years.

Perestroika laws, intended to make the economy more flexible, gave more discretion to top managers at production facilities, but failed to keep them accountable. The incentives became more perverse than ever. Managers and their party bosses began to treat facilities under their control as their own personal property. Toward the end of the 1980s, meeting the production target became less important than personal enrichment from producing for the gray and black markets.

By 1990, central planning was dying and everyone could see the economy weakening. Soviet economists Grigory Yavlinsky and Stanislav Shatalin (in consultation with Western economists) developed the 500-Day Plan to shift to a market system. The idea was to cross over slowly. The state would first sell small properties like apartments, trucks, and workshops, and gradually move up to large factories and oilfields. This approach would release savings bit by bit and soak up the ruble oversupply, and it might have been a smooth ramp to a market economy. In the next few years, such plans worked reasonably well in Poland, the Czech Republic, and other spin-offs of the Soviet empire. However, Communist Party traditionalists resisted, and Gorbachev dithered.

In August 1991, plotters took him prisoner as he was relaxing at his $20 million vacation home in the Crimea. Led by Gorbachev's appointees on the right, the coup failed, partly through their drunkenness and waffling. Appointees on the left had already drifted toward free-speaking Russian President Boris Yeltsin. In the center, Gorbachev was suddenly all alone. Within a few months, Yeltsin and his counterparts in other Soviet republics shoved him aside by dissolving the USSR.

Shocks

This fragmentation stunned the Russian economy, for, overnight, it raised huge barriers to trade. Imagine Florida, New England, and Texas seceding and hindering normal shipments across their borders. In fact, the consequences were even worse in the ex-Soviet Union because, with a highly centralized industrial structure, many factories had neither alternative suppliers nor customers within their republics.

Yeltsin's economic team and its Western advisors had such faith in the magical powers of the market system that they chose this moment to remove price controls. The "shock therapy" turned out to be all shock and no therapy. People cashed in their ruble bank deposits and started buying. The volcano was erupting. Money flooded the system, inflation skyrocketed, and to the surprise and dismay of the economic team, it roared on for several years. Inflation vaporized the life savings of most families and retirees as their rubles lost 99.99 percent of their value in less than a decade.

Could economic policy get any worse? In Russia, the problems had just begun. Members of the economic team rightly regarded private ownership as essential to a market system, so they began privatization in late 1993. It was an enormous shift of wealth, since the state had owned almost everything except minor personal household goods. As a first step, all Russian citizens got vouchers, which they could use to buy state property for themselves. But with their income, savings, and faith in government all exhausted, most people sold their vouchers immediately—often to glib operatives—for less than 1 percent of the potential value. Then, over the next three years, the state distributed virtually all its assets in the noteworthy auctions described below.

Meanwhile, according to journalist Paul Klebnikov, the insiders of the Communist Party and KGB had been effecting their own exit strategies. In alliance with black market figures, they looted the nation and stashed the pelf in safe places like Switzerland.

Pillage is essentially a medieval operation, but in Russia the looters used twentieth-century tactics. These included:

- *Bank fraud.* In this ploy, especially favored by Chechen gangsters, two shell companies fake a transfer of money and collect a real payout. It was veiled robbery, telecom Bonnie and Clyde. The first company sends a wire transfer of funds to the second, and it goes through the Central Bank, as all transactions did in Russia. The Central Bank checks the first company's account, okays the deal, and places the funds in the second company's account. The second company withdraws them and disappears. Then the Central Bank discovers that the first company never really had that money after all, and it also has already disappeared. How could such a scheme work? It requires a carrot and a deadly stick: (1) relatively modest payoffs to Central Bank employees who provide the codes to approve the bogus transfers, and (2) mortal threats to resisters. Over twenty-five bank officials met violent ends between 1992 and 1995. In a particularly exotic murder, banker Ivan Kivelidi died in 1996 after swallowing a nerve toxin placed on the lip of his cup. Bank fraud worked especially well in 1990–92, and overall involved tens of billions of dollars.
- *Capital flight.* The Soviet Union had kept prices artificially low, so that people could afford basics like bread and gas. To prevent operators from selling these goods abroad and making a fast ruble, the government enforced strict export controls. In this ploy, the looter evaded them. He first bought oil, natural gas, or even wheat at the low Soviet price. He then got permission to export (sometimes with a bribe) and sold the goods at a low price to a foreign partner or foreign shell company. The foreign partner, in turn, sold on world markets at a much higher price and earned a huge profit in hard currency. The booty went into a Swiss bank account, or the equivalent. This scam became easier after 1991 "reforms" eased most export controls. Some $100 billion was involved in the 1990s, wiping out the Soviet Union's entire gold and foreign currency reserves, as well as large loans from the IMF.
- *Monopoly pricing.* After shock therapy in January 1992, factory owners could set their own prices, often unchecked by real competition. So if you owned the only blue jeans company in Russia, you could charge exorbitant prices. And you could discourage potential rivals by asking your bureaucrat friends to harass them or shut them down, or by turning your gangster partners loose on them.
- Basic *organized crime*, such as protection rackets, smuggling, drugs, and prostitution. Protection schemes were hookworms in the economy, sucking away business profits, boosting costs, and slowing trade. And once the Mafiya got rolling in the early 1990s, it began to move upscale. For example, it opened new casinos and took over many legitimate hotels. In 1993, Russian President Boris Yeltsin estimated that two-thirds of all commerce was connected to organized crime—an astounding figure but in line with subsequent expert estimates.
- *Auction rigging.* This was the biggest scam of all, yielding several trillion dollars in plunder. The basic idea is childishly simple: hold an auction and gag the other bidders. Looters often bid less than 1 percent of fundamental value for a government asset, such as an oil field or factory, while their partners in the

government and the mob suppressed rival offers. For example, Gazprom, with natural gas reserves worth about $500 billion, sold to insiders for one-twentieth of one cent on the dollar. Almost all state assets went on the block, in the largest and most corrupt auctions the world has ever seen.

Some top "conservatives" in the KGB and Communist Party commenced this looting around 1990, as the Soviet system was melting. But even more ruthless men soon displaced them. In economies, as well as ecosystems, evolution is at work: when the environment shifts, success goes to those best suited to the new conditions. In Russia, people at the edge of power often saw the opportunities sooner and more clearly than the old rulers. Of course, everyone still needed a "roof"—protection against government intervention (legal or military) and other thieves—so the old-timers and their minions still got some of the loot. But Russia's crown jewels went to men like Boris Berezovsky.

Oligarchs and Kleptocrats

The most notorious of the oligarchs, Berezovsky illuminates the breed. He was the only child of a factory builder and a nurse, and became a top student in the USSR's elite science universities in the 1960s. By the late 1980s, he was directing a research lab developing software for production management. But he was a better networker than researcher. He developed consulting ties to Autovaz, a vast factory producing 1960-era Fiat clones, and as the Soviet system unraveled around 1990, he took advantage of his client. In partnership with Autovaz managers, government officials and Chechen gangsters, he acquired the bulk of auto dealerships and soon had "privatized the profits" of much of the auto industry. That is, Berezovsky's operation paid the factory less than the cost of making cars, and using tricks like fake exports and reimports, sold the vehicles to customers at inflated prices. Thus, the scheme exploited the workers and suppliers, while extracting up to half the sales revenue. Berezovsky and his partners made a fortune.

This sort of scam destroys value: Autovaz was, in effect, subsidizing the Berezovsky ring, so its productivity and quality suffered as it slid toward bankruptcy. But these problems brought larger subsidies from the state, allowing Berezovsky and friends to pocket even more money. His gangster allies came out relatively well in spectacular street wars of 1993, in which hundreds of mobsters died in shootouts and assassinations, and they held down the competition. His government allies headed off criminal investigations and kept the loot flowing, from the state to Autovaz to Berezovsky and friends.

Soon other opportunities opened up. The shock therapy of 1992 did not apply to the whole economy, and domestic prices remained quite low for oil, gas, strategic metals, and other commodities. Berezovsky partnered with fugitive U.S. financier Marc Rich to pioneer capital flight, Russian style. They made a second fortune looting Russia's aluminum, lumber, and oil. Berezovsky increased his political influence by doing personal favors for Boris Yeltsin, such as publishing his memoirs and advancing him huge royalties. These connections allowed

Berezovsky to acquire Russia's national TV network. Berezovsky's media dominance and campaign contributions gave Yeltsin a come-from-behind victory in the 1996 reelection.

Government and Mafiya ties enabled Berezovsky to rig some major privatization auctions. In one, he paid only $100 million to acquire Sibneft, whose oil and gas reserves rival Mobils', and whose market value soon rose to $5 billion. He also gained control of the state airline Aeroflot and several banks.

Yeltsin appointed Berezovsky to a high government post in late 1996, where he managed to outmaneuver reformist rivals like Anatoly Chubais and old-line conservatives like Yevgeny Primakov. By 1999, Berezovsky had achieved political, as well as economic, dominance, and he helped Yeltsin's surprise choice of a successor, ex-KGB official Vladimir Putin, win the 2000 election. But Putin detested political rivals and quickly moved to consolidate power in his own hands. Within a year, Berezovsky fled into exile in London, just ahead of criminal charges of complicity to fraud and money laundering.

As oligarchs like Berezovsky soared in the 1990s, Russia's economy starved. The final blow was a huge default on international debt in July 1998. Once the world's second largest, its economy fell to less than half its former size and ranked behind those of Brazil and Mexico.

You could see the impact everywhere. As black-windowed Rolls-Royces purred through the streets and the new elite drank $150 nightclub Scotch, the justice system and government agencies crumbled. Taxes were huge and often bizarre— there was a tax on business losses, for instance—but went unpaid by companies with good connections, like Gazprom, the world's largest natural gas company. At the same time, Russia's world-class medical and educational systems collapsed. Teachers could no longer earn a living wage, and doctors gave their own blood in transfusions.

Among the police and military, morale and discipline vanished, and officers survived mainly by selling weapons and protection services to the highest bidder. The 1993 Russian murder rate set new records, quadrupling that of the United States in one of our worst years ever. Thugs assassinated prominent individuals, yet seemed beyond the reach of the police and courts. Live birth rates dropped, while alcoholism and disease reached new highs. Life expectancy plummeted, especially for men, resulting in about six million excess deaths.

Moral Fiber for Markets

In sum, Russia's transition from Communism was among the twentieth century's worst disasters. Why? Why did the invisible hand that bred wealth in the West merely steer it to the crooks in Russia?

To work their magic, markets need the right kind of competition. When firms vie to offer customers better quality and lower prices, we get a value overflow that markets split among customers, suppliers, and owners. The magic vanishes when competition, instead, is for currying government favors, stealing property, and murdering rivals. That sort of competition killed economic growth in ancient empires and in medieval times, and did so again in Russia under the oligarchs and Mafiya.

Ultimately, it is morals that channel competition in productive directions. A story I heard in the late 1970s shows how a moral code protects the world's most liquid market—the interbank market for foreign exchange. On a rare holiday when markets were closed, Giuseppe, the head trader at a large American bank, got a call at home from a young trader at a foreign bank. He asked Giuseppe to help him out of a tight spot by buying his Pasetas at yesterday's closing price. The request was very irregular, but Giuseppe agreed. The next trading day, he discovered that the young trader had exploited breaking news that the Peseta was about to devalue, and had just made tens of thousands of dollars at the American bank's expense.

The young trader thought that his sharp dealing would enhance his reputation, but he misunderstood the traders' moral code. Giuseppe honored his agreement and spread the word on what had happened. The other traders—all of them—stopped dealing with the miscreant. It was as if the Law Merchant handed down an adverse ruling. Later that week, the young trader begged to return the money, but Giuseppe refused it. The trader's boss soon fired him, and he had to find a different line of work.

Markets live on voluntary exchange, which requires trust. You have to feel that strangers won't be cheating you before you'll deal with them. You have to believe your property is secure before you'll work to improve it. You have to think the banks are honest before you'll put your money in them. You need confidence that your profits won't drain away in protection payments before you'll start a business in the first place.

The market system didn't really take off until the moral infrastructure matured. Chapter 3 showed how that happened: bourgeois virtues and markets nurtured each other, and the rule of law tied monarchs' greedy hands. People trusted the system to enforce contracts, shield property from confiscation, keep banks sound, minimize violence and corruption, and foster real competition.

In Russia, such trust didn't take root. Honest economic reformers did their best but never gained traction. Part of the problem was the old socialist dream—happy workers laboring for the common good. Three generations of Soviet citizens had learned at school that property is theft, and that capitalists are parasites and crooks. Their experience in Soviet black markets reinforced that lesson. So when criminals flourished in newly capitalist Russia, public outrage was muffled.

The upshot was that politicians and officials found it more expedient to join the looting than oppose it. The courts and police were toothless, and legitimate businesspeople feared for their possessions and lives. The incentive from the top down was not to invest and improve, but to strip and loot. The Russian pie shrank as the oligarchs feasted.

Russia Recently

In 2007, Russia looks much better. Moscow's Great Mob War of 1993–94 is a receding memory, and the murder rate has declined toward a more civilized level.

The government is more coherent since Yeltsin turned over the reins to Vladimir Putin in May 2000—for example, it seems safe to say that the legislature will never again have gun battles as it did with Yeltsin in October 1993. The economy is moving forward, as internal barriers to trade shrink, and as oil prices float near historic highs.

Russia's recent stability is itself an economic boon. As noted in earlier chapters, economies dominated by stationary bandits do better than those dominated by insecure roving bandits, who constantly have to be ready to take the loot and run. In that sense at least, everyone agrees that the Russian economy has greatly improved since the Yeltsin years.

Observers differ on whether Russia's recent economic gains are sustainable, and I tend to side with the skeptics. Clearly, the economy will take a huge hit if and when oil prices return to the historical average. Russia's fundamental problem, though, is its threadbare moral infrastructure, illustrated in the following stories of the Putin era.

Judge Olga Kudeshkina seemed a model citizen until the trial of police investigator Pavel Zaitsev. It seems Zaitsev had zealously pursued a case of smuggled furniture in two shopping centers, and his findings implicated high officials. So prosecutors charged him with conducting searches without a warrant, and Judge Kudeshkina's supervisors told her to falsify court records and rule against him. Instead, she went public with the story on a radio station. A more malleable judge later convicted Zaitsev, and in April 2004, Judge Kudeshkina was fired.

A top oligarch, former Young Communist League activist Mikhail Khordorkovsky, created Russia's most efficient oil company, Yukos. But he started to negotiate with a foreign buyer, and made large donations to Putin's political opposition. Putin had him arrested in October 2003. "After a bogus trial conducted by servile judges," says one Western observer, "Mr. Khordorkovsky was sent to a Siberian prison camp and Yukos was broken up and pushed into bankruptcy through [clumsily rigged] back tax claims." Using rigged auctions, the oil assets were transferred to a more pliant oligarch. Since 2006, Putin's government has used bogus legal procedures to grab control of new eastern fields developed by BP, Exxon, and Royal Dutch Shell. The Russian oil and gas industry, once again, is under direct state control.

Moscow still has thirty-three billionaires, more than New York City, according to *Forbes Russia*. In 2004, the magazine listed the oligarchs along with a summary of how they acquired their wealth. Their unhappiness with this publicity may account for the 2004 assassination of the magazine's American editor, Paul Klebnikov. Or possibly, it was due to his detailed explanation to local journalists of how the pliant oligarchs' crimes exceeded those of Khordorkovsky. Shot four times after he left his Moscow office on the night of July 9, Klebnikov was taken slowly in a badly equipped Russian ambulance to a stripped-down local hospital. He died in a stalled elevator.

Western television covered the November 2006 thallium poisoning of KGB defector Alexander Litvinenko in London, but two other assassinations seem more typical. Anna Politkovskaya, a prominent journalist already banished from all major Russian media for her reporting on the Chechen war, was shot and killed at point blank range as she stepped out of the elevator in her apartment building on October 7, 2006. Like Klebnikov's, and those of a dozen other dissident journalists since 2000, her murder remains unsolved.

Andrei Kozlov, the forty-one-year-old first deputy chairman of the Russian Central Bank, was shot dead by contract gunmen in a soccer stadium parking lot on September 13, 2006. Contract murders usually remain unsolved in Russia, but within three months, the authorities had wrapped up the case, saying that the assassins were working for a small time banker who had recently been sanctioned by Kozlov. However, the authorities' evidence seems far less compelling than that of Austrian police, who say that Kozlov had recently uncovered a large money-laundering scheme involving current government officials.

What to make of all this? As of late 2007, Russia seems to be jelling as a classic dictatorship, with the government controlling key industries. Her citizens seem unlikely to resist, given their traumatic experiences under Yeltsin-era oligarchs and the Soviets. Eventually, perhaps when oil prices are lower, a new generation of Russians may try to lay, at last, the moral foundations of a true market economy.

Japan's Bubbles and Zombies
When Morals Choke Markets

World War II left Japan a rubble. Atomic bombs had leveled two cities, fire-storms had charred huge tracts of Tokyo, Osaka, and other urban areas, and the economy was on its knees. Yet, when the U.S. occupation ended in 1952, Japan began one of the most amazing spurts of wealth creation the world has ever seen. By the late 1980s, her economy was the world's second largest and one of the fastest growing. Pundits, including Lester Thurow, dean of MIT's prestigious Sloan School of Management, argued that Japan would leave us far behind unless we copied her policies.

Even more remarkably, Japan seemed to have overcome the conflict between morals and markets by stressing social harmony (*wa*) and tradition. Firms enjoyed friendly ties with regulators, as management did with labor, while bosses made decisions by consensus with their underlings. Karl Marx would scarcely have believed it. Japan's economy seemed different, and better, than everyone else's.

But Japan's growth collapsed in 1990, and its financial system stopped functioning. For fifteen years the economy stagnated and endured deflation reminiscent of the Great Depression. Stocks lost more than two-thirds of their peak value.

Why? This chapter argues that the problem was too much *wa*. The moral ties that had helped it for so long strangled Japan's economy when it needed to run in a different direction.

Looking Back

The argument reaches deep into Japan's history and geography. An island nation at the edge of the Middle Kingdom, Japan kept its independence for over two thousand years by a remarkable mix of adaptability and cultural unity. Japan, again and again, copied from China, taking not just ideograms and the Confucian social structure, but techniques of metallurgy, military technology, city planning, architecture, and much more. At the same time, Japan's internal networks spanned the islands, maintaining a single culture and a single ethnicity. Her cultural unity and up-to-date military capacities protected her from invasion century after century.

Around 1600, as Europe was starting to lead the world toward the market system, feudal Japan barricaded itself for two-and-a-half centuries. Why? The first Tokugawa shogun had just triumphed after decades of bloody wars and didn't want outsiders—especially Christians—whispering sedition to his vassals. Japan was also imitating China, which disdained contact with foreigners. But it was also calling on its historic in-group ties, cutting a chasm around itself in response to alien influences. Intriguingly, scholars see the beginnings of a homegrown Japanese market economy in this period, and indeed, from 1600 to 1853, Tokyo grew from a marsh side village to a metropolis of over one million, the largest city on earth.

National seclusion ended in 1853 when Commodore Matthew Perry sailed his "black ships" into Tokyo Bay. This display of military muscle and the not-so-subtle message—trade or else—soon created a consensus among top leaders for drastic change. It culminated in 1868 with the Meiji Restoration, essentially a takeover by technocrats. Japan then modernized rapidly and in a novel fashion.

The government guided development, selecting promising industries and funneling resources to them. It acted as a super-lender, spurring faster, better-targeted growth. Meanwhile, businesspeople cooperated with their neighbors to look like better modernizers than rival groups in different industries or locales. Business in-groups spanned the islands, and military and religious leaders also joined the mutual support system.

In late nineteenth-century Japan, production became concentrated in conglomerates, the great *zaibatsu* like Mitsui and Mitsubishi. Each *zaibatsu* was an enormous family of companies, all linked together. Typically, a bank stood at the center, and satellite firms in manufacturing, mining, and other fields revolved around it. The bank loaned funds at low rates to its members, and members sold products at similarly low rates to other members.

Meanwhile, Japanese delegations ransacked Europe for new ideas and brought them home, much as their ancestors had from China. In 1905, Japan's modernized armed forces startled the world by defeating a European power, czarist Russia, giving the nation a tremendous boost in morale and military prestige.

But the next generation overreached. The military dominated the government and pushed the old samurai warrior ethic, *bushido*, to fanatic extremes. This moral code, like those in fascist Europe, glorified the destiny of the nation and reflex obedience to its leaders. Those leaders gave Japan a colonial empire in Korea and China, but their aggressiveness led to atrocities against civilians and eventually pulled them into World War II. Stunning strategy and tactics—the surprise attack on Pearl Harbor, for example, and suicide plane crashes called kamikaze—were not enough to bring victory.

Economic Sunrise

Defeat and U.S. occupation opened Japan to new influences. In July 1950, business guru William Edwards Deming (1900–1993) toured the country. "I told them that Japanese industry could develop in a short time," Deming recalled later, and his shrewd ideas about quality control, continuous improvement, flexible work teams, and delegating decisions to the shop floor took root there, even as they faded into obscurity in his native United States. In the 1950s, the young Toyota engineer Taiichi Ohno (1912–90), inspired by his experiences in American supermarkets, conceived *kanban*, or "just-in-time" inventory control. Such techniques fit well with prewar Japanese corporate traditions of lifetime employment and close links to suppliers and customers, including joint ownership or owning large blocks of each other's stock. Revamped *zaibatsu*, now called *keiretsu*, emerged and competed for handouts from the government. The combination amounted to a new, distinctively Japanese, system of manufacturing.

The new system had favorable tailwinds. Japan's stress on *wa* and solidarity remained intact, as did its cultural and ethnic unity. The Japanese sense of "us versus them" shifted from military to economic competition with foreigners. Moreover, the U.S.-led postwar world order featured a reopening of global trade, so Japan had excellent opportunities to sell abroad, and export-oriented manufacturing soon dominated its economy.

Although the war had devastated factories and equipment, Japan had an exceptionally deep and talented labor pool in the decades following 1950. Compared to the United States, its workers were young and poor, but educated, disciplined, and keenly motivated. Its people saved a remarkably large share of earnings, and deposited them in banks and other institutions that loaned the funds to corporations, in close consultation with government officials. Within two decades, Japan had built (or rebuilt) world-class manufacturing facilities.

Politically, Japan became a vast back scratching system, with bureaucrats, business managers, and politicians all helping each other. A lone political party, the Liberal Democratic Party (LDP), has dominated Japan for sixty years. The LDP favors consensus decisions that maintain *wa* within its coalition of corporate interests and traditionalists such as farmers and small shopkeepers. For most of its time in power, the LDP has rotated the top position—prime minister—among factional leaders in the party. Real power lies with career bureaucrats in key executive departments such as the Ministry of Finance (MOF) and the Ministry of Trade and Industry (MITI). It is a cozy deal for all. Thanks to generous campaign contributions from industry, politicians seldom face annoying challengers, bureaucrats subsidize farmers and encourage savings and low-cost financing for key industries, and top bureaucrats often retire to lucrative positions in industry, a practice called "descent from heaven."

Mutual support is the linchpin everywhere. Workers are expected to actively aid others on their team (and generally do), and the team is expected to take initiative in improving performance. The moral code also calls for management to consult extensively with workers, and for everyone to build consensus before changing anything important. In-group morality softens market competition within and across firms in the *keiretsu* (and to some extent, within the country) to make them tougher competitors in foreign markets.

When something went wrong, it was taken care of quietly, usually within the *keiretsu* family. Nobody wanted to lose face. For example, Maruzen, an oil refinery company, expanded too fast in the 1960s and became unable to meet its financial obligations. The lead bank in its *keiretsu*, Sanwa, in cooperation with government officials of MITI and a host of supporting banks, gently encouraged the family owner-managers to retire, brought in a professional leadership team, reduced the workforce (mostly through attrition, not layoffs), infused capital, and restored profitability. Maruzen never formally declared bankruptcy. Similarly, when the car manufacturer Mazda got into financial trouble in the 1980s, its lead bank stepped in. Working with MOF officials, the troubleshooters from Sumitomo eased out the founder's grandson Kohei Matsuda, and the bank's own top manager, Tsutomu Murai, took over. He cut costs, partnered with Ford, and nursed Mazda back to profitability.

By 1970, manufacturers like Matsushita and Toyota were setting the world standard for quality and efficiency. Japan's new manufacturing system had unprecedented agility, and it grew adept at meeting rapid, but small, shifts in demand for product variety, as is common with cars and consumer electronics. (By contrast, the traditional corporate system of mass production and top-down hierarchical control works better when demand is either very steady, or when drastic changes require massive layoffs and quick redeployment.)

Supported by their partners in the *keiretsu*, by government ministries, and by cheap long-term loans, Japanese manufacturers could plan deeper into the future. They could build market share without worrying about next-quarter profitability, and could give each other price breaks until they had driven out foreign rivals in export markets. Meanwhile, a snarl of very adhesive red tape discouraged foreign firms from entering Japan. Its economy delivered breathtaking growth, and in the 1980s, it appeared destined to rule the world.

Except all was not as it seemed.

Bubble and Crash

In retrospect, everyone can see that Japan entered a bubble in the late 1980s. Land and stock prices, which had risen steadily since the 1950s, shot upward. The Nikkei stock index first hit 8,000 by about 1980 and 10,000 by about 1986, but then rocketed to just under 39,000 by the end of 1989. Even with very rosy views of profitability, stock prices were exorbitant. The textile sector sold for 103 times earnings, for instance, and fishery and forestry firms for 319 times earnings. The stock prices implied that Japanese companies were worth more than all those in the United States and most of Europe combined. Land prices in Japan also ballooned, and by 1990, they reached about one hundred times the U.S. level. The ground beneath the Emperor's palace in central Tokyo famously had a higher market value than all of California or Canada. When Nippon Telegraph and Telephone (NTT) opened an office building in downtown Tokyo with rents at $3,000 per square meter (quickly sold out), citizens dubbed it "The Tower of Bubble."

Japan's policy makers had grown incautious. They deregulated banks in the 1980s, letting them invest in stock and real estate schemes directly, and via loans to customers investing aggressively in similar schemes. Funds were going out to people who had less chance of paying them back. Deregulation also loosened *keiretsu* ties, so banks no longer reliably vetoed risky ventures by other firms in their family. Yet, government agencies were slow to take up the regulatory slack. Forty years of prosperity and government protection gave Japanese investors a false sense of security.

Moreover, as in the U.S. Savings and Loan industry a few years earlier, deposit guarantees created what economists call a "moral hazard." Remove the danger from risky or unethical behavior and it increases. Why not sit down at the blackjack table if someone else will cover your losses? Furthermore, the Bank of Japan (BOJ), the monetary authority, kept interest rates artificially low too long in the mid-to late 1980s.

Loans were easy, as well as cheap. A borrower could use inflated stock or land as collateral for a new loan, and use the funds to buy more stock or land. But habitable land is scarce in Japan, and domestic stock is also in limited supply. Increasing demand chased limited asset supply, and Japan's land prices and stock prices spiraled upward.

Why not buy foreign assets instead? Japanese international investors for decades have shown a remarkable knack for buying blue-chip properties—like Pebble Beach golf course, the Lincoln Center, and Dutch Master paintings—at all-time high prices, and selling years later near historic lows. With such experiences, foreign investment didn't seem so attractive. As a result, the two Japanese bubbles—land and stocks—continued swelling for several years.

The air supply eventually runs out in all bubbles, and it happened in Japan in 1990. The public had fully invested and began to worry about the oil price spike due to Iraq's invasion of Kuwait. Then the Bank of Japan let interest rates rise to more realistic levels. Money cost more. Borrowing got harder.

Stock prices paused.

Then the self-feeding dynamics halted and went into fast reverse. After peaking at 38,912.87 in late December 1989, the Nikkei lost about half its value in a year. Later, it lost half of the remaining value, and in late 2007, it still lingered below 16,000. Land prices dropped more gradually, but continued to fall for fifteen years. Transaction volume plummeted—the buyers had vanished—and people found it very difficult to sell their property. As stock and land prices fell, bank assets shrank, so the banks stopped lending to finance new purchases. Many of the more aggressive speculators were unable to pay back their loans.

Three company presidents faced this problem in 1998. One, Masaaki Kobayashi, had been highly successful, and his two friends grew wealthy as his suppliers. Kobayashi loved spending money, buying racehorses and flashy cars, and when the economy went into first gear, he kept spending, though his two friends begged him to halt. The Internet brought further woe as customers abandoned him for online retailers. Finally, he realized he was badly in debt and turned to his two pals. Both felt they owed him, and not just as a friend, but as a patron. So they embezzled from their own firms and passed him cash on the sly, $650,000 from one and $225,000 from the other. It didn't help, and Kobayashi's quicksand soon became theirs. Unable to face disgrace, on February 25, they all committed suicide.

But why didn't they just declare bankruptcy a year earlier?

Bankruptcy law is crucial to modern society. When borrowers can't pay back their debts, the law spells out which lenders get what. Bankruptcy laws should induce debtors to swiftly abandon unprofitable business, to sell the assets and distribute the proceeds to lenders. Good bankruptcy laws cleanse the system, quickly redirecting resources so as to minimize the overall loss. Confidence in bankruptcy procedures encourages lenders, and thus benefits borrowers. It is essential to financial markets in good times and bad.

Zombie Finance

The next chapter explains what is supposed to happen when bubbles burst: the overspent firms go bankrupt and their assets are sold off. The government makes sure that healthy companies have the chance to recover from their links to bankrupt firms. Asset prices once again reflect fundamental value, and restore their tie to reality. The financial system is back in business and the economy recovers.

That's not what happened in Japan. Encouraged and even pressured by government regulators, Japan's banks gave first priority to loans to firms facing bankruptcy, and kept them afloat. Such walking dead or "zombie" firms cut the profitability of their sounder competitors, who had to match their subsidized prices. They were also money sinks, absorbing loans that could energize more promising enterprises. The invisible hand of loan selectivity that guides healthy economies was pushing the wrong way. The zombie effect depressed investment, new job opportunities, and economic vigor throughout Japan, especially in construction, retail, and real estate.

We know a lot about one zombie, Sogo. Founded as a kimono store in 1830, it was a second-tier department store chain with three branches by 1962. In that year, Hiroh Mizushima took over. He had been an ambitious executive at the Industrial Bank of Japan (IJB), a semiofficial spigot of bureaucratic largesse about to be privatized, but he bailed out at age fifty when he realized he probably wouldn't reach the top spot.

Known within the firm as the "Emperor" or "God," Mizushima ran Sogo like a real estate speculator. He'd buy up property near busy train stations, install a department store or mall, and rent out the extra space. When the land rose in price, he'd sell it off or borrow against its now-greater value, and buy more land near the next train station. His method worked well from the beginning, and looked brilliant during the land bubble. But then the bubble burst.

Mizushima had never run Sogo's department stores efficiently, and they made little profit. During the 1990s, they racked up increasingly large losses. Mizushima, by then an autocrat in his eighties, was unwilling to switch tactics. With his goal of being Japan's largest retailer almost in sight, he continued to open new stores, even as the value of his holdings sank alarmingly. So he needed huge bank loans.

In a proper market economy, Sogo would have declared bankruptcy by 1991 or 1992, and Mizushima, along with thousands of employees, would have lost his job. The government might have retrained some employees, and helped basically sound suppliers make the transition. Instead, it kept the zombie upright and walking.

Mizushima called on his old friends from IBJ. Soon IBJ became the lead bank, and its prestige and close ties to government ministries encouraged other banks to pitch in. It seemed reasonable: join in and help make powerful men happy, gain reflected prestige, and contribute to *wa*. Everyone was doing it. The fact that Sogo's property was unsaleable, and that cash flows were negative, seemed beneath the notice of the lenders. (Echoing Louis XIV, Mizushima liked to say, "Collateral? It is me.") Eventually, Sogo ran up more than $17 billion debt to seventy-three banks.

In 2000, the government introduced new accounting rules, which showed that Sogo had a negative net worth that began at $5 billion. (The total was surely worse, but Sogo didn't have to disclose it.) Mizushima and his pals worked out a typically quiet, backroom deal. The banks would cancel about $6 billion of debt and the government ministers and elected officials would earn the gratitude of Sogo's employees, suppliers, lenders, and customers. Would all seventy-three lenders go along? Normally, they probably would have. When the herd began moving, no one wanted to get caught walking against it—especially when the well-being of everyone in the Sogo empire seemed at stake.

But this time it was different. A few months earlier, the government had sold off a failed lender called Shinsei Bank to an American group, which had insisted on guarantees of bad loans. So the bank was able to pass its hit, about $1 billion, back to the government, which had to disclose the deal. Insiders were embarrassed— one of IBJ's key officials committed suicide—and the public was outraged. The deal unraveled and Sogo declared bankruptcy in July 2000.

Mizushima publicly stepped down, but kept power behind the scenes. Despite his age and government connections, his legal problems mounted. In March 2005, he was convicted of hiding personal assets he'd skimmed from Sogo. Other lawsuits are pending.

We know so much about Sogo because it was a fluke. Mizushima ran into bad luck with the timing of the crisis, and especially the presence of the American-controlled lender, outside the system of *wa*. Thousands of other zombies remain in operation, their losses unknown.

But where did the banks get the money to give to firms like Sogo? Most banks fear dud loans, since they can be fatal. Indeed, Japan's banking industry had a net operating loss every year from 1993 through 2003. The banks' international credit ratings, once the envy of the world, crashed to Third World levels.

The natural result should be that some banks themselves declare bankruptcy, their assets are sold, and the banking sector recovers. Instead, in the 1990s, Japanese bureaucrats and politicians propped them up. The bureaucrats encouraged an accounting scam known as "evergreen lending": when a borrower can't repay, instead of classifying the loan as nonperforming, the bank lends the borrower more money to make payments on the old loan. Politicians kept weak banks alive by dipping into the public treasury. They funneled taxpayer money to bank subsidiaries called *jusen*, which specialized in real estate lending. Voter outrage at the huge giveaways to these firms (or to their parent banks) in the late 1990s then persuaded the politicians to use more covert handouts, such as subsidizing megamergers among Japanese banks.

By 2001, the total debt of Japanese banks was over one trillion dollars. Due to the disproportionate role banks play in the Japanese financial sector, the impact was huge. Subsidies, direct or hidden, also shored up the two other major financial market subsectors: insurance and government-run financial institutions such as the Postal Savings bank. The result was a zombie financial sector, no longer able to do its job, and an economy on Ambien.

Why did government regulators and the public tolerate this mess? Why didn't they demand that banks and other financial firms restructure, and start lending for activities that have a real future?

The reason was *wa*. Bankruptcy in Japan is not a simple risk of doing business, but a moral transgression, "regarded as close to a crime," according to Seiichi Yoshikawa, a Tokyo attorney. The bankruptcies Japan needed would have shamed important people in government and industry, and increased unemployment for awhile. Some of the disgraced, like the three company presidents, might take their own lives. Friends don't do that to friends. They lock arms with them, even if they wind up in freefall, too. So in-group thinking spreads success in good times, and spreads trouble in bad. *Wa* has two sides.

The personal traits that help you succeed in markets are quite different from those that help you socially. For instance, good stock investors make money by quickly spotting chances to buy at a low price or to sell at a high one. They don't buy shares in firms as favors to the CEO. Economies, too, must know how to impersonally jettison losing efforts like Sogo, as through bankruptcy, and how to reward promising ones. Where moral feelings—like gratitude, loyalty, and *wa*—get tangled in the process, they can knock it awry.

A Second Sunrise?

Eventually, good sense should prevail and get Japan's economy back on track. By 2007, it appears that this might finally be happening. Japan's working-age population is shrinking and her corporations have outsourced many manufacturing jobs, boosting profitability. China's amazing growth spurt (surpassing even postwar Japan) is driving demand for Japanese goods. High profile foreigners, like Carlos Ghosn at Nissan Motor and Harold Stringer at Sony, bring a more competitive attitude to top management. Junichiro Koizumi pushed economic reform very hard during his 2001–6 tenure as Prime Minister. He privatized Postal Savings, while the banks cut the nonperforming bank loans by more than half, and are starting to repay the taxpayer bailouts. Consolidation has reduced the zombie count in some industries like oil refining, paper, and cement. Japan still has the world's second largest economy, so it has ample resources for recovery.

But sustained growth is not yet assured. Japan's workforce is graying, and its cultural barriers make it difficult to tap foreign talent or professional women. There are still lots of nonperforming loans, but more worrisome is a large, but unknown, fraction of supposedly good loans. They are performing now because, like subprime mortgages in the United States, they require only easy payments at first, but eventually, they call for an unrealistically large "balloon" payment. And, of course, some industries like construction are still wandering in zombie land.

What are Japan's longer-term prospects? Quite possibly, Japan will look like Britain after World War II, enduring a full generation of genteel decline. But the nation has always responded adaptively to external forces, from the unification of China in 589 BCE to the door knocking of Perry, and more recently, to defeat in World War II and the oil price shocks of the 1970s.

Now Japan must respond to an internal threat. The in-group coherence that helped it so often in the past has become the root problem—it must pull back a bit and open some space for competitive market forces.

Happily, change is in the air. Many companies are turning to "freeters," young part-time and temporary employees who give firms a new flexibility. A long-time observer writes, "The Japanese are, for all else, pragmatic . . . '100 yen shops' (basically dollar stores) are everywhere now. Department stores actually have sales. . . . Like in everything, the Japanese have taken to this full-force (they tend to be all-or-nothing, very little middle ground) and are now competitive shoppers." Japan already has a vibrant urban youth culture, ready to do things its own way. The country just might find new ways to combine morals and markets, and once again become a world leader.

7

Towers of Trust

The Rise (and Occasional Crash)
of Financial Markets

A Tale of Two Bubbles

Tirana 1997

Albania was Europe's poorest and most isolated nation when it renounced communism in 1991. Then the new Democratic Party took over, radically reformed the economy, and touched off an economic boom. The official banking system, burdened with bad loans to Communist era enterprises, couldn't keep pace, so financing came mainly from unofficial and unsupervised financial institutions.

Vefa was a prime example. Founded in 1992 by Vehbi Alimucaj, a former Army officer with $700 in the bank, Vefa started to build shopping centers, to finance trade with Italy (which lies just across the Adriatic), and to begin a host of other new activities. Vefa promised investors a return of at least 6 percent per month (or about 100 percent per annum!) and delivered on that promise month after month, for several years. The business activities produced some revenue, but mostly Vefa paid old investors with funds raised from dazzled new investors. Families poured in their life savings (especially remittances from sons and daughters working in the West), and Vefa's assets soared to hundreds of thousands of dollars in 1993 and to hundreds of millions in 1996.

By then, rivals offered even higher interest rates, up to 50 percent per month without ever investing the money. They relied entirely on funds from a growing pool of new investors—pure Ponzi schemes. Legitimate investments couldn't compete, nor could wages. People quit their jobs and looked for ever-quicker ways to get rich. Outsiders warned that collapse was inevitable, but government officials gave their blessings to Vefa and several rivals.

Ponzi schemes fail when they run out of naïve investors. In Albania's capital city, Tirana, things started to unravel with a prominent default in November 1996, and by January 1997, Vefa and the other major players shut down. Many of the owners fled with whatever cash they could grab. Alimucaj was caught transferring funds to Switzerland. He was arrested and charged with fraud.

Spring 1997 was bitter. A majority of Albanians had lost their life savings, totaling about half of GDP—an all-time record. Citizens were outraged to learn that officials who blessed Vefa and its cousins had been on the payroll. Some rose in revolt, stole weapons from police stations, and burned and looted government buildings. The government fell and over two thousand people were killed before order was restored.

Decisive action in late 1997 helped heal the wounds. National and international authorities imposed martial law, and seized and sold off assets of the bankrupt companies. A new government was elected and, remarkably, the economy began to grow again in 1998.

London 1720

Another episode took place centuries earlier at the other end of Europe. In 1711, the British government awarded Robert Hartley's South Seas Company (SSC) a Royal charter—a monopoly franchise—to pursue overseas trade in the southern Atlantic and Pacific. But the trade opportunities fizzled out and the franchise looked worthless by 1719. Instead of folding, SSC came up with a bold new business plan: to buy up England's entire public debt. While the government was considering the offer, SSC launched an aggressive advertising campaign. Several leading politicians and some eager Dutch investors helped push up the stock price, from 128 pounds sterling per share in January 1720 to 175 in late February and to 380 in late March.

The government accepted the offer in April, and SSC's stock price climbed further. Middle class and wealthy people became obsessed with buying stocks, including those of startup companies with vague plans. One entrepreneur simply advertised, "A company for carrying on an undertaking of great advantage, but nobody to know what it is." He raised two thousand pounds in five hours and then absconded. SSC shares looked solid by comparison, especially after Parliament's "Bubble Act" in June outlawed selling stock in companies without a royal charter.

Savvy investors such as Sir Isaac Newton (the immortal physicist at that time was also Master of the Mint) remained skeptical about SSC and the "bubble" companies, but it was hard to sit idly while everyone else got rich. Newton finally gave in to pressure and bought SSC shares near the peak price of 1050 in late June. Then the supply of dazzled new investors ran out, and it became increasingly obvious that managing the national debt was not going to be exceptionally profitable.

SSC's stock price trended down and then began to tumble. By December 1720, it had crashed back down to 128. Huge fortunes were lost, along with many family nest eggs, and charges of bribery and fraud were filed. SSC officials fled the country or prepared themselves for prison. Newton lost twenty thousand pounds of public funds and was traumatized for life. "I can calculate the motions of the heavenly bodies," he wrote, "but not the madness of people."

*   *   *

The great South Sea bubble was not the first, and the Albanian crash was not the last. The dot-com and telecom bubbles roiled the U.S. economy just after the turn of the millennium, and Japan is only now recovering from her 1980s bubbles in real estate and stocks. The Great Depression of the 1930s, precipitated by the U.S. stock market crash in October 1929, blighted an entire generation.

How and why do financial markets run amok? And why do we tolerate financial markets when they can cause such misery? The rest of the chapter seeks answers and, along the way, finds some enduring mysteries. We begin with the moral roots of finance, and trace the tensions deep beneath modern financial markets.

Promises, Promises: The Moral Finance of *Eranos*

Promises are the heart of finance. As borrower, I promise to give you, the lender, money later in return for the money you give me now. The idea is as old as written history—indeed, the first known writing, in ancient Sumeria, records just this sort of promise. Probably, the idea is older than that, and even older than money—prehistoric villagers must have promised shares of the coming harvest to those who gave them needed seeds or tools or labor.

In classical Greek civilization, some promises took the form of an *eranos* loan. An Athenian merchant with a customer in Alexandria for 100 amphorae of olive oil, say, would not want to buy all the goods himself. After all, a storm might sink the ship, and then he'd be penniless. He could share the risk and the reward by borrowing from extended family, neighbors, and wealthy friends. Such *eranos* loans were at zero interest and obliged the borrower to reciprocate by lending later to others in his circle. The lenders could see when the borrower was making an honest effort to repay, and would show forbearance when bad luck delayed the promised repayment. Or, if the borrower was not trying his best to repay, the lenders could see that too, and exert pressure through the social network. Moral codes encourage efficient renegotiation when promises are not fulfilled.

This is just the sort of thing the moral system is designed for, and it works pretty much the same way in farming and fishing villages throughout the world, even today. Members of a closely-knit group provide financing (and insurance) to each other, and the promises are enforced by the group's moral code. Recently, the same sort of financing has emerged spontaneously in towns in Africa, Asia, and Latin America. Roscas (rotating savings and credit associations) typically involve about half a dozen families who pool their savings and take turns purchasing things like bicycles or roofing materials. By pooling their resources, they can purchase sooner on average, reduce risk, and encourage each other to save more.

Why is there any other sort of finance? Polonius, father of Hamlet's sweetheart Ophelia, pointed out a problem: "loan oft loses both itself and friend." You might have relatives that you love dearly, but would never lend to because their lifestyles make repayment problematic, and unrepaid loans can be very awkward. The point is that *eranos* lending is vulnerable to social disruption and, as Polonius hinted, can even cause it.

More importantly, *eranos* lending draws only on the resources of your own personal circle. If you are like most people in recorded history, those resources are quite limited, and won't allow you to take advantage of great opportunity or to get enough help in an emergency. Even if you belonged to the wealthy ruling elite, you probably would find most resources tied up trying to maintain power, and not much would be available for really new opportunities.

In sum, *eranos* finance is not especially dynamic. It doesn't scale up very well as societies get larger and more diverse. Other forms of finance become increasingly important.

The Dark Side of *Daneizein*

Professional moneylenders took up the slack as Athens' commercial empire expanded. Their *daneizein* were interest-bearing loans backed by collateral. This sort of finance goes back at least to Uruk, and by 2,500 years ago it was an accepted part of city life from the Mediterranean to China.

Most Greek moneylenders were lower class, not citizens. The moneylender Pasion, for example, was born a slave, but gained his freedom and started his business around 400 BCE. Twenty very successful years later, and after conspicuous public philanthropy, Pasion was made an Athenian citizen. By the time of his death ten years after, his net worth of seventy talents made him the city's richest man.

Pasion's rise to citizenship was an exception. Plato's *Republic* disparages moneylenders as parasitic wasps, and in general, Greek citizens regarded them as a necessary evil. Most ancient civilizations (and those since) seem to share the Greeks' ambivalence. But, why? Why wouldn't people welcome something so important and useful?

Giving *eranos* loans to friends feels morally virtuous—you are helping a friend in need, you share in good outcomes and bad, and you expect reciprocation. In contrast, the *daneizein* loan feels unfriendly. The moneylender collects interest without actually working for it, and if you are down on your luck and can't repay, he multiplies your problems. He takes the family heirlooms or family land you put up for collateral. If you didn't have any collateral, he might have you put in prison or sold as a slave. Not nice.

The ancient rules on collateral and default, though morally distasteful, have a compelling economic logic. Once the borrower has received the resources, his direct incentive is to delay or avoid repayment. He will be better off if he can evade his promise, and will be tempted to abscond or to pretend that he can't repay. Economists now call the problem "moral hazard," and theoretical biologists would recognize it as a version of cheating. It must be solved for lending to be viable.

Of course, the borrower may feel morally bound by his promise, and that solution works just fine for *eranos* loans from in-group friends. The borrower's reputation is at stake, and everyone has an interest in seeing the loan repaid. But moral bonds are much looser for *daneizein* loans from an outsider, and the borrower's friends are far less likely to sympathize with the lender when things go wrong.

Daneizein lenders who rely entirely on the borrower's good faith tend to go out of business.

The standard solution is collateral plus enforcement. Borrowers will do their best to repay if they know that they otherwise will be worse off materially. Thus, the collateral must be something precious to the borrower, more valued than the repayment.

Unfortunately, the collateral solution is not perfect. Even very scrupulous borrowers sometimes get into trouble. Crops might fail, or robbers or invaders might strike, and the borrower forfeits the collateral. A decent hardworking family could lose everything to a low-class moneylender, a stranger who doesn't even work for a living. It seems terribly unjust.

This tension between moral sensibilities and economic logic has predictable consequences. First, moneylenders seldom belong to the social mainstream. As outsiders, they can tap resources beyond those in the borrowers' circles, and their threat to seize collateral is more believable. Therefore, moneylenders tend to have relatively weak moral ties to borrowers, and often have a different ethnicity. For example, overseas Chinese dominate the money lending business in Southeast Asia, as do Lebanese in the Mediterranean and beyond, and Jews in medieval Christian Europe.

A second consequence is what lenders now call political risk: as outsiders, moneylenders are an inviting target for ambitious politicians. *Daneizein*-style lending is forbidden by Christian and Muslim teachings, but, of course, it often crops up anyway in a black or gray market. The Old Testament calls for some debt contracts to be cancelled every seventh year, and other debts every half century, at Jubilee. This would cause credit to dry up as cancellation approached, and the custom apparently was soon abandoned. Whether or not *daneizein* lending is officially tolerated, widespread moral feelings make it vulnerable to expropriation.

An early example occurred in 1788 BC. Perhaps to clear his own debts, or to curry favor with borrowers, King Rim-Sin of Ur declared all loans null and void. Surviving cuneiform texts show that the edict ruined a moneylender named Dumuzi-gamil and all his competitors. The texts also hint that such events occurred occasionally in previous and subsequent reigns.

Plato was hostile toward moneylenders but even more scathing about demagogues who buy off the people by confiscating moneylenders' property. He praised Sparta, the archrival city, for never repudiating debts, and rightly so, because that policy surely strengthened Sparta's economy. The danger of politically motivated debt forgiveness and expropriation always has the same sad effects: higher interest rates to cover the extra risk, stunted finance, and a weaker economy.

A Princely Paradox

Imagine that you suddenly become the absolute monarch of your realm, with no legal constraints. You can just take whatever you want. No more financial worries, right?

Well, maybe. Here's the problem. From time to time, you'll need a loan for castle improvements, or for diplomatic ventures, or maybe just to fight that nasty baron across the river. Since you control the local courts, after you get the loan, you can easily declare the promise to repay null and void. You could declare a state emergency, for example, and if a local lender objects, you could throw him in jail and seize his property. But the lenders know this and will stay away. You have a royal case of moral hazard, and are a very bad credit risk.

To get a loan, you have to find convincing collateral, something that wouldn't entice you to change your mind later. The usual royal collateral turned out to be tax collection rights and tax exemptions. Unfortunately, the highest bidder for collection rights was usually the most ruthless, and such people often offend taxpayers' sense of fairness. Tax exemptions put the burden on a smaller and smaller number of people, who naturally resent those who don't have to pay. Eventually, the system seems unfair and illegitimate.

Minting coins, the other steady source of royal revenue, also suffers from moral hazard. When you need quick cash, you can debase the coinage by lowering its gold or silver content. Of course, this creates inflation. It amounts to stealing from lenders (whose repayments will be worth less than they bargained for), and it will disrupt markets and financial affairs throughout your realm.

Paper money brought similar problems to China. First introduced in Sichuan province around 1000 CE as a stopgap measure (not enough bronze for coins), paper money seemed wonderful at first. The rulers got the same revenue as with coins, but at lower cost, and the people found it more convenient to use than heavy strings of bronze coins. But after awhile, to cope with military emergencies, the Sichuan rulers printed lots of extra money, with the same ill effects as debasing coins. Later, the southern Song emperors also overprinted. By 1276, they had totally trashed the economy, and that year, the empire fell to Kublai Khan. His Yuan dynasty also eventually overissued paper money and fell to the Ming dynasty, which soon followed the same pattern. In 1430, and for the next five hundred years, the Chinese banned paper money.

The corrosive effects of royal finance helped bring down dynasties all over the ancient and medieval worlds, not just in China. (Robin Hood's legendary campaign against the corrupt Sheriff of Nottingham comes to mind.) More recently, such corrosion triggered the French Revolution and hastened the fall of czarist Russia. There had to be a better way.

Banks Branch Out

The Italian Renaissance is famous for new forms of artistic expression, but arguably, the real spark came from new forms of finance. Beginning in Florence around 1250, interpersonal networks of *fiducia* (trust) crossed family lines, soon embracing most of the city's elite and, eventually, their contacts across the continent. These supple credit networks could eventually draw on resources throughout Europe. For example, in May 1399, banker Giovanni da Pessano in Milan reported to senior partner Francesco Datini in Florence about a new loan he extended to a merchant traveling to Venice, funded by a repayment arriving from Avignon.

The network was dispersed and powerful enough to deal with local rulers as well as merchants. The royals soon learned that a default to the local banker would cut them off from the whole network. Best of all, the Florence-centered system multiplied resources, since one florin of bank capital could typically support five florins of bank loans. It was financial magic, and for over two hundred years, it energized the economy in Florence, in Northern Italy, and throughout Europe.

How did it work? Complex networks in previous eras soon collapsed in mutual recrimination, or never got off the ground. The Florentine banks reinforced their exacting moral code of *onore* (honor) with new political and technical structures:

- Double-entry bookkeeping. By 1300, Florentine merchants and bankers wrote exact debits and credits for each transaction. There could be no self-serving bias or ambiguity about who owed what to whom.
- Letters of credit and other business forms. A simple letter sufficed to transfer resources to borrowers, economizing on cash. Business letters often used the language of *amicizia* (friendship) and *fratelanza* (kinship), but were quite precise about the amounts owed and conditions of repayment.
- Partnerships and correspondents. Individuals joined forces to reap mutual gains, either by sharing the costs and benefits as partners, or by forming credit and informational links as *corrispondenti*.
- Republican government. In this golden age of Florence, holders of high office were generally bankers or merchants who had earned highest *onore* and respect in the business world. This practice helped limit corruption and nepotism, and strengthened both the Florentine state and Florentine commerce.

Eventually, one of the leading banking families, the Medicis, consolidated power, and the system became less flexible and dynamic. But by that time, banking networks had taken hold throughout the continent. Some families rose to great prominence—for example, the Rothschilds in the early nineteenth century, and later, the Wallenbergs—but the real magic was always in the network. As an expansive moral in-group, the network allowed bankers to confidently extend loans to each other, thus giving their customers access to a vast pool of resources. The network continued to guarantee promises as it did in Florence and earlier among the Maghrebi traders: the threat of ostracism kept everyone honest because one's career (and perhaps one's place in the family) depended on being a member of the network in good standing.

Promises for Sale

Financial markets are what allow modern economies to really soar, but they only got started a century or so before the South Seas Company. Why did it take so long? Why are they so powerful, and why do they sometimes let the economy crash and burn?

Let's start with the basic description. Financial markets are where promises are traded: borrowers sell new promises to the highest bidder in the primary market, and investors buy and sell old promises in the secondary market.

Most promises are too personal to trade. Financial markets need special sorts of promises, ones that are standardized and depersonalized. To make his promise tradable, the borrower (whether a person or organization) must publicly reveal a lot of information about his circumstances, and often another person or organization vouches for the information or for the promise itself. In the United States, for example, the Securities and Exchange Commission requires extensive disclosures from companies issuing new stock or bonds; the companies often promise not to incur additional debt and to keep liquid assets; other companies, called underwriters, offer additional guarantees; and rating agencies, such as Moody's, monitor and report on the companies and their guarantors.

Something is lost in making promises tradable. No longer do we have a rich human relationship between the person making the promise and the person who accepts it. We put aside feelings of trust, gratitude, worry of betrayal, and guilt and vengeance if the promise isn't honored. Tradability pushes these social emotions to the background, and creates more space for opportunistic behavior.

Yet, much is gained. An investor will pay more for a promise that she can sell whenever she wants than for a promise that she must hold until it matures—the secondary market gives her valuable flexibility. Since she will now pay more in the primary market, the borrower gets a better deal, too.

Moreover, the investor doesn't have to assess the trustworthiness of a buyer in the secondary market, nor does the buyer have to assess her trustworthiness. Special networks of trust are unnecessary. Investors selling and buying a promise only need to know about the original borrower and the guarantors, not about each other. This opens financial markets to anyone, and they can directly tap the resources of all savers.

Financial markets can tap mental, as well as physical, resources. As we will see, they pull together everyone's ideas on how best to provide for the future, and this is the deep source of their power in the modern world. But these powers beg the earlier question: why did it take so long for financial markets to emerge?

I suspect that the underlying obstacle was moral repugnance. Financial markets tend to corrode the traditional social order. When financial assets can be freely bought and sold, some people will stop being farmers or craftsmen and, instead, become full-time traders. Occasionally, through skill or fraud or perhaps blind luck, a trader will acquire wealth beyond the dreams of ordinary folk. Often, traders go bankrupt, sometimes bringing ruin to their families. Traditional morals find both extremes deeply offensive, and resent the siphoning of talent from "honest" activities. Moreover, successful participants in financial markets often have offensive motives and personality traits: think of Ebenezer Scrooge's shriveled heart (and his Protestant work ethic) in Charles Dickens' classic 1843 story *A Christmas Carol.*

Therefore, like moneylenders, financial markets are a tempting target for politicians. Twentieth-century despots Lenin and Hitler (and Robert Mugabe in early twenty-first century Zimbabwe) found it politically advantageous to expropriate the "leeches and parasites" who make their living in financial markets. Even representative governments may find it politically expedient to outlaw financial markets when their citizens see them as no different from casinos.

Financial markets thus become viable only when there is a strong rule of law that can trump social norms and political expediency. Arguably, such law first appeared in the Roman republic, and recently, scholars have discovered a prequel there to financial markets. Organizations called *societas publicanorum* contracted with the government to provision temples, to construct and repair other public works, and to collect taxes. Surviving texts suggest that these organizations had a continuing existence beyond their specific members, and were owned by shareholders who could trade shares in the Forum. This proto stock market apparently disappeared after the Roman emperors seized absolute power in the first century BCE.

The rule of law advanced fastest in the Netherlands and Britain, as we have seen in earlier chapters. So it should come as no surprise that modern financial markets began in the seventeenth century port cities of Amsterdam and London. From 1602, investors traded Dutch East India Company shares in the Amsterdam stock market. (Shares are promises to a given fraction or share of a company's profit. Another sort of financial asset that appeared early was a bond, which promises a regular sequence of cash payments.) In 1688, Penso de la Vega described more complex promises traded in Amsterdam's secondary market, including what we would now call forward contracts and options. He also described some episodes that we now might call bubbles.

Financial markets spread once it became obvious that the cities that housed them attracted more efficient investment and prospered. Local morals and local laws adapted to accommodate the new markets.

Financial Market Magic

Casinos and financial markets might attract people with similar motives, but financial markets have a far more elevating effect on the economy. Indeed, for the last four hundred years, the world's most advanced economies have relied mainly on financial markets to make crucial choices: how much of available resources should be consumed now, and how much invested for the future? And, among all the competing ideas on how best to provide for the future, which should be ignored, which should be tried, and which should be expanded?

Financial markets answer these questions in a remarkably simple way. When financial assets are generally cheap, investors buy more of them, steering resources away from consumption and toward building the future; and when investors think an idea is particularly good, they buy more promises (assets) based on that idea, sending more resources in its direction.

Why are these simple answers so powerful? To explain, we take a short detour into theory. The Appendix includes a longer tour.

Financial markets are efficient when the market price of every financial asset is equal to its "fundamental value." As explained in section A9 of the Appendix, the fundamental value is the expected present value of the promised repayments, taking into account everything that anyone currently knows about the borrower's prospects. When asset price and fundamental value are equal, then trades in financial markets funnel resources into the best bets for the future.

For example, suppose that you need childcare and, after shopping around, you discover that an up-and-coming local franchise, KidsRUs, has some wonderful new ideas on providing high quality care at an affordable price. You buy their stock and so do your wealthy friends and relatives. Then KRU has more resources to invest in training and development, and in spreading the franchise. If you are right about KRU, you gain wealth from the higher share price, but at the same time, society benefits from funneling resources into the most promising childcare facilities.

The general point is that financial markets encourage everyone to buy or sell assets based on their personal information and best understanding, and the price reacts to their purchases and sales. Investors gain wealth when they buy undervalued assets or sell overvalued assets that the market later prices correctly. When the asset price settles down, it should reflect the personal information and best thinking of all investors. Financial markets, thus, can combine the information dispersed throughout society. The markets gather information, summarize it as fundamental value, and use it to decide the most productive courses of action.

The Sorcerer's Apprentice

Thus, financial markets work their magic when they are efficient, expressed mathematically as asset price equals fundamental value. Bubbles are defined as deviations of price from fundamental value. When the deviation is positive or negative for some assets, the financial market is inefficient. It funnels resources into bad bets, and diverts resources from sounder investments.

Negative bubbles shouldn't last long. Investors who think price is less than value can personally profit and help society by buying the undervalued asset. These purchases will drive up the price and help restore efficiency.

Positive bubbles are a bit trickier. If you think price is above value for some asset, you could sell it if you had any, but what if you already have sold or never owned it? You might want to borrow shares at the current price and repay them later, at what you expect to be a lower price. This practice is called short selling. It is discouraged in most financial markets, including major exchanges in the United States. The main reason, I think, is because short selling goes against our moral sensibilities. It seems, somehow, like picking on someone down on his luck, or like profiting from others' misfortunes. Unfortunately, legal restrictions on short selling reduce market efficiency and stop pessimistic investors from deflating bubbles.

But this doesn't yet explain how bubbles get started and grow. Economists still argue these matters and have not yet reached a consensus. The perspective I personally find most convincing is due to economist Hyman Minsky, who drew on themes of John Maynard Keynes that later were elaborated by Charles Kindleberger.

The Keynes-Minsky-Kindleberger (KMK) perspective can be summarized as a sequence of phases. Phase 0 is normalcy, and efficient financial markets. Investors share a broad consensus on the earnings prospects for tradable assets, the prices closely track fundamental values, and investors earn normal returns.

Phase 1 begins when an unusual opportunity appears. For example, Albania opened its economy in 1992, and in 1720, the South Seas Company proposed to privatize Britain's national debt. Here are two other examples: in the late 1980s, innovative Japanese car and consumer electronic manufacturers gained world leadership in efficiency and quality; and in the late 1990s, the rapid rise of the Internet created a host of new business opportunities.

Normally, shared experience leads to rough consensus on the value of available opportunities. But Phase 1 opportunities are so unusual that different investors hold very different opinions. Optimists think they can make once-in-a-lifetime profits. Mary Meeker and Henry Blodgett, for example, predicted that dozens of Internet startup companies would each be worth hundreds of billions of dollars, while pessimists (including most economists) argued that, although the Internet might attract a substantial share of commerce, it would tend to lower profit margins and, therefore, few of the startup companies would ever be worth very much.

Phase 2 begins if and when the optimists reap impressive profits. Think of the Albanians whose Vefa investments doubled in value each year from 1992 to 1996, or the SSC investors who did even better in early 1720. The market value of Netscape shares increased sixfold in five months from the initial offering in August 1995. Such returns attract trend-following investors, who, in turn, attract financial innovators. For instance, venture capital firms mushroomed in the late 1990s, inundated by new investors, and day trading became popular.

Optimists, of course, put everything they can into the new financial assets. But in Phase 2, the pessimists don't cancel out the optimists' impact—the pessimists must either play along or get left out. As a young financial analyst in the late 1970s, I personally watched top managers at a large U.S. bank decide whether to expand energy lending, despite warnings that the sector was overextended. The clinching argument was that the bank had to make the loans to remain a major player. The pressure on pessimists was even more intense in Albania in 1996, and we've seen how Sir Isaac Newton succumbed in the summer of 1720. In Phase 2, prices in the financial market no longer reflect consensus beliefs. The tie to reality frays, and asset prices float upward.

Asset quality deteriorates as the bubble inflates. Lulled by favorable recent experience, some investors eagerly pay high prices for promises that can only be fulfilled in good times. Financial market innovators make sure that there is no shortage of such promises. Subprime home loans are a recent example: the borrower has little equity, and will be able to make promised payments only if home prices continue to rise briskly, and if refinancing remains easy to obtain. Lower quality assets make the financial sector more vulnerable to unfavorable events.

Phase 3 begins when the supply of dazzled new investors and financial innovation is exhausted, as must eventually happen in our finite world. A minor event can then touch off a cascade, and one broken promise leads to another. It's hard to remember what event in March 2000 ended the run up of the NASDAQ index to over 5,000, or what stopped Japan's Nikkei index just short of 40,000 in January 1990. But once asset prices start to decline, the most leveraged investors have to sell, and the decline accelerates. Such declines erode collateral, and borrower defaults can cause lender defaults, so a financial crash can be contagious. Phase 3 generally runs faster than Phase 2, and a national or international recession may result.

Phase 4 begins when asset prices are so low that savvy investors purchase again. The NASDAQ was a good buy at 1200 in the summer of 2002. With effective bankruptcy laws, the losses accrued in Phase 3 are quickly parceled out, productive assets are redeployed, and recovery begins promptly, as in Albania in 1998. Consensus beliefs return, and financial asset prices are again grounded in reality. Phase 0, normalcy, begins anew and usually lasts for decades.

The crash causes lasting damage when it is unclear who gets stuck with the losses, as in Japan recently, or in Latin America in the 1970s and 1980s. A political struggle determines the outcome, and it can make Phase 4 quite long and painful. (The Great Depression of the 1930s involved inept government policy as well as inadequate bankruptcy laws.)

In the KMK perspective, bubbles inflate when the financial market magic goes wrong. Naïve investors are dazzled by the success of early optimists, pundits exaggerate the opportunities, and the skeptics play along. The market stops combining dispersed private information and instead amplifies over-optimism. Abraham Lincoln was right that you can't fool all the people all of the time, but you can fool lots of them occasionally. The eventual crash restores realism and inoculates investors. Hence, bubbles tend not to repeat themselves: it takes a rather different novel opportunity, in a distant market segment or location or era, to touch off the next episode.

Lessons Learned and Unsolved Mysteries

Financial markets loom large in the modern world not because of their intrinsic charm, but rather because they usually work. Countries that let them flourish tend to grow faster than economies that rely on more traditional ways of providing for the future.

Financial markets work their magic by pooling the resources and information of all participants, and steering resources toward the most promising ideas. Someone with a great new idea doesn't have to convince the powers that be; she just has to convince some greedy investors. Within a few months, modern financial markets can put billions of dollars behind an attractive idea.

Financial magic is powerful, but at the same time, it is subtle and error prone. According to the KMK perspective, financial markets sometimes build a tower of trust too high for its foundation, and the tower can topple, crash, and burn. Good bankruptcy laws and monetary policy can limit the damage.

The KMK perspective seems fine as far as it goes, but it leaves open some of the most crucial questions. What, exactly, does it take for investors to converge on a consensus belief? Or, to put it the other way, how unusual must an opportunity be for consensus to fail? What sort of financial markets are most susceptible to bubbles, and how (besides bitter experience) can they be made more resistant?

Academic research from the 1950s through the mid-1980s mostly ignored bubbles. Some researchers argued that famous historical episodes, like the South Sea Company and the earlier Tulip mania, were not really bubbles at all, just examples of unusually rapid movements in fundamental values. It is hard to prove the point one way or the other, since the fundamental value is a combination of private information that (by definition of private) is not directly observable by the researcher.

The academic tide began to turn in the mid-1980s. Dozens of studies found indirect evidence that markets are not always efficient. For example, several authors pointed out that, historically, stock prices are much more volatile than the discounted stream of eventual earnings. Also, the stock market crash of October 1987 (it dropped 22.6 percent in a single day) was hard to justify in terms of new information about future earnings.

Laboratory evidence helps sort things out. A researcher can create simple assets in the lab, and give different pieces of information privately to different traders. The traders (usually college or MBA students) get to keep the trading profits, and so, for them, the financial market is quite real. The researcher controls the fundamental value and can observe the asset price as the traders buy and sell from each other, and so has an exact measure of any bubble. In the 1980s, I and several other researchers verified that laboratory asset markets are quite efficient (and bubbles are much smaller and shorter lived than I had expected) when traders are experienced and the lab environment is stable.

On the other hand (economists always seem to have another hand!), 2002 Nobel laureate Vernon Smith and his coauthors found a reliable way to produce quite sizeable bubbles in the lab, using long-lived assets and inexperienced traders.

The evidence from the laboratory helps us sharpen the questions and recognize the deeper mysteries. When do financial markets cancel out the biases and errors of individual traders, and when do markets amplify them? Recent lab studies have shown that bubbles are more prevalent when the traders are paid based on relative performance (as are most mutual fund managers), and when there is some chance (but no certainty) that some traders have inside information. The market format—whether all participants get access to all bids and asks, for example—also seems to matter.

Accumulating evidence from labs and from ongoing financial markets around the world will continually increase our understanding, but it may never solve all the mysteries. In the meantime, policy makers must do the best they can. The perspectives in this chapter suggest that they should try to keep access to financial markets open to everyone, including pessimists, and to build incentives for transparent and honest behavior by all participants. Then, promises of all sorts will trade widely, and their prices will more closely reflect our pooled knowledge.

8

From Hudson's Bay to eBay
Why Do Some People Like Going to Work?

> The more evolved and psychologically healthy people get, the more will enlightened management policy be necessary in order to survive in competition and the more handicapped will be an enterprise with an authoritarian policy.
>
> —*Abraham Maslow*, Business Reader

In 1805, the venerable Hudson's Bay Company was sinking fast. Since 1670, its Royal Charter had given it a monopoly on the best trade routes to Europe for fine Canadian furs, but the lucrative business recently attracted a new firm, North West. Its trappers and traders had to haul furs an extra fifteen hundred miles in birchbark canoes, often over killing portages. Despite that huge cost disadvantage, North West had somehow managed to seize over 80 percent of market share, and Hudson's Bay's stock was in freefall.

How did North West do it? Not with superior technology, but instead, with superior organization. North West offered trappers incentive pay and partnership opportunities. It bred a self-reinforcing trust, and aligned the trappers' goals with those of the organization. Hudson's Bay, on the other hand, was a feudal hierarchy. It passed orders from London down through the ranks, paid employees low, fixed salaries, and flogged them for disobedience. In 1809, new owners took over and it began to emulate North West. Hudson's Bay profits rose quickly, and in 1821, it bought out its pesky competitor. Today, it is the world's oldest company still in its original line of business.

The Hudson's Bay revival is a parable for the twenty-first century, as upstarts like eBay threaten established organizations. Some of the older firms are adapting, for example, HP, Wal-Mart, and IBM. Both the upstarts and the older firms seek the North West advantage: quick reflexes and motivated workers. Nowadays, good organizations of all sorts reward hard work materially, as by bonuses and promotions, and socially, through the respect of coworkers and superiors. They follow the Maslow prescription, encouraging autonomy and soliciting good ideas from every level.

But why did corporate hierarchies rule for so long? Why are moral codes mutating in today's workplace, and how do they intensify market competition? This chapter investigates the underlying forces. It spotlights the social dilemmas that lurk in any human organization, and recounts the rise of corporations to dominate twentieth-century economies. Then, it examines the fracture lines in today's corporate world, and shows how new fission-fusion networks are expanding in the cracks.

Not Going to Extremes

What is the best way for human society to organize work? Thinkers from Plato to Lenin believed that the answer was obvious: let the most talented experts plan everything, and let loyal citizens follow the plan. They thought that a single unified organization, run by philosopher kings, would eliminate all the chaos, waste, and confusion. Ancient Sumerian cities might possibly have worked this way, but since then, monolithic planned societies have performed badly.

Why? The quick answer is that a unified organization can't properly coordinate and motivate large numbers of people in complex settings. As we will see, much better results come from smaller organizations coordinated by the market system.

So why not go all the way to the other extreme? Atomize organizations so that each individual person operates directly in the market. Imagine a complete set of markets: at every moment, anyone could buy or sell every kind of raw material, labor, equipment, good, or service at a competitive price. You would make your living by renting out your own labor and other resources to the highest bidder, or else by renting other people's labor and resources in order to produce and sell a product. Everyone would do this on an individual basis. Markets would coordinate everything, and firms would vanish. But this is not the way things have ever worked.

Why not? The answer is that markets, especially labor markets, can never be perfect. There are inescapable frictions. Coordinating activities across individuals is costly, sometimes very costly. Even for something as commonplace as remodeling a house, and even with blueprints already in hand, it takes a lot of time and energy to line up the carpenters, roofers, sheetrockers, tilers, plumbers, electricians, and building inspectors, and to get the right materials and right specifications to each of them at the right time. The general contractor usually gets about 25 percent of the entire cost just to coordinate the work.

Dilemmas and Holdups

The problem isn't just coordination and communication—social dilemmas lie just beneath the surface. The goals and priorities of an organization do not automatically align with those of its members. In the contractor example, each workman would like more money and a more convenient schedule. If an agreement isn't worked out in advance, quarrels might stop the job. The whole point of contracting, of course, is to avoid such quarrels by writing down an agreement.

But written agreements are not a complete solution because unforeseen contingencies often arise. The special tile for the remodel job might be defective and have to be backordered, and the tiler might not be able to reschedule. Or maybe dry rot has ruined the wall studs and the job turns out to be much more complicated than expected. It is impossible to know everything in advance, so quarrels can still arise.

The problem is especially tricky when you have to make specialized investments. For example, about ten years ago, Caligula University (the episode is fictionalized to protect the guilty) hired TSC Software to modernize the student record system. Unfortunately, lots of problems surfaced once the CU registrar started using the system. Grade point averages for alums out more than four years were incorrectly reported, for instance, and the system froze when everyone tried to enter new grades at the end of the semester. Meanwhile, TSC had been purchased by software giant Orator. Backed by an impressive legal team, Orator executives argued that the problems were due to CU's bad specifications. They offered to fix and guarantee everything for an extra $5 million. CU had no practical alternative, so after intensive negotiations, they signed a new $4 million contract. Happily, everything has worked well recently, but CU budget analysts now guess that the fix more than doubled TSC/Orator profits, and (due to the registrar's lost productivity) the unanticipated cost for CU exceeded $6 million.

Economists call this sort of episode a "holdup problem," and it can arise in all sorts of activities, from selling advice to building a zoo. We already encountered it in the Duke-Serf game of Chapter 3. The Serf invests his time and care into growing a crop, and is vulnerable at harvest time. You may have encountered it if you bought a printer for your computer. Maybe you got a great price on the printer, but have to pay ridiculous amounts for compatible ink cartridges.

Here's a general description. You put resources into a specialized system, a system that is valuable as long as you maintain a relationship with a customer (or a supplier), but is not worth much if the relationship breaks. The bargaining power you once had now evaporates because, having sunk the resources, you have little recourse if there is a disagreement. The customer (or supplier) can hold you up, demanding better terms at your expense. Long-term contracting can help, but it can't eliminate the problem because special circumstances might arise (or be invented).

The larger danger is that, fearing eventual holdup, you never create the specialized systems, even when they are extremely valuable. The holdup problem cripples market transactions for all sorts of goods and services that require specialized investment.

Markets Meet Morals: Organizations and Motivation

Multi-person organizations are the universal solution to such dilemmas and holdups. Each organization—not just businesses, but also colleges, government agencies, and charities—can transact with other organizations and individuals. It can acquire inputs from suppliers, hire labor, own equipment, and create outputs of value to someone. Having established its own identity, an organization can function well, even with turnover of its individual members.

Each organization ideally finds the size and activity set that best meet its goals. It often makes its own specialized investments, thus avoiding holdup problems. It undertakes activities that need close coordination, for example, the assembly, testing, and delivery of printers. It doesn't undertake activities that others can do better, say accounting or training engineers or building delivery trucks, but instead, buys what it needs under contract or in the spot market.

To keep everyone on task, organizations require regulation, internal and external. The tools of internal regulation are material—wages, benefits, bonuses, and promotion opportunities—and also moral—the corporate culture, formal and informal.

Corporate culture sounds vague, but it refers to the everyday social experience within an organization. Its core is a unique moral code, a shared understanding of how to work together to achieve the organization's goals. For example, when I worked at Bank of America headquarters in the late 1970s, a printed copy of the formal rules—the *Standard Practices Manual*—occupied an entire bookshelf. Weeks might go by without anyone in my department looking at it, but we were all well aware of the main informal rules. For example, it was quite acceptable to take a long lunch break on a slow day, but carelessness was unacceptable in checking facts for the boss's presentation to top management—that could hurt your chances of being promoted. The informal corporate culture rewarded some sorts of efficient specialized investment, such as mastering some unique software, but did not reward other sorts, such as measuring the performance of the bank's regular consultants.

Business firms and other organizations divide up into departments or other small groups of people that work together on a daily basis. The department manager uses all the ancient moral devices to increase productivity: exchange of favors, appeals to friendship and team spirit, reminders of threats posed by rival teams, and promises to improve things later if current goals are met.

Some department managers are more successful than others at motivating people. Success obviously depends on the manager's skill, but it also crucially depends on external market conditions. As with hunter-gatherers, members of a modern organization have the alternative of quitting and going elsewhere. In the modern world, the labor market determines how good that alternative is. So it is the labor market that sets limits on how hard managers can push, and how lucrative and pleasant an experience they must provide.

The market environment and the moral codes for internal regulation are the main forces that determine whether a business firm expands or shrinks, merges or splits up, and enters or exits new activities. Occasionally, the same forces create a major transition in the way firms organize themselves, as happened about a century ago.

The Corporate Takeover

Early capitalist firms were mostly family operations. In the United States around 1800, "apprentices, journeymen, and clerks typically lived in the master's household and were subject to his discipline in the same way as children were," according to one account. These firms mainly dealt with local suppliers and customers. To cope with motivation, coordination, and communication problems, the firm used the old-fashioned moral devices, reputation, and hierarchy. Of course, difficulties remained, like apprentices running away to the U.S. western frontier.

Francis C. Lowell helped change things. He watched firms like Rhode Island's Almy & Brown earn good profits in the new cloth manufacturing business. They would build a mill on a river, and pay local parents to send their children in to work. But as textile and transportation technology advanced and more distant markets opened, Lowell came up with a more profitable business model. Around 1820, he and his partners started to build entire new towns in Massachusetts. The towns centered on huge factories that turned stretches of river into brick-lined canyons, and also included dormitories, stores, and churches. Lowell recruited unmarried young women throughout the region, and paid them piece rates to run the specialized equipment. The factories pirated basic technology from England, got cotton bales from the South (cheap, thanks to Eli Whitney's recent de-seeding device), and used giant water wheels to power the spinning and weaving equipment. The factory-made cloth sold throughout New England and beyond, and made Lowell's partners rich.

In later decades, with the development of steam powered equipment and national markets, the leading textile firms became more specialized and clustered. By 1870, over six hundred such firms operated in Philadelphia. The New England factories went out of business, but the brick canyons can still be seen along the Merrimack River near Lowell, Massachusetts.

Adam Smith was the first to explain the factories' underlying logic, called "economies of scale." A bit ahead of his time in 1776, Smith began his most famous book by explaining how factory assembly lines could manufacture vast numbers of pins at far lower unit cost. Instead of a skilled craftsman doing everything himself, the factories divided the process into tiny tasks (drawing wire, cutting it, sharpening the pin point, etc.) so that each task could be done by unskilled workers using specialized equipment. The idea spread to the textile industry and, along with the idea of interchangeable parts, to clock and gun manufacture. In the early twentieth century, Henry Ford's assembly line pushed the idea even further. Such economies of scale could cut labor costs to 10 percent of those of an independent craftsman.

Of course, economies of scale aren't much use without mass markets. The new manufacturers' cost advantage depended on operating near full capacity over long periods of time, and local customers couldn't absorb all that output. Itinerant peddlers helped expand markets in the early 1800s, but some of them overcharged customers or palmed off damaged or inferior goods. Markets function much better when buyers trust the quality of the merchandise, and the seller's reputation can make all the difference. Some manufacturers, like Singer's sewing machines, built national brands through their own retail networks. Others earned buyers' trust by selling to mass retailers, like Sears or Woolworth, who developed their own reputations for quality.

Transportation is an important piece of the puzzle. Expanding to (or beyond) national markets works only if shipping costs are low. The supply of transportation networks expanded to meet demand, and costs plummeted, spurring (and spurred by) advances in shipbuilding, canals, railroads, and highways.

Transportation networks themselves demanded new sorts of organization. For example, railroad companies earned much greater profits when shippers and passengers could choose from a wide set of destinations and expect to reach them quickly and reliably. Meeting these expectations required unprecedented coordination and communication. Successful railroad companies like Southern Pacific honed methods used during the Civil War for military operations and logistical support. The internal organization began to look less like a family and more like a specialized army, with general staff, commanders, and geographically dispersed units pledged to execute the orders passed down the ranks. (Shades of the old Hudson's Bay? The late nineteenth-century companies had the advantage of rapid communication via telegraph, and they offered attractive pay and promotion opportunities.)

In the late 1800s, the corporate form of organization began to invade a wide variety of industries: manufacturers like Singer, chain stores like Woolworth, mail-order retailing like Sears Roebuck, new industries like petroleum, and old ones like tobacco, coal, and steel. The process was contagious. Some company in a new industry, or an innovator in an established industry, would figure out how to make specialized investments that ensured economies of scale, how to tap low cost inputs, and how to distribute the product to masses of customers. To survive, the other companies in the industry had to follow the leaders, or leapfrog them.

Corporate organization evolved further in the early twentieth century at companies like General Motors, Standard Oil, Du Pont, and Bank of America. The competitive advantage went to firms whose organization allowed them to produce a wider range of higher value products at lower unit cost. This increasingly meant managing a multi-unit hierarchy involving workers and several levels of managers, as well as professionals such as engineers, accountants, and lawyers. Besides the chain of command in the production process itself, the organization needed to coordinate purchases of materials, to hire and train workers, and to manage marketing and distribution. It also needed to engage in research and development, and to coordinate planning. Making it all work together smoothly is an intricate problem.

Corporate hierarchies are built to solve just that problem. The law regards a corporation as an individual person, with a separate identity from its owners, managers, and workers. This allows the corporation to make deals that survive changes in management or ownership, and helps stabilize reputations with customers and suppliers. Just as important, the owners are not personally liable if the corporation gets in trouble. Owners don't have to worry so much about everyday activities of the corporation or its other owners. The upshot is that ownership shares can be freely traded in a stock market. This makes it much easier to raise money by selling shares or issuing debt. In 1814, Lowell financed construction of his first textile mill by selling stock to the general public, and ever since, American corporations have raised money the same way.

Throughout the first half of the twentieth century, the corporate transformation created new resources to fuel further growth. It became a positive feedback loop. More efficient corporate forms, combined with lower transportation and communication costs, helped expand and stabilize markets. The growth of mass markets created dynamic new industries. As national wealth increased, more children survived, but fewer were needed in agriculture, as it, too, became mechanized. So the pool of blue-collar workers deepened. The white-collar pool—managers and professionals—also grew as families and governments invested more in education.

Profits went to innovators who found new ways to serve the corporate machine at lower cost. The innovations drove transportation and communication costs even lower, expanding the mass market and building new corporate industries like advertising, broadcasting, and consulting. Corporations went conglomerate, adding new product lines and merging with firms in distantly related (or even unrelated) activities. Despite the distractions of two world wars and the Great Depression, the corporate bulldozer chugged forward.

The Union Label

The overriding goal of a firm is to earn money for its owners, but in so doing, it touches the lives of other stakeholders: managers, workers, suppliers, and customers. As the corporate system developed, there was little problem in motivating the managers—the prospect of climbing the corporate ladder did the trick. The corporate system catered to customers, and prosperity served suppliers well.

Blue-collar workers were always more problematic. Neither piece rate pay nor intrinsic satisfaction work well on the assembly line, since each worker's personal contribution is hard to see. Effective worker incentives were mainly negative: punching the time clock, close supervision and intrusive monitoring, and the threat of being fired. When the alternative was subsistence farming or worse, plenty of workers were willing to take factory jobs, but they paid a personal price. As noted in Chapter 4, critics ranging from Karl Marx to Charlie Chaplin, echoing predecessors like Adam Smith and William Blake, decried the corporate factory as a moral wasteland, alienating and demeaning.

Trade unions helped fill the void. Workers found that joining a union made them part of an in-group that could stand up to corporate management and demand better pay, better working conditions, and more respect. At first, the corporations fought the unions fiercely, but that didn't always work. For example, Lowell's successors defeated the Factory Girls Association strike in 1834, but three years later, they went bankrupt in a recession. Strikes and boycotts hurt corporate profits: some unions turned out to very effective in holding their members' loyalty and in arousing sympathy from consumers and voters. Unions in the United States slowly gained ground as the corporate system matured, especially in the New Deal years before World War II.

Following that war, unions in Japan and Germany worked closely with corporate officials and government to rebuild their countries and enrich everyone. In the United States, many industries found that the most profitable course was to sign industry-wide union contracts. For example, General Motors, Ford, and Chrysler wrote contracts with the United Auto Workers that tended to equalize their labor costs. This reduced the incentive to compete on price or quality, and made it more difficult for new U.S. firms to enter the industry. Thus, the unions helped make the Big Three a stable oligopoly. Of course, soft competition in domestic markets later helped foreign automakers catch up and become tough rivals, but the danger seemed distant at the time.

As a student in the late 1960s, I worked summers in union jobs on San Francisco's docks and warehouses. The International Longshore and Warehouse Union (ILWU) still had older members who told me stories of their service with the Lincoln Brigade, fighting fascists in Spain on the eve of World War II, and how they brought racial equality to the union. Their fierce moral code and militancy had made the union strong, but their influence already was fading. All the younger union members I met had only personal material concerns: better wages and benefits and easier work for themselves. As these younger folks took over, the ILWU, like many other unions, slowly lost bargaining power, as well as its moral edge.

A Delicate Balance

A few years ago, a research team studied internal regulation by having human subjects play games in a Zurich laboratory. Some players (the managers) offered a wage, either high or low, and other players (the workers) chose which offer to accept and how much costly effort to exert. Standard economic theory predicted that the workers would take the highest offer and still shirk, but that wasn't what happened. Players who accepted higher offers tended to exert more effort. The experimenters interpreted their results in terms of gift exchange. The workers wanted to repay managers' generosity, and realizing this, the managers were more generous.

Surprisingly, explicit incentive contracts didn't work well in this experiment. Workers tended to make more selfish choices when their take-home pay was directly tied to how much effort they exerted. When workers could see exactly how much their effort helped the manager, they again tended to behave more selfishly, especially when the managers earned more.

The lesson is clear. There is a delicate balance between workers' financial incentives and moral imperatives. Workers' willingness to give a good effort is among the most valuable assets an organization can possess.

A nasty counterexample surfaced a few years ago. Ford Motor Company's profits in the late 1990s came largely from its best-selling sports utility vehicle, the Explorer. In 2000, sales started to drop on reports of fatal rollover accidents. Tread separation on Firestone tires produced at the Decatur, Illinois plant turned out to be the main cause of more than 270 deaths. Firestone and Ford barely survived the huge tire recall and marketing disaster.

A careful study showed that the problem at Decatur was not technical, but moral. In 1994, despite improved profits, the tire company decided to play tough with the Union of Rubber Workers. It demanded a large wage cut, and longer hours rotating between day and night, and immediately hired replacement workers ("scabs") when the union went on strike. The union eventually went bankrupt and capitulated. After that, the workforce at Decatur was a mix of scabs, union men who broke the strike, and men returning from the broken union. Morale was poisonous. Workers had no loyalty to the company or pride in their work, and they produced lots of defective tires. Everyone lost: workers, company managers and owners, customers, and the driving public.

Times Change

On the whole, though, in the second half of the twentieth century, the balance held. Big business—Coke and Pepsi, the Big Three automakers, U.S. Steel and its brethren, the five major airlines, the six money center banks, the seven sisters of Big Oil, the Big Eight accounting firms, and so forth—dominated the industrialized world. Union wages and benefits climbed steadily, pulling millions of families into the middle class. Nonunionized workers did almost as well because their employers had to offer prevailing wages, set, in part, by big union contracts. Prosperous workers became a force for stability and economic growth, and corporations thrived.

Now things are different. A transition is underway in the way organizations operate, and once again, markets are corroding the old order and opening things up. Big Business and Big Labor are fragmenting, and company loyalty has become passé. Networks are taking root in huge sectors, including retail, manufacturing, services, and high technology.

But, why now? What changed?

Twentieth-century corporations thrived on large, stable, predictable markets. The corporations, with major investments in specialized capital, reaped economies of scale. Economic stability and predictability allows such investments to pay off. But in the last quarter of the century, things began to shake loose. The 1970s and 1980s saw oil price shocks and two major recessions. A wave of deregulation swept through airlines, banking, and other industries. Markets became more fluid and powerful than ever, and less predictable.

The pace of change accelerated in the late 1980s and the 1990s as the cold war wound down. The market system invaded Eastern Europe and China, and advanced in much of Asia and Latin America. The accessible pool of labor tripled. Vast new investment opportunities opened, along with a flood of new savings. Wealthy consumers grew more numerous and their tastes became more fickle and fragmented. Containerization drastically lowered shipping costs: sealed cargo from the factory could be trucked to the dock, put on a boat, offloaded to a train, and then delivered in a eighteen-wheeler truck, with minimal costs for labor, inspections, and delays. Most famously, advances in semiconductors and fiber optics touched off the information technology revolution, enabling new organizational structures as well as novel products and a new generation of competitors.

These changes rocked the cozy world of big business and big labor. Many of the largest employers, facing global competition, could no longer afford the customary wage increases. To tap the growing labor pool, corporations increasingly built new manufacturing facilities abroad, and also started to outsource some service and professional jobs. Most firms that tried to maintain the old ways were unable to compete on price and quality, and had to shed jobs. Leading unions also suffered from demographic changes. Worker solidarity and political influence waned as older members moved to suburbs and retired.

In this unstable environment, corporations faced unpredicted new threats and new opportunities. All of the sudden, being nimble trumped being big.

But why not be both? Of course, some giants are nimbler than others. Later in the chapter, we'll look at the growth of corporate Tim Duncans like IBM and Wal-Mart. But first, let's consider why it is so difficult for large corporations to be agile.

The laws of physics prevent a three-hundred-pounder like Shaquille O'Neal from changing direction as quickly as Tony Parker. The problem for corporations is not physical, of course. Their economic inertia has three main sources. Probably most familiar, but least important, is the fact that it takes longer to coordinate more people using a longer chain of command. A second source arises from the fact that giants always have major profit streams from current technology and current business models. When they innovate, they must trade off losses in these current streams against the gains from the innovation. For example, when Apple jumped into the music industry with its iPod player and downloadable tunes, the giant of the industry, Sony, worried about losing CD sales and reacted too slowly. Cannibalizing current profit streams is a cost for giants but not for newcomers.

Third, any giant has to allocate resources among its units. Managers of the units will try to influence the decision, and will squander resources to do so: time and talent devoted to producing dueling PowerPoint presentations, to puffing their own performance, or to spreading rumors about the other units. The comic strip Dilbert features endless examples. Small companies, run by an entrepreneur who already knows the entire business, face much smaller influence costs. They can devote more of their resources to dealing with customers and suppliers because they are not so tied up with internal politics.

Big corporations can bear cannibalization and influence costs and still prosper in a stable environment. When serious threats and new opportunities bombard the firm from all directions, however, these costs can be killers.

But what's the alternative to big corporations? Old-fashioned family firms? Why would they work any better now than a hundred years ago?

Good Old Networks

Interpersonal networks, of course, have been around even longer than family firms. They dominate tribal life, and in medieval times, the Maghrebi trader networks and the Florentine banker networks spurred economic progress. The largest networks in medieval Europe, however, were the guilds. Each trade in each town had a guild with connections to its counterparts in other towns and in other trades. The guilds worked together to exclude rivals and to maintain the incomes of their senior members. These cozy networks thrived on the status quo and feared innovation. The great market transformation swept them away—or most of them.

A few guild networks adapted to the new market system and prospered. Consider, for example, the Italian wool trade, centered in the city of Prato, near Florence. Recently home to about nine thousand factories with forty-five thousand workers, Prato is laced with independent small to medium operations, each with a specialty in spinning, twisting, warping, weaving, dyeing, or finishing. The owners, called *impannatori*, form temporary teams to design new products, and to produce and market the finished products. This fission-fusion network has enabled them to set world-class standards in speed and quality for hundreds of years. In the last five years, however, they have had trouble meeting price competition from large Chinese factories and from newer, even more agile networks in Spain.

Hollywood has always relied on a similar network. A unique team of writers, directors, cinematographers, actors, producers, and crew creates a film, and they split up once it's done. Commercial success makes reunion of key team members more likely for a new project.

The major production studios (MGM, Fox, Paramount, Warner Bros., etc.) once controlled distribution and financing, and signed many participants to exclusive contracts, but now the interpersonal networks are wider and more flexible than ever. Financing now comes from hedge funds as well as media conglomerates, revenues come increasingly from DVD sales and foreign distribution, and production often takes place outside of California. Next time you watch a movie, read all the credits. The span of the participating networks will amaze you.

The higher education industry may have the world's oldest professional network. Even in the first colleges (founded in eleventh century Bologna and Oxford), the loyalties of the professors went more to students and to distant colleagues than to their nominal bosses, the deans and provosts, or to their wealthy sponsors. Like members of some prehistoric tribe, and probably like members of the original academies of ancient Greece, the scholars formed bands that sometimes split up and sometimes gathered together. Learned societies took root, like the British Royal Society, founded in London in 1660, and sponsored regular meetings and circulated journals reporting new findings. Young scholars moved from one campus to the next, building their personal networks and spreading ideas.

Market forces roared through most industries in the 1800s, utterly transforming them. Higher education was an exception: it sailed along nicely, growing briskly, while only gradually changing course. In leading nations, wealthy industrialists and governments spread around their increasing wealth, and universities got a share. These sponsors eventually realized that innovation promoted industrial leadership, and that innovators often drew on new scientific knowledge generated in the universities. For example, the new sciences of thermodynamics and chemistry helped craftsmen design better steam engines, and advances in organic chemistry spurred the discovery of new dyes. European governments began to support university science and engineering more generously, and the Untied States also sponsored land grant colleges aimed at boosting farm productivity.

Germany, Europe's most ambitious rising power in the 1800s, introduced a more corporate university system. The government funds each Herr Doktor Professor directly, and each of them hires his own team of assistants. The system worked well and spread, but never displaced the decentralized networks in the English-speaking world and beyond. Since the World War II, U.S. universities have dominated the industry with an especially competitive fission-fusion network. Ambitious campuses bid against each other to sign up the most promising new researchers, and they often try to hire away other schools' established stars.

A researcher's prospects in academia depend mainly on her reputation among network members sharing her specialties, and on the importance and trend of those specialties within the wider research network. Multi-campus teams of researchers assemble themselves to write grant proposals to national agencies. Teams that get grants present their work at conferences and write it up for journal publication, then dissolve and reform in different configurations. For example, I am presently a member of three research teams funded by the U.S. National Science Foundation. One team includes assistant professors of economics at liberal arts colleges on both coasts. A second team includes an emeritus professor of mathematics at my home campus. The third team includes members of a leading industrial lab, as well as economists and computer scientists from research universities in the southeast and the southwest. Some members of each team have worked together before, but none of the full teams existed before their current project, nor is expected to continue beyond its completion.

The New Networks

Recently, networks have expanded their domain. They have invaded some of the old, corporate dominated industries, and started to take root in industries that never existed before.

The network advantage is always agility. For example, one night in December 2003, an Italian system administrator detected a dangerous virus attack on his Linux server. He contacted Linux network experts in Australia and Atlanta, who identified the vulnerability in the code. They linked up with specialists in California and elsewhere to build a patch, test it, and disseminate it to users. Despite the fact that they had never previously worked together, or even met face-to-face, the team finished the job just twenty-nine hours after first detection. It might have taken a traditional organization days or weeks just to identify the problem, and months to fix it.

This story illustrates the boost that networks get from twenty-first century specialized education and mobility, as well as from the new information technologies. The span of networks is no longer a single town—they can reach to the other side of the world to find just the right person or equipment to add to the team.

The story also illustrates decentralization and scalability. Any well-connected person can get the ball rolling. Once she becomes aware of a new opportunity or threat, she can begin to assemble a team from her network contacts. The new teammates can draw on their own contacts to complete the team, and the team can grow (or shrink) as appropriate.

Such teams avoid the overhead costs of large corporations, who must keep paying for their specialized equipment and employees, even when there is a lull. Networks, by contrast, have minimal ongoing expenses—phone, email, IM, blogs, occasional travel, and meetings—that their own members are happy to cover. When teams form, they can offer key members very intense material rewards, such as stock options or a substantial share of the profit. The profit stream belongs to the particular team, not to the network itself, so the network avoids cannibalization and influence costs.

Fission-fusion networks also bring a new solution to the holdup problem. Many sorts of specialized skills (or human capital, in economics jargon) are valued in the network. You can build these skills and your reputation in your network over time and not lose bargaining power, because you can always look for another team if your present one doesn't reward you properly.

Life in the NetZone

Even more important, however, is the human advantage. Networks are far better than hierarchical organizations at mobilizing our moral sentiments. Being a member of a team handpicked for a special project is like playing on an elite basketball team. Each person's efforts are crucial and are easy for teammates to recognize, and the team can generate incredible bursts of energy and creativity for many months. That's what pays off in unstable times.

Google's famous story illustrates the point. In 1996, two new computer science PhD students at Stanford University found that they enjoyed arguing with each other. Sergey Brin and Larry Page collaborated on class projects, and worked overtime on one they called BackRub. It improved Internet search by tracing links backward and ranking each Web site by the popularity of the links pointing to it. By the summer of 1998, their search engine was up and running with impressive results. "Angel" investors raised a million dollars, and Sergey and Larry moved out of their dorm rooms, hired their first employee, and launched their start-up company from Susan Wojcicki's spacious garage. A few months of hard work and five employees later, they moved into a real office and started signing up clients. In 1999, two top venture capital firms took a piece of the action for $25 million, which allowed Google to move to its own building, hire professional staff, and grow.

Google grabbed a great new market niche. As Internet content mushroomed, search became crucial. Existing search engines got their revenues from advertisers, who could buy higher rankings in user searches and bombard users with unwanted ads. Google offered sharper, faster, and more honest searches, with ads shown only to those who wanted to see them. Its moral code also made Google more attractive to young talent. The egalitarian atmosphere, at once whimsical (starting with the company name) and serious, encouraged everyone to try out wild new ideas and to work around the clock to develop the best ones. Google's 2004 initial public stock offering was also unconventional, using an equal access auction instead of the usual IPO procedure that favors investment banks and their top clients. At the time of this writing, Google's market value puts it among the world's top thirty companies. Hundreds of employees are multimillionaires and can do whatever they want. What most of them want to do is to keep on working with talented teammates on exciting new projects.

Ordinary startups, not just supernovas like Google, draw on their networks, and not just in good times. Kntek, a 1996 Silicon Valley startup, began with a core of Russian engineers. The company went through several cycles of expansion and contraction, constantly increasing the web of personal and professional contacts. Layoffs in bad times mainly hit the less productive departments and individuals. (Larger companies generally have worse aim.) In good times, they heeded the saying, "A players hire A players, but B players hire C's." They found several A players trained at the Indian Institute of Technology, and a few more at American schools.

In the summer of 2000, Kntek's engineering team faced its toughest test. The key customer pushed the key product harder than usual, found it defective, and gave Kntek a deadline to get it working properly. The problem turned out to be fundamental—an inadequate software engine. Working around the clock from a single room, leaving only to gather specific information and report back, the seven-person "brain trust" team found a way to replace the engine. But the huge job remained of retrofitting and debugging everything that the engine drove. After a week, the brain trust was able to parcel out specialized tasks to the rest of the engineering staff, and it was their turn to work around the clock for the next two weeks. The company met the deadline with a day to spare, and survived. Indeed, it became stronger than ever, because the shared experience—mortal danger averted by outstanding teamwork—brought everyone closer together.

Bonding can take many forms. An American Buddhist temple supplemented the usual classes in meditation and philosophy with offerings in martial arts and Java programming. In northern California, programming seemed as natural a spiritual practice as raking gravel in Japan, or Thangka painting in Tibet. You bring your mind to one point, see the connections that need to be made, and then type in the code. The class took on increasingly ambitious joint projects. The teacher suggested that they build a software company, and a dozen of the top students signed on.

For the next eighteen months, the team spent virtually all waking hours together. Most days, they'd carpool to a large office and program for at least ten hours, the key clatter punctuated by occasional bursts of chatter and laughter. They'd end the workday with a martial arts class and meditation, and then return to a decaying mansion that most of them called home. After eighteen months, they had a prototype product but money was running low. Even team members with no prior experience had accumulated skills in high demand, so most of them moved to a different city and took outside programming jobs. With coffers replenished, but no major customers for their product, the team recently moved once more to a city noted for its angel investors.

What has kept the team together for five years and three long moves? Partly, it is the prospect (not yet realized) of getting lots of money and recognition for their unique products. Money is handy, even for those uninterested in fancy cars and vacations: it could be used to build a great Zendo, for example. The larger motivation, though, is the teamwork itself—they love being part of a working spiritual community, and want to keep it going.

Nets at Work

Google is not the only startup to reshape an industry, nor is it the most net-driven. The world's fourth largest retailer now is eBay, on track to sell over $50 billion of merchandise in 2007. It outsources almost everything to its network of 700 thousand sellers, who acquire the merchandise, price it, sell it to the highest bidder, and ship it. The network of registered users totals 200 million, but the organization relies heavily on much smaller networks of teachers, shippers, and web consultants that serve the sellers' needs. For itself, eBay retains only the market core: the electronic auction platform that the sellers and buyers plug into, and trust-building institutions like buyer and seller reputation records and PayPal, a secure payment mechanism.

Fission-fusion networks are not just to make money. They also have revolutionized military tactics. In April 2003, the U.S. Army captured Baghdad with remarkable speed and very few casualties using fission-fusion combat teams with peer-to-peer communication. Since then, Iraqi insurgents have formed at least three different networks. The insurgent networks all seem very decentralized, and they exploit the Internet and cell phones to share information, recruit new members, coordinate actions, and disperse. Unfortunately, the networks help both sides to become more lethal.

Networks are also taking over several more peaceful activities. Consider the open source movement. It has produced the leading Web site server software, Apache, as well as Linux, the impressive computer operating system mentioned earlier. Perhaps its most famous product is the online encyclopedia *Wikipedia*, which now has far more articles and readers than *Britannica*. Open source contributors aren't paid directly, but the teamwork is emotionally rewarding and builds valuable reputations in the professional network. The open source communities also provide a livelihood for companies that repackage and customize the product for paying customers, as Red Hat does with Linux software.

The U.S. construction industry at first seems to represent a countertrend. Traditionally dominated by a network of small, independent contractors and subcontractors, the industry lacked economies of scale. National corporations began to seize a larger share of the industry over the last decade or two, profiting especially from McMansions (large upscale homes with region-independent floor plans and features) and opulent retirement communities. But this is not the first corporate invasion. Many homes in my town built in the 1920s, for example, came from Sears Craftsman kits, but the Great Depression drove Sears out of the industry. At the time of this writing, the U.S. housing market is softening and the corporations are losing money. Perhaps home construction has too many ups and downs, and buyers' preferences are too regional and idiosyncratic, for corporations to thrive. Networks just might be the industry's future, as well as its past.

Networks and Corporations: Conflict and Cooperation

Are fission-fusion networks poised to take over the world? I don't think so. The future will probably be much more interesting and complicated than that. Networks and corporations are already partners as well as rivals, and are coevolving in new directions.

Take, for example, two of the most important networks in my region, venture capitalists and engineers. They absolutely need each other—VCs exist to invest in new ideas, and engineers with new ideas are always looking for financing. But the two networks have different moral codes and conflicting incentives, and things don't always go as smoothly as they did with Google.

An engineer recently told me of a life-and-death struggle for control of his company. Its technology showed real promise in early tests, and the company received a very generous offer letter of second round finance from a new VC partner. However, the original lead VC (with the new CEO's support) first wanted to get rid of a charter provision that gave veto power to the founding engineers. The engineers refused, the new VC got spooked, and the financing fell through. The original VC then issued an ultimatum: fire the founding engineer and change the charter, or no more money. The engineers held their ground and the company went bankrupt. The VCs got nothing back on their $20 million investment. However, a new company quickly snapped up the engineering team and gave them even better options than before.

The boundaries between corporations and networks are starting to blur. Most corporations are dissolving some units and functions traditionally under central command and control. They often can reduce costs and increase shareholder value by spinning off some units or splitting up into several smaller companies. For example, in 1999, Hewlett-Packard, one of the original Silicon Valley firms, spun off its huge scientific instrument unit, under the hopeful name Agilent. About the same time, HP opened the VC Café. Its mission is to spin off startup companies led by HP employees. Toyota and Boeing now emulate the Linux community, emphasizing knowledge sharing, peer recognition, and reputation systems.

Outsourcing is becoming ever more important. The idea is to hire out some corporate functions, like information technology or payroll processing (or even manufacturing or purchasing or distribution) to specialized service companies that can do the job at lower cost. Due to globalization and information technology, the specialist companies now can offer real-time service to many different clients in different cities, and reap economies of scale. They also can draw on low cost pools of skilled labor in Eastern Europe, India, or even Indiana. By now, most corporations have outsourced some functions to reduce overhead and influence costs, and to become more flexible. Some have outsourced so many functions that they look almost like a network, or like eBay.

Of course, outsourcing can lead to holdup problems. Once you have outsourced your specialized computer systems, for example, you might have a hard time switching to a new vendor if the current vendor gets too greedy. It is a dilemma. Joint ventures and cross-holdings are sometimes a good compromise.

Fission-fusion thinking undermines traditional hierarchical organizations. Once a network begins to form, workers begin to put more value on personal contacts with peers in different parts of the firm, and among the firm's suppliers, customers, and even competitors. They become less concerned with pleasing the boss and being loyal to the employer. Young workers now expect several career changes, maybe every two or three years. Flatter hierarchies mean fewer promotion opportunities. What really matters is the size and quality of your professional network, and your reputation among peers. Thus, loyalty shifts from firm to network.

Traditional corporations are trying to adapt to the new worker attitudes and to the new unstable environment. In the 1980s, IBM couldn't properly exploit the personal computer because really aggressive shifts would cannibalize mainframe computer services, its core business at the time. In particular, IBM didn't react quickly to the new opportunities for better PC operating systems and microprocessors. This allowed Microsoft and Intel to seize what soon became the most profitable parts of the computer industry. In the early 1990s, squeezed between the two nimbler firms, IBM had a near death experience.

Lew Gerstner, an outsider who became CEO in 1993, saved IBM by radically transforming it. Internally, IBM dissolved its traditional silos and helped weave personal networks across the research labs, business consultants, and computer systems specialists. The new IBM still sells lots of hardware and software, but most of its revenue now comes from global services. These consist of business solutions, such as showing a client how to reconfigure its business to take advantage of outsourcing opportunities, as well as information technology services, such as running the client's computer systems. Now Microsoft and Intel have the more traditional business plans, trying to exploit market power in maturing industries. They all want to be agile giants, but at the moment, Big Blue seems to do it better.

Wal-Mart has deployed a unique blend of techniques to become the world's largest retailer, with annual revenue now almost $350 billion. Its hierarchy is lean, and rather flat, for a giant corporation. Borrowing Japanese labor practices, Wal-Mart calls its workers "associates" and engages them in company cheers and morale building exercises but offers rather low pay and benefits. Wal-Mart's supply chain is a marvel. Using advanced information technology and local decision making authority, Wal-Mart responds almost instantaneously to customers' purchasing trends, and with unmatched efficiency, moves the goods from manufacturers to warehouses to stores. It aggressively outsources production to a network of suppliers, especially to new Chinese mass manufacturers. Most of the suppliers would find it difficult to survive without Wal-Mart orders, so the corporation retains bargaining power. Wal-Mart's captive supplier network gives it flexibility without sacrificing economies of scale.

The old union model is collapsing in the private sector as blue-collar jobs are outsourced to worldwide supplier networks and the remaining corporate jobs become more professional and shorter term. Sara Horwitz, the daughter of a union lawyer and granddaughter of a top union official, recently created a new model. The thirty-seven thousand members of her Freelancer's Union do not pay dues or bargain with employers. Instead, these self-employed workers use their union's networking Web site to strengthen their professional and social links and, more concretely, they save lots of money by buying health insurance through the union. The union also plans to offer something like a 401(k) defined contribution pension plan.

As the twenty-first century advances, we can expect more cooperation, more conflict, and increasingly blurred boundaries between corporations and interpersonal networks. It is not the world Maslow imagined, but his upbeat prediction on work life may yet come true.

Markets for Crime and Markets for Punishment

Victorian philosophers confidently predicted that vice and crime would fade away as the human species evolved. That doesn't seem to be happening. For example, the State of California used to spend twice as much on universities as on prisons, but now, despite a record number of students, it spends far more on prisons. The War on Drugs, which costs U.S. taxpayers about $40 billion each year, has been about as effective as Caligula's war against the sea.

Why does the United States spend so much on fighting crime, and why don't we get better results? The search for answers begins by looking at the nature of crime, and at crime prevention before the rule of law matured. It traces the rise of courts and the fall in crime until the twentieth century. Then, progress somehow went into reverse. We will see how the market system in the United States has recently amplified vice, together with dubious policies for fighting vice and crime.

The Roots of Crime and Vice

Why are some activities called crimes? In today's world, the direct answer is simple—those activities are forbidden by law—but that begs the real questions: why do societies outlaw some activities and not others? Which sort of activities *should* society outlaw, and which should it tolerate or discourage by other means?

This chapter will try to sort it all out. The starting point is a certain type of social dilemma. Activities like robbery, theft, fraud, embezzlement, extortion, rape, and blackmail are self-serving. So, usually, are assault and murder—the perpetrator will be better off materially if he can get away with it. But these activities harm the victim, usually far more than they benefit the perpetrator. Almost every society regards them as crimes, and preventing them is clearly in the social interest.

As with other human social dilemmas, the first lines of defense are moral. Most potential crime is prevented by internal restraints—social emotions like empathy for the potential victim, the prospect of guilt and (if caught) shame. External moral restraints—social sanctions, informal and formal—stop most of the rest.

Vices are not social dilemmas simply because they don't benefit anyone. Self-interest alone should turn us away from personally harmful activities such as gambling and substance abuse. Why, then, is vice tempting? Why do most societies try to suppress some vices? And why do vices still flourish?

The answer to the second question is that the harm spreads. Vices divert resources from the actor's family, undermine trust, and coarsen conduct. They weaken internal restraints to crime. So vices are not really victimless, and often, it is in society's interest to resist them.

The third question hinges on the first. Vices are tempting because they hook into pleasure centers in the brain that support gene propagation. Take the clearest case—prostitution. Nature has endowed us with sex drives that can overpower common sense. The client might realize he'd be better off passing up the opportunity, but still might find the temptation irresistible.

It is less obvious that substance abuse and gambling have similar roots, so let me explain. Nature has tuned our brains' pleasure centers to encourage behaviors that enhance biological fitness, or would tend to do so in ancestral hunter-gatherer environments. Some responses are immediate and automatic—to cool spring water when thirsty, for instance—while others, like a taste for chili, are acquired gradually. Alcohol, opiates, cocaine, and other addictive substances hijack the brain's pleasure mechanisms and weaken self-control. The temptation to continue abusing the substance can overpower rational self-interest.

Some evolutionary psychologists argue that gambling is a variation on the same theme. They note that recent studies show that the prospect of higher status and higher wealth can trigger measurable changes in brain chemistry. But why would nature want you to gamble in situations where, on average, you come out behind? The argument is that if you are a low-status adolescent male in a premodern society, you are destined to have few, if any, surviving children if you play it safe. If you take a big risk and lose, your fitness can't decrease much since it is already close to zero. But if you win big and achieve high status and wealth, then you will have far better opportunities to father many children, legitimate or otherwise. Although payoff in wealth may be negative on average, the fitness payoff (the average number of descendents) is positive. Hence, nature endows us with a taste for risk-taking, especially when we are low-status, adolescent, or male. The fitness calculation may no longer apply in the modern world, but the taste for risk persists.

Whatever the merits of this evolutionary argument, it is indisputable that some people become addicted to taking risks that occasionally pay off, but not often enough to make it personally worthwhile.

The Moral Response

Hunter-gatherer societies fight crime the old-fashioned way, with the moral system. Everybody knows the norms of proper behavior, and knows which sorts of norm violations are minor and which are serious. When people observe a serious violation, they spread the word. Until the culprit repents, people in his group will be outraged and put him under increasing pressure. He can expect ridicule, insult, avoidance, and reduced status, and if he persists, the group will expel him or even kill him. Within a well functioning group, socially inefficient crime doesn't pay because the social sanctions are too costly. Awareness of these external constraints reinforces the internal restraints, and serious crime is uncommon.

Consider how a twentieth-century tribe dealt with a murderer. Hunter-gatherers in Africa's Kalahari Desert, the !Kung have been called "the harmless people" because they favor verbal sanctions and generally avoid violence. Still, anthropologists documented about two dozen homicide cases among them over three decades. Four of the cases concerned a bad tempered man named /Twi. After a second episode in which /Twi killed another man, relatives of the victims and others achieved a widespread consensus that he had to go. One winter day in 1948, a distant kinsman named /Xashi ambushed /Twi, and shot a poisoned arrow into his hip. /Twi tried to stab /Xashi but /Xashi escaped, aided by his mother-in-law. Some people in the encampment offered /Twi sympathy and started to suck out the poison, but /Twi lashed out at them, wounding one woman and killing her husband with a poison arrow. After that, everyone took cover and shot poison arrows into /Twi until he "looked like a porcupine." After burying him, the encampment split up to avoid confronting /Twi's relatives. An anthropologist describes this as an example of "collective action and collective responsibility in a . . . nonhierarchical society."

The Corsican Connection

No one ever called the Corsican people harmless. But owing to its unique geography and history, nineteenth-century Corsica became an ideal place to observe traditional morality at work. Although it is the Mediterranean's fourth largest island, Corsica has never been especially important strategically or economically. Invading powers—Phoenicia, Rome, the Vandals, Byzantium, the Moors, Lombardy, Aragon, Genoa—regarded it as a minor outpost and controlled only a few coastal towns. Their civilizations hardly touched most Corsicans, who lived in isolated mountain villages connected (after the winter snow melted) only by mule tracks.

Things started to change in 1769. That year, the French took over Corsica, and a boy named Napoleon was born to the Buonapartes, one of the wealthier families in the coastal town of Ajaccio (Ajax). The boy was raised in France, and after he rose to power, the French court system reached deep into the Corsican interior. Beginning around 1800, the French compiled a vast archive of official documents (and unofficial memoirs and novels) on life in "the land of the vendetta."

The Corsican people—mainly herdsmen, farmers, and chestnut growers—spoke a variety of dialects related to ancient Tuscan. They were quite egalitarian and had no separate class of nobility. Family and *honore* (honor) were paramount: the larger your family (including first and second cousins and tenants, and sometimes, third cousins) and the better their reputation, the stronger your position. *Honore* for a man demanded that he avenge insults to himself or kinsmen, and especially threats to female chastity. A Corsican proverb put it this way: "At weddings and in trouble, one knows one's own people."

The French records show relatively little property crime, despite poverty, and most of that was banditry or theft from distant merchants or peddlers; stealing from neighbors or within the family brought serious *bergogna* (dishonor or shame). On the other hand, the records contain stories like the one that follows.

In June 1835, wonderful news spread in the troubled Corsican village of Arbellara: the rich and handsome Guilio Forcioli, returned from his medical studies in Rome, was to marry Maria Giustiniani, the mayor's beautiful daughter. The marriage would bring together the two leading families of the village and end the bad blood between them. In half a dozen recorded episodes over the last several years, the families had found their oxen, cows, and horses poisoned or shot, and now everyone in the village was afraid to go out after dark.

But in July, more Forcioli livestock were found dead and, amid finger pointing and threats, the marriage was called off. On July 22, Guilio's brother Antono and his cousin ambushed four members of the Giustiniani clan, killing one and seriously wounding the mayor. The gunmen disappeared, and everyone barricaded their homes. On August 11, a third Forcioli brother, Rocco, was shot in the leg, and in the ensuing melee, one of the Forcioli women stabbed Maria three times. Despite a string of truces and peace pacts, some of them celebrated in church, the vendetta sputtered along for decades, eventually claiming half a dozen more lives.

Corsican male honor demanded ownership of guns, and young men sometimes humiliated others to impress the girls. For example, if someone took your gun and spit down the barrel, you had to retaliate when you got the chance. If you didn't, you were *rimbeccu* (a wimp), a disgrace, and a liability to your family. Etiquette required that you give fair warning (once) before launching a vendetta, and if you couldn't get to the culprit, then attacking a close relative was almost as good.

That moral code might sound completely dysfunctional, but most of the time it worked pretty well. It maintained order within Corsican families, despite increasing overpopulation and crowded homes during the 1800s. It normally enforced good behavior across families and villages as well, since the potential cost of impoliteness could be so high to your family. Even when a man raped or killed a member of another family, cooler heads in both families usually would discuss the matter and often would agree on punishment, perhaps exile or even being shot by his own kinsmen. For example, in January 1848, Susino Maestrati killed Bastiano Guidicelli in the village of Zonza, and the same afternoon, Bastiano's nephew killed Susino's brother. The elders saw a balance of *honore*, and to keep things from getting out of hand, they made everyone tell the authorities that the two victims had killed each other.

Of course, the French records mainly tell us about times where the moral code failed to keep order, as in Arbellara and hundreds of other episodes. The problem is that even cooler heads suffer from self-serving bias. It is easy to disagree on fault and proper punishment, and on whose *honore* had been slighted most. The moral code demanded vengeance to obtain a favorable balance of *honore* and, too often, that in turn demanded counter-vengeance. The result was a homicide rate about one hundred times higher than in most modern societies.

Rule of Law

When you move from villages to towns to cities, you interact with strangers more often, and you have less and less reason to expect that they will share your understanding of the proper way to behave. Also, group boundaries in cities are often fuzzy and overlapping. Therefore, traditional morals break down. Something different must emerge, or cities would dissolve in chaos.

All civilizations have responded to the problem in the same way. The people at the top of the hierarchy announce explicit rules—maybe that's why they are called rulers. They designate specialists to write, interpret, and enforce the rules; it is no longer an equally shared responsibility. The system is called law, and it partially displaces the unwritten moral codes.

Hammurabi, King of Babylon around 1700 BCE, posted all 282 of his laws publicly, carved in stone. The laws spelled out the penalties for murder, rape, property theft, injury, false accusation, and so forth, contingent on the status of the culprit and victim. A much shorter list of laws, the Ten Commandments, governed the Hebrews a few centuries later. The rules expanded and changed somewhat when written down in the Book of Deuteronomy and other parts of the Bible. Interpretations and modifications accumulated over the centuries, and were collected in the Talmud about fifteen hundred years ago. About the same time, Emperor Justinian published his codex. It described itself as a compilation and reconciliation of earlier Roman law, but, in fact, many earlier laws were altered to meet the needs of the early Byzantine Empire. Thus, even written codes evolve.

In the modern world, the specialists have their own separate spheres. Legislators write and change laws, responding to their constituents; courts interpret (and create) law and apply it; lawyers are hired to help their clients get more favorable court decisions; government bureaucrats and police enforce the law; prisons carry out punishments prescribed by the courts; and the press reports on how everyone performs his job.

The formal legal system has never replaced the informal moral system. For one thing, the moral system can discourage all sorts of selfish behaviors that weaken the group: not just murder, rape, and theft, but also bullying, laziness, and general troublemaking. Laws must define crimes more narrowly, with a focus on antisocial acts that outsiders can identify and sanction relatively easily. Biblical laws are a mix, not designed for court enforcement.

Laws do not always trump the unwritten moral rules, or norms. For example, cattle ranchers in Shasta County still rely on local norms regarding trespass and fence maintenance, even when they conflict with California state law. The relation between the law and norms is now a hot topic among legal theorists. Do changes in norms drive changes in the law, or is it the other way around? Everyone agrees that laws are more effective when they reinforce a group's norms, and that laws that oppose widely held norms are problematic. Indeed, some scholars believe that the French legal system worsened Corsica's vendettas in the mid-1800s. The courts weakened the traditional moral code (e.g., on who was a combatant) long before gaining enough traction to deter violence.

Jeremy Bentham and Rational Crime Fighting

The modern world surely needs a legal system, but what specific laws and enforcement policies should it employ? Where should legal boundaries be drawn in defining crime and vice? How many of our scarce resources should be devoted to police, courts, and prisons?

Jeremy Bentham (1748–1832) was among the first modern thinkers to tackle these big questions. Exhibited as a child prodigy by his father, a prosperous London solicitor, Bentham emerged at age sixteen with an Oxford law degree, a taste for philosophy, a fear of rough company, and a distaste for the actual practice of law. In 1769, he read Joseph Priestley's slogan—"the greatest happiness for the greatest number"—and found his life's mission, to spread utilitarian ideas. His 1776 "Fragment on Government," caught the attention of leading scholars, who rescued him from his "miserable life" as an unemployed lawyer, and he blossomed as a public intellectual. When his father died and left him a tidy fortune, Bentham bought poet John Milton's former London home and, for the last forty years of his life, was seldom seen outside its gates.

Bentham lived to write. Every day he rose at 6 a.m., walked around his garden, and then wrote steadily until evening. He wrote to people all over the world, and to officials and scholars in London. He wrote notes to himself, and, once in a while, he even wrote for publication. Bentham proposed inventions, such as refrigerators and pneumatic tubes for messages, and most notably, the panopticon. The idea, rather Orwellian, was to build a jail so that a few centrally positioned guards could see hundreds of isolated jail cells, but the prisoners couldn't see the guards, who could thus take frequent (but randomly timed) coffee breaks. This would be much cheaper, Bentham argued, than conventional, heavily guarded jails or transporting criminals to Australia.

Although he didn't actually enjoy human company (he was inordinately attached to his walking stick and cats), Bentham's goal, above all, was to make more people happier. When he died, he donated 172 boxes of his writings to the new University College of London—they are still sorting them out. He wanted his corpse to be useful, too: following his will meticulously, it was dissected before medical students and reassembled into a wax-enhanced mummy, the "Auto-Icon," which still sits in a glass case, walking stick in hand, in the lobby outside the university's finest lecture room.

Bentham's lasting legacy is his "hedonistic calculus," a sometimes subtle (and sometimes obtuse) cost-benefit analysis. Here's an example, slightly updated. Suppose that a thief steals an heirloom bracelet a family values at $1,000 and sells it for $100, and afterward, the family spends $2,000 changing locks and installing an alarm system. The associated direct cost of the crime is $900 = 1,000 − 100. (Yes, the thief's benefit counts just as much as the family's.) The $2,000 is an extra private cost of crime prevention. We should also account for public costs of crime prevention and law enforcement, including those for police, courts, and prisons.

The greatest good for the greatest number (or efficiency, to use modern jargon) in this context comes down to minimizing the total social cost, the sum of all prevention and enforcement costs, as well as the direct costs of crime. The test for the minimum is whether an additional expenditure on any sort of crime prevention or enforcement would lead to a greater reduction in the cost of crime. Spending another $100,000 on catching jewel thieves, for example, is efficient if it will reduce the costs of theft and other crimes by more than $100,000, and it is inefficient if the reduction is less than that.

But how can you know in advance what effect a policy might have on crime rates? Bentham assumed (as do his modern followers) that potential criminals try to maximize profit. A rational thief will steal the bracelet if the revenue he expects ($100) exceeds his own expected cost. His cost includes time spent on the crime and disposing of the loot, plus expected jail time (the probability of being caught and convicted times the length of sentence served) and other losses due to conviction.

For example, consider three different ways to increase the cost of theft: increase the probability of catching suspects 10 percent by increasing police patrols; or increase the probability of convicting a suspect 10 percent by increasing the prosecutor budget (or allowing weaker evidence); or increase punishment for convicted thieves 10 percent. Rational thieves would respond equally to any of the three ways, so the more efficient policy would be the cheapest, usually the more severe punishment.

Bentham's approach is a useful starting place but it has its limits. Criminals are not always rational profit maximizers. Many of them share, to some degree, the social emotions that restrain most people from crime, but their social emotions can also push in the opposite direction. For example, a small-time criminal may commit a spectacular, but unprofitable, crime in hopes of gaining higher status among his peers. Young criminals seem to respond much more strongly to the probability of conviction than to the severity of punishment. Also, dollar values can be problematic: what is the direct cost of a rape or murder, for example? For this and other reasons, estimation of total social costs is quite difficult. Fortunately, gauging efficiency relies on estimating *changes* in social costs, which is easier.

Do Markets Suppress Crime?

Murder and other major crimes are more prevalent in hunter-gatherer cultures. This assertion was taken for granted by civilized people until about two hundred years ago. But then, Rousseau and other Romantics argued persuasively that "savages" were naturally noble and moral, and many twentieth-century anthropologists agreed. Evidence accumulated by the late twentieth century, however, favors the original assertion. Even !Kung homicide rates are higher than in any modern nation, and rates in some Amazonian tribes and Borneo highland tribes are about ten times higher, similar to those of nineteenth-century Corsica. Archaeological evidence suggests that murder rates among our ancestors tens of thousands of years ago were also pretty high.

Wartime casualties aside, homicide and other serious crimes seem to decrease as civilization advances. Historians combing the archives of medieval European towns estimate an annual homicide rate of about 50 per 100,000 residents. The rate dropped by about half in the sixteenth and seventeenth centuries, and by the time of the great market takeover, it was below 10. The trend continued downward throughout the 1800s with the introduction of modern courts, police, and prisons. Fifty years after Bentham's death, the annual homicide rate in London was less than 2 per 100,000 and headed lower. No wonder the Victorian philosophers were so optimistic.

The trend in many advanced industrial countries justifies their optimism. Japan and Iceland now have rates less than 0.5, and most of the others have rates in the 1 to 3 range. By contrast, developing countries often have rates of 10–100.

Did the market system itself cause the drop in crime? Some pundits think so. The main point of a 2006 book by Benjamin S. Friedman is that economic growth (i.e., increasing income for the average person) seems historically, more often than not, to coincide with a more tolerant, mobile, and democratic society, presumably with lower crime rates.

Why might that be? One possible explanation is that a wealthier society has more resources to devote to crime prevention. If it does so efficiently, it should have a lower crime rate. A second possibility is that, if wealth is widespread, people will have better legitimate opportunities and will find crime less tempting. A third explanation goes beyond the standard economic perspective. The process that leads to market takeover involves a transformation of the moral system. As noted in Chapter 3, personal traits like patience and prudence tend to displace traits favored in feudal societies, such as a strong sense of honor. The new personal traits seem less conducive to violent crime.

This logic suggests that the United States, with the world's most advanced market economy, would have the world's lowest crime rates over the last few decades. Unfortunately, instead, we have among the highest crime rates in the developed world. The U.S. annual homicide rate, for example, is 5.5 per 100,000, similar to some developing countries. Crime rates in other industrial countries, although lower than in the United States, stopped falling in the last quarter of the twentieth century, while their economies continued to grow. Something else must be going on.

Do advanced market economies somehow boost crime? The rest of the chapter pursues this question. It shows how misplaced moral instincts boosted modern markets for three vices. Then it looks at three crime-fighting industries that have prospered in recent decades, and shows how they increase demand for their services.

Markets for Vices

Economically naïve pundits, and most voters, assume that outlawing an industry will make it disappear. The direct effect, however, is to increase the cost of delivering the product. That increases the price and reduces the amount sold. It decreases revenues only if demand is elastic, that is, if consumers respond strongly to price. If they don't, then the price increase more than offsets the decreased amount sold, and revenues actually increase. Production costs decrease (since less is sold), partially offsetting the increased delivery costs. Thus, outlawing an industry with inelastic demand will increase revenue, and might increase profit.

Demand for vice (as for all addictive products) tends to be very inelastic. Anyone who discovers a business model that keeps down the cost of delivering an outlawed vice, then, stands to profit. Such a business model is bound to spread, expanding the industry. In sum, economic logic tells us that outlawing a vice can make it into a larger industry than ever.

So much for economic logic. How did modern markets for vice actually evolve? We'll look at three of the largest.

* * *

Gambling. Demand must have expanded in the transition to agricultural societies, in part because low status is more prevalent than among hunter-gatherers and mobility is lower. Humans are not temperamentally well adapted to such a station in life, and seek outlets. Demand expanded further in the transition to the modern world as people of all classes became wealthier and could afford larger and more frequent bets. To meet the increasing demand, innovators developed a wider variety of wagers, such as new games of chance and bets on regularly scheduled sporting events.

State sponsored lotteries in the United States go back to the Virginia colony in 1612, and gambling was widely tolerated until the late 1800s. A wave of scandals—payoffs to state officials, rigging winning numbers, and so on—together with religious opposition and Progressive era ferment ("muckraking" journalism, and movements to "improve the working classes") led to prohibition by 1900, with legal gambling restricted to racetrack bets in a handful of states.

Of course, demand for gambling turned out to be inelastic. Revenues, and profits, soared as entrepreneurs found ways to deliver gambling services to customers. The Mafia business model worked especially well: monopolize the local action, pay winners reliably, but keep a large rake (fraction of the total bets) and bribe local police and officials to maintain lax enforcement.

Political support for prohibition began to fade in the 1960s, and in the 1970s, an unholy alliance of gambling moguls and starved public schools brought back state-run lotteries. Over $550 billion annually is now legally wagered in the United States. The net revenue (or rake) expanded from $10 billion in 1982 to over $40 billion by 1994, and doubtless is much higher today. Some 80 percent of U.S. adults report having engaged in gambling at some time in their lives, but about 5 percent account for half of the wagers. Experts estimate that 1 or 2 percent of Americans are addicts whose gambling habit dominates their lives. As predicted by evolutionary psychology, the addicts are more often male and come disproportionately from lower income groups.

Three new business models seem to be catching on.

Mega-casinos. The gaming industry dominates Las Vegas and Atlantic City, and has showered cash on obscure Indian tribes. It turns out that bigger is better—casinos with thousands of slot machines and hundreds of tables and rooms have lower per-guest labor costs and can afford entertainment that keeps guests longer. U.S. casinos now rake in over $40 billion annually, and grew three times as fast as the overall economy in recent years. Casinos and official lotteries have become the third largest (and fastest growing) source of revenue for state governments: typically 55 percent of wagers are paid out to winners, 10 percent goes to promotion, salaries, and so forth, and the state keeps the remaining 35 percent.

One can begin to see a backlash, as the social costs become apparent and the benefits to education disappoint. Recent academic studies suggest that the social costs—increased crime, reduced demand for other goods, and especially other forms of entertainment—exceed the gains for most communities. But states are not yet killing their cash cows. For example, in his 2003 election campaign, Arnold Schwarzenegger strongly opposed Indian casinos, but as Governor of California, he soon made a deal to expand the casinos in return for $1 billion up front and larger tax payments in the future.

Online betting on events. Sites such as TradeSports.com allow people around the world to wager 24/7 on the outcome of soccer, basketball, tennis, and other sports events. Their product line has expanded to include wagers on financial markets (e.g., will the DJIA end the year above 14,000?), weather events (will a category 3 hurricane hit the U.S. coast this season?), political contests (who will be elected U.S. President?), and current events (will the Israeli airforce strike Iran next month?). Potentially, such markets can provide valuable insurance and information—for example, you can hedge your stock market position by betting that the DJIA won't end the year above 14,000, and you might want to cancel a trip to the Mideast when the price of war bets increases. Overall, the prediction markets have proved remarkably accurate, more so than published expert opinion.

Online wagers of all sorts—for electronic slot machines, roulette, and so forth, as well as events—are growing rapidly and probably exceeded $20 billion worldwide in 2007. The convenience to bettors, and the ability to shift easily to low tax jurisdictions, suggests that online sites will become major players in the gaming industry.

Online poker may be the most dynamic part of the industry. Its roots stretch back to China a thousand years ago, when playing cards first appeared and soon spread across Eurasia. The current fifty-two-card deck took shape in France about five hundred years ago, but allowing the ace to outrank the king may be a product of the French Revolution three hundred years later. Poker emerged as a distinct game in New Orleans in the early 1800s, with published rules beginning in 1850.

Decks of cards are inexpensive to produce, easy to transport, and can entertain up to a dozen people for months or years. Hence, card games spread across the United States in covered wagons, during the Civil War, and in World Wars I and II. Poker is especially appealing to players since it requires skills in detecting and disguising intentions, and in building and exploiting a reputation outside the normal confines of the moral code. The varieties of poker have evolved, and Texas Hold-em has tended to displace Draw and Stud Poker.

Poker's commercial appeal seemed limited until quite recently. Unlike blackjack, slot machines or roulette, it doesn't funnel much income to casinos. At best, the players just rent a table and buy drinks. However, Hollywood profited from poker, and increased its popularity with movies like "Big Hand for the Little Lady," "The Cincinnati Kid," "The Sting," "Maverick," and "Rounders." Since 2000, TV coverage has exploded. Tournament viewership now exceeds even NBA basketball, and now the big winners are instant celebrities.

Poker became an industry in its own right as the Internet grew. Computer screens capture poker action much better than that of rival sports like darts or billiards, and the Internet reduces players' participation costs. Tens of thousands of players now frequent sites like pokerstars.com and fulltiltpoker.com every night, and wager tens of millions of dollars. The media run occasional horror stories of young lives ruined by an online poker addiction, and new legislation makes it more difficult to transfer money, but the online sites always find work-arounds and continue to grow.

In sum, the gaming industry is not fading away. It is taking new forms, some socially beneficial and others less so, and business is booming.

*   *   *

The **alcoholic beverage** industry provides interesting parallels and divergences. Laws and norms encouraged moderate beer and wine consumption for most of the history of Western civilization. Distilled spirits with higher alcoholic content, first developed by Persian alchemists, reached Europe in medieval times. Cheap versions ("demon rum") and spreading abuse among the urban lower classes spurred a paternalistic prohibition movement in the United States by the mid-1800s. The movement pushed through the Eighteenth Amendment to the U.S. Constitution, which outlawed the alcohol industry in 1919.

Prohibition led to a tripling of average price, to consumption decreases of perhaps 25 to 50 percent, and to a reduction in liver cirrhosis of zero to 50 percent (estimates differ). Enforcement turned out to be much more difficult than prohibitionists had predicted—but that really shouldn't surprise anyone who does the math: the estimates imply a doubling, more or less, of industry revenues. Illegal brewing, distilling, importing ("bootlegging"), and sales (in "speakeasies") became widespread and condoned by local norms, encouraging a general disrespect for the law and for hypocritical authority. Organized crime got a major boost, and homicides and police corruption increased. Consumption shifted toward beverages with higher alcohol content (easier to smuggle) and greater health risks. Of course, government revenues from alcohol taxes dried up while enforcement expenses increased. Public support for prohibition collapsed after 1930, and by 1933. the Twenty-first Amendment ended the "noble experiment."

The current legal regime supports several major subindustries in the United States with quite diverse business plans. Winemakers, brewers, distillers, distributors, and retailers generate annual retail sales of about $100 billion. The industry is a cash cow for government, delivering annual tax receipts of about $20 billion, even though the tax rate now is rather low. At about twenty-five cents per ounce of alcohol, it is only about one-third of its level fifty years ago (after accounting for inflation). Enforcement remains a major enterprise—one cognizant federal agency, ATF, has a $1 billion annual budget. (Supposedly, most of it goes to firearms control and "anti-terror activities" but at least 2 percent of it goes to pursuing alcohol and cigarette tax evaders.)

Alcohol abuse continues to be a major problem, and leads to over 100 thousand excess deaths annually in the United States. The rehab industry has experienced rapid growth. Since 1934, Alcoholics Anonymous has provided peer support to recovering alcoholics—its decentralized networks currently include millions of members, and it has spawned several other "twelve-step" programs for drug abusers, compulsive overeaters, and so on. In 1982, former first lady Betty Ford helped launch a more commercial line of residential clinics. Perhaps the most encouraging sign is that binge drinking seems to be in decline among eighteen-to twenty-four-year-olds. Social norms, at last, may be coming into line with reality.

* * *

Tobacco consumption is a vice even deadlier than alcohol. According to impartial estimates, cigarette smoking accounts for over 400 thousand excess deaths each year in the United States, and so is the largest preventable killer. The industry is huge, with worldwide annual revenues currently around $300 billion.

Throughout most of the twentieth century, the U.S. industry was a cozy oligopoly, insulated from competition, and raking in extraordinary profits from addicted customers. It recruited generation after generation of new customers with sophisticated marketing campaigns featuring rugged cowboys and cool camels. Fueled by massive campaign contributions, expensive lawyers and lobbyists, and well-funded research labs, the tobacco industry always prevailed in the legislature and never lost in court. It seemed a juggernaut.

The industry had just one little problem: its product posed a subtle long-term health threat. Life and health are the ultimate currencies, and our social and political institutions eventually responded. Academic research laboratories finally isolated the threat, and eventually showed that tobacco consumption was the main cause of lung cancer and emphysema, and contributed to other fatal diseases. They also demonstrated that nicotine, a molecule prevalent in tobacco smoke, was addictive. Various non-government (and eventually government) organizations publicized the danger. Anti-smoking campaigns started to take hold.

The first breakthrough, in 1969, was the mandatory printed warning from the U.S. Surgeon General that "smoking may be dangerous to your health," later strengthened to "smoking causes lung cancer." In 1994, trial lawyers allied with state government officials and launched an epic legal battle. Success came suddenly in late 1998. The landmark Master Settlement showered over $250 billion on state governments over twenty-five years, with tens of billions more going to lawyers and to educational funds.

You might think that the settlement was bad for the industry, but savvy investors saw a bright silver lining. Altria's stock price, for example, increased about 25 percent during the second half of 1998 as investors realized that the settlement locked in a 50 percent market share for the company's Phillip Morris brands, led by Marlboro. State governments now rely on revenue from the tobacco industry, and so have become industry stakeholders. The states can't bring further legal action, and the settlement might actually reduce the industry's future tax liability. It makes it easier for the cartel to raise prices, extracting even more money from nicotine addicts.

Changing norms seem to be reducing the health risk. Smoking has become disreputable in much of the United States, and most of Western Europe seems to be moving in the same direction. (On the other hand, industry growth remains impressive in Asia.) Teenagers are the key to the future, and their norms began to turn against smoking in the late 1990s. However, the decline in smoking among U.S. high school students apparently ended by 2006, as antismoking campaigns wound down and cash-strapped states diverted more settlement funds into other activities.

Overall, then, markets seem to be amplifying the three vices. Prohibition has not been an effective answer. When in force, it increased gambling and alcohol industry revenues and perhaps profits. The prohibited vices spread to new clienteles, and cause secondary damage, such as corruption of police and officials. But simple legalization inspires marketing campaigns to spread the vice further.

Bentham would have called for efficient vice reduction, minimizing the total cost of efforts to suppress vices, plus the cost of harm they actually cause. From that perspective, the most efficient approach would be to combine market with moral disincentives. Keep the activities legal, but tax them heavily and use the tax revenues to finance antimarketing campaigns. These campaigns should aim to spread the social codes found most effective in reducing demand, especially among young people. The idea is to make it seem uncool to engage in smoking, serious gambling, and heavy drinking.

Crime-fighting Industries

All developed countries have a court system, but only in the United States does the trial lawyer industry loom so large. Roughly 2 percent of GDP, over $200 billion each year, passes through the system, and the trial lawyers extract about $40 billion, a major increase over the last thirty years. The industry's current profit centers (like asbestos, tobacco, and insurance) help finance the exploration of potential growth markets (like lead paint, mold, and regulated industries), and new products (like suits against the fast-food industry). The industry's government relations and public relations arms are among the most powerful of business lobbies. They contribute to both political parties, but are a core constituency for the Democrats.

The business model is laid out in the movie *Erin Brockovich*, which earned Julia Roberts an Academy Award. Find sympathetic victims, like young families with major health problems. Find an unpopular defendant who may be responsible, like Pacific Gas & Electric. Appeal to the jury's moral sentiments and ask them to help the injured innocents get even with the evil bully. (Of course, the defendant's lawyers will counter by portraying the plaintiffs as lazy gold diggers, and will remind the jury that exorbitant fines will hurt the defendant's workers and customers.) Since the trial lawyers can get up to 50 percent of any award, and may be able to win a substantial settlement prior to trial, they can profitably sue, even when the probability of winning is not especially large.

Defendants, like asbestos and pharmaceuticals firms, have recently found more effective ways to fight back. Their political campaign contributions now rival those of trial lawyers. The Bush administration has tried, with partial success, to put limits on the amount of damages that juries can award, and to make it more difficult to file class action lawsuits. Judges are now more likely to throw out claims they believe were "manufactured for money," and one of the most aggressive class action law firms is under indictment for paying people to become plaintiffs. Industry growth has slowed.

Is the U.S. trial lawyer industry too large? Consider the costs and benefits. The main benefit is to push manufacturers to find safer production processes and safer products. PG&E is much more careful now about toxic chemicals, for example. The obvious cost is higher consumer prices, but other costs are subtler. For example, the threat of lawsuits has pushed medical doctors to prescribe defensive tests or therapies of dubious value, and the same threat has destroyed the small airplane industry.

As Bentham taught us, efficiency is served when the last dollar spent on safety actually reduces harm by more than one dollar on average. The trial lawyer industry is efficient to the extent that the threat of lawsuits pushes everyone toward efficiency, and does so more cheaply than alternative inducements. I don't know of any broad studies on the question, but I'd guess that the threat has gone past the efficient point.

Prisons are as old as civilization, but only in the United States have they become a major industry in their own right. The United States, with less than 5 percent of world population, now holds about 25 percent of the world's prisoners. Our incarceration rate is ten times higher than most of Europe and Japan. It is difficult to find any country in any era that kept a larger fraction of its population behind bars.

The cost to taxpayers is enormous. The U.S. prison population grew from half a million in 1980 to 2.2 million in 2006, and annual prison expenditures grew even faster. California State prisons house 168 thousand of those inmates at a cost $10.1 billion, more than combined state spending on our 400 thousand Cal State students and 200 thousand University of California students. The prison system is one of the state's larger industries, and its revenues come almost entirely from taxpayers.

What do we get for our money? Prisons have always served four distinct purposes. The first is punishment: make the culprit suffer and pay a price for harming others. It is negative reciprocity, carried out on behalf of the victim and of society as a whole. The second purpose is incapacitation: take the culprit out of circulation so he can't harm anyone else. There is also rehabilitation: let the culprit mend his ways so that he will contribute to society when released, and won't commit more crimes. The final purpose is deterrence: make crime less attractive by demonstrating that culprits are punished.

Punishment and incapacitation certainly happen in California. We lock up lots of criminals and, since the facilities are desperately overcrowded, few of them have a pleasant experience. Indeed, so many inmates died that the federal authorities intervened in 2006 to force improved health care.

Rehabilitation was proudly added to the California Department of Correction's name in 2003 by its new boss, Rod Hickman. He resigned in frustration after less than three years. While serving time, California's prisoners learn new crime skills from other inmates and build their criminal networks, but very few have the opportunity to develop skills, contacts, and attitudes that would help them succeed in legitimate society. More than half of former prisoners are back behind bars within two years of release, and only 21 percent successfully complete parole. This "catch-and-release" syndrome is rehabilitation in reverse.

Deterrence is hard to measure, but available evidence is not encouraging. A recent, statistically sophisticated U.S. study suggests that in the 1980s, an additional year behind bars prevented about two violent crimes, but now it prevents less than one-half of one violent crime. The authors conclude that we are now locking up less dangerous criminals, reducing the incapacitation effect. It seems that the (marginal) deterrence effect was never very strong, and is now almost negligible.

None of the purposes of prison are served in a cost-effective manner. California spends more than $30,000 per prisoner each year, about one-third more than the national average. Only Massachusetts spends more per prisoner, and they at least get average results. California's rehabilitation statistics are among the nation's worst, and are disgraceful by international standards.

How did California get such a dysfunctional prison system? The answer is actually pretty clear to most policy analysts, though they differ on emphasis and terminology. It is the unfortunate by-product of very successful business models employed by the prison industry, its labor union, state and national politicians, and television news.

Let's start with the union, the California Correctional Peace Officers Association. In the early 1980s, Don Novey put CCPOA together from fragmented groups of low-paid prison guards. He increased dues and used the money to build public relations and influence in Sacramento. The timing was excellent, and guards' salaries climbed steadily, while employment zoomed. By 2006, members received an average annual base salary of $57,000, the highest in the nation, and with overtime, more than a tenth of them earned more than $100,000. The union collects about $22 million in dues each year and uses it to run a sophisticated operation. More than a third of the union's budget goes to political activities. In the aftermath of the 2003–4 state budget crisis and the recall election, the new governor, Arnold Schwarzenegger, tried to reduce prison payrolls by a mere $300,000. The union and its allies forced him to back down and, in the end, he offered concessions that make the union stronger and richer than ever.

The union's goals dovetail nicely with those of the construction industry and suppliers of prison services such as food and medical care. All benefit from more convictions and longer sentences, and from larger expenditures per prisoner. The expansion of the state system from thirteen prisons in 1985 to thirty-one in 1995 increased their revenues and political power.

Politicians are key players, since they choose policies and allocate the resources. A politician's business model always involves raising campaign funds and finding messages that resonate with voters. A recipe for success in the late twentieth-century United States was to get contributions from prison industry (especially, in California, from the union) and to talk "tough on crime."

Consider, for example, the 1994 "three strikes" initiative sponsored by the CCPOA and by "victims' rights committees" funded by the union and its allies. Endorsed by politicians in both parties, the initiative passed with over 70 percent of the vote. It requires life sentences for conviction of a third felony, and generally forces the court to impose longer sentences. "Three strikes" is one of the reasons why California's prison population has soared. But it does little or nothing to protect the public. For example, Leonard Scott, a fifty-year-old who had stayed out of jail for twenty years following two burglary convictions, was sentenced in January 2000 to twenty-five years to life for misrepresenting his financial condition on a car lease. The law prevents judges from using their professional judgment, and makes taxpayers fund an expensive, but unpleasant, retirement for those who no longer pose much danger to society.

Why do voters support such foolish policies? Local TV news is part of the explanation. Its business model is to build ratings, and to hold viewers through advertisements. In-depth analysis of sentencing guidelines and their cost effectiveness don't help. Their goals are served much better by stories and images that appeal to strong social emotions, such as our urge to find and punish bad people. Crime rates and actual danger to the public have little to do with what works for TV.

*　*　*

The last crime fighting industry we shall examine is the U.S. "war on drugs." The war's history reprises some familiar themes. In some states one hundred years ago, you could legally purchase heroin and cocaine, but not tobacco or alcohol. The medical profession initially encouraged those drugs as general and local anesthetics, but early in the twentieth century, it turned to substitutes like morphine and Novocain that produced fewer side effects. Cocaine continued to be used as a minor ingredient of patent medicines, while consumption of opium products, confined mainly to Chinese immigrants, was trending down. Nonetheless, sensational (and often racist) newspaper stories, combined with reformist zeal and foreign policy concerns (mainly, ending opium trade in the Far East) spurred Congress to pass the 1914 Harrison Act. It required a doctor's prescription for these and many other drugs. U.S. consumption dwindled until mid-century, and then began to rise as organized crime discovered the profit potential.

Since then, we've been caught in a runaway growth cycle. Advances in the industries that supply illegal drugs provoke growth in the repression industry, which in turn leads to further innovations on the supply side. Harry Anslinger, the entrepreneurial chief of the new Federal Narcotics division in the 1930s, increased his mandate and budget by leading a successful campaign to outlaw marijuana use. The youth culture of the 1950s and 1960s glamorized the use of illegal drugs, especially marijuana and the new psychedelics. Norms can be a bit fuzzy, and the youth culture of the day led to more abuse of the harder illegal drugs.

President Nixon escalated in 1971 by announcing his War on Drugs, with a much expanded enforcement budget. This drove up prices, which (since addicts are not very price responsive) greatly increased illegal drug revenues. The market system responded in the predictable fashion: producer and distributor networks expanded, fought each other for turf, tried to corrupt enforcers in the United States and overseas, expanded their product lines, and sought new customers in the suburbs and small towns.

The War on Drugs has, so far, brought prosperity to the illegal drug supply industry and to the enforcement industry, but has brought only misery to taxpayers and ordinary citizens. Illegal drugs now generate about $60 billion in retail sales annually in the United States, and account for some twenty-five thousand excess deaths—less than tobacco or alcohol but still depressing figures. Drug War enforcement expenditures by federal, state, and local governments exceed $40 billion every year, and drug arrests account for well over half of the federal prison population. These figures do not count indirect costs, such as robbery, theft, and embezzlement by addicts trying to finance their habit, or assaults and homicides from turf battles among drug dealers.

Prevention programs like DARE are politically popular, but scientific studies are all inconclusive or negative. Drug rehabilitation programs have success rates well under 50 percent. Although that doesn't sound impressive, scientific studies still end up estimating benefits at three to seven times cost. Society surely would benefit from further growth of the rehab industry and the development of more effective prevention programs.

When the "noble experiment" of alcohol prohibition unleashed perverse market forces, public opinion changed quickly and terminated the experiment in short order. Why hasn't this happened for the War on Drugs? It is far more expensive and seems even less effective than Prohibition, and has terrible side effects. It surely ranks among the worst public policy mistakes of all time. Yet, it continues to receive almost unanimous support among elected officials. Why has our system failed us so badly?

Morals Help Markets Run Amok

The disastrous War on Drugs can be explained in the same way as California's prison-industrial complex, or the outsized trial lawyer industry. Key players found business models that succeeded for them, and it just so happens that some of the results hurt the general public. Whatever its failings, the War on Drugs has been very profitable for politicians, news media, law enforcement agencies, and prisons.

But this explanation raises a deeper question: if the public is seriously harmed, why don't political and business entrepreneurs come up with some way to cure the problem? Almost by definition, an inefficiency is a profit opportunity: there is some lower cost way to meet society's goals, and whoever steers society in that direction should be able to pocket some of the cost savings. Such entrepreneurs ended Prohibition in 1933. Why haven't they stopped the War on Drugs, or reformed our prisons?

As I see it, the underlying difference is in the workings of the moral system. Widely held norms supported moderate alcohol use before Prohibition, and the onset of the Great Depression helped focus people on Prohibition's unfavorable balance of costs and benefits. By contrast, the substances prohibited by US drug laws had not previously enjoyed mainstream acceptance, and few citizens are aware of far more effective drug policies in the Netherlands, Switzerland, and elsewhere. As a result, taxpayers and voters misperceive the benefits and don't clearly see the costs.

Perhaps even more important, most people put alcohol and tobacco in different moral categories than heroin and cocaine. For example, former drug czar William Bennett writes "drug use degrades human character," and philosopher James Q. Wilson (1990, 26) writes,

> Tobacco shortens one's life, cocaine debases it. Nicotine alters one's habits, cocaine alters one's soul. The heavy use of crack, unlike the heavy use of tobacco, corrodes those natural sentiments of sympathy and duty that constitute our human nature and make possible our social life.

With such moral stakes, it is unnatural to give much weight to routine costs and benefits. Our instinct is to absolutely forbid the corrosive influences, damn the cost.

Such instincts often work well in small cohesive groups, but in the modern world they are manipulated by sensationalist journalism (stories sell well about addiction and violence, and parents' heartache), by politicians seeking higher office and by bureaucrats seeking larger budgets. Competitive political markets and media amplify the appeals to moral outrage and don't help us focus on the actual consequences of current policy. Like Ahab's quest for the whale, these policies hijack our urge to punish and send us on a mad voyage.

Mullahs' Revenge

Gangs, Cults, and Anti-terrorists

The Symbionese Liberation Army (SLA) got off to a bad start in November 1973. A ragtag collection of leftist activists, Vietnam vets, and escaped convicts, the SLA wanted to make a splash by killing some authoritarian figure. A careless reading of a news clipping pointed them to Oakland's Superintendent of Schools, Marcus Foster, and they ambushed and killed him with eight bullets dipped in cyanide. But Foster was actually a beloved progressive, and everyone condemned the action, even other radicals.

The SLA hit pay dirt on their second action, a February 1974 kidnap of heiress Patty Hearst. Two months later, Patty shocked the nation by joining her captors in a bank robbery. Six SLA members died in a subsequent shootout and fire in Los Angeles, but the remaining three, including Patty, eluded capture for more than a year. Then she was caught, deprogrammed, brought to trial, and convicted. President Carter released Patty in 1979 after two years in jail, and since then she has led a quiet, domestic life with her husband (her deprogramming bodyguard) and their two daughters.

Why did Patty join her bumbling kidnappers? Indeed, why would anyone join such a deviant group? Rational explanations, of the sort Jeremy Bentham would understand, go only so far. This chapter goes farther, and examines the moral codes of gangs, cults, and terrorist cells, and their market plans. It shows how they evolve with mainstream society, and how they coevolve with anti-terror tactics.

The Mafia

To begin, consider the most famous collection of American criminal gangs, the Mafia. Everyone knows elements of their moral code, if only from movies like *The Godfather* and TV shows like *The Sopranos*. Respect is paramount. A mix of fear and admiration, it holds together a paramilitary organization and weakens opposition in the community. *Omerta*, the code of silence, prohibits telling outsiders about Mafia activities, and enjoins everyone never to help the police. All this is supposed to support *la famiglia*, and somehow protect wives and children.

The Mafia's market plan has changed over the years. The gangs got started in the United States about one hundred years ago, led by young Italian immigrants (with a few Jewish and other ethnic variants). At first, revenues mostly came from extorting local Italian shopkeepers, who were easily discouraged from seeking police protection. Some Mafia entrepreneurs developed a second product line, gambling or "numbers rackets." The threat of violence (and codes of respect) helped maintain profitable local monopolies. After 1920, Prohibition created very profitable new product lines, bootlegging and distilling, and the rise of organized labor unions over the next several decades expanded the scope for extortion rackets.

Heroin, the emerging market in the 1950s, created tension between Mafia markets and Mafia morals. Coppola's classic movie, *The Godfather* (1972), hinges on the decision by Vito Corleone (played by Marlon Brando) to stay out of narcotics. His advisors favored getting in because "there's a lot of money in that white powder," and, "If we don't get into it, somebody else will . . . with the money they earn, they can buy more police and political power; then they come after us." But Vito refuses Sollozzo's partnership offer and that touches off a bloody war among the Mafia's Five Families. Eventually, Vito brokers a peace agreement, saying, "When did I ever refuse an accommodation, except one time. And why? Because I believe this drug business is gonna destroy us in the years to come," since "even the police departments that've helped us in the past with gambling and other things are gonna refuse to help us when it comes to narcotics."

In part due to the narcotics trade, federal prosecutors began to go after the Mafia in the 1960s and, a few years later, legalized gambling began to undercut the numbers rackets. The Mafia market plan responded by spinning off legitimate gambling and entertainment units, which have merged with ordinary corporations to run mega-casinos in Las Vegas, Atlantic City, and numerous Indian reservations. It has also spun off (or ceded to more recent immigrant gangs from Russia and elsewhere) the higher-margin drug and prostitution product lines. Traditional Mafia activities continue, but overall, their style of organized crime seems to be in decline.

Youth Gangs

American youth gangs are also ethnically based, and celebrated in movies and TV. The African-American dominated Crips and Bloods are probably the most famous, but I'll focus on the Chicano gangs in my home state.

When the United States annexed California in 1850, the Hispanic families already there were pushed aside. Some of the young men joined bandit gangs, such as the one run by the "Robin Hood of El Dorado," Joaquin Murieta. Ever since those gold rush days, migrants have swarmed into the state, especially Anglos from other parts of the United States and Hispanics from Mexico. Tensions between old and new arrivals from differing cultures have occasionally flared into violence. For instance, in Los Angeles during World War II, the Zoot Suit riots pitted local Hispanic youths against sailors and cops.

Today's Chicano street gangs got their start in California prisons, especially the Deuel facility in Tracy. There, in the late 1950s, the nucleus of the Mexican Mafia or *Eme* (Spanish pronunciation of the letter "M") took shape among first and second-generation Mexican immigrants. Once they met their first goal, mutual protection from Anglo and African American prison gangs, the *Emes* quickly developed profitable in-prison product lines such as gambling, narcotics, extortion, and male prostitution. Their *Surenos* (southerners) network spread outside the prison and, within a few years, dominated Latino *barrios* (neighborhoods) across Southern California, with connections south of the Mexican border.

The *Nuestra Familia* formed in the late 1960s to resist *Eme* bullying. It favored the letter "N" and its numerical equivalent, 14, in contrast to *Eme*'s 13/M. Its *Nortenos* (northerners) network entered the same product lines as *Surenos* but recruited mainly young Chicanos born north of the border, or living in northern California barrios, or in the north side of large barrios. The gangs are mortal enemies, yet feed off each other: if you live in the wrong neighborhood (or in prison), the best protection against one gang is to join the other.

Chicano gangs have distinctive codes of behavior. They advertise their power and territory using eye-catching graffiti featuring 13/M or 14/N. Personal fashions include tattoos, shaved heads, or slicked-back hair and bandanas, baggy pants, and speaking in Spanglish, an eccentric blend of Spanish and English.

Their codes promote loyalty and tend to foreclose other options. For example, the initiation oath for *Nuestra Familia* reportedly is: "If I lead, follow me. If I hesitate, push me. If they [rival gangs] kill me, avenge me. If I am a traitor, kill me!"

Above all, the moral codes value honor, or respect, among peers. Greater respect brings better access to revenues and to *cholas* (girlfriends). A gangster earns respect by attacking rival gang members and defending his own. A wannabe member can gain acceptance by shooting rivals targeted by senior members—these underage attackers receive lighter sentences and shield the senior leadership from the law.

Before the mid-1980s, weapons of choice included fists, knives, and clubs. Then a new product line, crack cocaine, changed everything. Gang revenues exploded, and so did membership and territory. Conflicts spread. Soon everyone had guns and drive-by shootings became an everyday event in larger cities, and even in some smaller towns. By 1995, Los Angeles and Fresno, two major M vs. N battlegrounds, had violent crime rates that put them among the four worst U.S. cities.

Gang activity seems to have stabilized since then, but the problem remains acute. As recently as 2004, half of Los Angeles' homicides were considered gang related, and more than a quarter of the nation's. Gang revenues still come mainly from illegal drugs, with major sidelines in extortion and robbery.

Deviant Morals, Deviant Markets

Evidently, the Mafia and the youth gangs have roughly parallel morals and basically similar market plans. How about the SLA?

Their moral code was a mishmash of leftist rhetoric ("Death to the fascist insect that preys upon the life of the people") and occult symbols (a seven-headed cobra), but it served its purpose. It gave SLA members the feeling that they were part of something noble and important, and that they had special ties to each other. Their bonds were strengthened by life-and-death shared experiences. Sexual bonds also contributed, and some journalists are convinced that Patty Hearst fell in love with William Wolfe, a core SLA member who also had a privileged childhood.

The SLA's market plan had a short but memorable run. At first, the gang got what they needed by robbing fellow leftists, then by bank robbery and ransom. Amateurish luck helped considerably: most kidnap victims would have run at the first opportunity, but Patty's conversion took hold and brought priceless publicity, and inept police work compensated for inept SLA actions.

Do the SLA and the gangs really have anything important in common? After all, almost any organization has some sort market plan and a code of behavior, even Cub Scouts and Rotarians. Listing parallel market plans and codes doesn't necessarily provide any real insight.

This chapter hinges on the argument that modern gangs and cults, despite obvious differences, really do have roots in the same moral ground and face similar market realities. Before turning to cults, let's see how the argument goes for gangs.

Humans evolved in close-knit bands that met their material and spiritual needs, but in a Pleistocene world far different from today's. Overall, the modern world is much better at providing material goods—food, shelter, personal security, medical care, and so forth—but it can fall short in matters of the human spirit.

As argued in Chapter 1, a sense of community appeals to our evolved psychology. Some of us feel that tug more strongly than others, of course, and most of us are reasonably satisfied with what we can find in the modern world. As noted in Chapter 8, some modern jobs offer a very intense communal experience, in startup companies, for example, or in the military or some corporations. The modern world also offers opportunities to join a wide variety of part-time communities—regular churches, parent-teacher associations, bowling leagues, and Elks, to name just a few.

Cults and gangs offer a much different proposition. Membership is full-time, and it cuts ties to the mainstream. In-group bonds become exceedingly intense. Once you join the Mafia (or M or N) family, you are supposed to be in for life, and to forget your old friends and ambitions.

Many cults and gangs focus recruitment on a single ethnic group, and their codes appeal to our innate chauvinism. They praise the nobility of their own group, and hammer away at real or imagined oppression or disrespect by the mainstream. In a variant on the theme, the SLA and rival leftist groups claimed to be acting on behalf of the underprivileged of the world. Some of their members (and leaders) grew up in comfort, but felt guilty about it and tried fervently to identify with oppressed minorities.

The proposition offered by deviant groups obviously has more appeal where the mainstream is unattractive: in countries and neighborhoods where markets and state don't function well, and for low-status individuals with poor mainstream prospects. The SLA and the Chicano street gangs both started recruitment in an ideal center: California's prison system. Its vast population lives in humiliating conditions, sees little chance of rehabilitation, and urgently needs protection. The Mafia traditionally recruited its foot soldiers from among recent immigrants. So did the *Emes*, once their network began to grow. The *Nuestra Familia* also recruited school dropouts in barrios throughout California.

But still, why would a young person join up? It's not just that kids in the barrios and ghettos see very few examples of mainstream success. Just as important, they see an upside. Top gang leaders seem to have a glamorous life, with lots of money, girls, and respect. Of course, not many make it to the top, and those that do seldom last long. It's a bad gamble but, as noted in an earlier chapter, it is just the sort of gamble that appeals to low-status young men.

A market plan is essential. Every group (indeed, every living thing) has to acquire resources to sustain itself, and in the modern world, the market is the dominant source. Even groups that reject the mainstream must somehow deal with that reality. There are four basic options:

- Legal selling. For example, the Amish cling to the old ways and aim for self-sufficiency, but many of their communities compromise by selling food and handicrafts to tourists.
- Illegal selling. Smuggling, theft, gambling, and prostitution are gangs' traditional mainstays, but now drugs are what bring the big bucks.
- Extortion. Protection money, ransom, robbery, and sweetheart contracts are one-sided revenues paid to avoid injury.
- Voluntary contributions. Sometimes, one-sided revenues are paid to return a favor, or just to help out, as with charitable foundations. Of course, the boundary with extortion can get fuzzy, as in *The Godfather* or in ancient royal gift exchange and tribute.

The market plan must mesh with the moral system. For example, the Palestine Liberation Organization's mission is to resist the Israeli occupation of the West Bank and Gaza, and to build the Palestinian nation. Their market plan degenerated into diverting foreign aid donations and extorting local businesses to build the bank accounts of their top officials. That disconnect led to a crushing defeat in Palestine's January 2006 elections and to a collapse of their revenues.

Religion

Religion brings new moral dimensions into the equation. As noted in early chapters, hunter-gatherer moral codes don't separate religion from everyday activities, nor do they call for extravagant self-sacrifice. To evolve among wandering tribes, a code can only ask for personal sacrifices that are likely to be eventually repaid, to kin if not personally to the donor.

Civilizations can evolve more extreme religious codes. From Uruk onward, religions have, above all, demanded that believers honor the gods and obey their earthly representatives. Religions that inspire extreme loyalty tend to last longer, especially in times of conflict. For example, in 167–160 BCE, Alexander's successors tried to stamp out Jewish religious practice. A band of fanatics called the Maccabees rebelled, risked near-certain death, and ultimately prevailed. The Zealots, another band of Jewish fanatics, rose up against the Romans in 66 CE and had some initial military success, but none survived their defeat at Masada in 73 CE.

A few years earlier, Christianity split from its parent faith when Apostle Paul eliminated the circumcision requirement, and after that, it spread quickly, especially among the lower classes throughout the Roman empire. Early Christians faced persecution, and the willingness of many martyrs to die for their faith was a convincing advertisement. Christianity spread so widely over the next few centuries that Emperor Constantine made it the empire's favored religion after 313 CE. The faith continued to inspire extreme loyalty, even as it became established throughout Europe over the next millennium.

Islam was a militant faith from the start. True believers were willing, even eager, to die in the service of their religious leaders. In the century following Muhammad's death in 632 CE, the new faith spread from Spain to India. Islamic conquerors didn't usually force their new subjects to convert, but those who did paid lower taxes and had better access to power. Over the centuries and across the vast swath of Africa and Eurasia, Islamic religion and politics became quite varied and complex.

A Terrorist Cult

The world's first true terrorists, according to historian Bernard Lewis, were a cult of Islamic heretics known as the Assassins. As a high school student, I read that the Assassins would train a young man in the martial arts, give him a week in palace gardens surrounded by beautiful young women anxious to please, and then send him out on missions to kill the Old Man's enemies. The cannabis extract known as hashish supposedly had something to do with Assassins. That part of the story seemed garbled, and I wasn't so sure about the missions, but the gardens of paradise inspired some wonderful daydreams.

Sad to say, Lewis debunked the whole story, which seems to go back to fables recounted by Marco Polo. Assassins were actually followers of an ascetic warlord and theologian, Hasan-i Sabbah. After joining the Ismailis, a mystical and messianic strain of Shiite Islam, young Hasan visited their Cairo headquarters in 1078. He returned to preach in Persia and, in 1090, acquired a stronghold at Alamut, commanding a narrow valley in the northern mountains. There, he built his band of believers, custodians of circles within circles of sacred mysteries.

Hasan plotted world domination for his brand of the true faith, but he faced very long odds. Ismailis were regarded as evil heretics by most Muslims and their rulers, and were periodically rounded up and slaughtered. On the other hand, that part of the world was run by autocrats who relied on transient personal loyalties of henchmen and notables. Whenever the autocrat died, things fell apart until one of the heirs (or usurpers) gained the upper hand. Hasan and his Assassin successors exploited that weakness by perfecting their eponymous craft.

Their first victim, in 1092, was Nizam al-Mulk, the brains behind the Seljuk dynasty and a fierce anti-heretic. A pious volunteer named Bu Tahir Arrani disguised himself as a Sufi, sidled up to Nizam as he was being carried to the tent of his women, and buried a dagger in his heart. The Seljuk dynasty fragmented, and over the years, many of the more Ismaili-hostile rulers from Syria to Iran fell to Assassin daggers. The executioners were often secret agents who had gained the ruler's trust after years of service, and they showed no remorse or fear once caught.

Often, a threat was enough. Sultan Sanjar awoke one morning in 1119, staring at a dagger stuck in the ground beside his bed. A messenger from Hasan delivered a short note: "Did I not wish the Sultan well, that dagger which was stuck into the hard ground would have been planted in his soft breast." For the rest of his reign, Sanjar appeased the sect. He and many other rulers (including several Christians holding territories captured the Crusaders) sent payments to the Assassins and took it easy on the local Ismailis, and these rulers slept better at night.

Fanatical discipline and loyalty, and inaccessible mountain citadels in northern Persia and Syria, gave the Assassins power far beyond their numbers. Their reputation for systematic terror protected Ismaili enclaves throughout the region and brought revenue to the citadels. A notable exception: in the mid-1200s, the Assassins paid out tribute to the Christian Templars and Hospitallers. Partly, it was the Christians' skill in assaulting mountain citadels and their often hostile relations with the Assassins' enemies. But according to the historian Joinville, the main reason was that the orders' corporate structure immunized them from Assassin terror. If one master was killed, then another who was just as good would replace him immediately; the Assassins would lose a top operative and gain nothing.

In the later 1200s, the Mongols wiped out the Persian Assassins, and the Syrian branch submitted to Baybars, the Mamluk Sultan headquartered in Egypt. Some groups of Ismailis survived, and today, most are followers of the Aga Khan, a very modern Imam whose family has held high positions in the League of Nations and the UN. Fanaticism passed to other branches of the Muslim faith.

Who is a Terrorist? What is a Cult?

Terrorist cults have been much in the news since the SLA, and especially since al-Qaeda's September 11, 2001, attacks in New York and Washington. Things have changed considerably since the days of the Zealots and Assassins, so it seems useful to sort out what cults and terrorism mean in the modern world.

A cult is a small group whose shared beliefs cut it off from the mainstream. (Of course, most such groups reject the epithet.) Some groups, like the Amish, coexist peacefully with the mainstream. A few groups, like the Mormons (or the early Christians, for that matter), started out as cults, but over time, they grew so large and accommodated themselves so well that they became part of mainstream. Cults put their core beliefs ahead of mainstream law, but illegal activity is seldom their reason for existence. Criminal gangs fall on the other side of that fuzzy line: their core activities are illegal, and they are usually less tightly tied to an ideology or a charismatic leader.

Terrorists try to achieve political objectives by threatening opponents' lives. This description could include military threats from powerful countries, but I'll restrict the term to small groups not run by national governments. Criminal gangs also threaten lives, but their motive is to acquire money and respect rather than political objectives. Of course, this line also can get fuzzy.

Insurgents try to oust an established government, or foreign occupiers. Many insurgent groups can fairly be described as terrorists, but they usually prefer to call themselves freedom fighters. Some insurgents reject terror tactics and try to maintain high moral standards of conduct, even toward enemies. Gandhi's campaign against British colonialists in India is the prime example; other examples include the American Revolution and young David's struggle against the Hebrews' first king, Saul.

The history of Hamas illustrates the connections between a cult's moral codes and its product lines, including terror. In 1971, Sheik Ahmed Yassin founded *Mujamah* (Arabic for Congress) in Gaza to provide local services like medical clinics, schools, sports clubs, and mosques. The Israeli government offered tacit support, and revenues mostly came from families using the services and from wealthy outsiders. The moral code involved strict Islamic piety, ethical personal behavior, and political support for an eventual Islamic Palestine state.

Until 1988, the movement was nonviolent, aside from occasional skirmishes with the secular Palestine Liberation Organization (PLO). But as the PLO began to lend support to a violent popular uprising that year, now called the first intifada, the Mujamah leaders worried that their organization would lose out. They founded a secret militia called Hamas. It adopted a more extreme position than the PLO, calling for immediate holy war (jihad) to conquer all of Palestine and Israel.

Despite intense repression (sometimes by the PLO as well as Israeli authorities), Hamas grew into one of the most effective terrorist organizations in history. Relying on donations from Iran, Palestinian expatriates, and wealthy individuals in Saudi Arabia and other parts of the Arab world, Hamas recruited Mujamah clients and other Palestinians, especially young men from Gaza, and instructed them in a strict version of Sunni Islam. It selected a few to participate in deadly attacks, featuring car bombs, roadside mines, and suicide bombings. Hamas took the lead during the second intifada (2000–present). It is responsible for about half of the roughly one thousand Israelis killed so far—some soldiers, but mostly civilian victims of suicide bombers.

Hamas entered uncharted waters when it won an upset victory over the PLO in Palestine's January 2006 elections. No longer a mere cult, Hamas has wavered between taking on government responsibilities and continuing to organize terrorist actions. In June 2007, Hamas ousted the PLO from Gaza, and the PLO clamped down on Hamas activity in the West Bank. Now that it has sole responsibility for Gaza's 1.4 million residents, Hamas must completely revise its tactics and strategy. It needs a new market plan and moral code, but at the time of this writing, the new direction remains unclear.

Classic Anti-terror Tactics

Some cults are harmless or even productive (the American Buddhist programming team, for example), but others impose costs on the rest of us. For example, many Israelis believe that the settlers' movement, a cult of extremists who take land from the Palestinians and require protection from the army, is largely responsible for the second intifada, at incalculable cost in lives and treasure. The U.S. Mafia is more or less indifferent to the mainstream, but it still imposes significant costs: protection money, labor racketeering, and so forth are like a very inefficient tax. The Italian Mafia, most observers agree, is largely responsible for the chronic underperformance of southern Italy. Clearly, it is in society's interest to find effective ways to reduce these costs, and to suppress the most harmful gangs and cults.

What methods are most effective? From the dawn of recorded history, the favored tools have been torture, slaughter, and scorched earth. The Romans were masters of this extreme package of deterrence and incapacitation—in Carthage, Judea, and countless other places, "they made a wasteland and called it peace." The Mongols used slaughter and scorched earth (they didn't care much for torture) to break the Assassins, along with their Sunni opponents. More recently, Syrian dictator Hafez al-Assad dealt with a revolt by the Muslim Brotherhood centered in one of the country's largest cities, Hama. In February 1982, an all-out artillery attack leveled the city, and Syria's best troops, reportedly using poison gas, went after surviving militants. The massacre claimed somewhere between ten thousand and forty thousand lives, most of them bystanders. A quarter of a century later, the city still hasn't recovered, but neither has the Brotherhood nor their Syrian allies.

But this heavy-handed package doesn't always work, and sometimes it backfires. Despite its best efforts, Rome was never able to completely crush the barbarians to the north and east. When they got their chances in 410, 455, and 546 CE, the Visigoths, Vandals, and Ostrogoths sacked Rome, and the Ostrogoths left it a zero population wasteland. The Mings took revenge on the Mongols after a century under the yoke. Turkey's current problems with Kurds and Armenians can be largely traced to heavy-handed treatment almost a century ago.

Torture, slaughter, and scorched earth don't seem to work very well for modern nations. These brutal tactics undermine our own moral system. As a result, military morale sinks, civilian support weakens, and alliances fray. The Vietnam War is surely the textbook example. By comparison, the Iraq war so far (late 2007) has involved less wholesale slaughter and scorching, but more egregious torture, at Abu Ghraib and elsewhere, and overall, has had similar ill effects on American alliances and civilian support.

Moreover, our rule of law (especially since the Nuremberg Trials and the Geneva Conventions) keeps us from being as thorough as the Romans, but halfway measures are often counterproductive. Persecution of minorities boosts radicals, and makes the mainstream less attractive. Normal prison terms help Chicano gangsters, and jihadis, build recruitment networks.

So what other tactics are there? Recently, the U.S. government has offered large cash rewards for apprehension of top terrorists. A $25 million bounty might (or might not) have helped U.S. troops capture Saddam Hussein, but so far, it has not helped in Pakistan's tribal areas where Osama bin Laden and other top al-Qaeda and Taliban leaders are thought to be hiding. A tribesman going for the reward would have to balance mortal danger to himself and family, and a permanent loss of his entire social network, against the possibility of starting a new life of leisure in some distant part of the world. Evidently, it hasn't seemed like a good gamble.

Infiltration is another classic tactic. Israel's intelligence service, Mossad, reportedly penetrated the PLO and the governments of its neighbors; the CIA seemingly has been less effective. The tactic is especially powerful against terrorist groups, for two reasons. A single defection can enable authorities to wipe out lots of terrorists, perhaps including top leaders. And the fear of double agents impairs communication and coordination within the terrorist group, and slows recruitment.

Terror and Anti-terror Tactics Coevolve

Around 1980, the string ran out for the SLA, as well as for the more competent leftist terrorists in the United States and Europe, such as the Weather Underground, the Baader-Meinhof gang, and the Red Brigades. The FBI found more subtle and effective infiltration tactics after J. Edgar Hoover's departure in 1972, and recruitment dried up in prisons (as gangs became more attractive) as well as among middle class youth (with the end of the draft and Vietnam War). Former sympathizers lost their taste for kidnap, robbery, and murder, and lost their belief that society was ripe for revolution. Donations dwindled and these secular cults fizzled out.

The PLO and other secular Palestinian groups stayed alive, but with crumbling moral foundations and market plans. On the other hand, as we've seen, Hamas mushroomed, and so did Hezbollah in Lebanon, and other religious terrorists. It's time to examine the reasons why.

Economist Laurence Iannaccone pointed out that religious groups like Mujamah (the precursor of Hamas) are alternative providers of essential public goods, like education, health care, and emergency assistance. Originally, tribes provided such goods, and in well-functioning modern states, the government assures them. Cults and gangs thrive where governments don't deliver these goods and people have poor mainstream alternatives. Extreme political demands and boycotts disrupt delivery of public goods and so help groups like Hamas expand. Cults also undermine their members' attraction to the mainstream, for example, by discouraging them from acquiring marketable skills. This is the logic behind the Taliban insurgents' efforts to drive the Red Cross and school builders from southern Afghanistan.

Economists Eli Berman and David Laitin take the argument a step further. The key to success in the modern terrorism business is to prevent defection: if the authorities can infiltrate or persuade even one person in the cell to cooperate with them, then the terrorist action will fail. The sacrifices Hamas demands of its recruits—years at religious schools that teach no marketable skills, five prayer sessions each day, and so forth—drives out those individuals most susceptible to defection. As a result, Hamas is better than the secular PLO at screening out Mossad agents and finding suicide bombers who will follow through.

How about the Israeli settler movement? It, too, is dominated by religious fanatics who spend vast amounts of time in prayer. One of its members, Yigal Amir, assassinated Israeli Prime Minister Yitzhak Rabin in 1995, derailing the Mideast's most promising peace initiative. However, since then, Israeli authorities have managed to break up the settlers' most egregious plots. Screening by religious fervor doesn't seem to work as well against home-country authorities, once they recognize the danger.

Terrorists must choose their targets carefully. We saw that the Assassins' narrow focus on the top leader was ineffective against the corporate Crusaders. The same logic, and tough security for the military and top officials, push modern terrorists to target ordinary people. (Rabin was an exception, since he didn't have a successor just as good at achieving his goals.) The terrorists hope that resulting media attention will bring them more donations and recruits from their friends, and weaken the resolve of their opponents. The first part, at least, has worked all too well in the Mideast.

Terrorist cults face an organizational dilemma: tight central control, or a loose network? The first is more natural—cults are sometimes defined as followers of a charismatic leader. The medieval Assassin cult usually had such a leader, and it worked well because his mountain citadel was so hard to attack. Osama Bin Laden and Ayman al-Zawahiry seem to have found mountain refuges on the Afghanistan-Pakistan border, but central control still faded as counter-terrorists successfully targeted the next layer of al-Qaeda's hierarchy. Until he was captured by Turkey in 1999, Abdullah Ocalan ran the Kurdish insurgency (PKK) the way his hero, Lenin, ran the Russian Communist Party. Since then, however, the PKK has become much more decentralized.

Anti-terror tactics have thus pushed terrorists toward loose networks. This brings several advantages, as noted in Chapter 8: flexible response to changing opportunities and threats, and the ability to draw on dispersed resources. Islamic mosques span the globe, and extremists can troll them for donors and recruits. Mosques are open to all believers; unlike the Catholic Church, Islam has no central hierarchy to close the door on people who might give it a bad name.

New Anti-terror Tactics

What new tactics might be effective against modern gang and terrorist networks? More than ever, these organizations need cohesive moral codes and compatible market plans. Anti-terror campaigns will be more effective when they tarnish the codes and disrupt the plans.

Decentralized political and religious movements are especially vulnerable to internal division, to splitting into hostile factions. That has always been the downfall of the militant left. Many medieval wars were among Muslim sects, and competing Christian creeds battled almost nonstop in Europe between 1550 and 1650. Modern anti-terrorists can stoke internal battles by well-timed covert support of minority factions. It's a tricky business, though, and can backfire. Israel's authorities surely regret their attempt to undermine the PLO by supporting Mujamah.

Religious roots can make a group susceptible to moral suasion. Since 2002, Yemen's High Court Judge Hamood Al-Hitar has organized theological debates with captured militants. He asks them to justify attacks on innocent civilians. They cite various passages in the Koran, but none bear close scrutiny. Then Al-Hitar points out numerous passages commanding Muslims not to attack civilians, to respect other religions, and to fight only in self-defense. One of his favorites: "Whoever kills a soul, unless for a soul, or for corruption done in the land—it is as if he had slain all mankind entirely. And, whoever saves one, it is as if he had saved mankind entirely." According to a 2005 report, the judge had released 364 young men who promised to obey the Koran, and none of them had left the country to fight anywhere else. Al Qaeda's top commander in that country was killed in late 2002 on a tip from a reformed prisoner. Yemen has deported foreign militants and shut down extremist madrassas, and has become an "indispensable ally in the war on terror." Similar good results are reported in Indonesia.

Militant morals can also be undermined by satire. A scene in the 2005 film *Paradise Now* shows endless flubbed takes for a would-be suicide bomber's martyr videotape. After seeing that, it would be harder for anyone to take such propaganda seriously. Monty Python films skewer leftist pretensions, and self-righteous Muslim fanatics should be even more vulnerable. A caveat: effective ridicule appeals to the terrorists' potential donors, recruits, and support network. Ridicule that appeals to their enemies, like the infamous Danish newspaper cartoons, is counterproductive.

Similar tactics can help fight youth gangs, and perhaps the Mafia. According to a recent account, a satirical radio broadcast crippled the once-powerful American terrorist cult, the Ku Klux Klan. Respect is vital for these groups, and ridicule is fatal. However, standup comics might find themselves in personal danger if their riffs get too popular. Perhaps convicted gang leaders should be given the choice between maximum-security isolation, or time off for community service on education campaigns that vividly portray gang life as stupid, ugly, and ridiculous.

Jihadis now rely on the Internet to spread their faith and their techniques. It should be an equally effective medium for undermining their moral message and market plans. The medium is ideal for circulating jokes and video clips, and for misdirecting browsers seeking jihadi propaganda. It should be cheap and easy to flood the Internet with counterfeit Web sites that carry counterpropaganda.

U.S. antiterrorists have not yet done a very good job at disrupting terrorists' market plans. Their focus has been on revenue flows through fake Islamic charities. But blocking one channel doesn't do much to stop the flow. As long as donors have lots of money and want it to go to terrorist networks, it will get there somehow. Far more effective is to cut off the supply at its source.

New York Times columnist Thomas Friedman (again, no relation) has repeatedly argued that the best way to do it is with a serious carbon tax. He is probably right. The funds to Islamic terrorists come mainly from the oil revenues flowing to Saudi Arabia, Iran, and other regional oil producers. Demand for oil is extremely inelastic in the short run, and in the long run, a tax that put a floor on the price at the pump would encourage alternative energy production and conservation. So taxes should take money from the Wahhabi and Shiite firebrands and bring it back home.

Likewise, our homegrown gangsters' revenue comes mainly from selling addictive drugs, also extremely demand-inelastic. An anti-drug policy more like the Dutch—legalize, but discourage by heavy taxes and restrictions—would cut off gangs' air supply.

Details matter, and are hard to get just right. To take advantage of the modern world's great strengths—science, pragmatism, adaptability—we should systematically try out different forms of oil and drug taxes and restrictions, figure out what works best, and then do more of it.

In the long run, the mainstream's best defense against hostile cults and gangs is to provide good prospects for social and material advance, and to offer membership in attractive part-time groups that encourage pro-social behavior. But, of course, that's exactly what we should be doing anyway.

Cooling the Earth
Environmental Markets and Morals

Just off New England's coast, the cold, mineral-rich Labrador Current mixes with the warm Gulf Stream above a series of underwater plateaus, called banks, and nurtures a startling variety of marine plants, animals, and birds. Some, like pollock, lobster, and scallops, are quite valuable commercially.

But the real prize was cod, "so thick you can scoop them up in a basket," according to sailors returning from Cabot's famous 1497 voyage. Basque fishermen had discovered the banks decades earlier and kept them secret. By 1550, and for the next two hundred years, more than half the fish consumed in Europe were salt cod, most of them caught in these banks. The proceeds paid for England's first colony in Newfoundland and then the New England colonies, and powered their economies for centuries.

Cod's bounty seemed eternal. The great English biologist, Thomas Huxley, wrote in 1883 that cod fishery was inexhaustible. But by 1991, fishermen like Billy Tyne of Gloucester, Massachusetts had to sail far beyond the banks to fill their boats. Catches were down 80–90 percent from what Billy had seen as a young man, despite (or because of) rapid advances in fishing technology. His search for fish that summer brought him to the middle of the Atlantic Ocean, where his ship, the Andrea Gail, sank in the "Perfect Storm."

Another storm, slower but even more powerful, soon sank cod fishery. The Grand Banks, off Newfoundland, was closed to commercial fishing in 1992, and then the Georges Bank, off New England, in December 1994. Gloucester plunged into economic depression, joining dozens of other Northeast coastal cities and towns. Even now, more than a decade later, most of the young people are gone and recovery is uncertain. That manmade storm must rank among New England's worst environmental, social, and economic disasters.

How could an "inexhaustible" resource just disappear? Afterward, of course, everyone involved blamed someone else: out-of-touch scientists, inept government officials, greedy foreign fishermen, local fishermen, or ignorant consumers. Where does the fault really lie?

This chapter will investigate. It will examine several other episodes where the environment and the economy collide, and will identify the underlying problem,

the tragedy of the commons. The chapter explains how our own species traditionally averted the tragedy, using the moral system. It shows why modern markets and
dysfunctional morals inflame the problem, and threaten our planetary future. But
there is a better way. Reformed markets, supported by more sophisticated morals, have brought some local success, and the combination offers hope for lasting
global solutions.

Anatomy of a Tragedy

"The Tragedy of the Commons" is the title of ecologist Garrett Hardin's famous
1968 article in *Science*. Inspired by game theorists, he identified a variant of
the basic social dilemma as the underlying cause of virtually all environmental problems.

Hardin explains the tragedy by means of a parable. There is a group of herdsmen, and each of them decides how many of his own cows to let graze on a pasture,
the "commons." The individual herdsman enjoys the full benefit of an additional
cow, but he bears only a fraction of the additional grazing costs: less grass available, more trampling of new growth, and so forth. For example, with ten equal
herds, each herdsman bears only a tenth of the cost of an extra cow. Consequently,
each herdsman will keep adding cows far past the point that the additional cost
equals the additional benefit, and the pasture will be ruined by overgrazing.

This sort of social dilemma crops up in all times and places. I grew up in the
San Francisco Bay area, and have fond memories of enjoying fresh Dungeness crab
in late fall. In recent years, the local haul has been good to excellent for the first
two weeks of the season, as large crab boats pile in from further north. But the rest
of the seven-month season is often meager. The personal benefit is clear to being
the first crab catcher to arrive at a good spot. The cost is that, later, it is harder to
catch crabs there, and most of that cost is borne by the other local crabbers. The
result is a minor tragedy: fishermen over-invest in crabbing equipment, unused
except for a few weeks each year, and crab consumers like me have slim pickings
most of the time.

Easter Island witnessed a much more acute tragedy. After first arriving around
900 CE, the island's residents personally enjoyed the benefits of cutting another
tree (or raising another child), but shared the cost with everyone else. Around 1600,
the island's last tree was felled, while soil eroded and wildlife vanished. The human
population crashed, from perhaps as many as thirty thousand. In 1774, Captain
Cook found a few thousand survivors, "small, lean, timid, and miserable."

To cite a larger example, many anthropologists believe that an opening of the
Canadian ice sheet thirteen thousand years ago allowed Clovis big game hunters to
expand in a wave that swept through the Americas in a few centuries, and caused
the extinction of mammoths, horses, giant sloths, and dozens of other large mammals. Similarly, humans with advanced hunting skills first arrived at the vast commons now called Australia about thirty-five thousand years ago, and all sorts of
big game went extinct there over the next few centuries. The cost of killing the last

breeding stock in an area is shared by all future residents, but the current hunters monopolize the benefits.

Moral Management

Other animals, herbivores as well as carnivores, face the same problem. It is in an individual animal's interest to exploit a depletable resource far past the point that is optimal for her species.

As Hardin notes, there are ways to cope with the tragedy, or in less poetic language, to more efficiently manage common pool resources. Nature's main device is territoriality. That is, creatures restrict access to the common pool, or, in economic jargon, they privatize it. For example, an adult male red-tailed deer will stake out a grazing area and threaten other males who trespass, or who show an interest in the local females. Likewise, prides of lions drive off intruders who try to hunt in their area. Aquarium owners are warned about territorial fish such as groupers and seahorses that will attack new arrivals.

The human moral system evolved to cope with social dilemmas of all sorts, including the tragedy of the commons. As discussed in Chapter 2, as our ancestors adopted more sedentary lifestyles, their moral codes began to include territoriality, defending against outsiders. For example, in Akira Kurosawa's film *Seven Samurai* (1954), villager Katsushiro recruits samurai warriors to protect his poor village against bandits. Audiences everywhere are thrilled to see samurai leader Kambei Shimada rally the villagers and outwit and pick off the bandits one by one.

So humans have a traditional way to escape the tragedy. A local group takes control of the common pool resource and evolves a moral code, finely tuned to local circumstances, for excluding outsiders, sharing the resource, and contributing to its maintenance. Cultures that fail to do so fall apart, and cultures that succeed are the ones that last—this seems to be the main lesson of Jared Diamond's 2005 book *Collapse*. For example, the descendents of the Clovis hunters eventually evolved cultures that, over the next ten thousand years, efficiently managed the remaining North American grazing animals, such as bison and caribou.

A wonderful example concerns rice farmers on the other side of the planet. Bali's rice terraces rise in stair steps from white sand beaches toward ten thousand-foot volcanic peaks. Tourists from around the world are drawn to the equatorial island paradise, and are struck by the beautiful landscapes and by the harmonious culture. Both have the same source—a moral code that has sustained Bali's people for many centuries.

The Balinese call their system *Agama Tirtha*, the religion of holy water. Rivers rush down the mountainside and hit diversion dams or weirs, and the water then enters a network of tunnels and canals. Each farm family has a small shrine at the top of their terraces, at the gate of the local irrigation canal. The farmers along each canal belong to a *subak*, an organization with its own local temple. Each *subak* has fraternal relationships with the other *subaks* drawing on the same weir, and each pays homage to those upstream. Religious ceremonies focus on the exchange and mixing of waters from upstream and downstream *subaks*, and they promote close ties throughout the watershed. As part of their religious duties, the higher priests adjudicate conflicting claims among *subaks* and larger units, for example, whether to develop a new spring or to dig a new water tunnel. The *subaks* and larger units stagger planting cycles to balance water use within the watershed, and they control pests by coordinating fallow times, burning, and flooding.

As part of the "green revolution," the Asian Development Bank launched the Bali Irrigation Project in 1979. Outside experts, who knew nothing about Bali's water temple system and its unique artificial ecology, took over about 10 percent of the island's *subaks* and began continuous rice cultivation. Within five years, an "explosion of pests and diseases" and water shortages during the dry season had caused major crop failures, and the usual remedies only created dangerous pesticide pollution. By 1988, the World Bank acknowledged the problems and its 1997 final report celebrates working with the water temple system instead of trying to impose a standard structure.

Markets Corrode Morals

Moral management worked well in Bali as the *Agama Tirtha* religion came to embrace entire watersheds, and eventually, the whole island. At that point, all costs and benefits of water management and pest control were contained within the moral order, and the commons tragedy evaporated.

When farmers produce for distant markets, however, the tragedy can easily recur. The moral regulation breaks down when individual farmers receive the revenues while the costs are still shared by their neighbors.

A prime example begins with the "sod busters" who first farmed North America's Great Plains in the late 1800s. Most of them had to mortgage the property to purchase machinery and seed, and later fertilizers and pesticides. To meet payments, every year they needed to sell wheat and other cash crops in the national and international markets. The farmers had little scope for worrying about longer term costs, such as depleted soil and falling water tables—the price signals from global markets drowned out these faint local signals.

In the early 1930s, a drought triggered rapid desertification called the Dust Bowl. Remaining topsoil dried up and blew away, destroying crops hundreds of miles downwind. Bankruptcies spread, and the region has never recovered its population and vitality.

Today things are very different, yet oddly similar. Corporate farms draw down a common pool resource called the Ogallala Aquifer—a vast underground lake stretching from north of Nebraska down through the Texas panhandle, filled thousands of years ago. Even a huge corporation bears only a tiny fraction of the cost when it depletes the aquifer, and it gains the entire benefit. On present trends, the aquifer will run dry in a few decades and decimate the regional economy.

The tragedy strikes at sea as well as on land. Market imperatives penetrated even the deep commons, the great banks of the northwest Atlantic. Steam powered fishing boats allowed their owners to sell more fish at lower cost. Other fishermen had to copy, or find an even cheaper way, or retire. Then came otter trawls, large nets that stayed open by being dragged across the sea floor. Other waves of inno-vation swept through the fishing fleets, such as rock hoppers to cope with rocky floors, and drag-chains to flush out the fish. Eventually fishermen needed onboard fish processing and freezing facilities to remain competitive.

By the late 1960s, factory trawlers dragged nets the size of several football fields across the underwater plateaus, and turned sea gardens into sea desert. The young cod had nowhere to grow, and sonar (first developed in World War II) tracked down the dwindling schools of adults. Prices rose as cod became scarcer, and higher prices intensified the hunt—all forces that Huxley failed to foresee.

Could territoriality prevent tragedy? The Basques used secrecy to exclude outsiders, but that only lasted until the great age of exploration began around 1500. Four-and-a-half centuries later, Iceland was the first to expand its territorial waters, from three miles from shore to four in 1950, to twelve miles in 1958, and to fifty miles in 1972. Victory in three "cod wars" enabled Iceland to enforce the new boundaries, and in 1976, most countries, including the United States and Canada, declared a two hundred mile limit.

Many observers thought the problem was solved. Surely, national control would now internalize the costs, preserve the offshore resources, and halt the tragedy of the commons. Governments could harness science and technology to keep the fishing industry healthy over the long term, to the benefit of all. But it didn't work out that way, for reasons that will gradually become apparent.

The Great Green Crusade

Let's look at a larger story unfolding about the same time, and begin with toxic pesticides. The benefit to a farmer of spraying poison is obvious: he sees dead bugs and his crops are saved for the harvest. The costs are less obvious and are mostly borne by others: (a) the surviving insects evolve greater pesticide resistance; (b) the pesticides kill insect-eating creatures, allowing pests to multiply later; and (c) pesticides accumulate in the crops, soil, rivers, and oceans, imperiling the health of wildlife and ourselves. As usual, the dispersion of costs leads to overuse and ineffi-cient pollution. The kicker is that effects (a) and (b) create an accelerating demand for pesticides, and the chemical industry acquires a vested interest in expanding demand yet further for some of its most profitable products.

At first, Rachel Carson's 1962 book *Silent Spring* seemed quixotic in so strongly criticizing a very powerful industry, but the book gave clear insight into the new science of ecology. Even more important, it evoked a moral obligation to protect the environment for its own sake and for the health of our children. *Silent Spring* was a surprise best seller, and the political response was huge. Environmentalism became a moral crusade, one of the great causes of the 1960s and beyond. Nongov-ernmental organizations mushroomed, such as the Sierra Club and Greenpeace, and Earth Day gained semi-official (or even official) status around the world.

Like the original Crusades a thousand years ago, the environmental move-ment enjoyed initial success. The chemical industry was taken by surprise and was overwhelmed. Most industrialized countries passed laws banning the worst toxic chemicals. Other new laws curbed air and water pollution. New agencies such as the U.S. Environmental Protection Agency set standards and monitored compliance.

By 1972, the leading pesticide, DDT, was banned in the United States, and bird populations soon began to recover. For example, as a student in the early 1970s, I seldom saw any pelicans in coastal Santa Cruz, but since returning in the late 1980s, I frequently see dozens, or even hundreds, of brown pelicans dive-bombing the anchovies just beyond the surf line.

Air and water quality improved impressively in the United States and Western Europe during the 1970s and 1980s. Even in Los Angeles, the air is far better today than in the 1960s. Recycling programs and anti-litter campaigns have spread across the industrialized world. Large new swaths of land are preserved as wilderness, and many cities have new green belts. The list of environmental improvements is long and varied.

The green crusade took the high moral ground. Its leaders proposed environment-friendly laws, and masses of foot soldiers wrote letters of support and packed public hearings. Supporters donated generously, time as well as money. They all saw themselves as creating a legacy for generations as yet unborn, fighting the good fight against evil corporations. The battle seemed to go their way in the 1970s as they pushed through lots of legislation, and the new laws gave them leverage in the 1980s and beyond, as they filed class-action lawsuits.

Industry Strikes Back

Like the original Crusaders, the green movement didn't really understand its sworn enemy. In the market system, economic interests have large stakes in the political process. The value to an industry of favorable law or regulatory decision or legal ruling is often in the hundreds of millions of dollars, and occasionally it is in the tens of billions. Economic logic dictates that firms will spend up to that amount to gain a favorable decision.

Now, as always, "money is the mother's milk of politics." Well-funded industry groups can wear down watchdog agencies by litigation and lobbying. They can use strategic campaign contributions to sponsor friendly politicians, and get former employees and consultants appointed as the top regulators.

More imaginatively, industry groups threatened by environmental regulations can learn from Rachel Carson. They, too, can try to harness moral outrage and scientific research to meet their goals. Consider, for example, the "sagebrush rebellion" of the late 1970s, a populist campaign funded by the mining, oil, timber, and grazing industries in Nevada and nearby states. Under pressure from environmentalists, the federal Bureau of Land Management (BLM) began in the early 1970s to raise grazing and logging fees, and to restrict access to the more fragile habitats. The foot soldiers in the rebellion—ranchers with property adjoining the vast BLM tracts—demanded a rollback of rules and a transfer of the lands to state or county control, or privatization. The rhetoric was quite heated, and likened the BLM to communist commissars or to King George's minions. The sagebrush rebels formed a core constituency for Ronald Reagan, and helped him win the 1980 Republican nomination, and then the White House.

Michael Crichton's thriller *State Of Fear* is a more recent example of fighting moral fire with fire. The novel's scientist hero battles evil environmentalists and debunks their fear campaigns on climate change. We'll take our own look at the issue later in the chapter.

Scientific research is itself a major front in the battle. For the last hundred years or so, governments in the advanced industrialized countries have funded basic scientific research at universities. The political goal is to catalyze new products and industries that will increase national wealth and prestige. In recent decades, however, government finances have weakened, and a larger share of funding now comes from industry.

Industry has always funded research that translates fundamental science into commercial products; indeed, that is exactly what the biotechnology and computer hardware and software industries do in my own region. Some corporations and foundations also fund research for political purposes. The tobacco industry, for example, sponsored researchers who raised doubts as to whether cigarette smoking really caused cancer; such work delayed consensus for decades. As we'll see shortly, something very similar happened on crucial environmental issues such as climate change.

Coda for Cod

Scientific uncertainty and self-interested skepticism helped kill New England's cod industry. In 1976, the United States and Canada established national control over the offshore banks. Scientists assessed the fish populations, while regulatory agencies set total allowable catches (TACs), allocated the rights among fishermen, and monitored compliance. The system was supposed to maximize the economic yield, so that fish and fishermen could live happily ever after. Yet, in less than twenty years, the cod fishing industry was dead, and cod almost went extinct.

The fatal dynamics began with uncertainty. Underfunded researchers, relying largely on industry's reports of cod catches, put wide bands of possible error around their estimates of the live population. For example, in 1977, U.S. scientists estimated that a TAC of fifteen thousand tons would allow the Georges Bank cod population to sustain itself. Industry advocates argued that the data could justify a TAC of twenty-four thousand tons. The regulators set the TAC at twenty thousand tons, and an "emergency amendment" late in the fishing season raised the TAC about 10 percent. The actual catch was probably considerably higher due to "recreational" fishing, as well as underreported catches and misreported species counts. Nevertheless, under industry pressure, the TAC was set even higher the next year. From then on, regulations and quotas were constantly juggled in response to political pressure and overly optimistic interpretations of the data.

Canada's dynamics were even worse. Hoping that the new two hundred-mile limit would bring prosperity to her impoverished maritime provinces, the Canadian government heavily subsidized factory trawlers and onshore fish processing facilities. The bureaucrats then had a short-term interest in seeing the facilities used, and their pressure (combined with pressure from industry) may have pushed up scientific estimates of the fish population. These pressures certainly biased the TAC and allowed the industry to continue to destroy fish habitat with outsize trawling nets. Also, U.S. and Canadian authorities squabbled over management of banks that lay partly in each other's territory.

As fish populations declined in the late 1980s, public interest groups and scientists filed lawsuits in the United States and Canada, demanding more realistic measures to protect the fish populations. Industry leaders dug in their heels and delayed decisive action. Perhaps they truly believed the more optimistic reports, perhaps they suffered from self-serving bias, or perhaps they were planning early retirement and wanted to leave on a prosperous note. Whatever the reasons, they kept the bureaucracy from lowering the TACs as fast as necessary. Cod populations collapsed in the early 1990s, and so did the fishing industry.

Theories of the Long Run

The point should now be clear. Environmentalists were naïve to believe that a moral crusade will, by itself, secure a sound and durable environmental policy. Laws may be passed and bureaucracies built, but inevitably, they will be eroded when they conflict with market imperatives.

What are the long-run consequences? An optimistic theory is based on the graph of national environmental quality against average family income. The U-shaped relationship is called the environmental Kuznets curve. It shows that the environment is in pretty good shape in most of the world's poorest and most isolated countries, such as Bhutan. Environmental quality falls sharply as we move to poor countries in early stages of industrialization, but it begins to move up again as we move to wealthier countries, and becomes quite good for the wealthiest. Some economists conclude that greater prosperity automatically creates a greater demand for a healthy environment, and eventually, the whole world will clean up as it becomes richer.

There is also a pessimistic theory, called the race to the bottom or the pollution haven hypothesis. The key here is international trade. When a country enforces stricter environmental controls, it raises the costs of manufacturing, especially for the industries that generate more pollution, so these industries export less and face more competition from imports. Freer trade then may shift pollution-intensive industries to poorer countries, more than offsetting the pollution decrease in richer countries. Alternatively, competition for export industries could lead to laxer environmental standards across the board.

Economists have not yet reached consensus on either theory; there are many countervailing trends and the evidence is ambiguous. In my opinion, the long-run outcome is not yet determined. Rather, it depends on the policies that governments will adopt during the next decade as they respond to pressures from industry and from green interest groups.

Marrying Markets to Morals

There is another way to look at environmental problems. The tragedy of the commons can be seen as the result of missing markets. The herdsman didn't pay the full cost of grazing the extra cow because of a missing market: access to the meadow. If there were a competitive grazing fee that reflected the full cost, then there would be no overgrazing. In the market-oriented modern world, often the best way to solve environmental problems is to build the missing markets, and to buttress them with appropriate moral codes.

Here is an example of success. Halibut, some over two hundred pounds, still abound in the waters of southeastern Alaska. Seasonal limits prevented over-fishing until the 1960s, when more and more fishing boats began to enter at the beginning of the season. The resulting "derby" got much worse than among San Francisco Bay area crabbers. As Alaskan fisherman Arne Fuglvog recounts, "In the derby days we would set as much gear as possible because we would only have twenty-four or forty-eight hours to fish. And a lot of times, you didn't get all of your gear back, especially if the weather was really bad. So there'd be all of this lost gear on the bottom, ghost fishing, and catching and killing millions of pounds of fish. There was an unlimited number of vessels, all trying to race and catch as much fish as possible in this set amount of time. We knew we only had one, maybe two shots at it, to make our entire living."

In the late 1980s, local fishermen, environmentalists, and officials agreed on a market system that solved the problem. Based on estimates of the current halibut population, scientists set an overall limit to the allowable catch that season. Shares of that limit, called ITQs (Individual Transferable Quotas), were awarded to people who had historically fished in those waters. The ITQ holder can catch the fish himself, or rent or sell his ITQ to the highest bidder. The usual market magic should put the ITQs into the most efficient hands. Fuglvog explains, "Under the present ITQ system, we have an 8-month season. We can choose when we go out and fish. We can go when the prices are high. We can work it around our crew schedule, our family schedule. We fish totally different now. I do think it's true that ITQs have fostered better stewardship. And one of the main reasons is that we do own part of the resource. We want to keep the resource healthy."

The ITQ market works with the moral system, not against it. Enforcement is aided by peer monitoring: it is in the interest of law abiding fishermen to watch out for violators and to report them. A fisherman who needs to increase his fish quota to cover fixed costs, or who just wants to expand, no longer must hire a lobbyist or a professional expert witness. Instead of trying to bend the political process or the legal system, he can simply go on the open market and purchase the ITQs he wants. Likewise, discouraged fishermen can simply sell their ITQs and probably end up with more money than they could expect to get by lobbying for a government subsidy. ITQ markets are now under development for fishing in the Gulf of Mexico and elsewhere.

Of greater national importance, in 1990, Congress and the first President Bush introduced the Acid Rain Trading Program for sulfur dioxide (SO_2). The science was pretty clear by then. Coal-fired electricity generating plants produced this air pollutant, which could lead to high concentrations of sulfuric acid in lakes and streams hundreds of miles downwind, killing off fish and other wildlife, and endangering human health. The trading program puts a national limit or "cap" on SO_2 emissions each year—about ten million tons in 2001, for example—and doles out pieces of the cap, called "allowances," to every generating plant. The EPA measures emissions from each plant, and the owner must have enough allowances to cover the emissions. Extra allowances may be saved for next year or sold to other plants that fall short. Plants that can't come up with enough allowances must pay hefty fines and get fewer allowances the next year.

So far this "cap-and-trade" program is a great success. Overall SO_2 emissions are already about 40 percent below 1980 levels, and even more at the Ohio valley plants that were the biggest polluters. The lakes and streams seem well under way to recovery. The economic, bureaucratic, legal, and political costs are quite low—50 to 80 percent lower than those incurred under traditional "command-and-control" programs, according to estimates reported by the EPA. Congressional hearings were held a few years ago on a program to extend the cap-and-trade method to the other major regional air pollutants, nitrogen oxides and mercury, and to lower the SO_2 caps quite a bit further. It seems likely that such a program will eventually become law and will work well.

Greenhouse Gas Markets

Could the market approach also solve the world's biggest and most contentious environmental problem—global climate change? The problem arises from three factors: (a) carbon dioxide, methane, and other greenhouse gasses (GHGs) trap solar energy and warm our planet's surface; (b) the atmospheric concentration of GHGs has risen dramatically since the beginning of the Industrial Revolution, and especially in the last thirty years; and (c) current and projected future concentrations of GHGs threaten to warm the globe, make rainfall more erratic, and melt icepacks and raise sea levels, all of which would disrupt the world's environment and economy.

But climate science is notoriously complex, and doesn't allow controlled experiments. It leaves a lot of room for uncertainty and self-interested skepticism. A few of the largest industries—oil, cars, and coal—would probably bear a disproportionate share of the costs of reducing GHGs. It should come as no surprise, then, that Exxon and other industry leaders funded think tanks and researchers who argued that the oceans might absorb excess GHGs, or that there might be natural causes for observed changes. One important puzzle—that average temperatures recorded in the lower atmosphere didn't seem to be rising in parallel to average surface temperatures—was solved only in the summer of 2005 when researchers identified incorrect adjustments of the atmosphere data.

Now, however, there is a solid consensus that human activity is raising global levels of GHG to such an extent that it will significantly change the global climate.

But how much? Will the changes be comparable to those seen in recent centuries, or will they be catastrophes of Biblical proportions? Science can't yet say.

For greenhouse gases, the entire planet is a single commons. Since we live in a world of many nations, Garrett Hardin's logic shows that we are in deep trouble. Economist Scott Barrett first worked out the math (and game theory) in a simplified setting with symmetric nations, and came to the dismal conclusion that pursuit of national self-interest will lead to only a tiny fraction of optimal GHG reduction.

Of course, nations differ in their vulnerability to climate change—much of the Netherlands and Bangladesh and some Pacific islands might be wiped off the map, while Russia and Canada might almost break even—and on their costs of reducing GHGs. For example, China and India have lots of primitive coal-fired power plants and, by modernizing, they could reduce GHG emissions much more cheaply than countries like Japan or the Netherlands.

It might seem that such asymmetric benefits and costs make bargaining even more difficult. But economist Matt McGinty remembered Ricardo's lesson that diversity increases the gains from trade. What if firms could trade GHG allowances internationally as well as domestically? McGinty worked out the math and reached a much happier conclusion: self-interested countries with realistic distributions of costs and benefits would have the incentive to form a large coalition, agree on a cap, and trade allowances. This could provide more than half of the potential gains from full cooperation.

If there were a single world government, or if national governments cared more about the good of the planet than about their own economies, then an even better solution would be a uniform tax on GHG emissions (mainly on carbon) that reflected the costs to the global commons. However, serious new problems would arise from a carbon tax that gradually ratchets up, or that differs across countries, or that is not fully enforced in some places. So a global carbon tax strikes me as unrealistic in today's world.

So much for theory. What is actually happening? The first serious attempt to deal with the problem, the 1997 Kyoto Protocol, called for industrialized nations to roll back GHG emissions to about 95 percent of their 1990 levels. The goal is a bit arbitrary, and not related to estimated costs or benefits. More importantly, it doesn't apply to the fastest growing countries, such as China and India, and the United States refused to join. (Australia finally joined following her November 2007 elections, but at least one of the original joiners, Canada, now seems unlikely to meet its obligations.) As a result, climate change is a bigger problem now than in 1997.

If nothing else, the Kyoto Protocol has been a valuable learning experience. It spurred research, debate, and the first markets for trading carbon allowances. European nations are bound by their Kyoto limits, and their companies can trade allowances in the European Emissions Trading Scheme (ETS). Prices rose gradually and erratically after the ETS opened in 2004, but crashed in early 2006, when the word leaked out that the initial allocations had been far too generous. ETS trading recovered for later year allowances, and total trading volume reached about $30 billion in 2006. California passed its own GHG regulations in late 2007, and cap-and-trade markets are planned for 2009. Several other states are considering similar laws.

Recent reaction from industry has been remarkably positive. Economist Michael Porter once argued that environmental regulations induce efficiency and innovation, and make an industry more competitive. This hypothesis is far too sweeping, but it is true that some companies can profit from cleaning up the environment, and that those who move first have an advantage. Since 2004, the corporate giant GE has focused on making money from products like wind turbines and fuel-efficient jet engines, and lobbied for national and international environmental standards. Green startup companies are now the darlings of Silicon Valley VCs—as I write this section, Google announced it was putting up $200 million in venture capital to develop sources of renewable energy cheaper than coal. The banking industry recently figured out that that GHG allowances could become the world's largest commodities market, and they would like to launch the market sooner rather than later.

Firms in the energy industries realize that uniform national (or international) rules are less costly than a patchwork of individual state and local rules. Another inducement: initial allocations of cap-and-trade allowances should be worth something like $40 billion in the United States, and the power companies want to get them for free. If they drag their feet, they might end up having to buy them at auction, or face a carbon tax. As a result, even traditionalists like Exxon and Duke Energy no longer actively oppose doing something about climate change. Now they too are looking for ways to profit from going green.

The stars have never been better aligned for a global trading of GHG allowances. However, the crucial next step—assigning initial allowances—is quite tricky, for moral and economic, as well as technical, reasons. A larger initial allowance is a prize worth billions of dollars to most countries, so, as with the cod TAC in the late 1970s, everyone will look for ways to get more. Bargaining is likely to take the form of dueling approaches to fairness. Countries like China and India will argue that fair means allocations proportional to population, while countries like Russia will argue that it is fairer to set allocations proportional to historical emission levels. To break the bargaining logjam, one should perhaps take a closer look at McGinty's coalition calculations, and then reverse-engineer an appealing moral rule that assigns allowances that support the best feasible coalition. Once a sufficiently large coalition stabilizes, it could impose carbon import taxes that give the holdout countries the incentive to join.

Here's the bottom line: environmental problems are now too pervasive to be dealt with solely by local morals or traditional markets. We need well-engineered replacements for the missing markets, supported by a pragmatic moral code insisting on a healthy planet for our grandchildren.

Future Morals and Markets
Can This Marriage Be Saved?

For millennia, the Persian Gulf oasis of Al Qatif was famous for its date palms and shrimp, and its marketplace, the *suq*. Now a Saudi Arabian oil boom city of 500 thousand people, Al Qatif made international headlines in late 2007 when a government-backed religious court there sentenced a young woman to two hundred lashes and six months in jail.

Her crime? She was abducted from a car driven by an ex-boyfriend, and gang raped by seven men. The twenty-year-old victim said that she had just been trying to recover a photo she gave the ex-boyfriend, whom she knew only from secret phone conversations years earlier. She thought the rapists' motive was to ruin her recent marriage and her reputation. She also said that once the word got out, her own brother attacked and tried to kill her.

The Saudi court punished the young woman to uphold an ancient code of honor. The code holds that any suggestion of extramarital sex, even just being in a car with an ex-boyfriend, defiles a woman and her entire family. The remedy is often death. As many as five thousand women are killed each year in the name of family honor, most of them in rural parts of Pakistan, Egypt, Jordan, and Iran, but some in other parts of the world such as Brazil and Italy. A 1980 PBS docudrama on the honor killing of a Saudi princess, ordered by her grandfather, provoked serious diplomatic crisis.

Perhaps you are shocked that anyone—much less a grandfather or brother— would want to murder a harmless young woman. How can any moral code condone such behavior, much less make it mandatory?

Then again, our own mainstream morality can seem shocking to outsiders, and sometimes even to our own young people. How can we condone breaking up a family over mere personal differences? How can we tolerate a vast and widening gulf between rich and poor? How can we drive so many other species to extinction?

Here's the underlying question: what sort of morals *should* we want? For that matter, what sort of markets should we try to build? This chapter will nibble on these big questions.

Origins of Honor

Suppose that, as you walked down a narrow hallway, some guy bumped you and called you an asshole. Would your blood boil? Psychologist Richard Nisbett and three colleagues showed that that is much more likely if you are male American who grew up in the South. In their experiment, following the insult, Southern men were less inclined to make room for the next person walking down the hall. Compared to Southern men who were not insulted, they also tended to talk tougher and to call for more violence in a story completion exercise. Their blood testosterone and cortisol levels rose dramatically, indicating that they were physically primed for aggression. By contrast, the insult had no detectable effect on men from the northern United States.

What causes such different emotional (and physical) responses to an insult? The experimenters are convinced that it is different moral codes. Strict honor codes persist in Southern states, but lie outside mainstream in the rest of the country. For a man, honor means a personal reputation for bravery and for defending his in-group against insults and threats, and implies that he can enforce his will on others. For a woman, it means a reputation for chastity.

Maintaining honor is paramount. One observer of Arab culture writes, "If honor so demands, lying and cheating may become absolute imperatives," and "Whoever feels dishonored cannot be talked out of it or reasoned with. Shame sears the soul, and it has to be wiped out and avenged in a public way that all can witness and appreciate. No cost is too great for this end"—even if that means putting yourself in mortal danger, or killing your sister or granddaughter.

Honor codes, and honor killings, go back long before Islam began, possibly to early herdsmen in the hills beyond Mesopotamia. As noted in Chapter 1, herdsmen must maintain a reputation for vengeful behavior, individually and as members of a group. Rustlers can take a herdsman's entire wealth in a single raid, or chip away at it with nighttime theft. They pick on those they perceive as most vulnerable, and are deterred by those with highest honor.

Homer's *Iliad* and *Odyssey* are tales of honor, beginning with Helen's abduction to Troy and ending with Odysseus' slaughter of dozens of suitors besieging his faithful wife Penelope. Variants of honor codes governed noble Romans, medieval knights, the Mongol hordes, and, after the reintroduction of horses to North America in the 1500s, Plains Indian tribes. Mutant honor codes still govern Chicano street gangs, as noted in Chapter 10. The logic is the same as for herdsmen: if you live outside the law (or above it), then lesser honor means greater vulnerability to attack.

When Moral Codes Collide

Other groups have prospered with kinder, gentler moral codes, which may go all the way back to the first humans. The "fat Venus" figurines and other Upper Paleolithic artifacts found throughout western Eurasia, for example, hardly suggest a female chastity fetish. Nor does Uruk's worship of Inanna/Ishtar, a goddess famous for her torrid affairs. Greek merchants, if not their rulers, tended to be tolerant and pragmatic, and such dis-honorable virtues were apparently widespread among residents of ancient and medieval cities.

Chapter 3 examined how, in recent centuries, bourgeois moral codes spread over the modernizing world. Truthfulness and tolerance, and working hard and playing by the rules, paid off as the rule of law took hold. The old rules of honor withered. For example, in the early 1800s, dueling was outlawed and became unfashionable in the modernizing countries, and honor killings declined in Corsica even before 1800. Honor codes softened and changed, even in the military. Nowadays, the U.S. Navy and Marines still list honor, courage, and commitment as their core values, but they define honor not in terms of insult and vengeance, but rather with modest imperatives like "Deal honestly and truthfully with others," and "Abide by an uncompromising code of integrity, taking responsibility for our actions and keeping our word."

The rise of bourgeois virtues, however, has neither been smooth nor universal. We saw earlier how Portugal's vibrant and tolerant new culture of the 1400s was squeezed by Spain in the 1500s. New World plunder gave Spain the luxury of retaining an antimodern honor culture, and of financing religious fanatics at home and halfway around the world.

The recent court decision in Saudi Arabia is a symptom of the Spanish syndrome. The Kingdom enjoys a stream of unearned wealth that would make Phillip II jealous. To maintain power, the Saudi Royals don't need a productive populace—they just need to deflect challenges to their control of vast oil revenues. It helps to have the backing of the most fanatical religious groups, such as followers of the puritanical and intolerant eighteenth-century Sunni cleric Ibn Abdul Wahhab, and the Royals have always been very generous in financing Wahhabi preachers overseas as well as at home. The city of Al Qatif has modern cars and roads, but its Wahhabi-dominated courts are medieval.

Chapter 4 began by recounting moral outrage at modernity: Carlyle, among others, seemed concerned mainly about the loss of honor. The culture clash really began much earlier, perhaps as far back as Uruk. The hill country shepherds often see moral decadence in the cosmopolitan city dwellers, who, in turn, see the country folk as ignorant and superstitious. Many of history's great conquerors, including Caliph Umar (581–644 CE) and Genghis Khan (1162–1227 CE), came from herdsmen tribes and launched cleansing missions. After such a conquest, the culture of honor takes top place for a while.

Three episodes in the late twentieth century echo the same theme. China's cultural revolution (1966–76) was supposed to sweep away bourgeois thinking and to purify the Maoist creed, and Cambodia's genocidal Khmer Rouge regime (1975–79) had the same goal. The siege of Sarajevo (1992–96) was much smaller scale (about ten thousand dead rather than millions), but it, too, was honor-driven. The Serb nationalists in the surrounding mountains wanted to ethnically cleanse a cosmopolitan enclave.

Noxious Nostalgia

We all have a natural tendency to regard morals as absolute and unchanging—it can make you queasy to think hard about changing your views on what is right and what is wrong. Sometimes contemporary morals are obviously out of joint, and then it is comforting to think that moral systems of the past worked better. Fundamentalists of all stripes go a step further and demand that we return to an older moral code.

But in all times and places, there has been a gap between the prescribed proper behavior and actual behavior—that's the way the moral system works. And, as we saw in Chapter 1, codes always evolve. As conditions change, believers deemphasize some injunctions and expand on others. Not even fundamentalist creeds are exact replicas of the past. Christian fundamentalists must reinterpret what the Bible says, for example, to condemn the sale of "morning-after" pills. Suicide bombers targeting civilians stretch, or overstretch, historic Islamic doctrine.

Does awareness of a code's evolution weaken its hold? Do we become less moral and more opportunistic? That, I think, is a fear that drives fundamentalism. It has a grain of truth, in that truly fanatic enforcement of moral codes is hard to reconcile with awareness of their changing contents. But normal adherence to codes, and normal enforcement, should not be affected, and greater awareness may bring a side benefit.

An analogy may help make the point. Biologists and psychologists know more than most of us about the origins and evolution of human sexuality. Such awareness doesn't kill romance or long-term relationships for them, or make sex any less pleasurable. Indeed, as a side benefit, awareness may help overcome morbid fetishes.

Likewise, it feels good to most people to follow the prevailing moral code, and to encourage others to do so. Knowing the evolutionary basis of morals should make us even prouder of our moral accomplishments, and of the bonds of love and friendship that we are able to forge. The viability of a moral code comes from its emotional resonance (for internal enforcement), from the sanctions and rewards it inspires (for external enforcement), and from the productivity it generates (for spreading adherence). It doesn't come from ignorance.

Is Religion the Problem?

This book hasn't said much about religion, despite its strong connections to morals. The topic is just too big and complicated for a satisfactory treatment here—it would require an entire book, or maybe a library, and surely a different author. However, in *The God Delusion*, Richard Dawkins tried his best to kill off religion, which he blames for war and a variety of psychological ills. Another 2006 book by another leading evolutionist, Daniel Dennett, has the same thrust.

Are these authors right? Should we try to improve our moral codes by getting rid of religion? Let me offer a few skeptical words on that question before moving on.

Religion is deeply rooted in the human psyche. As evolved social creatures, we automatically intuit intentions behind the actions we observe. Our "theory of mind" modules work overtime, even when individuals are not physically present, and so notions like "soul" or "spirit" come to us naturally. We are primed to search for order and meaning in the world. We observe, for example, winter storms and spring flowers every year, and welcome explanations involving unseen agents called gods.

Equally important, group cohesion is enhanced by shared beliefs about the proper way to behave, and such beliefs are reinforced by stories about their divine origins. For example, the traditional Hopi lifestyle (closely related to the Chaco Canyon civilization mentioned in Chapter 2) centers on growing and storing corn. The original underground storage chamber, called a kiva, became a religious object, sort of an umbilicus to the ancestral world. Religious practice gave transcendent meaning to the intrinsically boring activities of maintaining good storage facilities. Or, to take another example, Jewish kosher laws are obeyed because of God's commands, but they spread partly because they promoted health and good hygiene, and partly because they helped a dispersed people maintain a separate identity. The point is that religious practice can help the group survive and prosper.

I see no reason why these insights should lead us away from religion. We are adapted for it, and the danger comes not from religion as such, but from fanaticism. Nazis, ultra-Maoists, Tamil Tigers, Serbian hardliners and other secular in-groups have launched savage wars of ideology and poisoned young psyches. They are no better, and no worse, than Islamic jihadis, or Hindu fundis, or ultra-orthodox Israeli settlers.

What Sort of Morals *Should* We Want?

The real problem with honor-based moral codes is their relative nature. My in-group gains honor if men in your group submit to our will. We gain if you bow down to us and, if you won't, we gain by killing your men and taking your women. In short, we gain honor by dishonoring your group. So, if we succeed, your group licks its wounds and plots revenge, and my group has to defend itself. That diverts society's attention (and resources) from more productive activities. Honor-driven rivalries of this sort impoverished Corsica, and much of the ancient and medieval world.

Could an honor-based moral code ever overcome the problem? If the in-group expanded to include everyone, then the problem would disappear, but so, too, would the in-group identity and the sense of honor. Rival groups seem essential. Longtime dominance by a unified in-group is very rare, since factions normally emerge within the ruling group. Also, as noted in the first few chapters, men in power tend to sire too many offspring raised by women outside the ruling class. A remaining logical possibility is a rigid caste system—a true "fascist insect" regime, perhaps along the lines of Huxley's *Brave New World*. But breaking up the gene pool like this is inhuman, maybe even invertebrate. It is abhorrent and probably infeasible.

Honor codes dominated the ruling classes in the early Bronze Age, but, at that time, the world population was only about ten million and the average newborn would live only twenty years. In the days of Basil II of Constantinople, the world population had grown to a quarter billion, but most of them still had desperately poor and rather short lives. Average lifespan, income, and population all crept up over the next several centuries, but then really took off after 1800. More than 6.6 billion people are alive today, life expectancy is sixty to seventy years in most countries, and world average income is $10,000 per person. As argued in Chapter 3, the take-off was associated with modern morals that support the market system.

Unless we wish to rid the world of billions of people and impoverish most of the survivors, then we must rely mainly on moral codes that are conducive to the market system. At least, that is the way I read the evidence. If so, moral codes should emphasize bourgeois virtues like tolerance, honesty, prudence, working hard, and obeying the law. Noble virtues like justice and courage still have a place, but no longer at the center. The moral codes we should want, then, are perhaps not the most thrilling, but rather those that help support a healthy, wealthy, and populous world.

What Sort of Markets?

Ultimately, the logical outcome of the market system is a single world market, with goods made and services performed wherever costs are lowest, for consumption by the planet's highest bidders. Should we encourage such global markets, or try to keep things more local?

Resistance to globalization has spread in the last decade or two. It brought the 1999 "Battle of Seattle," the largest and most violent demonstration in recent U.S. history, and several other protests around the world. Critics from the political Right (Pat Buchanan, Lou Dobbs, and Ross Perot, for example) blame global markets for loss of national sovereignty and excessive immigration. Their counterparts on the Left (Noam Chomsky and Ralph Nader, say) worry more about threats to the environment, to worker health and safety, and to economic equality. Critics from both wings claim that global markets destroy local jobs and depress real wages, and transfer too much power to international organizations like the World Bank and the World Trade Organization.

Columbia University economist Jagdish Bhagwati has written a very readable refutation. He summarizes lots of careful studies and concludes that, on balance, opening global markets has slightly boosted real wages in the United States and elsewhere. Bhagwati doesn't quite say so, but our us-versus-them moral instincts and self-serving biases may prevent us from clearly seeing the gains that globalization brings to our exporting industries and to our consumers. Likewise, we may attribute lost jobs to low-wage foreign competition when the main cause is technological advance.

Bhagwati eloquently points up the cultural gains from global exchange, and the economic and political gains when foreign competition breaks local monopolies and cartels. He recommends direct measures to deal with environmental problems that arise when export-oriented businesses expand. For example, when shrimp farming starts to destroy mangrove swamp habitat, the recommended solution is to make sure the shrimp farmers pay the full cost, not to ban shrimp exports.

UCLA economist Edward Leamer argues that most jobs in the United States (and elsewhere) are not vulnerable to offshore competition because they can't be commodified. For example, typing is offshorable, but editing a journal (or writing a book) is not. After discussing the disruptive textile markets in late 1700s England, Leamer concludes, "The lesson is that infrastructure and workforce quality can create deeps roots that hold the best jobs firmly in place."

Along with a large majority of other economists, I am convinced, by evidence as well as theory, that expanding global markets make the world far wealthier. The global market system boosts incomes, especially in the poorer countries that join. China and India are the most prominent recent examples, but they follow a path blazed earlier by Japan and many other countries.

Nevertheless, thoughtful critics of globalization raise three points that deserve more careful analysis. First, joining the global economy brings new vulnerability: distant events are more likely to cause local disruption. For example, suppose that my county becomes specialized in growing brussels sprouts for export. Normally, that would bring in more income—otherwise, we would not have specialized—but if some new root fungus killed our crop then we'd be in much deeper trouble than if we had stayed with mixed agriculture for local consumption. The risk is also economic: New Zealand farmers might suddenly flood the market with lower cost brussels sprouts, or our sprouts might go out of fashion in key foreign markets.

The global economy also brings new opportunities to diversify and share risk. In the premodern era, risks could only be shared locally, within the extended family or village, and that can still be part of the mix. For example, the farmers in my county might rotate the sprouts with other crops. But risks now can (and should) be partly shared with people on the other side of the world. For example, imagine a brussels sprouts futures market, or an event market of the sort mentioned in Chapter 9. Local farmers could hedge the risk, accommodated by distant investors seeking diversified financial assets. There is also a role for government. "Wage insurance" is a good example: the government could temporarily and partially subsidize workers who take new jobs after losing higher-pay jobs due to foreign competition. Even Bhagwati approves of this sort of safety net.

A second and related point is the loss of local diversity. Global chain stores replace homegrown operations, eBay and Amazon drive out local antique dealers and bookstores, and regional shopping malls suck the life from towns' Main Streets. Everything looks pretty much the same everywhere.

Except that it doesn't, if you look just a little further. Quirky little businesses spring up that use eBay or their own Web sites to sell some tiny specialty to the whole world. Three random examples: vintage postcards of Massachusetts' Pioneer Valley, or consulting services to biotechnology companies appealing their tax assessments, or a bed-and-breakfast catering to loyal fans of poet Robinson Jeffers. Long ago, Adam Smith observed that the larger the market, the more specialties it could support. Global markets promote world-class narrow specialties that ambitious people can exploit wherever they have full market access. Diversity doesn't diminish, it just changes shape.

What's Wrong with Inequality?

> The League of Shadows has been a check against human corruption for thousands of years. We sacked Rome. Loaded trade ships with plague rats. Burned London to the ground. Every time a civilization reaches the pinnacle of its decadence we return to restore the balance. Over the ages our weapons have grown more sophisticated. With Gotham we tried a new one. Economics.
>
> —*Ducard (Liam Neeson) in* Batman Begins, *2005*

The critics' third point is inequality. Batman fans know that the League of Shadows' sophisticated new weapon was to increase economic inequality until it tore apart Gotham's social fabric, and rendered the city defenseless against the League's final assault. However, in the real world, not everyone fears that weapon. Bhagwati, for example, argues that since globalization boosts incomes for the poor and middle classes, it shouldn't bother anyone that the rich profit so fabulously that they get a larger share of the pie than ever.

I'm not so sure about that. This may be one time when Hollywood screenwriters have better insight than an eminent economist. Before jumping to conclusions, though, let's take a closer look at the facts.

Although the rise of developing countries has reduced income inequality for the world as a whole, recent analyses confirm that inequality is increasing within most countries. Economists Pinelopi Goldberg and Nina Pavcnik find it in developing countries like Mexico and China. In developing countries, people with more education and greater mobility apparently reap most of the gains from globalization because they are better able to take advantage of the new opportunities. Leamer points to parallel trends in developed countries. Workers stuck in jobs that are offshorable are hurt by global competition, but those with jobs rooted in local relationships do well. The fabulous gains at top incomes are due more to modern communications technologies, which create huge talent premiums and superstars. For example, a part of Oprah's income is due to international distribution, but most of it is due to national TV and merchandising networks.

Inequality does fray the social fabric, especially when it comes from unequal opportunities. Modern nations got started when their citizens' sense of in-group expanded from village and region, but people with far different opportunities and lifestyle always seem more like "them" than like "us." So inequality undermines the national sense of shared purpose, and can also undermine the moral infrastructure markets need to thrive. We have already looked at extreme cases, like France in the late 1700s, or Russia a century later, and have seen that revolutionary cures for inequality can be as toxic as the disease.

Traditionally, economists paid little attention to inequality, but that is finally changing. Larry Summers and other prominent economists have launched intensive research programs, and I'll not try to anticipate the results. To refocus on the connection to globalization, recall the "creative destruction" insight from Chapters 2 and 3. The market system showers money on those people who first seize the biggest new opportunities, and drains income away from the old ways—but only during the transition. Once globalization becomes routine and everyone has made their adjustments, the income distribution in all countries should become less extreme.

The policy implication is not to fight globalization, say, by putting up new trade restrictions, nor to subsidize it, as, for example, allowing exporters to freely pollute the air and water. Instead, we should try to make the adjustments as smooth as possible. For example, we should encourage risk sharing and safety nets, and think carefully about the best sequence when removing trade restrictions. Of course, the other causes of inequality remain, and they may require additional prescriptions.

Can Global Markets Prevent War?

At least since John Stuart Mill, thinkers have suggested that international trade reduces the chances of war. Europe is a prime example. From pre-Roman tribal battles to World War II, one bloody war followed another in a continent divided by political boundaries and trade barriers. Yet Europe is now a single market, and war between France and Germany, say, is unimaginable. It seems that markets have made Europe more moral than morals alone ever did.

Could markets spread peace across the globe? There are some hopeful signs. Open trade helped Slovakia peacefully split away from the Czech Republic in 1992, and now both are full members of the European Union. Some observers think that a similar separation might bring Belgium, the unhappy combination of Dutch-speaking Flanders and French-speaking Wallonia, greater harmony and prosperity. Hostilities between China and Taiwan were among the Cold War's greatest dangers, but over the last twenty years, the two have become so commercially bound that, despite posturing, war now seems unlikely. The global economy helped defuse the India-Pakistan crisis in 2002. There is, as yet, hardly any trade between Israel and her Arab neighbors, despite tremendous potential gains. The world's future would surely brighten if trade took off within the Mideast.

But is it really that simple? Trade ties tightened around the world a century ago, and many thought that they made war obsolete. Then the First World War destroyed everything—young lives, trade, and the dream of lasting peace.

What causes war, and how can it be prevented? These questions are far too big for this book, but it might be worth looking again at how they connect with trade. The second chapter argued that organized warfare begins with capturing and defending transferable wealth, such as livestock herds and stored grain. Military imperatives profoundly changed moral codes, and brought back hierarchy. To prepare for battle, leaders stoked their warriors' sense of honor, and their sense of us versus them. "They" are evil or corrupt or bullies that need to be taught a lesson, vengeance is our due, and we must defend ourselves, preemptively if necessary. Such are the moral clarion calls, even to the present day.

To end war, it seems to me that we must make the fruits less tempting and the means more difficult. Chapter 3 noted that, even for transferable wealth, trade often was a good substitute for war. Fortunately, modern services are less transferable. In the old days, you might try to capture the silver mines (or the oil fields nowadays), but today's software designers and film studios are not tempting military targets, even when they generate greater wealth.

As for the means of war, one way to make them more difficult is to soften the edges of us versus them. Hitler had excellent material to work with in Germany after World War I—widespread chauvinism, resentment, and poverty. After World War II, however, Germany's schools and media encouraged their prosperous younger citizens to think of themselves as Europeans first and Germans second—a profound cultural change that also softened edges in neighboring countries.

Building Better Markets

Markets, according to earlier chapters, played a subordinate role in the premodern world, but not any more. Most people now spend most of their work lives producing things to be sold, and purchase most necessities as well as luxuries. Yet, there are still crucial activities that remain outside the market system. Should the line be drawn differently? Which sorts of services should be provided by the market, and which should come from government or remain inside the household?

To answer the question, I'll first perform triage, and sort services (including goods) into three categories. Assume good infrastructure—transportation and communication networks, and courts that enforce contracts and punish fraud. Then the market can reliably provide items in the first category, such as bread, shoes, computers, and other commodities. The second category consists of things the market could not or should not provide, like slaves or legislation or parental care.

The third category needs the most attention: services that markets can easily screw up, but that they might be able to efficiently provide if they had special infrastructure or engineering.

For example, take California's electric power industry. A partially deregulated power market opened in 1998 with great fanfare, but it blew up between May 2000 and September 2001. Enron and other power suppliers and traders carved out tens of billions of dollars in windfall profits, while consumers suffered from rolling blackouts, bankrupt local utilities, and inflated bills.

What went wrong? The official report blamed the traders and suppliers who "violated the anti-gaming provisions," but the real problem was bad design. The politicians and lawyers in charge of deregulation mainly worried about satisfying powerful interest groups. They consulted some economists and engineers, but gave them little latitude in proposing and testing new designs. When the market opened, customers had no real-time information about prices. The market format and special rules were dysfunctional and, even worse, concentrated ownership of generating facilities encouraged suppliers to artificially restrict production and extract monopoly profits. You can't patch those problems with "anti-gaming provisions." Of course, it is not straightforward to build a competitive market for electric power—if it were, it probably would have emerged spontaneously—but I have no doubt that economists and engineers could now do so. Most likely, it will be a while before politicians dare to let them try.

For services in the third category, the basic principle is to design the market so that the best profit opportunities come from competitive behavior, from supplying at low cost and from bidding aggressively. It should be less profitable to "game" the system so as to impair market performance. The theory of mechanism design, developed largely by the three 2007 Nobel Laureates in economics, gives some guidance on how to do it—how to align participants' incentives with market efficiency.

The basic principle is not enough, however, because there are always crucial details left outside the theory. Laboratory tests, small-scale trials in the field, and tinkering are therefore necessary.

Perhaps even more important are the political obstacles. There are usually interests vested in the current way of doing things, and they will try to strangle the new market. For example, as a naïve assistant professor in the 1980s, I tried to persuade New York Stock Exchange officials to consider an all-electronic double auction format. They didn't go for it. Eventually, the reason dawned on me: the NYSE was owned by specialists who prospered in the current system, but who would sidelined in an all-electronic system.

On small scale, the problem is the same as that faced by medieval markets. Chapter 3 argued that Western Europe's solution began in the backwaters, in towns beyond the reach of the politically powerful. Likewise, to spread a new market format, one should seek hungry upstarts at the fringes, build strong enough coalitions to launch, and expand into neighboring niches as they become profitable. In the 1990s, local entrepreneurs brought all-electronic double auctions to new exchanges in Europe, Asia, and Canada, and to U.S. dealers in thinly traded securities. In 2006, the new market formats finally reached the power center, the NYSE, when competition pushed it to merge with Archipelago.

Building a Better Marriage

The greatest challenge is to realign morals and markets so that they work together, rather than at cross purposes. To take a small example, consider e-mail spam. The underlying cause is that it costs almost nothing to e-mail a thousand more strangers about how to make a fortune or improve their sex appeal. A spammer can make money even if only one person in ten thousand goes for the bait, but all ten thousand suffer from clogged in-baskets and wasted time. It's a classic social dilemma, and the profit opportunity has defeated all technical fixes tried so far.

Perhaps it would be more effective to harness peoples' moral outrage. For example, require all e-mail senders to post a bond, perhaps twenty dollars for an ordinary user, and a much larger sum for anyone who wants to send bulk mail.

Have routers confirm the bond balance before forwarding messages, and let recipients click a "spam" button to take a nickel or so from the sender's bond. This cheap form of vengeance would, I believe, soon raise the cost of sending another unwanted email enough to make spam unprofitable.

Health care is a far larger example of the third category. In the United States, health care accounts for a huge share of the economy (currently 16 percent, and on course to rise to 20 percent within the decade), but it is delivered by a dysfunctional mix of market and government programs. Most coverage comes from the employer (who gets a tax break), but that distorts workers' decisions on taking and keeping jobs, and artificially raises employers' costs. An increasing part of the coverage comes from government programs, and they create even worse problems for all the usual reasons. To top it off, large numbers of people have no health coverage and they clog the emergency rooms, where they get extremely expensive, but not very effective, treatment while putting a burden on everyone else.

Simple market solutions are stymied by informational problems. The doctor must have detailed personal knowledge to find the proper treatment, and few patients can judge the quality of the medical services they receive. Insurance is appropriate because, occasionally, very expensive treatments are required, and that risk is diversifiable. Unfortunately, the usual sort of insurance is undercut by adverse selection: patients have a better idea than insurers on whether they will need lots of expensive care, and the healthiest patients are most likely to opt out, raising insurance premiums for those who remain.

Altogether, then, health care reform is one of the great policy challenges of our time. Several major industries—notably insurance and pharmaceuticals—have large stakes in the current dysfunctional system. Ideologues of the Left and the Right cling to obsolete ideas about the role of the government. Perhaps the Dutch model is the place to start, with taxpayers ensuring a basic level of care for everyone, and some sort of specially-engineered competitive market supplying higher quality care to those willing and able to pay for it. One hopes that less ideological political entrepreneurs will be able to harness moral conviction to economic practicalities, and put us on the path to good health care.

Reform of U.S. primary and secondary education is another great challenge, and it, too, will require an imaginative blend of moral fervor and mechanism design. Education in premodern times was a simple market good—some wealthy families hired tutors or sent their children to a private academy. The other kids became apprentices or learned a trade from their parents. But in the modern world, education brings important external benefits. You are much more productive when your coworkers (and customers and suppliers) can read and write the same language, and when you know that strangers learned the same things in school that you did. Standard economic theory suggests that education should therefore be subsidized.

In the nineteenth century, the United States led the way in offering free public education, eventually covering all children from kindergarten to high school. But we fell behind in the last third of the twentieth century. Most other industrialized countries now have better K–12 public education and, despite President Bush's "no child left behind" program, recent U.S. trends are not encouraging.

U.S. public education has always been run locally, by elected school boards and superintendents, and financed mainly from local property taxes. Most teachers feel that they are sacrificing personal income to do something truly worthwhile, and unions see their mission as preventing exploitation. Such strong moral claims, and fragmented control, greatly complicate reform. Some call for vouchers or other privatization schemes. The unions resist, and call for smaller classes, higher salaries, and more respect. Taxpayers are skeptical: more money might not be well spent, especially by distant schools. We seem trapped in a bad equilibrium.

As with our other pressing problems, the answer is not to launch a new moral crusade to shame corporations (or schools) into social responsibility, nor to build big bureaucracies to micromanage them. Neither is the answer simply to let the global markets rip. There is a better way forward: to experiment, test, and build new market structures on proper moral foundations.

Fortunately, both morals and markets are adaptable and, with some patience and care, they can accommodate each other. Morals have already undergone two major transitions, at the dawn of civilization and again at the dawn of the modern era. The transitions wove new elements into the moral code but did not eliminate the old—for instance, egalitarian impulses remained even as we became civilized. To solve our present problems, we don't need a third moral transformation—a little readjustment of existing elements should do just fine. Remaining elements of honor—especially young peoples' eagerness to fight corruption and willingness to sacrifice for greater good—are tremendous resources that could be better brought to bear on our problems. For example, a national program could bring college students back to poor high schools near where they grew up to serve as teaching assistants, activity leaders, and researchers. It could be largely financed by student loan forgiveness, but animated by idealism.

Markets adapt very quickly. The profit motive is like an ever-flowing stream, and, if unattended, it can erode the social fabric (as seen especially in Chapter 9 and earlier in the present chapter) and the environment (as in Chapter 11). But good ground rules can channel competition to serve the public purpose. The rules must be readily enforceable by the rule of law (or nearly so, with a nudge from conscience or peers), and ensure that everyone profits most by creating value. Chapter 3 recounted how markets rechanneled themselves two centuries ago, and the last several chapters have pointed up new possibilities. Global markets for greenhouse gas allowances, heavily taxing dangerous drugs with the proceeds going to the most effective anti-drug campaigns, spam bonds, anti-jihadi oil taxes—all work basically the same way. They join morals and markets so that, together, they help build a better world.

Appendix

Technical Details

This appendix is not necessary to understand the text or notes. It should be skipped by readers not interested in technical details. Other readers will find it a convenient distillation of material scattered in existing literature, together with a few minor new contributions to the literature.

A1. Social and Biological Evolution

Evolution derives from a Latin word meaning "unfolding" or "unrolling." Imagine an ornate hall rug just off the delivery truck. As you gradually roll it out, more of its patterns emerge and finally it is revealed in its full glory.

Popular use still reflects this original meaning. As most people use the word, evolution refers to any cumulative process of change or development, of unfolding over time. The word retains overtones of gradualism, of continuous improvement and increasing complexity over time, and of direction toward some final goal.

The technical meaning of evolution is quite different. In biology, the word has a much narrower and more specific meaning. Biological evolution certainly is a cumulative process, but it may or may not be gradual or increase complexity. It certainly does not have a preordained goal.

Since Darwin (1859), biological evolution refers to the process governing the changes over time in all life forms. The process, also called "natural selection," involves variations among individuals and selective transmission of characteristics to offspring. The variants that more successfully reproduce themselves become more prevalent in later generations. In modern perspective, what evolves are the genes—sequences in DNA molecules that encode biological characteristics.

In this book, the word evolution is used somewhat more broadly than in biology, but not so broadly as in popular use. Human social behavior can change over time because of biological evolution, but over shorter time scales—years or decades—the major genetic factors are almost constant. More rapid social change comes from nongenetic mechanisms such as (a) turnover in the population via entry and exit or migration (or war); (b) resource redistribution; and (c) changes in individual behavior via imitation and learning (see Boyd and Richerson, 1985).

Societies can change dramatically from one decade to the next due to the evolution of transmissible cultural characteristics, sometimes called "memes."

Social (or cultural) evolution and biological evolution follow the same abstract logic. It begins with a set of alternative characteristics or traits. New alternative traits are generated in some fashion, for example, by mutation or innovation. Evolutionary logic then analyzes how the population distribution changes over time. For example, in biology, one might look at a trait such as the number of eggs a bird lays. A simple set of alternatives would be one, two, three, or four eggs, and the biologist would keep track, over many seasons, of how many times each number was observed in the nest. A social scientist might be interested in a social custom like primogeniture (the eldest son inherits all the parents' land) and would track its prevalence in some region over the generations. Or, on a more rapid time scale, one might track a particular style of tattoo versus alternative styles and other sorts of body decoration.

Fitness summarizes the result of competition among existing traits. It determines the growth rate for each alternative trait, and thereby alters their prevalence over time.

Fitness has two components: the survival rate of carriers of the trait, and the transmission rate from carriers to the population as a whole. Fitness depends on the general environment in which the traits operate: changes in the environment can alter fitness and thereby shift the outcomes. For example, four eggs might have highest fitness when food is locally plentiful, but one egg might have higher fitness when the parents have to fly far to find food.

A2. Coevolution and Dynamics

The current prevalence of each alternative trait can also affect fitness by altering survival or transmission rates. Biologists call this frequency dependence. Here is a cultural example. A particular style of tattoo may transmit rapidly when worn by only a few trendsetters, but may lose its cachet if it becomes too popular, and the transmission rate could collapse.

Traits do not evolve in isolation. Their fitness depends on other traits in relevant populations. For example, sharp talons enhance the fitness of an osprey with the eyesight, wingspan, and nesting location to capture large fish swimming near the water's surface. But such talons won't enhance fitness of birds living in many other habitats. Like the osprey's physical and behavioral tool kit for fish hunting, the main traits in all creatures coevolve.

In particular, social traits coevolve with biological traits. A classic example is sickle cell anemia. The biological trait can be traced to a single point mutation in human DNA that substitutes one amino acid for another at one place in the hemoglobin protein. The altered protein precipitates more readily than the normal form when it releases the oxygen it carries, and this tends to collapse the red blood cell into a sickle shape. Such red blood cells tend to clump and to not take up as much oxygen. The body compensates by shortening the life cycle of red blood cells.

Individuals whose DNA carries two copies of the sickle cell trait have poor health. They usually don't survive long enough to have children, so their biological fitness is far below normal. In most environments, individuals with one copy for normal hemoglobin and one for sickle cell have fitness just a bit below normal. However, in environments where malaria is prevalent, their fitness is boosted by the shorter life cycle of red blood cells, because the malaria parasite infects red blood cells and has fewer opportunities to spread when the hosts are not around very long. On balance, the sickle cell gene boosts fitness in malarial environments when it is sufficiently rare, but always impairs fitness when it is so common that most babies inherit two copies.

The story is coevolutionary because the environmental prevalence of malaria depends, in part, on human activity. Traditional yam growing cultures require people to live near pools of standing water that help mosquitoes breed, and the mosquitoes spread the malaria parasite from one individual to another. The net effect is that the sickle cell gene boosts the yam growing meme and vice versa. The story is told in greater detail in Goldsmith and Zimmerman (2001) and Durham (1991).

Coevolution and frequency-dependent fitness make for nontrivial dynamics. Most evolutionary theorists look only at equilibrium, where all surviving traits have zero fitness and the alternative traits have negative fitness. There is a fascinating technical literature on the stability of equilibrium, launched in the 1980s by John Maynard Smith and George Price (see Smith, 1982).

Of course, convergence to equilibrium is not guaranteed. Traits may indefinitely cycle among three or more alternatives. They also can fluctuate chaotically. The book presumes that, normally, the most important social traits are near equilibrium, but occasionally—in a major evolutionary transition—they are pushed out of a "basin of attraction" and a runaway dynamic carries the system rapidly toward a new equilibrium. Detailed theories about runaway (or positive feedback loop) dynamics are not yet very well developed, but the general perspective comes from the literature on nonlinear dynamics. See Friedman (1998) for a relatively accessible summary aimed at economics graduate students, and Gould and Eldridge (1993) for a nonmathematical collection of ideas.

A3. Social Dilemmas and Coordination Problems

Social creatures face a fundamental dilemma. Evolution selects for traits that increase the carrier's fitness, whether or not those traits help or harm other individuals. This individual imperative contrasts with the social imperative to help other members of the group and to avoid harming them, whether or not that is personally advantageous. A successful social group must somehow reconcile the individual imperative with the group imperative.

Figure A3 makes the point abstractly. The horizontal axis depicts the net fitness benefit ($x > 0$) or cost ($x < 0$) to a creature, denoted "Self," associated with some activity. The vertical axis depicts the net fitness benefit ($y > 0$) or cost ($y > 0$) that Self's activity brings to all other creatures, denoted "Other."

Figure A3: Payoffs to Self and Other

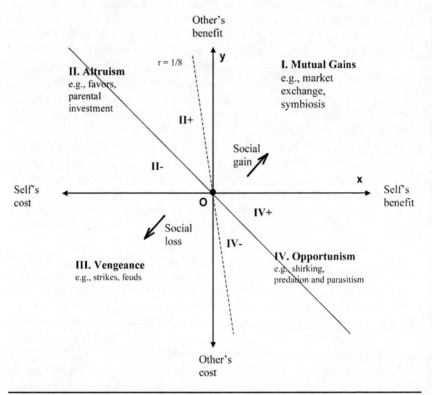

First appeared in Huck, *Advances in Understanding Behavior*, 2005, Palgrave Macmillan. Reproducer with permission of Palgrave Macmillan.

Quadrant I is the region where both x and y are positive because the chosen activity simultaneously benefits both Self and Other. Biologists call this case mutualism or symbiosis, and cite examples like bees pollinating flowers while they gather nectar. Economists call this mutual benefit, and emphasize examples like voluntary trade. In quadrant I, there is sociality but no dilemma: we have a win-win situation.

The dilemma appears in quadrants II and IV; here, there is a conflict of interest between Self and Other. A quadrant II example is that Self gives food to Other. Such behavior is often called altruism. Quadrant IV is the region where x is positive but y is negative: the chosen strategy benefits Self at the expense of Other. For example, Self might steal food gathered by Other. The biological terms are parasitism and predation, and the economic terms are opportunism or exploitation.

It is important to realize that altruism doesn't always improve social efficiency, nor does exploitation always impair it. Social efficiency (i.e., the group imperative) is served to the extent that the sum $x + y$ increases, as indicated by the arrow labeled "social gain." The portions II+ and IV+ of quadrants II and IV above the diagonal line represent efficient actions. For example, a well fed vampire bat loses only a little fitness (say $x = -1$) when it regurgitates blood into the mouth of a starving bat, but that other bat gains a lot (say $y = 3$) so the action is efficient ($x + y = 2 > 0$). The other quadrant portions II- and IV- are inefficient. Thus, it is not socially worthwhile for Self to incur a large personal cost that brings only a small benefit to Other, or to grab a small personal net benefit that creates large cost to Other.

Coordination problems are different. The idea is that mutual gains (a win-win outcome in quadrant I) are possible if Self and Other act in compatible ways. The standard example of a coordination problem is deciding on which side of the road to drive. If everyone drives on the right, as in the United States and continental Europe (or everyone on the left, as in Britain and some of its former colonies), there will be fewer accidents and everyone benefits. However, if some people drive on the left and some on the right, then accidents will be much more common.

There is no dilemma in a coordination problem: Self and everyone else is better off when she picks an action that coordinates with others in her group. But there can still be a problem, because group members might not choose compatible actions.

Why wouldn't they? Coordination failures can easily arise when the group hasn't worked together very long. For example, Team USA has more skilled basketball players than the other national teams, but, sometimes, the other team coordinates better and wins.

Another reason for coordination failures is that the benefits to coordinating may not spit equally. The standard example (from 1950s textbooks) is a couple that wants an evening out together, but the man prefers a prizefight and the woman prefers opera. Each is least happy when they go separate ways, but that could happen in a struggle to choose the evening's event.

Many coordination problems are resolved by means of a hierarchy. The individual with highest status gets the first choice, then the second highest-ranking individual, and so on down the line. Wolves divide up the kill in exactly this way.

A4. Coping with Social Dilemmas: Kinship and Reciprocity

Abstractly speaking, the way to solve the social dilemma is to somehow rotate, counterclockwise, the vertical line in Figure A3 separating Self's gains from losses. Rotating the line forty-five degrees would completely solve the dilemma.

The main biological device is inclusive fitness, or kin selection (Haldane, 1955; Hamilton 1964; Williams, 1966). If Self and Other are kin, then the line rotates in the right direction. The amount of rotation depends on the degree r of relatedness. I haven't seen the diagram in textbooks, so the analytic geometry might be worth spelling out. If Self incurs a personal cost $x = -C$ to provide benefit B to Other, then the act increases inclusive fitness as long as $F = rB - C > 0$. The neutral line $x + ry = 0$ (like other iso-fitness lines) therefore has slope $-1/r$.

When Other is unrelated, then $r = 0$ and the line is vertical. The dashed line in the diagram has slope -8, corresponding to $r = 1/8$, as with first cousins. If Self and

Other are clones or identical twins ($r = 1$) then the line rotates forty-five degrees and the dilemma completely disappears. Evolution pushes individuals toward socially efficient behavior because there is no distinction between self-interest and group interest when the group shares identical genes. An example: all cells in your body have a common interest because they share the same DNA and depend on specialized germ cells to reproduce. Slime mold amoeba also come close to $r = 1$.

The degree of relatedness r is as high as 3/4 in hymenoptera, which includes social insects such as ants and bees. Primates like ourselves (along with most other creatures) have $r = 1/2$ between siblings and between parents and offspring. Relatedness drops off fairly quickly from there: for first cousins $r = 1/8$, as shown by the dotted line in Figure A3, and for second cousins r is only about 0.03.

Reciprocity is another device recognized by biologists since Trivers (1971). The idea is that when Other receives a favor $y = B > 0$ (or an injury $y < 0$), he will try to reciprocate with a return favor later. Such reciprocation brings fitness $F = dB - C$, where $x = - C$ is the cost to the donor. The discount factor d summarizes the probability that the favor will be returned, the delay in returning the favor, and the relative size of the return. Specifically, $d = q/(1+i)t$, where q is probability that the favor will be returned, i is the real interest rate, and t is the delay time.

The abstract representation of reciprocity is exactly the same as inclusive fitness, with the discount factor d replacing r. Reciprocity supports a larger fraction of all socially efficient behavior as d gets closer to 1. Large d means that the group is stable and faces repetitive symmetric opportunities for mutual aid, as with vampire bats. But d is small for typical members of a fission-fusion group facing once-off opportunities for mutual aid.

A5. Schematic Overview of the Moral System

Table A5 summarizes the main aspects of the human moral system. It contains prescriptions for proper behavior, possibly contingent on status; a means for monitoring actual behavior; and a means for transmitting observations, status updates, and prescriptions.

For example, a particular moral code might include the following prescriptive elements:

- share big game equally among all heads of households within the current group;
- mildly punish cheaters on this rule;
- threaten any outsiders entering our valley and try to kill them if they stay overnight;
- exile any insiders who fail to support this rule.

The code evolves as groups that embrace it are more or less successful than groups with differing codes. For example, a group that is more hospitable to outsiders may (or may not, depending on the social and physical environment) enjoy greater

Table A5 The Moral System	
Shared Understanding of Proper Behavior	

Proper Behavior	*Actual Behavior*
Coordinate mutual benefits	Enthusiastic support, "above and beyond"
Encourage efficient altruism	Adequate support
Discourage inefficient opportunism	Visible shortfall
Encourage costly punishment of particular sorts (e.g., in finding and sharing food, creating shelter, raising kids, finding mates.)	Hidden shortfall: cheating
	Hidden shortfall: lying
. . . depending on:	. . . shared via:
Status	*Transmission*
Age, sex, health, kinship, and marriage	Direct observation
Ingroup/outgroup	Stories, myths, and songs
Personal reputation	Gossip within group
Group reputation	Travelers' tales

military success due to fewer losses and wider alliances. If so, the more hospitable code will spread.

The moral system relies on capacities for:

- Sharing understandings and information, via speech, memory, and cognition.
- Tracking individuals, using face recognition, memory, and cognition. That allows us to employ a code that depends delicately on status. (By contrast, ants can't track individuals, just classes within the colony and outsiders.)
- Detecting intentions or "mind reading" using cues like body language, gestures, laughs and moans, and speech. This is key to adjusting reputation, hence, status, and to code enforcement. (Dogs and other social mammals are pretty good at this, too.)
- Emotions: guilt (internal reputation), anger (supports punishment codes), love (supports altruism, anti-opportunistic codes), joy of teamwork. The code must hook into these emotions to gain traction.

A6. The Unpleasant Arithmetic behind Hierarchy

As the group size increases, the probability of reaching consensus in a given amount of time drops rapidly. The difficulties of monitoring and keeping track of even bilateral relationships increase sharply as numbers increase.

Some arithmetic (or combinatorics, to use a fancier expression) shows the problem. In a group of size n there are $b(n) = n^*(n-1)/2$ bilateral relationships. For a dozen people, this is $b(12) = 66$ relationships, quite manageable for humans. For a thousand people in a large village, it is $b(1000) = 499,500$, or about half a million relationships, far more than a normal person can track.

Multilateral relationships are important in many cases. For example, I might not be willing to work with a particular teenager unless his dad is along to keep him in line. These explode even faster. There are $n^*(n-1)^*(n-2)/6$ three way relationships, and using the factorial notation (!), there are $n!/(m-n)!m!$ relationships among m of the n people. Adding them up over all m between 0 and n, the total is 2^n relationships. Even for a dozen people this is $2^{12} = 4,096$ relationships. A socially adept person can quickly find the most important of them and keep track. But with a thousand people, the total number of relationships is 2^{1000}, more than the number of atoms in the universe. Keeping track of them, or even scanning a small subset, seems beyond human reach.

The solution is a layered hierarchy. For example, suppose the big boss has a dozen subordinates, each of whom has a dozen foremen in charge of a dozen ordinary workers. The three hierarchical steps allow the big boss to manage more than a thousand workers. (Taken literally, the number in the example is 1,728.)

A7. Markets' Inner Workings

Vernon Smith and many followers have conducted thousands of laboratory markets, using a variety of trading rules, different schedules of costs and values, different numbers of participants from all sorts of backgrounds, and so forth. The results are rather surprising. Given the right sort of trading rules, very high efficiencies can be consistently achieved, even with only a few buyers and a few sellers, say three or four of each. Standard economic theory predicts efficiency, but only with lots of buyers and lots of sellers. So the laboratory results, at first, deepen the mystery of how markets really work.

However, the best thing about laboratory markets is that you can rerun them, varying one thing at a time, and thus dissect their inner workings. Researchers have discovered four hidden forces that push toward competitive equilibrium (CE) prices and efficient exchange.

1. Market formats matter. The discussion in Chapter 2 suggested that posted prices (as in the farmers' market or in the supermarket) promote more efficient trade than haggling, and this is confirmed in the laboratory (e.g., Cason et al. 2003). Vernon Smith found that other market formats (or trading rules) are even more efficient. The continuous double auction (CDA, used in major financial markets) typically achieves 95–99 percent of the potential gains in the lab. At each moment in the CDA, traders can make public offers to buy ("bids") or to sell ("asks"), and a transaction is completed whenever anyone accepts an existing offer. Indeed, the CDA allows even random bidders to achieve very high efficiencies (Gode and Sunder, 1993).

2. Good trading rules discourage traders from acting too tough. Textbook monopoly theory says that sellers will hold back some low cost units when that will drive up price, even though this strategy creates a "deadweight" efficiency loss. Buyers who can affect price are similarly motivated to play tough by understating the quantity they wish to purchase. But CDA rules make it difficult for such strategies to work. Instead, the rules encourage traders to reveal the full amount they wish to trade, but to shade the prices they offer toward CE. This supports 100 percent efficiency while protecting against exploitation by traders on the other side of the market. Friedman and Ostroy (1995) show how this works in a simpler market format, the Call Market (CM).

3. Good trading rules can also use human learning biases to promote efficient trade. For example, suppose there are four buyers, each hoping to purchase a single unit, and four single unit sellers. Modern economic theory (available in advanced textbooks) predicts that each trader will offer a tough price that optimally trades off the probability of transacting against the transaction profitability. We have found in CM experiments that human traders, on average, start out offering prices about as tough as theory predicts, but that with experience, they make more generous prices and achieve very efficient trade. Careful data analysis indicates that traders react strongly when they miss a profitable transaction (by being too tough) and react much less when they could have obtained a better price (by being tougher). These reactions bias learning toward generous behavior and efficient trade (Cason and Friedman, 1999).

4. Good trading rules can drive out inefficient rules. Suppose that traders are used to a haggle market, and a new CDA market opens. Will traders move to the new market? At first, one might think so (efficiency is good), but there are two serious obstacles. First, buyers want to be where there are more sellers competing, and sellers want to be where the buyers are, so the existing market has a huge advantage. Also, even though the new market would be better, on average, if everyone used it, not everyone is average. Some buyers and some sellers are better off in the haggle market. Still, careful theory indicates that the better rules will prevail, and this has been confirmed in recent lab experiments. Here is the key insight. Buyers with the highest values and sellers with lowest cost have the most to gain by leaving the haggle market and going to an auction market, where they can keep a larger portion of their surplus. So these most valuable trading partners peel off first, leaving the haggle market less attractive. Now it's worthwhile for the most valuable remaining traders to peel off, and so on, until nobody is left in the haggle market that can trade in CE (Kugler et al. 2006; see also Friedman, 2007).

*   *   *

Friedrich Hayek shared the 1974 Nobel Prize for pushing the competitive equilibrium efficiency argument a bit further. His point is that nobody needs to know much for the markets to function well. All you need to know is your own personal circumstances plus the prices for the goods you buy and sell. When you buy carrots, you don't need to know restaurant chefs' menus, matrons' dinner plans, or farmers' luck with weather and irrigation systems and seasonal labor. In gift exchange, by contrast, you do have to know quite a bit about the personal circumstances of the people with whom you exchange. Acquiring such information becomes increasingly problematic when a larger number of more diverse people engage in exchange, so markets have a huge informational advantage at larger scale.

The last paragraphs of the "Market Magic" section of Chapter 2 offered a short list of limitations to markets. Here is a more detailed list:

1. Gift exchange has a built-in tendency to split gains in some manner that participants regard as "fair." Markets have no such tendency. The CE price is determined only by supply and demand. It can turn out to be quite different than expected, and might produce a split that gives the lion's share of gains to some undeserving lout and might bankrupt some worthy citizen.

2. The arguments so far assume that trade has no effect on third parties. But if production or consumption helps or harms other people not involved in the market exchange, then we have an "externality" that may undermine efficiency. For example, people who live downwind of a large hog farm bear a cost, and a sculptor's neighbors may get an unpaid benefit. Markets that fail to recognize such external costs and benefits are generally not efficient, and sometimes, extremely inefficient. Chapter 11 mentions several examples like air pollution.

3. The arguments so far assume that people have secure ownership of the goods they buy and sell. But investment disappears and markets freeze up when people fear expropriation. Robert Mugabe's Zimbabwe and Afghanistan under the pre-Taliban warlords immediately come to mind.

4. The argument on price adjustment assumes that producers and consumers can respond to price in timely fashion. This is not always the case. For example, homeowners and most businesses have no idea what electricity costs until the bill comes at the end of the month. Chapter 12 notes how this lack of timely information helped create the 2000 California energy crisis.

5. Hayek's argument assumes that each person knows the personal benefits or costs of the goods he or she transacts. In financial markets, most investors have considerable uncertainty about the returns they will receive. Their perceptions may change suddenly, at tremendous personal and social cost. Chapter 7 examines some of the consequences.

6. Good market formats like the continuous double auction make it difficult for any one trader to push the price around, but in some situations a single trader is able to do so. (Or a group of traders might form a cartel to manipulate prices.) The lack of real competition can lead to inefficiency. Many observers believe that Microsoft's dominance in computer operating systems in the 1990s was a prime example. The text examines several other examples, beginning with Thales of Miletus.

7. Competition and efficiency are also hampered by informational obstacles. For example, if the seller of a used car knows more about its quality than the buyer, then a sensible buyer will bid on it very cautiously. This point comes up in Chapter 12.

8. The personal traits that help you do well in markets are quite different from the traits that help you do well in personal exchange. Success in auction markets comes from quickly recognizing opportunities to buy at a low price or to sell at a high price. Social emotions that are essential in personal exchange—empathy, gratitude, loyalty, and so on—are excess baggage in auction markets.

A8. The Duke and Serf Game

Player #1 (the Serf) first chooses an amount $k \in [0, 10]$ of corn to plant and consumes the rest of his initial endowment, so his current consumption is $c_0 = 10 - k$. Player #2 (the Duke, or Lord of the Manor) sees k and chooses the tax rate $t \in [0, 1]$. The crop size is $C(k) = (1+r)\sqrt{k} = 4\sqrt{k}$, reflecting diminishing marginal returns and productivity parameter $r = 3$. The Duke takes $T = tC$ and the Serf keeps $c_1 = (1-t)C$. The Duke seeks to maximize T and the Serf seeks to maximize $c_0 + c_1 - 10$, assuming that he needs to consume 10 over the year to stay alive.

To analyze this game, first note that the socially efficient outcome is to maximize the net surplus, $S = T + c_0 + c_1 - 10 = 4\sqrt{k} - k$. By standard calculus arguments, the solution satisfies $0 = dS/dk$, whose solution is $k^* = 4$. Plugging this into the appropriate expressions, we get the social optimum, $C^* = 8$ and $S^* = 4$. A minor technical qualification: if $r > 3.48$ in this example then the boundary condition $k \leq 10$ comes into play.

We solve the game via backward induction, that is, we find the subgame perfect Nash equilibrium. Whatever crop the Serf harvests, the Duke is personally better off by taking more of it. Rationally he will choose $t = 1$ or $T = C$. The rational choice of $k = K(t)$ by the Serf given anticipated take rate t will maximize his payoff $P = 10 - k + (1-t)4\sqrt{k}$. To find it, set $0 = dP/dk$, which yields $K(t) = 4(1-t)^2$. Given the (roving bandit) Duke's choice $t = 1$, the Serf will choose $K(1) = 0$, resulting in $C = 0$ and $S = 0$. This is a social dilemma: the equilibrium leaves both players far worse off than at the social optimum.

One way to cope with the social dilemma is to change the game so that the Duke chooses the tax rate before planting, and can't change his mind afterward. Giving the Serf access to an independent court would do the trick. Rationally, the Duke then would want to commit to a tax rate that maximizes $T(t) = tC(K(t)) = 8t(1-t)$. The first order condition $0 = dT/dt$ yields $t = 0.5$, which implies $k = K(0.5) = 1$ and $C = 4$, with net social surplus $S = 3$. This gets us 75 percent the social optimum. We can do even better if the courts enforce a take rate more favorable to the Serf.

Standard game theory texts (e.g., Watson, 2007) show how to set up the stationary bandit version as a repeated game in which Player 2 has discount factor $d \in [0, 1)$. A higher d means more patience, typically reflecting greater confidence in the future. Player 2 rationally restrains his greed up to the point that the discounted present value (see A9 below) of a steady take, $(1 + d + d^2 + \ldots)tC = tC/(1-d)$, is as good as taking the entire harvest C now and getting nothing ever after, that is, up to the point that $t = 1-d$. Thus, a more patient Duke can tolerate a lower take rate t.

Another way to expand on the basic game is to allow the productivity r to depend on the Serf's prior investment in farm equipment, fertilizer, crop rotation, and so on. Since such investments take longer to pay off, the preceding arguments apply with greater force: the Serf will invest more when he has good reason to believe that the Duke is committed to a lower take rate.

A9. Asset Price and Fundamental Value

The Generalized St Ives Problem. Although every standard finance textbook explains the mathematics of expected present value, it might be helpful to begin here with a self-contained explanation, using a medieval theme.

Recall the ditty from Chaucer's era: "As I was going to St Ives/ I met a man with seven wives/ And every wife had seven sacks/ And every sack had seven cats/And every cat had seven kits. / Kits, cats, sacks, wives[, man]/ How many were going to St Ives?"

It appears that we are asked to sum the geometric series $1 + 7 + 7^2 + 7^3 + 7^4$. Instead of grinding it out, let's find the general formula. Let $S(x, n) = \sum_{t=0}^{n} x^t$, whose value we seek for $x = 7$ and $n = 4$. The math trick is to notice that $xS(x, n) = \sum_{t=0}^{n} x^{t+1}$ is the same as $S(x, n)$ except that it is missing the first term, $x^0 = 1$, and has an extra term, x^{n+1}. Therefore $1-x^{n+1} = S(x, n) - xS(x, n) = (1-x) S(x, n)$. As long as $x \neq 1$, we can divide both sides of the equation by $(1-x)$ to obtain the answer:

$$S(x, n) = (1- x^{n+1})/(1- x). \tag{1}$$

In particular, for the St Ives menagerie, we get $S(7, 4) = (1-7^5)/(1-7) = (1-16807)/(-6) = 16806/6 = 2801$. (When $x = 1$, of course, the sum is simply $S(1, n) = 1+1+ \ldots +1 = n+1$.)

The ditty has a catch, however. Maybe the menagerie was returning from the fair, not going to it. But it seems likely that the narrator would travel faster, and so might have overtaken them. Using a bit of calculus and a lot of guesswork, we might say that the probability that the menagerie was going to St Ives was 25 percent. In that case, the expected number going to St Ives was $(.25) 2801 + (.75) 0 = 700.25$.

* * *

Fundamental Value. The fundamental value of an asset is the expected present value of the promised cash stream. "Present value" refers to the fact that a dollar in hand now is worth more than a dollar received later. If the interest rate at your bank is 5 percent, then you could put the present dollar on deposit and get back $1.05 one year later, or get back $(1+.05)^2$ two years later, and so on. The present value of, say, $10 received two years from now is the amount $10/(1+.05)^2$, about $9.07, that you would have to deposit now to have the $10 in two years.

The present value of a stream of regular cash payments (such as that promised by a conventional bond) is simply the sum of the present value of each payment. It is the sum of the geometric series $B + B/(1+r) + B/(1+r)^2 + \ldots + B/(1+r)^n = B\ S(1/(1+r), n)$, where B is the amount received each period, r is the interest rate (e.g., .05 or 5 percent) and n is the number of periods over which the payment is promised. Plugging $x = 1/(1+r)$ into formula (1) above, multiplying numerator and denominator by $(1+r)$ and simplifying slightly, you find that the present value of the promised payments is $W = B(1+r-x^n)/r$. If you don't count the current payment, and so subtract B from the sum, you get the textbook formula

$$W = B(1 - (1/(1+r))^n)/r. \qquad (2)$$

The value of a bond must take into account that the promise is not 100 percent certain to be honored. For example, if the probability were 90 percent of it being honored in full, and 10 percent of receiving nothing, then the "expected present value" would be

$$V = EW = 0.9W, \qquad (3)$$

and that would be the fundamental value of the bond.

*   *   *

Great Expectations. With these technical points out of the way, we can ask the more interesting conceptual question: whose beliefs lie behind the expectation? A hypothetical outside observer who knows the future? The smartest investor? An average investor?

The first answer is wrong because financial markets in our world must rely on information that is actually available at the present time. We might enjoy "Monday morning quarterbacking" after the fact, or wish for divine revelation of the future, but in forming expectations, we must rely on what is known at the time. The second and third answers are also wrong, but for the opposite reason: they neglect useful information that is available. Smart as he (or she) might be, the smartest investor typically is unaware of important facts known by some other people. Friedrich Hayek received the 1974 Nobel Prize in Economics mainly for making this key point:

> The knowledge of the circumstances of which we must make use never exists in concentrated or integrated form but solely as the dispersed bits of incomplete and frequently contradictory knowledge which all the separate individuals possess. The economic problem of society is thus not merely a problem of how to allocate "given" resources—if "given" is to mean given to a single mind. . . . It is rather a problem of how to secure the best use of resources known to any of the members of society, for ends whose relative importance only those individuals know. Or, to put it briefly, it is a problem of the utilization of knowledge which is not given to anyone in totality (1945, 77–78).

Thus, the expectation should incorporate all information presently available to anyone. Imagine investors not as gods who know what the future will bring, but rather as mind-reading angels who are willing to share everything they know with each other and to combine their information without bias or distortion. That is the nature of the beliefs behind the fundamental value *V*.

*   *   *

Information Aggregation. Of course, investors are not mind-reading angels. To the contrary, they are probably at least as greedy and selfish as the average human, and not generally inclined to share their private information with other investors. Hayek's claim is that the market gets the same result from human investors. If Hayek is right, the magic is not in the investors, but rather in the way that financial markets work. Somehow markets get selfish and greedy investors to reveal their knowledge and to summarize it all in asset prices. If this trick works, then price equals fundamental value and financial markets are efficient.

Getting investors to combine and summarize their knowledge into market prices would be a remarkable trick in its own right. As mentioned in the introduction, it would also be of crucial importance in economies like ours that rely on financial markets to allocate resources for the future. So how might the trick work?

Hayek never spelled it out, but the KidsRUs (KRU) example in the text makes the point. When you and your wealthy friends buy its stock, your purchases are often amplified by day traders and other investors who follow order flow and price changes. So the stock price goes up, and KRU can borrow more given the appreciated stock, or use its appreciated stock to buy up other firms, or use more valuable stock options to pay its managers and employees. These activities all increase the resources available to KRU.

A10. Notes on Networks

Networks are described mathematically as a set of nodes, together with a set of links (or edges or connections) between some pairs of nodes. The mathematical theory, called graph or network theory, has developed in fits and starts over two hundred years, and has gathered lots of applications, for example, in physics, computer science, and epidemiology. In most social science applications, each node refers to an individual person, and two people are linked if they have some specified relationship, for example, they work together or are they spend leisure time together.

Chapters 1 and 2 contrast societies with fission-fusion networks to societies with fixed hierarchies. The difference can be described in terms of the network architecture. For example, in 1203 CE, Genghis Khan reorganized his army as a strict hierarchy (or "tree" in graph theory jargon) as follows. Each ordinary warrior belonged to a ten-person squad called an *arban*. Each member of an *arban* was linked to every other member, and one of them was designated the leader and belonged to a group of ten other leaders called a *zagun*. Members of the *zagun* were linked to each other and they selected a leader who, along with nine other *zagun* leaders, formed a *mingan*, sort of a battalion staff. It, in turn, had a leader who, with nine others, formed a *tumen*, whose leader controlled an army of 10,000 and, like nine or so others, reported to the great Khan, or to his top general. Genghis Khan believed in meritocracy and in delegating decisions to the lowest possible level, so this hierarchical organization—call it GK—was quite effective. Over the next several decades, it became the backbone of the most extensive empire the world had yet seen.

Fission-fusion networks have a different sort of architecture, recently called "small-world." To sharpen the contrast, assume that there are again ten thousand people in the society, and that working groups consist of ten people all linked to each other, as in an *arban* of the great Khan. But in the present example—call it FF—the working groups are temporary and don't have leaders. Instead, most people have links to a few others outside the current working group, and a few people (call them hubs) have hundreds of links, scattered fairly randomly throughout the society, including some to other hubs. Random collections of groups fuse when it is in their interest to do so, and form new links. Then they fission back to working groups, sometimes with the membership rearranged. The Shoshone and !Kung networks worked something like this FF example.

Mathematicians use various sorts of summary statistics to describe networks. For example, the *density* is the average number of links per node, a bit over ten in both examples. The *mean path length* is the average number of links needed to get from one randomly chosen node to another. It is almost eight in the GK example, because most pairs of random nodes are ordinary warriors in different *tumen*, so the connecting path has to pass all the way up through the ranks and back down again. The mean path length is only about four in the FF example because most people are linked to a hub, and any two hubs are likely to be linked directly or through a third hub; see Travers and Milgram (1969) and Watts and Strogatz (1998). The *clustering coefficient* is the probability that two nodes linked to a randomly chosen node are themselves linked. It is over 0.9 in the GK example, but less than that in the FF example.

To get everyone moving on the same battle plan in the GK example, the top general can reach each soldier via a set of four links. In the FF example, even if someone somewhere had a battle plan that everyone agreed to, it would probably reach more than half the people in four links, but it might take seven or more links to reach some people. On the other hand, by virtue of its fluctuating work groups, the FF architecture seems much better at generating novelty and, by virtue of its shorter path length, also better at spreading it. Those advantages would seem to be very important in the Pleistocene, and surely are crucial in the business world of the early twenty-first century.

Notes

The ideas presented in this book have many sources. It was my great fortune to learn from a series of generous mentors. Mathematicians Stephen Smale and Ralph Abraham taught me new ways to think about dynamic processes. Economists Robert Clower and Jack Hirshleifer (and watching the interbank FX market at Bank of America) helped shape my thinking about the inner workings of markets. My approach to evolutionary games, and especially to social dilemmas, owes much to Ken Binmore and Reinhard Selten. I gained philosophical and historical perspective from Axel Leijonhufvud.

Numerous colleagues helped at crucial junctures. A dinner conversation with Ernst Fehr convinced me think more systematically about social preferences and their market impact. Repeated contacts with Santa Fe Institute researchers and MacArthur Preference Group members—Sam Bowles, Herb Gintis, Rob Boyd, Pete Richerson, and Stu Kauffman are the first who spring to mind—helped sharpen my thinking about the nature and evolution of morals. Intellectual debts to other individuals are acknowledged in the chapter endnotes below.

I accrued more debts while putting the book together. Dan McNeill and I talked about it for years, and during the process, he taught me much about how to write. It was my huge disappointment that, when the time came, Dan was not able to coauthor the book. Many of the chapter titles are his, and some of the more graceful turns of phrase, particularly in Chapters 5 and 6. His ideas on content as well as style shine through every chapter.

Several other people read chapter drafts and helped me correct errors and clarify my prose and my thinking: Art Argiewicz, Nick Despota, Bernie Elbaum, Benjamin Friedman, Sara Hendrix, Joel Leventhal, and an anonymous Palgrave reviewer. My deepest debt is to my dear wife, Penny Hargrove, who put up with me during countless preoccupied hours and, in the end, did a complete round of copyediting.

The people at Palgrave helped me turn a pile of drafts into a tidy volume. Jaime Marshall introduced me to the organization, Aaron Javsicas signed me up, and Airie Stuart kept the project alive. I am especially grateful to acquisitions editor Laurie Harting for helping me finish what I started, and to the production crew, led by Rosemi Mederos. Marshall Somers compiled the bibliography and endnotes, and Kathryn Tobisch compiled the index. My heartfelt thanks to all.

This book is dedicated to the memory of my mom, Marion Thelma Siegel Friedman (1918–97). Humanist and skeptic, biology teacher and spiritual seeker, she first got me thinking about many of questions asked in this book.

Prologue

Healy and Palepu (2003) summarizes the facts about Enron. The next two articles in the Spring 2003 issue of *Journal of Economic Perspectives* discuss accounting issues and conflicts of interest arising from the scandal wave. Several popular books on Enron have sold well, and one was made into a movie (see McLean and Elkind 2004).

Partnoy (2004) is a nontechnical discussion of the financial engineering behind the scandals. On the losses incurred by my pension fund, see "UC vies with Florida System to Take Helm in Enron Suit; 2 Pension Funds Top Losers in Collapse of Firm's Stock," by Lance Williams (*San Francisco Chronicle*, January 25, 2002).

Inappropriate mortgage loans are discussed in "Borrowers Face Dubious Charges in Foreclosures," by Gretchen Morgenson (*New York Times*, November 6, 2007). Some of the conflicts of interest are discussed in "A Catastrophe Foretold," by Paul Krugman (*New York Times*, op-ed page, October 26, 2007). I haven't yet seen a good article on the financial engineering aspects; my own information comes mainly from colleagues and former students working in financial markets.

McAfee (2004) notes that loss of public trust was particularly disastrous for Enron's pioneering product lines in market making.

"They lied about what they were doing": Tyco is a partial exception. Ex-CEO Dennis Kozlowski is serving jail time for taking company money for personal purposes. The TV show *60 Minutes* ran a story called "Prisoner 05A4820" (March 25, 2007) in which Kozlowski convincingly claims that his board of directors approved everything he asked for, and he hid nothing. Of course, that reinforces the point that boards of directors were ineffective safeguards.

Data on the high-powered incentives: see "CEO Compensation Survey: Goodbye to Pay for No Performance," by Joann Lublin (*Wall Street Journal*, April 11, 2005, R1). Chapters 8 and 12 discuss globalization and the other sources of threat and opportunity.

On lack of oversight by Boards of Directors, see "Deciding on Executive Pay: Lack of Independence Seen," by Diana B. Henriques and Geraldine Fabrikant (*New York Times*, December 18, 2002). The consult-audit conflict of interest is discussed in the *Journal of Economic Perspectives* symposium cited above.

John Olson's story is told in "Merrill Replaced Research Analyst Who Upset Enron," by Richard A. Oppel, Jr. (*New York Times*, July 30, 2002). Levitt (2002) tells his own story, and "S.E.C.'s Embattled Chief Resigns In Wake of Latest Political Storm," by Stephen Labaton (*New York Times*, November 6, 2002) tells Harvey Pitt's.

"Five Years Under the Thumb," (*The Economist*, July 28, 2007, 73–74) summarizes the mixed reviews of Sarbanes-Oxley act five years after its passage. "Sarboxed In?" by James Surowiecki (*The New Yorker*, December 12, 2005, 46) is a more sympathetic analysis.

Chapter 1

"Morals are what made us human." Of course, there is no shortage of competing opinions. Anthropologists in previous decades variously emphasized general intelligence, bipedalism, opposable thumbs, and tool-making. More recently, language seems to be the leading contender with morals gaining ground; see, for example, Klein (1999), and also McBrearty and Brooks (2000). Rhetoric aside, my point is no longer especially controversial: the moral system coevolved with language, tool-making, and do forth, and it is crucial to human cooperation.

On how amoeboids self-organize into a fruiting body, see Marée and Hogeweg (2001) and also Herbert et al. (2000). A theoretical investigation of what happens when spores from unrelated fruiting bodies are likely to mix is featured in Armstrong (1984). See http://dictybase.org/ for general background.

On social dilemmas, see Appendix A3. It uses a four-quadrant diagram to show that, one way or another, cooperation depends on converting social dilemmas into games with mutual gains. Social creatures thrive to the extent they find devices that share the costs and benefits or, in economics jargon, internalize the externalities. (Appendix A1 and A2 offer background discussions on evolution, and on ultimate versus proximate causes.) A wealth of examples of animal cooperation and a classification similar to mine of devices solving the social dilemma can be found in Dugatkin (1997).

Hamilton (1964) formalized inclusive fitness and kin selection. As explained in Appendix A3, the key insight is algebraic: if cooperative behavior costs the individual some direct fitness c but brings fitness benefits b to others, then its inclusive fitness is $f = rb - c$, where r is the average relatedness of the others ($r=1$ for clones, $r=1/2$ for siblings, etc.) Behaviors with positive inclusive fitness tend become prevalent, and those with negative inclusive fitness tend to die out.

George Williams (1926–) is another great pioneer in the evolution of sociality; see especially Williams (1966). Dawkins (1976) is the most widely read book on the topic of the selfish gene, and rightfully so. E. O. Wilson (1975) provoked a very noisy controversy, partly because it suggested that kin selection arguments could explain human evolution. For a recent account, see Segerstrale (2001).

These books include descriptions of cooperation among bees and ants. The mechanism involves sophisticated trace chemicals called pheromones. Producing and detecting these chemicals allows ants, for example, to follow trails, and to identify fellow workers. The ultimate cause of cooperation, however, is inclusive fitness. An unusual genetic aspect of *hymenoptera*, called haplodiploidy, results in relatedness r as high as 3/4 for sisters, who are unable to produce offspring themselves. Their best opportunity to pass on the genes they carry is to cooperate closely in feeding and defending the colony and helping to hatch eggs laid by their mother, the queen. With $r=3/4$, the fundamental social dilemma is not entirely eliminated, but it is greatly reduced; natural selection favors activities for which the social gains exceed 1.33 times the private cost. In most species, by contrast, r is only ½ for full siblings (and parents and children), corresponding to a required benefit–cost ratio of 2.

Recent research has complicated the textbook story. In many insect societies, queens mate with several drones and in others, there are multiple queens, reducing r, but possibly improving the division of labor. Indeed, colony-level selection, rather than classic kin selection, may play the dominant role among bees and ants. See, for example, Wilson and Hölldobler (2005).

On cooperation among lions, see Packer and Pusey (1997); on mole rat societies, see Milius (2006).

Reciprocity, as explained in Trivers (1971), hinges on the discount factor. The sooner and more certain is the return favor, the closer the discount factor d is to 1.0, and the greater the range of prosocial behavior that can be supported by reciprocity. Trivers (1985) offers an accessible textbook treatment of reciprocity and other aspects of social behavior. The classic sociology article on reciprocity is Goulder (1960).

Cooperators must avoid non-kin when they bestow costly favors. The textbook example is the European common cuckoo, which survives on a "cheater" strategy. It lays an egg in the nest of other species whose eggs look similar. The cuckoo egg hatches sooner and the chick grows faster, and often kills off the host chicks. Host species must evolve ways to detect and evict these brood parasites as they become more prevalent, or else the host species dwindles. For a recent twist, see Soler et al. (1995).

Wilkinson (1984) reports reciprocal food sharing in vampire bats. Skepticism about Wilkinson's findings appears in recent work such as Hammerstein (2003). The underlying problem seems to be Wilkinson's small sample sizes, and the lack of other nonprimate examples. In an October 2007 personal communication, Wilkinson writes "I don't think it is an accident that vampire bats have the largest brains for their body size of any other bat," and that these bats clearly have the capacities for reciprocity. He acknowledges that the data have limitations, but remains confident that they demonstrate true reciprocity.

For a nice summary of research on primate grooming, see Maestipieri (2005, 199). Some evidence that reciprocity builds on kinship is noted in Ligon (1991, 51).

Hauser (2006) argues that evidence for reciprocity in food sharing is rather weak in bats and capuchin monkeys, though stronger in chimps, and lately he has found it in tamarinds.

On bonobos and chimps, and numerous references to the primary literature, see de Waal (2005). Once called "pygmy chimps," bonobos are now recognized as a separate species that separated from common chimps about five million years ago, only about half a million years past the time of our last common ancestor. Genetically, bonobos and chimps are about equally related to us and to each other. Observations of bonobo social structure come mostly from zoos because these primates are hard to observe in the wild (see Parker 2007). The world's most celebrated captive ape, Kanzi, at Georgia State's Language Research Center, is a bonobo noted for his understanding of spoken English, his expressive language using a keyboard, and his kindness: see "Kanzi," http://en.wikipedia.org/wiki/Kanzi and "Meet our Great Apes," Great Ape Trust, Des Moines, Iowa, http://www.iowagreatapes.org/bonobo/meet/kanzi.php.

Sahelanthropus and Lake Chad (see Gibbons 2006, 237).

The human lineage first diverged from our closest cousins, the chimps and bonobos, about 6.5 million years ago, but DNA evidence points to a hybrid about 1.2 million years later that rebred back with chimps (or with our own ancestors)—see Patterson et al. (2006). On chimp lineages (see Wade 2006, 15).

Climate fluctuations (see Richerson et al. [forthcoming]). Its thesis is that extreme climate fluctuations, especially in the last several hundred thousand years, were a primary force behind the evolution of larger brains and human cultural evolution.

Patchy habitats . . . merge again . . . accelerating evolution. See Provine (1986), particularly the discussions of "shifting balance" equilibrium. Also see the discussion of plaid ecosystems versus the usual stripes in Richerson et al. (forthcoming).

Homo erectus: see Bobe and Behrensmeyer (2004). Some scholars give a separate name, *Homo ergaster*, to the early African lineages of *Erectus*. Naked skin: see, for example, Klein (1999, 292). Expensive brain: see Aiello and Wheeler (1995). They propose an evolutionary tradeoff between robust digestive systems and large brains. Specialists vs. generalists: see, for example, Potts (1996).

On sexual dimorphism and the emergence of male-female pair bonds: see, for example, "A Course in Evolution, Taught by Chimps," by Nicholas Wade (*New York Times*, November 25, 2003). Among the wider families of apes, pair-bonding is observed in gibbons, but not in species more closely related to humans, such as gorillas, orangutans, and so on.

Group size and brain volume: see Dunbar (1996).

Contributions of young and old: see Kaplan and Guitierrez (2006).

Grandmothers: see Hawkes (2004). Some controversies remain, summarized in the article "Evolution's Secret Weapon: Grandma," (*New York Times*, October 5, 2007).

See Lee (1979) and Murphy and Murphy (1986) on group fusion among the !Kung and Shoshone, respectively.

Controversies abound regarding the relative importance of cultural and genetic evolution in shaping *Homo Sapiens*. The text emphasizes their coevolution without discussing specific mechanisms. For differing perspectives, see Choi and Bowles (2007) and Henrich and McElreath (2003).

Emotions in animals also remains a controversial topic. Our instinctive empathy often leads us to mistakenly read human motivation and human traits into animals, especially pets. For example, a bird song may seem cheery to us, even though its function is to warn other birds away from the singer's territory. Scientists studying animal behavior are so wary of this mistake, known as the pathetic fallacy, that they often discount even very strong evidence on animal emotions. The balance is starting to return, as noted by de Waal and many other scientists: see for example de Waal (2005, 210) for evidence of envy in capuchins. The article "Scientist Finds the Beginnings of Morality in Primate Behavior," by Nicholas Wade (*New York Times*, March 20, 2007) summarizes de Waal's recent views.

I use the customary distinction between emotions contingent on others' reaction to one's behavior (pride and shame) and emotions that arise even when others are unaware of one's behavior (guilt).

Whether the cognitive advances (theory of mind) or the emotions (empathy, etc.) are more important is also hotly debated by academics. That debate is pointless, in my opinion; both are essential and they reinforce each other in the human moral system.

Mirror neurons: for a popular account, see "Cells that Read Minds," by Sandra Blakeslee (*New York Times*, January 10, 2006). On the connection to language, it cites an interview with Michael Arbib, a neuroscientist at the University of Southern California, who mentions an article he published in *Trends in Neuroscience* in March 1998. On the cup of coffee, it cites Iacoboni et al. (2005). Mirror neurons were first observed in macaques, where they play a very limited role; they are far more numerous and apparently more important in humans.

Spindle cells, the ventromedial nucleus and the two insulas are discussed in the popular article "Humanity? Maybe It's in the Wiring," by Sandra Blakeslee (*New York Times*, December 9, 2003).

The definition of morals is my own, though it seems consistent with views I recently encountered in Rawls (2001, 6): "Social cooperation is guided by publicly recognized rules and procedures which those cooperating recognize as appropriate to regulate their conduct," and in Hauser (2006). Hauser proposes an analogy to the universal grammar that, according to Chomsky and followers, underlies all human languages. Hauser's critics, such as philosopher Richard Rorty, emphasize the plasticity of moral codes and are skeptical about biological foundations. My argument doesn't hinge on this debate about how tightly biology constrains cultural evolution, or on a parallel debate about the efficiency of cultural evolution. My point is, simply, that all established human groups have moral codes that are subject to cultural evolution.

The dictionary definition of morals is circular, and refers to moral constructs such as goodness and character. The *American Heritage Dictionary, 4th Ed.*, for example, says:

> *moral* (adj.) 1. Of or concerned with the judgment of the goodness or badness of human action or character. 2. Teaching or exhibiting goodness or correctness of character and behavior. 3. Conforming to [moral] standards . . .
> (noun) 1. The lesson or principle contained in or taught by a fable, a story or an event.

The air we breathe: only in the last two hundred years have scientists discovered that air is not elemental, but has several components (nitrogen, oxygen, carbon dioxide, water vapor); that a simple mathematical expression (the ideal gas law) governs air volume, pressure, and temperature; that a more complex equation (Navier-Stokes) governs air flow; and so forth. Common sense is adequate for normal activities in normal situations, but the deeper scientific understanding helps us refine unusual activities such as scuba diving and mountain climbing, and gives us broader insight into the weather, the unity of the plant kingdom, and many other facets of our world. Likewise, common sense about morals works well for everyday activities, but a deeper understanding of their origins and dynamics should provide wider insights into our world.

The Ultimatum Game was introduced by Güth et al. (1982). Rejections of unfair offers correlate with brain activity in the anterior insula region associated with disgust, according to Sanfey et al. (2003).

Experiments in small-scale societies: see Henrich et al. (2001). More details appear in the authors' forthcoming book, *Foundations of Human Sociality: Experiments in 15 small scale societies.* The interpretation given in the text also appears in Hauser (2006, 83).

Recipients of your affection: see the famous Rotten Kid Theorem in Becker (1974).

Vengeful emotions deter antisocial behavior: see Friedman and Singh (2004) and also the article "Payback Time: Why Revenge Tastes so Sweet," by Benedict Carey (*New York Times*, July 27, 2004).

The desire to achieve and maintain good standing can overpower even our most basic instincts, such as avoiding pain and preserving fertility. Gruesome examples include clitorectomy in several contemporary African cultures, penile piercing in aboriginal Australia, and voluntary castration for male sopranos and harem attendants in medieval civilizations.

Leda Cosmides and John Tooby's classic 1992 collection, *The Adapted Mind*, argues that our minds are tuned to the tasks most important for our Paleolithic ancestors. In particular, it emphasizes the task of detecting cheaters.

Peter Richerson comments (in a November 2007 personal communication): "I think it is significant that the group that speaks the same language or dialect is also the group that delimits the boundaries of routine cooperation. The historian Benedict Anderson explains the rise of nationalism as a byproduct of our treating people who speak the same language as we do something like our ancestors treated fellow tribespeople."

Ngenika and Wolimbka: see Bernhard et al. (2006). The Swiss Army result appears in the immediately preceding article.

The cultural selection arguments advanced here and in the next section go back at least to Boyd and Richerson (1985). On the harsh codes of herdsmen, see, for example, Pettigrew (1975), Boehm (1999), and Kelly (1985).

Polyandry spread among the Nyinba: see Durham (1991, chap. 2). Primogeniture (only the first born male inherits) is an alternative moral solution to the same problem, quite prevalent historically in Europe, but it works better when agriculture is less labor intensive, or cheap agricultural labor is available.

Some anthropologists, such as Klein (1999), postulate that the Upper Paleolithic explosion was primed by some sort of genetic change, perhaps in speech processing circuits of the brain. Others argue for a gradual accumulation of the cultural prerequisites with no genetic break: see McBrearty and Brooks (2000). Either way, the explosion and its aftermath were cultural phenomena.

Kelly (1985) explains the Nuer and Dinka conflict.

Expansion out of Africa: see Wade (2006).

Anthropologists Diane Gifford-Gonzales and Peter Richerson gave me very helpful insights into the literature. Of course, they (like everyone else I acknowledge) should not be held responsible for remaining errors, misunderstandings, or idiosyncrasies.

Chapter 2

Uruk is called "Erech" in the Bible. The city's deity, the goddess Inanna, is also known by her Akkadian name, "Ishtar."

The little fantasy of early Uruk is consistent with current opinion of historians, as I understand it from De Mieroop (2006), Bottéro (2001), Nemet-Nejat (1998), and Kramer (1998).

On population and carrying capacity, see Hassan (1981).

Things change when there are no more frontiers: see MacArthur and Wilson (1967). The discussion is grounded in the distinction between r-strategies (expand quickly) and k-strategies (become more efficient at extracting resources).

Fagan (2003) has a wealth of general information on California lifestyles before 1500 CE. The population reached about 300 thousand by the end of that period.

The classic book on the transition to settled life is Sahlins (1972).

A sidelight on herding: although herding is the product of social evolution, it eventually affected human genetics. Children of herdsmen enjoy greater health when they retain their ability to digest lactose later in life, so genetic mutations allowing greater lactose tolerance have spread over the centuries in every herding culture. For an overview, see Durham (1991).

On the diffusion of bow and arrow technology, see Klein (1999, 477) and also Diamond (1999).

Vayda (1967) discusses gift exchange among the Pomo, two (modern) counties north of Costanoan territory. They, and their Yurok and Karok neighbors to the north, enjoyed even larger salmon runs than the Costanoans.

Paul Samuelson, the first Nobel laureate in economics, is said to have named the idea of comparative advantage in Ricardo (1817) when challenged to identify a simple but nonobvious economic insight. Every microeconomics textbook now explains the idea in excruciating detail.

On Costanoans and fur seals: see Cooper and Etnier (2005).

Dow et al. (2006) contains a more elaborate and technical explanation of why sedentary hunter-gatherers took the first steps in the transition to agriculture. It also mentions the main alternative theories.

Chapter 4 of Diamond (2005) is an excellent brief description of Anasazi civilization, focusing on Chaco.

Hawkes (1992) discusses some aspects of the moral transformation. Boone (1992, 333ff) discusses the emergence of hierarchy in the Hawaiian Islands.

I can find only one partial exception to the rule that transferable wealth goes with hierarchy: two sedentary tribes of the Pacific Northwest, best known for their totem poles and potlatch feasts. Boehm (1999, 88) writes, "Neighbors of the Kwakiutl such as the Tolowa and Coastal Yurok also lived in year-round villages with food storage, but they kept their leaders weak and were politically egalitarian." Why the exception? I conjecture that the villages were not such inviting targets for raiders, perhaps because they were small and hard to reach, or because the stored food was mostly acorns and other items with low value per pound.

In game-theory jargon, the participation constraint is much higher in hunter-gatherer life than in agricultural life, so utility levels will be higher. The same abstract argument applies to chimps: the alpha male and his supporters can bully other males, because they face mortal danger (from the males of neighboring groups) if they try to leave.

Joseph's story is Genesis 41.

Karl Polanyi and followers emphasized the role of redistribution; see, for example, Polanyi and Conrad (1957).

On Uruk in 4500 BCE, see Van De Mieroop (2005).

On self-serving bias, see Babcock and Loewenstein (1997).

For the emergence of economic organization, see Howitt and Clower (2000).

On market formats more efficient than haggling, see Cason et al. (2003).

On the magic of CE, see any microeconomics textbook. The insight goes back to *The Wealth of Nations* by Adam Smith (1776), who famously wrote (Book IV, chap. 2) that each market participant is "led by an invisible hand to promote an end which was no part of his intention. Nor is it always the worse for the society that it was not part of it. By pursuing his own interest he frequently promotes that of the society more effectually than when he really intends to promote it."

Vernon Smith's experiments are nicely described in Smith (1982). The original paper is Smith (1962).

On Assyrian trader networks, see Larsen (1976).

On the Phoenicians, see Aubet (2001).

On Athens, see Millett (1991).

On Rome's open market economy, see Temin (2001) and Cameron and Neal (2003, 39–40. On Rome's stock market, see Malmendier (2006). On Rome's economic decline, see for example Cameron and Neal (2003, 41–42).

My thanks to Charlotte Cooper for pointers to the literature on California's first inhabitants, especially those of the central coast.

Chapter 3

Previous evolutionary transitions are discussed in, among other articles, Szathmary and Maynard Smith (1995). See, also, the last paragraph of Appendix section A2 on transition dynamics.

The quotes are from Polanyi (1944, 42, 57). The book argues that the market system was an aberration of the nineteenth century, which was breaking down in the twentieth century with the Great Depression and two world wars. Many economic historians now accept his view that ancient civilizations did not have a self-regulating market system, but evidence is spotty and controversies remain. Of course, his view of the market system's twentieth-century demise was, at best, premature.

Leijonhufvud (2007) is the source of the quotes in the forth paragraph.

For more on Basil's life and times, see Holmes (2005), and for Theophano's story, see Gibbons (2003). The millennium edition of the *Wall Street Journal* (January 11, 1999, R6) lists the sources of wealth for Basil and his contemporaries.

For more on contract enforceability, see Greif (1993).

Olson (1993) coins the terms roving bandit and stationary bandit. The Duke-Serf game is formalized and solved in Appendix section A8.

On the political pyramid of ancient civilizations, see, for example, Cameron and Neal (2003, chap. 2, 4). That textbook also contains population estimates used in this chapter.

While revising this chapter, I encountered North et al. (2006). Its perspective overlaps my own, but its focus is more on political changes than on market evolution.

"Monopoly profits . . . economically very inefficient." Since Adam Smith, the point has been central to economic analysis. Actually, royal cartels are far less efficient even than a standard textbook monopoly, for three reasons. First, production (or trade) typically involves high cost producers. Second, over time, the barriers to entry raise costs. Third, the cartels often include double marginalization. For example, the Afghan silk traders would charge a monopoly markup and then the Byzantine traders would put a monopoly markup on top of that, raising the final price above that of a profit maximizing unified monopolist. Double marginalization is still discussed in some microeconomic texts: see, for example, Baye (2005, 420).

Europe's early lead on cannon technology and the fall of Constantinople: see, for example, McNeill (1989).

Grantham (1999) argues that the economic collapse of Western Europe in the Dark Ages and its rise in medieval times are largely due to changes in access to markets and trade.

European contact with more advanced civilizations was spurred by the Mongols opening of the Silk Road in the 1200s, as well as by the Crusades: see Weatherford (2004) and Fernandez-Armesto (2006, chap. 3).

On the role of political fragmentation and competition, see Jones (1981).

The Champagne fairs are mentioned in most standard economic histories; see, for example, Cameron-Neal (2003, 65). A popular account of Troyes and its summer fair can be found in Gies and Gies (1981). The spirit of a smaller fair at Shrewsbury is nicely captured in Peters (1992).

For more on the community responsibility system and impartial justice, see Greif (2006). The influential article Greif et al. (1994)—or its overinterpretation— has been criticized in a number of later articles, including Dessi and Ogilvie (2003), and Sachs (2006). For more on private commercial law, see Bernstein (1998).

Arguably the last and best book in the "heroic tale" tradition is Boorstin (1983). I've drawn on it for the story of Prince Henry the Navigator. See Chapter 4 of Fernandez-Armesto (2006) for a less generous account of Dom Henrique's career.

Weber is not as one-sided as some of his followers. Page 186 of Weber (1930) notes that the Protestant ethic "was in turn influenced in its development and character by the totality of social conditions, especially economic ones." See also Tawney (1926), Clark (2007), and Landes (1998). Landes criticizes politically correct revisionist accounts such as Goody (1996).

My account also draws on Rosenberg and Birdsell (1986), and Maddison (2001, 63), which contains the ship count estimates.

I found the Spanish gold and silver estimates on UC Davis professor Richard Cowen's page http://www-geology.ucdavis.edu/~cowen/~GEL115/.

Acemoglu et al. (2005) shows how "Atlantic trade and colonial activity enriched and strengthened commercial interests, including new groups without ties to the monarchy." This led to legal and political reform, and strengthened property rights, a primary driver of growth and modernization. Shimer (2007) points up other Acemoglu themes relevant to the current discussion, for example, that spreading the franchise makes redistribution irreversible, whereas coups by old elite, and revolutions, raise fears of expropriation, and so deter investment and growth. Cervellati and Sunde (2005) present another related positive feedback story.

On China's Treasure Fleet, see Levathes (1996). Shiue and Keller (2007) summarize trade institutions in China (and continental Europe) in the 1700s and analyze location/price data, concluding that there was rough parity on efficiency of grain markets at that time. For contrasting perspectives, see Landes (2006) and chapter 4 of Fernandez-Armesto (2006).

Olson (1984) explains how unified control squelches innovation. Vested interests find it worthwhile to unite to protect their interests. The benefits of innovation greatly exceed the costs to the vested interests, but the benefits are too diffuse and too uncertain to sufficiently create powerful countervailing coalitions. Once the vested interests become sufficiently organized, the nation or empire loses its momentum and slowly declines.

The end of the Polynesian golden age is an exception. Their golden age was spurred by the discovery of truly virgin islands between Hawaii and New Zealand, and highlighted by accumulated skills in navigation and raft/outrigger construction and colonization. It ended not with unified control, but with exhaustion of resources, for example, on Easter Island, and collapse of trade (see Diamond 2005, chap. 2).

Chapter 4

Schumpeter sadly predicts capitalism's eventual demise in Schumpeter (1942). I can no longer find a quote indicating that Henry Kissinger also believed that communism would eventually triumph.

"Bathe . . ." is from *Milton: A Poem*, Book 2, Plate 41, by William Blake, 1810, and the "dark satanic mills" are from his 1804 poem *Jerusalem*. See Blake (1997).

The law of supply and demand destroys social responsibility: see Carlyle (1843).

"Seep across the boundaries": see Lasch (1996).

Population boomed: see, for example, Lee (2003). Of course, Russia in the 1990s is the biggest exception.

Most history books include a summary of the enclosure movement, for example, Palmer et al. (2002, 430). Dahlman (1980) offers a deeper analysis. He points out that prior to enclosure, the open field system dominated northern Europe for a full millennium, and was quite efficient in providing local self-sufficiency. Enclosure became viable only with regional markets and specialization. The national wool trade provoked the first great wave of enclosure in England about 1550, but as late as 1750, about half of land under plow remained in the open field system. The next wave of enclosures virtually eliminated English open fields by 1850. Dahlman, like other observers, emphasizes the torn social fabric: whether or not small farmers received fair compensation for releasing their claims on the commons, they lost local ties and their children became rootless agricultural or factory workers.

Portsmouth block maker example: see Hicks (1969, 149).

The lines are from Blake (1997, Gnomic Verses viii).

For an excellent discussion of modernization and the labor market, see Leijon-hufvud (2007).

Of course, the "market" for dissident politics is only metaphorical. The discussion draws on conversations with Jonathan Beecher, as well as his books.

On Luddites, see Pynchon (1984), who, in turn, cites the *Oxford English Dictionary* and *Encyclopedia Britannica*.

On Charles Fourier, see Beecher (1986) and Beecher and Bienvenu (1983).

"generous, conciliatory . . ." is from Beecher (2001, 5).

On the events of 1848, see Dureau (1984).

Marx (1844) contains the quoted lines on alienated labor.

Ricardo (1817) is still considered an intellectual landmark. Some of Marx's contemporaries (e.g., the economists Gossens, Jevons, Menger, and Walras) discovered fatal flaws in Ricardo's labor theory of value, but Marx seemed unaware of their work. Despite heroic efforts of modern economists in the 1970s and 1980s (e.g., Roemer, 1986) to find intellectual underpinnings, the labor theory of value is now dead. The consensus view is that, typically, market values are determined by the intersection of supply and demand, and that labor cost is just one factor affecting supply.

Goldman (1923), Remnick (1994), and Moynahan (1994) contain much of the material on the Soviet system. On Fascism, see Paxton (2004). *Animal Farm* by Orwell (1945) nicely captures the moral hypocrisy and hierarchy of the Soviet system.

Chapter 5

Aleksanyan's quote is from Remnick (1994, 318). The book also contains lots of very useful background information.

Sachs' quotes are from Lipton and Sachs (1992). The authors, at that time, were official economic advisors to Yeltsin's government. Their paper includes many caveats, especially about the political power of managers of loss-making state owned enterprises. Commentators Edmund Phelps and Mancur Olsen presciently warned of the greater danger from insiders who might abuse the reform initiatives to accumulate power rather than to submit to market discipline.

Moynahan (1994) is a good general source. Khrushchev's corn fiasco is described on pages 199–201, gas filching on page 233, Gorbachev's mud cabin on page 223, his anti-alcohol campaign on pages 227–28 and 241, and the 1991 failed coup on pages 249–50. See also Richardson (1999).

The pervasive lack of trust, and predictions that the Soviet economy was headed down, come from Richard E. Ericson, personal communication, 1977.

An excellent summary of Russia's economic shocks and policies in the 1990s is Leijonhufvud and Craver (2001).

On the role of insiders—nomenklatura—in controlling productive assets since Gorbachev's reforms, see Grigoriev (1995). I thank Julia Urozhaeva for bringing this reference to my attention. Julia also rightly points out that Russian economic reformers did not intend to promote the oligarchs' crimes. In the 1990s, the oligarchs and their government allies managed to remove intended safeguards and to block serious reforms.

The rise of the oligarchs and looting of Russia, see Klebnikov (2000).

On pliant oligarchs, see the article "The Triumph of the Quiet Tycoon," by Peter Maass (New York Times Magazine, August 1, 2004). The articles note that Putin has arrested or chased out the top three oligarch—Berezovsky, Khodorkovsky and Gusinsky—and the remaining oligarchs have found that they can do as they want as long as they support Putin.

Shkolnikov et al. (2001) show an unprecedented drop in life expectancy from 1991 to 1994, especially for males, partially reversed by 1998.

Jack Hirshleifer and other academic economists such as Hershel Grossman and Stergios Skaperdas have written on competition in the absence of property rights; see, for example, Hirshleifer (1995).

Development economists are increasingly sympathetic to the propositions that (a) well functioning markets are the linchpin of economic development, and (b) good legal and moral infrastructure are the keys to well functioning markets. See, for example, Fafchamps (forthcoming).

See, also, the large related literature on rent dissipation. A popular account appears in a review of a 1998 book by Schleifer and Vishny that appeared in the February 13, 1999 issue of the Economist magazine. The book authors were major Western advisors in the 1990s Russian reform.

Putin-era stories: see the article "Business in Russia after Yukos," (Economist magazine, May 12, 2007, 67–68), which includes the quote about Khordorkovsky's trial; Specter (2007, 50–63) focuses on Anna Politkovskaya; "The Murder of Paul Klebnikov," (Wall Street Journal, July 14, 2004, A14), and also "Murdered US Editor Was Probing Russian Reporter's Death," (Wall Street Journal, July 16, 2004) by David Satter. The Kozlov murder was reported in the article "Austrians Cast Doubt on Russian Arrests in Murder Case," by Andrew E. Kramer (New York Times, June 15, 2007).

Bribery by, and extortion of, ordinary Russian businessmen are engagingly described in "Face Value: The Reluctant Briber" (*Economist* magazine, November 4, 2006, 79). "Russia under Putin" (*Economist* magazine, August 25, 2007, 25–28) documents the rise of KGB men to dominate government and big business in the Putin era.

Chapter 6

Vogel (1979) is an early book by a Harvard Business School Professor pushing Japan as a role model. Thurow (1985, 284) argues that the United States must subsidize key industries to compete with Japan. Page 298 asks the reader to compare U.S. policies like "propping up Harley-Davidson using high tariffs" to the self-evidently better "Japanese policy of subsidizing research on the fifth-generation computer." Punditry is a tough business: the intervening twenty years have stood Thurow's example on its head. Harley-Davidson, now a $15 billion company, dominates its industry, with almost a 50 percent market share in the United States, and a rapidly growing share in Europe and even in Japan (now over 25 percent). Japan's huge subsidy of fifth generation computing seems to have missed the technological boat and her computer industries are far less impressive now than twenty years ago.

The Tokugawa era and the Meiji restoration: see Landes (1998), and Jansen (2002). A more detailed look at the origins and impact of the zaibatsu can be found in Morck and Nakamura (2007).

Deming (2000) summarizes his ideas. His key speech to Japanese top management can be found at http://deming.eng.clemson.edu/pub/den/deming_1950 .htm.

Toyota production system: see Ohno (1988).

The Japanese manufacturing system: see Aoki (1988), and articles such as Milgrom and Roberts (1990).

Hoshi and Kashyap (2001) include the Mazda and Maruzen examples in Chapter 5. I adapted the jusen material from pages 270–71. International bank ratings are shown on page 274, and bank mega-mergers are described on page 296.

Hoshi and Kashyap (2004, 3–26) is another source for material in this chapter. For example, page 12 cites other studies that conclude that net operating profits for Japanese banking industry have been negative since 1993.

Cargill, Hutchison, and Ito (1997) is a third source for much of the material. Pages 99–108 discuss liberalization in the 1980s and related topics, and pages 130–44 discuss jusen.

Peek and Rosengren (2005, 1144–66) documents "evergreen lending," government pressure to misclassify bad loans as good, and so forth; see also Okada and Horioka (2007). This article points up banks' central role in propping up zombies to the detriment of typical solvent firms. "Dead Firms Walking," (*The Economist*, September 25, 2004, 81–83) discusses remaining zombie sectors. The Yoshikawa quote appears in: "Business Suicides: Japan's Death Trap" (*Business Week*, June 3, 2002).

Wood (1992) is a journalist's account of the bubble years and the beginning of the zombie era.

The story of the three suicides comes from the article "Death of Three Salesmen—Partners in Suicide," by Mary Jordan and Kevin Sullivan (*Washington Post*, October 7, 1998), http://www.washingtonpost.com/wp-srv/inatl/longterm/brokenlives/broken4a.htm.

The Sogo saga is pieced together from *The Economist* articles "Unforgiven" (June 29, 2000), "Japan's Bankruptcy Department" (June 13, 2000), "The Slow Death of Japan, Inc." (October 12, 2000), "New Tricks," (October 26, 2000), and "Fiddling While Marunouchi Burns" (January 25, 2001), together with the *Asia Times* editorial "Japan: That Revealing Sogo Saga" (July 14, 2000), the *Mainichi Shimbun* story "Captain of Sinking Store Guilty of Hiding Assets" (March 29, 2005), and McIntyre (2000).

"The Sun Also Rises: A Survey of Japan," (*The Economist*, October 8, 2005), is an eighteen-page survey with a generally upbeat assessment of Koizumi's reforms and Japan's prospects for the future.

On Harold Stringer, see, for example, "Sony Chief Executive Says Company Is Back on Track" (*The AP*, December 12, 2007).

On Carlos Ghosn, see, for example, the article "Expenses Cited for End of Nissan's 6-Year Run of Record Profit," by Nick Bunckley and Micheline Maynard (*New York Times*, February 3, 2007).

"U.S. Private-Equity Kings Negotiate a Maze in Japan," by Aandrew Morse and Yukari Iwatani Kane (*Wall Street Journal*, November 23, 2007, A1) illustrates remaining obstacles to bankruptcy and restructuring in Japan.

"Japan still has the world's second largest economy": true, as of late 2007, by the standard comparison using market exchange rates to compare across countries. However, according to purchasing power parity measures, favored by some economists, China now has passed Japan. See "Clipping the Dragon's Wings" (*The Economist*, December 22, 2007, 68).

On "freeters," see "Still Work to be Done: Japan's Labour Market is Becoming More Flexible, but also More Unequal" (*The Economist*, November 29, 2007).

The quote in the last paragraph is from a July 2006 personal communication from Jeff Baer, an American who has worked and lived mostly in Japan since the late 1980s. His perspectives contribute to several other parts of the chapter.

Chapter 7

For more on Albanian Ponzi finance, see Jarvis (2000), Bezemer (1999), and Schmidt (2000). Ponzi schemes are named after Charles Ponzi, who swindled many Boston investors in 1920. They are also known as pyramid schemes. The idea is simply to lure investors by offering very high returns. Early investors are paid the promised returns using the funds raised from the next wave of investors. The pyramid grows as long as ever-increasing waves of new funds pour in from dazzled investors. In a finite world, this can't happen forever. The swindler tries to abscond with the last wave of funds before investors realize that the most recent promises will be broken.

Temin and Voth (2004) and Kindleberger (2000) describe the South Sea Bubble. The absconder is mentioned in Mackay (1841, 55).

Millett (1991, 43) discusses Plato's attitudes, and the entire book discusses Athenian financial practices. In modern Greek, *eranos* refers to communal charity, for example, passing around a collection plate in church (Nikos Nikiforakis, personal communication, April 2007).

Fishing and farming villages; Thomas and Worrall (2002) refers to *eranos* loans as quasi-credit, notes its prevalence in villages in southern India, central Africa, and in the Philippines, and demonstrates its theoretical efficiency.

Roscas: see Besley (1995) and Besley et al. (1993). Roscas are not to be confused with microfinance as practiced by Grameen Bank and a host of similar institutions. Here, a bank or other lender (often subsidized by governments or NGOs) lends to a group of people who live or work together and who agree to joint responsibility for repaying the loan. This encourages the same sort of peer screening and monitoring and peer pressure as in eranos, although as in daneizein the lender is outside the group. See, for example, Yunus (1999).

"Neither a borrower nor a lender be; / for loan oft loses both itself and friend, / and borrowing dulls the edge of husbandry." William Shakespeare, *Hamlet*, Act I, scene 3.

A recent *Wikipedia* definition of moral hazard is "the prospect that a party insulated from risk may behave differently than it would if it were fully exposed to the risk." See moral hazard, http://en.wikipedia.org/wiki/Moral_hazard.

John Steinbeck's 1939 novel *Grapes of Wrath* captures the same moral intuitions in Dustbowl America: flinty-hearted bankers evict hard working families down on their luck from family farms.

Biblical rules on debt forgiveness are in Deuteronomy (15:15) and Leviticus (25).

Finance in Ur: see de Mieroop (2005).

Royal moral hazard: see Hicks (1969). He explicitly mentions prerevolutionary France and Czarist Russia as examples of the ill effects of tax exemptions and outsourcing tax collection.

The origins of paper money in China, see von Glahn (2005).

Palmer, Colton, and Kramer (2003) states that the French Revolution "was precipitated by the financial collapse of the government," due mainly to "tax exemptions and tax evasions of privileged elements" and bad tax collection procedures (348). Czarist debts are mentioned on page 700.

The Florentine banking discussion draws mainly on the work of John F. Padgett, for example, McLean and Padgett (forthcoming).

One florin of bank capital could typically support five florins of bank loans: the mechanics are carefully explained in every intermediate macroeconomics text (and many beginning texts). Here is a quick summary tailored to medieval banks. The loans took the form of deposits in the borrowers' bank accounts. Not all depositors withdrew all their deposits (or repaid all the loans) at the same time.

Reserves (here the same as bank capital, in the form of gold coins called florins) just had to be sufficient to meet the net withdrawals most of the time; extra temporary reserves could be acquired from correspondent branches, if necessary. It turned out that keeping as reserves about 20 percent of the amount loaned was sufficient in the Florentine system. Thus, 80 percent of each florin of capital could be loaned out, and that amount would appear somewhere in the banking system as it was spent. In turn, 80 percent of that 80 percent could be loaned out in a second round. Taking into account third-round lending and beyond, the total loans supported by an additional florin of bank capital is the sum of a geometric series $0.8 + 0.64 + \ldots = 5$. See Appendix section A9 for an explanation of such sums.

The nature of financial markets. This is an original spin on standard textbook material, for example, Fabozzi and Modigliani (2003).

Mugabe's impact on markets: see for example the article, "How to Stay Alive When it All Runs Out: Ordinary Zimbabweans Find Creative Ways to Survive" (*The Economist*, July 12, 2007).

Roman Republic: see Malmendier (2005). Amsterdam finance: see Penso de la Vega (1688/1996). See also Goetzmann and Rouwenhorst (2005, chap. 7). Efficient Financial Market Theory: the original insight is due to Hayek (1945). See also the very influential article Fama (1971)

Short sales restrictions: see the article "Get Shorty," by J. Surowiecki (*New Yorker*, December 1, 2003, 42).

See Keynes (1936), Minksy (1982), and Kindleberger (2000). Keynes' famous beauty contest metaphor ends as follows, "It is not a case of choosing those [faces] which, to the best of one's judgment, are really the prettiest, nor even those which average opinion genuinely thinks the prettiest. We have reached the third degree where we devote our intelligences to anticipating what average opinion expects the average opinion to be. And there are some, I believe, who practise the fourth, fifth and higher degrees." Applied to financial market bubbles, his point is that sophisticated pessimists should sometimes mimic optimists.

Malkiel (2003, 32) makes the point this way: "[Keynes'] theory might less charitably be called the 'greater fool' theory. It's perfectly all right to pay three times what something is worth as long as later on you can find some innocent to pay five times what it's worth."

Subprime lending. See, for example, "One Family's Journey Into a Subprime Trap," by James R. Hagerty and Ken Gepfert (Wall Street Journal, August 16, 2007, A1); "Burned by Real Estate, Some Just Walk Away," by Kemba J. Dunham and Rachel Emma Silverman (*Wall Street Journal*, October 18, 2997, D1), and Robert Kuttner's testimony to the House Committee on Financial Services (October 2, 2007).

As of October 2007, financial markets are suffering substantial losses on securitized home mortgages. The episode illustrates several themes of the present chapter. First, the spread of subprime mortgage contracts illustrates KMK Phase 2 demand-pull financial innovation. Second, promise guarantors such as Moody's and Standard and Poor's gave unrealistically high ratings to some of the securities (called collateralized debt obligations [CDOs]) engineered from pools of home mortgages. Possibly due to conflicts of interest, they didn't do their job properly.

Third, recent tightening of bankruptcy laws make it more difficult for homeowners to keep their homes when things go bad with a subprime loan, affecting the Phase 3 dynamics. Also, the homeowner is less likely to be dealing with the banks (or other entities) that originated the loan, with which he might personally negotiate a mutually beneficial workout. Instead, he is dealing with agents of a diffuse set of indirect lenders who are unaware of his personal circumstances. Foreclosure and cascading problems are then more likely, as in KMK Phase 3. Finally, the financial innovations (CDOs, private equity, hedge funds) make it difficult to see who will bear the losses. As in KMK Phase 4, this ambiguity slows financial recovery and hurts the real economy.

Unusually rapid movements in fundamental values: see, for example, Garber (1989). The academic tide began to turn: see, for example, Schiller (2002).

Sizeable bubbles in the lab: see Smith, Suchanek, and Williams (1988). Recent laboratory findings and open questions are summarized in Friedman (2008).

Chapter 8

See also Maslow (1943). The article and many other writings are collected in Stephenson (2000).

For the history of the Hudson's Bay Company, see Innis (1999) and Newman (2000).

Organization and management: see also Milgrom and Roberts (1992). This classic textbook mentions Hudson's Bay company, and analyzes organizations in terms of the coordination and motivation problems they must solve. While polishing this chapter, I encountered Roberts (2004), which also mentions Hudson's Bay and covers some of the same ideas as in the present chapter. See page 18 for a very compatible definition of corporate culture, and pages 174–75 for a discussion of "high commitment human resource management systems."

Plato (1945, Books 5–7, 175ff) explains why everything should be run by philosopher-kings. Lenin (1902) contains a different version of the same idea.

Many business books implicitly assume that coordination and communication are the only problems, and ignore social dilemmas and motivation problems.

Malone (2004) is one of the higher quality examples. Its message is that lower communications costs, due to new computer networks, and so on, will bring about decentralization and democratization in the workplace.

The hold-up problem was analyzed first in Klein, Crawford, and Alchian (1978). Classic empirical work includes Masten (1984) and Monteverde and Teece (1982). Good textbook explanations can be found in Baye (2005) and in Milgrom and Roberts (1992).

The Caligula University example is based on a conversation in October 2007 with university employees who choose to remain anonymous. The computer engineer also prefers to remain anonymous. The quotes are from a conversation in May 2007.

The original paper on the how firms lower transaction costs is Coase (1937).

A classic book on boundaries of the firm is Williamson (1975).

The limits on internal rewards set by labor markets are called participation constraints by game theorists. Such constraints are a standard part of abstract theory and are discussed less formally in Milgrom and Roberts (1992).

On the transition to corporations one hundred years ago, see Chandler (1977). The historical account in this section draws on Lamoreaux, Raff, and Temin (2002). On the textile industry, see Scranton (1983).

The image of the late twentieth-century Merrimack River as a brick-lined canyon comes from personal correspondence with Art Argiewicz.

Economies of scale: see Smith (1776, chap. 1). Also, chapter 3 notes the role of mass markets.

Interchangeable parts are attributed to prerevolutionary France by the *Wikipedia* article http://en.wikipedia.org/wiki/Interchangeable_parts. It notes that the idea was brought to the United States by Thomas Jefferson, and that Eli Whitney (of cotton gin fame) obtained the first U.S. contract to manufacture guns this way in 1798. Eli Terry is credited with developing mass production of clocks in 1808.

Hicks (1969) notes contemporary data on the extent of economies of scale.

Leijonhufvud (2007) insightfully discusses how economies of scale and more extensive markets feed on each other.

"When the alternative was subsistence farming or worse." In many ways, corporate blue collar jobs, although impersonal, were better than most nineteenth-century jobs in the old family firms. Think of Bob Cratchit's work life under Ebenezer Scrooge in Dickens' famous story, "A Christmas Carol."

On Lowell and the Factory Girls Strike, see Chapter 1 in Sobel (1974) and also Zinn (2005).

The Swiss laboratory experiments are reported in Fehr, Kirchsteiger, and Riedl (1993). Their interpretation is based on Akerlof (1982). The delicate balance is documented in Charness, Kagel, and Frechette (2004) and in Falk and Kosfeld (2006), and other studies cited therein.

The Ford/Firestone debacle: see Krueger and Mas (2004). See also Mas (2007), which analyzes less famous but still large ($400 million) losses in value due to labor problems at Caterpillar.

On the new environment, the particular list is the author's. Each item on the list has its own extensive bibliography. On deregulation, see, for example, Kahn (2004).

On China and India's entry into the market system, see, for example, the special (June 2006) issue of *CESIfo Economic Studies*.

Tim Duncan is a basketball superstar, almost seven feet tall, noted for his agility. Shaquille O'Neill is another basketball giant. Tony Parker, listed at six foot two, is a basketball superstar noted for his quick moves.

Cannibalization costs are featured in Christensen (2003). The iPod story is part of the book *Sony vs Sony*, by Nihon Keizai Shimbun (a business daily).

Influence costs are prominently featured in Milgrom and Roberts (1992).

On medieval guilds, see Dessi and Olgilvie (2003).

On Prato, see http://www.prato.turismo.toscana.it/comprare/eng/storia3.htm.

History of Hollywood: see, for example, Thomson (2006).

The German university system was pioneered in Berlin by Friedrich Wilhelm von Humboldt (1767–1835); see http://en.wikipedia.org/wiki/Humboldt_Universit%C3%A4t

The Linux response to the virus: see Evans and Wolf (2005).

I'm not aware of publications that spell out how networks reduce cannibalization and influence costs and solve the holdup problem, but the point is self-evident. Networks also help solve the holdup problem for physical capital: once the network is wide enough, it can also support specialized equipment that can find several uses throughout the network.

I have no citations on networks mobilizing moral sentiments, but the point, again, is self-evident. A qualification on "incredible bursts of energy and creativity": burnout eventually sets in. A dutiful corporate pyramid climber will give decades of steady effort, and that's what pays off in stable times.

Google's story is told in numerous books and magazine articles, for example, Vise and Malseed (2006).

Kntek is a pseudonym for a software company founded in 1996 that changed its name in 2005, and again in 2007, following mergers. Its story was recounted to me by MC, an engineer, on May 7, 2007.

The story of the American Buddhist software company was recounted to me by LM, an engineer, in June 2007.

EBay data can be found it its 2006 annual report. The figure of 700 thousand sellers comes from the article "EBay Moves to Recharge Its Auctions," by Bob Tedeschi (*New York Times*, January 18, 2007).

U.S. Army combat networks: see for example the article "The Army's $200 Billion Makeover March to Modernize Proves Ambitious and Controversial," by Alec Klein (*Washington Post*, December 7, 2007, A01). Countering evolved insurgent networks: see Hammes (2006).

On the open source movement, see *The Economist*'s special report March 18, 2006, 73–75.

U.S. construction industry: for example, see the 2006 annual report of Pulte Homes, the industry's largest corporation. But also see the article "Pulte Homes Cutting 1,900 Jobs: Builder Cites 'Difficult' Housing Market for Move," (*AP*, May 30, 2007). The cut is about 20 percent of Pulte's workforce, and the CEO acknowledges that the company "is larger than the market presently allows."

The life-and-death struggle was described to me by engineer RM in May 2007.

HP's VC Café is discussed in Malone (op cit., 2004, 93–95). The company had long been noted for its egalitarian moral code, called the HP Way, emphasizing trust and teamwork. Carly Fiorina (the CEO 1999–2005) tried to make the company more aggressive and star-oriented, touching off a culture war: Fiorina (2006) gives her side of the story.

Toyota's emulation of the Linux community is discussed in Evans and Wolfe (2005). Also see the survey "The New Organization: A Survey of the Company" (*The Economist*, January 21, 2006), which quotes the Toyota Way. Page 17 of that supplement notes that Boeing didn't design the 787 in-house; the development team includes one hundred partner companies around the world. Team members constantly videoconference and work from a common real time database.

On outsourcing and the holdup problem: "The outsourcing provider and the client company may form alliances and take financial stakes in one other to make sure their interests are aligned," Jon Watts of Booz Allen Hamilton is quoted on page 17 of *The Economist* survey just cited.

IBM: see the corporate Web site and annual reports. Although panned by Amazon critics as self-serving and shallow, Gerstner (2002) collects the basic facts.

Regarding business consulting services, see Hancock et al. (2005). A capsule summary from page 4: "dividing its business into components, focusing on those that really matter, responding rapidly to market changes, creating a variable [scalable] business model and operating in a resilient manner."

Wal-Mart: see its 2007 annual report. The raft of recent books includes Fishman (2006). See also Lichtenstein (2006), the proceedings of an academic conference.

For a negative take on Wal-Mart employee relations, see Ehrenreich (2001). A reporter's adventures in the minimum wage world of the working poor, the book discusses Wal-Mart's "industrial engineering" (page 208) of "associates"; the "cult of Sam" on page 143; the Wal-Mart cheer, adapted from Japanese factories on page 178. Page 185ff argues that the company's fictional family is worse than dysfunctional due to extreme inequality. In general, Ehrenreich notes that a single parent would have to have a $14/hr job to minimally support two kids, but less than 40 percent of American workers earn that much. The book's main theme is that the nation's poor, the bottom 20 percent, are invisible to affluent Americans.

Sara Horowitz is profiled in the article "Freelancers of the World, Unite!" (*The Economist*, November 11, 2006, 76).

Chapter 9

Here is a quote from a Victorian philosopher: "Let us . . . consider in what particular ways this further evolution . . . may be expected to show itself. . . . Will it be in strength? Probably not to any considerable degree. . . . Will it be in swiftness or agility? Probably not. . . . Will it be in intelligence? Largely, no doubt. . . . Will it be in morality, that is, in greater degree of self-regulation? Largely also: perhaps most largely. Right conduct is usually come short of more from defect of will than defect of knowledge. . . . A further endowment of those . . . sentiments responding to the requirements of the social state . . . must be acquired before the crimes, excesses, [etc.] that now so greatly diminish the duration of life, can cease. . . . [Evolution will] work unceasingly towards a state of harmony" (Spencer 1896, chap. 13).

State of California expenditures are included in Aker (2006) and its citations. For U.S. annual crime rates by category 1960–2004, see http://www.disastercenter.com/crime/uscrime.htm.

Besides self-serving crimes, there are also crimes of passion, and crimes of honor or duty. The next chapter will examine some of them. The text distinguishes vice (behavior in Quadrant III in Figure A3 of the Appendix), where the actor is among those harmed, from self-serving crime (opportunistic behavior in Quadrant IV). In traditional usage, vice is habitual sin. Catholic doctrine defines mortal sin as consisting of three elements (the sin is venial if some are absent): the matter is grave, the sinner has full knowledge, and he sins deliberately or gives full consent. The deadly sins are: pride, covetousness, lust, anger, gluttony, envy, and sloth. Those that "cry out to heaven for vengeance" are: murder, sodomizing, oppressing the poor, and defrauding laborers of wages. Thus, the focus is on character flaws, defective moral sentiments, and it includes opportunistic behavior. See for example http://en.wikipedia.org/wiki/Sin.

Bridgeman (2003) summarizes the evolutionary psychology approach to vice and other behavior. On chili, see Rozin and Vollmecke (1986). On adolescent male gamblers, see Rubin and Paul (1979). Paternity is much more concentrated than maternity in most premodern cultures. Technically, the point is that the left skewed wealth-paternity distribution creates a gap between expected wealth and expected biological fitness. Diamond (1992) notes an alternative explanation: risk-takers signal their otherwise unobservable talents, because risk-taking is more expensive for those less talented.

Fighting crime the old fashioned way: see Boehm (1999).

The harmless people: see Thomas (1958). On /Twi's execution and the quotes: see Lee (1979, 394–95).

Napoleon changed the spelling of his last name to "Bonaparte," more natural to the French eye.

Wilson (1988) is the main source of material on Corsica, and includes the following quotes: "Towns were relatively unimportant, and only 17 percent of the population lived in them in 1851, after a period of considerable urban growth" pp. 5. "Land of the vendetta," attributed to Maupassant, pp. 14. Egalitarianism is discussed on pp. 13. The proverb is quoted on, pp. 182. The Arbellara story is distilled from pp.17–21. On honore, see chapter 4, especially. Male honor demanded ownership of guns pp. 91. Mediation by elders, chap. 9. Zonza, pp. 253. Corsica's recorded homicide rate during most of the 1800s was 20–60 per 100,000 per year, and the actual rate probably was 2–3 times higher, pp. 15–16. The custom of her relatives killing a dishonored woman (especially if she would not divulge the name of her seducer) was fading in Corsica by 1800 pp. 108. Abduction was common, sometimes with the girl's consent, e.g., to overcome her family's objections pp. 102–10.

Bowman (2006), traces Western honor culture back to medieval times and discusses its decline in the twentieth century.

Any code of behavior inevitably has some gaps or inconsistencies by Gödel's theorem; see Gödel (1931). For an absorbing popular account, see Hofstadter (1979).

The Code of Hammurabi is presented in Johns (1903) and in http://en.wikipedia .org/wiki/Code_of_Hammurabi.

On Justinian's codex and the Talmud, see Rosen (2007, chap. 5).

"Courts interpret law and apply it": A lawyer friend comments, "Actually, courts create most law and judges introduce new rules when a case demands it."–Daniel McNeill (personal communication, September 2007).

Shasta county ranchers: see Ellickson (1991). Laws vs. norms: see Rosen (1997), Glazer et al. (1996), and Posner (2000).

"Feuding in Corsica was [probably] exacerbated by the process of incorporation into a modern state. The power of blood-vengeance sanctions to prevent or contain conflict was seriously weakened for a time and the internal balancing mechanisms of the traditional system were disrupted, all of which meant an increase, in the medium term, of feuding of a fairly unrestrained kind" (Wilson 1993, 53–54).

Some of the Bentham material was drawn from History of the University College of London http://en.wikipedia.org/wiki/History_of_University_College _London, and Jeremy Bentham http://en.wikipedia.org/wiki/Jeremy_Bentham, which cite sources such as Dinwiddy (1989). The Bentham Project Web site http://www.ucl.ac.uk/Bentham-Project/info/aims.htm notes that twenty-six volumes of Bentham's collected works have appeared as of mid-2007, but the total might ultimately reach seventy volumes. Keneally (2006) reports Bentham's panopticon proposal, and other schemes to profit from Britain's prison system.

The text omits some other items of possible interest:

- Bentham's panopticon proposal was resurrected and condemned by post-modernist writers, especially Foucault (1995, 195–228).
- Bentham's early proposal to decriminalize sodomy has made him a hero to many in the gay rights movement.
- His second publication, *Defence of Usury*, sought to straighten out Adam Smith on financial markets, and advocated dropping interest rate ceilings.

The modern version of Bentham's hedonistic calculus is the core of the academic field known as Law and Economics: see for example Posner (2006) and Wittman (2006).

"Murder occurrences vary wildly among different countries and societies. In the Western world, murder rates in most countries have declined significantly during 20th century and are now between 1–3 cases per 100,000 people per year. Murder rates of *Japan* and *Iceland* are among the lowest in the world, around 0.5; rate of *United States* is highest among all *developed countries*, at 5.5 (2004, *[9]*). On the other hand, developing countries often have rates of 10–100 murders per 100,000 people per year" (http://en.wikipedia.org/wiki/List_of_countries_by_homicide_rate).

Revenues and elasticities are a standard topic in economics textbooks, for example, Baye (2006, chap. 3).

On the history of gambling, see Ezell (1960). See Ernst and Young (1996) for the rake estimate. Other data comes from U.S. National Research Council (1999), National Opinion Research Center (1999), and Clotfielder et al. (1999).

"The $50 Ticket: A Lottery Boon Raises Concern," by Nelson D. Schwartz (*New York Times*, December 27, 2007, A1) reports detailed survey data from the Texas state lottery in 2006. Gamblers were more likely to make larger wagers when they had a high school education or less, or were younger, Black or Hispanic, male, or unemployed.

Grinols (2004) concludes that, after accounting for increased crime and reduced expenditures on other forms of entertainment, and so on, the social costs of the mega-casinos exceed the benefits in most communities. See also Grinols and Mustard (2006) and the article "As More States Look to Win The Economic Jackpot with Casinos, Evidence Suggests They are Playing a Losing Hand," by Mark White-house (*The Wall Street Journal*, June 11, 2007).

Schwarzenegger's deal with Indian casinos is reported in the article "More Slot Machines for Tribes; $1 Billion for California," by John M. Broder (*New York Times*, June 22, 2004). Also see "As Schwarzenegger Tries to Slow It, Gambling Grows," also by John M. Broder (*New York Times*, October 10, 2004).

The event contracts mentioned were available on Tradesports.com (now Intrade.com) on July 6, 2007.

The article by Amy Schatz, "Another Gamble for Online Betting," (*Wall Street Journal*, September 22, 2006, A7). The 2007 estimate is from page 34 of the *Economist* article on Poker cited below.

Prediction markets: see Wolfers and Zitzewitz (2004).

Much of the material on poker is collected from an unpublished 2004 term paper by Connor Egan. Hundreds of books are now available, for example, Gordon and Grotenstein (2004), not to mention innumerable Web sites. Also see "A Big Deal: Poker is Getting Younger, Cleverer, Duller and Much, Much Richer," (*The Economist*, December 2007, 33–38).

An example (one of many) of horror stories of youngsters addicted to online poker is "The Gambler: The Hold-'Em Holdup," by Mattathias Schwartz (*New York Times Magazine*, June 11, 2006).

Much of the information on U.S. alcohol consumption and regulation comes from *2005 ATF Annual Report—Publication 1000.4*, 47–49. Most of the history comes from MacCoun and Reuter (2001, chap. 8).

The math: $3^*(1-.25) = 2.25 > 2.0 > 1.50 = 3^*(1-.50)$, so doubling is in the estimated range.

The Centers for Disease Control collect data on binge drinking: http://www.cdc.gov/alcohol/datatable.htm.

Tobacco statistics appear in MacCoun and Reuter (2001, chap. 8). The terms of the Master Settlement can be found on The National Conference of State Legislatures Web site, http://www.ncsl.org/statefed/tmsasumm.htm. According to Yahoo Finance, Altria's share price was $39.38 in June 1998, and rose to $53.50 in December, with most of the increase taking place September through November. Coller et al. (2004) report the tobacco settlement damage award.

Reality is more complex than my quick summary of tobacco lawsuits. An expert witness for the prosecution reminds me that the tobacco industry settled many cases out of court prior to the Master Settlement in order to maintain the image of legal invincibility. He also notes that the industry's "'well funded research labs' ... never did any real science, as far as I can tell"; their real mission was to muddy the scientific waters (Glenn W. Harrison, personal communication, June 23, 2004).

The Web site http://www.monitoringthefuture.org/ summarizes what works and what doesn't for tobacco discouragement among teenagers.

"Decline in Daily Smoking by Younger Teens has Ended." University of Michigan's "Monitoring the Future" press release, December 21, 2006.

Worldwide industry calculated from http://en.wikipedia.org/wiki/Tobacco_industry#Production_by_Country. The 1999 figures are grossed up slightly for 2005.

The Web site http://www.triallawyersinc.com/ savages the trial lawyer industry. See also "Class Inaction: Plaintiffs' Lawsuits Against Companies Sharply Decline," by Paul Davies (*Wall Street Journal*, August 26, 2006, A1).

Prison industry sources include Doyle, "Behind Bars in the U.S. and Europe," (*Scientific American*, September 1999, 25); Marc Klaas, "A Bad Law, Set in Stone," (*San Jose Mercury News*, November 14, 1999, P1), on the three-strikes law; "Joe Arpaio, Tyrant of the Desert," (*Economist* magazine, March 20, 1999, 30); "Prisoners: More than Any Other Democracy," (*Economist* magazine, February 25, 2005, 27–29); "Hotel California," (*Economist* magazine, February 25, 2005, 27–29); and "California's Prisons: Packing Them In," (*Economist* magazine, August 12, 2006, 23).

Aker (2006) is a good overview of California's criminal justice system. See Unger (2007) for a U.S. overview. Some useful background information appears in chapter 3 of Gilmore (2007). See also the articles "High Court Justice Supports Bar Plan to Ease Sentencing," by Linda Greenhouse (*New York Times*, June 24, 2004) and "U.S. 'Correctional Population' Hits New High," by Fox Butterfield (*New York Times*, July 26, 2004). The $10.1 billion figure is Corrections and Rehabilitation, from State Government proposed 2007–8 budget; the corresponding figures for UC and CSU are $5.45 and $4.36 billion.

Johnson and Raphael (2006) is the source of the estimates on deterrence plus incarceration effects. (Unfortunately, the data don't permit a reliable separation of the two different effects.)

Governor Schwarznegger backs down on prison costs: see "Guard Union in Showdown," by Mark Gladstone (*San Jose Mercury News*, June 22, 2004, 1).

Leonard Scott's three strikes are cited in LaDoris H. Cordell's op-ed article (*San Jose Mercury News*, July 10, 2006, 16A). Of course, there are dangerous criminals out there, but three strikes only increases the danger. Consider a violent two-time loser who hates jail and is spotted by a burglary victim. Under three strikes, he has little to lose, and much to gain, by murdering his victim to avoid a third conviction. Likewise, if he sees police approach his car, he is much more likely to endanger bystanders in a high-speed chase.

Drugs and drug wars: see Spillane (2000). Drug use and human character: see Bennett (1989) and Wilson (1990). Bennett himself confessed to compulsive gambling in June 2003. http://www.washingtonmonthly.com/features/2003/0306 .green.html. I found a lot of information and useful perspectives in MacCoun and Reuter (2001).

Chapter 10

Patty Hearst story: see http://www.crimelibrary.com/terrorists_spies/terrorists/ hearst.

Marcus Foster: see "Murder in California" (*Time Magazine*, November 19, 1973).

Statistics on crime: see *New York Times Almanac 2004*, 308. The war against the American mafia: see Reppetto (2006).

Joaquin Murieta is the inspiration for the recent film *Legend of Zorro*, and earlier Zorro films and pulp fiction. He also figures in higher brow works such as *The Splendor and Death of Joaquin Murieta*, a play by Pablo Neruda.

Much of the material on Chicano youth gangs comes from 1994 University of California, Santa Cruz term papers by Rafael Trevino, Antonio Gomez, Jose Renteria, and Francisco Marquez for Economics 106. They, in turn, cite Harris (1988), Virgil (1983), Mirande (1985), and Romotsky and Romotsky (1976). See also "Highlights of the 2004 National Youth Gang Survey," Office of Juvenile Justice and Delinquency Prevention, U.S. Department of Justice, April, 2006.

Why would a young person join a gang? See LeBlanc (2003).

Levitt and Dubner (2005, chap. 3) offers some fresh evidence on how bad the gamble is: most ordinary gang members make less than the minimum wage and live at home with their moms.

On the importance of these part-time communities, see Putnam (2000).

Rance (2006) reflects a consensus view of outside observers. More recent analyses include the article "Hamas May Find It Needs Its Enemy," by Craig S. Smith and Greg Myre (*New York Times*, June 17, 2007).

The story of the Maccabees is told to Jewish children every Hanukkah.

Zealots: see Ben-Sasson (1976, 275) discusses a subcult called the daggermen, or *sicarii* in Latin, who assassinated Jewish leaders who opposed them, as well as Roman soldiers and officials.

On early Christianity, see, for example, Cannon (2005) and Maccoby (1986).

Cairo headquarters: At that time, ruled by the great Fatimid Caliph al-Mustansir, the successor of Basil II's contemporary, Al-Hakim. The entire Fatimid dynasty was Ismaili but the Assassins didn't recognize al-Mustansir's successors as legitimate. The remark about the Christian orders is on p. 307 of Joinville (1868.)

Aga Khan: see *The Institute of Ismaili Studies* Web site, http://www.iis.ac.uk/.

The *American Heritage Dictionary*'s primary definition of a cult is, "A religion or religious sect generally considered to be extremist or false, with its followers often living in an unconventional manner under the guidance of an authoritarian, charismatic leader."

The *American Heritage Dictionary*'s definition of terrorism is: "The unlawful use or threatened use of force or violence by a person or an organized group against people or property with the intention of intimidating or coercing societies or governments, often for ideological or political reasons."

I emphasize threats against lives. The dictionary definition above would include groups that target property. For example, the Animal Liberation Front aims to damage laboratories that test dangerous products on mice, but does not target human enemies.

Hamas revenues: see United States Department of State (2006).

"Gaza Fighting Kills Palestinian Coalition," CBS/AP dispatch, Gaza Strip, June 14, 2007

Goldberg (2004) reports on the Israeli settler's movement.

"They Make a Wasteland and Call it Peace," Tacitus, *Agricola*, chapter 30, quoting the British chieftan Calgacus.

T. Friedman (1998) has a chapter on the Hama massacre.

Thomas (2007) is a history of Mossad.

The argument in Iannocone (1992) is subtler than described in the text. It focuses on the social dilemma associated with contributing to public good provision, and shows that a cult can mitigate the problem by prohibiting mainstream activities and demanding personal sacrifices. Also see Berman and Laitin (2005). Again, the article contains far more theory and empirics than described in the text.

Rabin's murder: see Goldberg (2004).

For recent discussion of the PKK after Ocalan's capture, see the article "In the Rugged North of Iraq, Kurdish Rebels Flout Turkey," by Sabrina Tavernise (*New York Times*, October 29, 2007).

Brandon (2005) describes the Koranic duels. "Reforming Jihadists: Preachers to the Converted," and "A Jihadist Recants," (*The Economist*, December 15, 2007) report some success with similar strategies in Indonesia and Egypt.

For example, the scene "Dennis, the Constitutional Peasant," in *Monty Python and the Holy Grail*, 1975.

Danish newspaper cartoons controversy of September 2005: see the very detailed *Wikipedia* entry "Jyllands-Posten Muhammad cartoons controversy," http://en.wikipedia.org/wiki/Jyllands-Posten_Muhammad_cartoons_controversy.

Chapter 2 of Levitt and Dubner (2005) ostensibly concerns the role of asymmetric information, but the KKK episode far better illustrates the undermining of the cult's moral code. Likewise, the *Nuestra Familia* initiation oath has been trivialized in blogs and chatrooms; probably a new oath will be needed soon.

"The Battle of the Pump," by Thomas L. Friedman (*New York Times*, October 7, 2004, op-ed page) is a typical example.

Saudis fund mosques and madrassas: see, for example, "Al Qaeda and Saudi Arabia," by Khaled Abou El Fadl, on behalf of the U.S. Commission on International Religious Freedom, in *The Wall Street Journal*, November 10, 2003, op-ed page.

"Where Boys Grow up to be Jihadis," by Andrea Elliot (*New York Times Sunday Magazine*, November 25, 2007) mentions the role of Saudi-funded mosques and jihadi Web sites, but emphasizes the young Moroccan recruits' sense of moral outrage and personal ties to their buddies.

Dutch drug policy: see MacCoun and Reuter (2001, chap. 9).

Chapter 11

Kurlansky (1997) is the source for all assertions in the first paragraph and the first two sentences of the second paragraph, as well as material later in the chapter. The rest of the second paragraph alludes to Junger (1999).

"Commercial Fishing Industry Needs on Gloucester Harbor, Now and in the Future," a study by the Gloucester Community Panel, released June 6, 2005, contains some background information on the local economy and the role of the fishing industry.

Red tail deer, lions, and other territorial animals: see Hardin (1968) or a standard biology text such as Goldsmith and Zimmerman (2001). Hardin doesn't mention the moral system of open fields, which, as noted in Chapter 4 and in Dahlman (1980), prevented the tragedy in medieval European commons.

Dungeness crab derby: see the article "Troubled Waters for Local Crabbers," by Marke Krupnick (*San Jose Mercury News*, November 28, 2003, 3C).

Easter Island's environmental catastrophe: see Diamond (2005, chap. 2). Megafauna extinction in America and Australia, see Diamond (1999).

A chart on territorial fish for the home aquarium can be found at http://www .liveaquaria.com/general/compatibility_chart.cfm.

Lansing (1991) is the source of the material on Balinese water temples. A more recent book, Lansing (2006) discusses its origins and stability as an "emergent . . . complex adaptive system." The final Asian Development Bank report is "Reevaluation of the Bali Irrigation Sector Project Loan No. 522-INO in Indonesia," Asian Development Bank RES: INO XXX, December 1997, http://www.adb.org/ Documents/PERs/RE-27.pdf.

Sod buster sagas include Rolvaag (1927), and, of course, *Little House on the Prairie*, by Laura Ingalls Wilder, never out of print since its original publication in 1935.

Egan (2005) describes the Dust Bowl.

On the Ogallala Aquifer, see Kromm and White (1992), and the Web site http:// www.waterencyclopedia.com/Oc-Po/Ogallala-Aquifer.html.

On twentieth-century cod fisheries and territorial limits, again, see Kurlansky (1997).

"Economic logic dictates": see Demsetz (1984), for example.

"Mother's milk of politics": the quote is attributed to Jesse "Big Daddy" Unruh (1922–87), the leading power broker in California's legislature for most of the 1960s. Another great Unruh-ism: "Sometimes we must rise above principles."

Cawley (1996) reports on the sagebrush rebellion. See also the Colorado University Library's *Sage Brush Rebellion* (Collection No. 32), http://carbon.cudenver .edu/public/library/archives/sagebrsh/sagebrsh.html.

Coda for Cod material: see Committee to Review Northeast Fishery Stock Assessments (1998) and Serchuk and Wigley (1992).

Kuznets curve: the original version relates income inequality to economic development, as countries progress from agriculture to manufacturing to services. The environmental Kuznets curve incorporates the idea that primitive agriculture and advanced services are less polluting. See, for example, Bradford et al. (2005), available at http://www.bepress.com/bejeap/contributions/vol4/iss1/art5. A special issue of the same journal, *Advances in Economic Analysis & Policy* 4, no. 2, is devoted to the pollution haven hypothesis and the race to the bottom. See also Copeland and Taylor (2004).

Missing markets: economists recognize that markets go missing mainly for two related reasons—property rights are not well defined and/or transactions costs are high. The original insight is due to 1991 Nobel laureate Ronald Coase; see, for example, Coase (1960).

ITQs in Alaska: see Pautzke and Oliver (1997) and the Web site http://www.fakr .noaa.gov/npfmc/sci_papers/ifqpaper.htm. My thanks to Jon Sutinen for pointing me to this article.

The Fuglvog quotes are from *Viewpoints* in the Alaskan Halibut episode of the PBS series "Empty Oceans, Empty Nets." The Web site is http://www.pbs.org/emptyoceans/eoen/halibut/viewpoints.html.

My lab recently received a grant to find effective ways to organize the ITQ markets for fisheries in the Gulf of Mexico. Results will be posted on the Web site http://leeps.ucsc.edu/projects.

The Cap and Trade program for SO2 emissions: see U.S. Environmental Protection Agency (2001). On compliance cost reductions, see table 3-2, page 25.

The consensus on global climate change is summarized and elaborated in "IPCC Fourth Assessment Report: Climate Change 2007," a report in three parts by the Intergovernmental Panel on Climate Change. That panel shared the 2007 Nobel Peace Prize with former U.S. Vice President Al Gore. Their final synthesis report was released on November 17, 2007, and can be found at the Web site http://www.ipcc.ch/pdf/assessment-report/ar4/syr/ar4_syr_spm.pdf.

Global warming measurement errors: see "Heat and Light," (*The Economist*, August 11, 2005).

Exxon's campaign: see Web sites such as http://www.greenpeace.org/usa/campaigns/global-warming-and-energy/exxon-secrets and http://archive.greenpeace.org/comms/cbio/cancod.html. In early 2007, following the retirement of its longtime CEO and the Republican Party's defeat in congressional elections, Exxon announced that it was cutting off those funds: see "Exxon Cuts Ties to Global Warming Skeptics," (MSNBC report, January 12, 2007).

Self-enforcing international environmental agreements: see Barrett (1994) and McGinty (2007).

The pitfalls of nonuniform carbon taxes: see Sinn (2007).

California's climate policy: see Goulder (2007).

Porter hypothesis: see Popp (2005), available at http://www.bepress.com/bejeap/contributions/vol4/iss1/art6.

Ally of Bush is Defeated in Australia," by Tim Johnston (*New York Times*, November 25, 2007), mentions the new prime minister's promise to ratify the Kyoto protocol.

Special Report on Business and Climate Change," (*The Economist*, June 2, 2007) contains recent information on GE and Silicon Valley VCs. See also "Google's Next Frontier: Renewable Energy," by Brad Stone (*New York Times*, November 28, 2007), and "Banks Urging U.S. to Adopt the Trading of Emissions," by James Kanter (*New York Times*, September 26, 2007). The estimate of $40 billion is attributed to Paul Bledsoe of the National Committee on Energy Policy, and is cited on page 6 of *The Economist*'s special report.

Paltsev (2007) contains cost estimates for several recent GHG market proposals.

See also "Kyoto's Caps on Emissions Hit Snag in Marketplace: U.N. Mulls How to Fix Pollution-Credit System," by Jeffrey Ball (*Wall Street Journal*, December 3, 2007, A1)

Sara Hendrix and Matt McGinty helped educate me about environmental economics and gave me helpful leads to the literature.

Chapter 12

"Ruling Jolts Even Saudis: 200 Lashes for Rape Victim," by Rasheed Abou-Alsamh, (*New York Times*, November 16, 2007) notes that the rapists were sentenced to ten months to five years plus eighty to one thousand lashes—in several cases, lighter sentences than the victim's. See also "Saudi Rape Victim Tells Her Story: Victim to Receive Whipping and Jail for Being in Nonrelative's Car When Attacked," by Lara Setrakian (ABC News, November 21, 2007). Recent reports of a royal pardon include "Saudi King Pardons Rape Victim Sentenced to Be Lashed, Saudi Paper Reports," by Katherine Zoepf (*New York Times*, December 18, 2007). Tellingly, "the king fully supported the verdicts against the woman," according to the Saudi Justice Minister, but issued the pardon perhaps to mollify international opinion.

On honor killings elsewhere, see "Pakistan Tries to Curb 'Honor Killings,'" by Salman Massod (*New York Times*, October 27, 2004). The figure of 5,000 comes from a *Wikipedia* article, http://en.wikipedia.org/wiki/Honor_killings, which cites an estimate by the *United Nations Population Fund*.

The docudrama aired in the United States in May 1980, and has a page on the PBS Frontline Web site, http://www.pbs.org/wgbh/pages/frontline/shows/princess/. The diplomatic fallout is discussed in White and Ganley (1983). "The behavior of his granddaughter was an intolerable blot on his [Prince Mohammed's] family honor and, say private Saudis, in similar circumstances they would have done the same thing themselves."

The experiment on the Southern honor culture is reported in Cohen et al. (1996). Supporting evidence comes from capital punishment in the United States. In 2007, all but six of the nation's forty-two executions took place in states south of the Mason-Dixon line, most of them in Texas. See the article, "At 60% of Total, Texas is Bucking Execution Trend," by Adam Liptak (*New York Times*, December 26, 2007, A1).

The quote on honor culture among Arabs is from Pryce-Jones (2002, 41); see also his follow up piece in *National Review*, April 21, 2003, 36–38. Also, see Bowman (2006, chap. 9). Bowman includes material from Western great books and twentieth-century popular sources to document honor culture's decline, especially following World War I. He hopes, with some caveats, for a revival in the twenty-first century.

"Enforce his will on others": Nisbett and Cohen (1996, 4). The authors argue that extreme honor codes come from herdsmen cultures, and they trace the distinctive cultures in the Southern United States to immigrants forced by the enclosure movement from ancestral pasture lands in Scotland and Ireland.

Upper Paleolithic culture: see, for example, Soffer et al. (2000).

In Tablet 6 of the *Gilgamesh* epic, Inanna offers herself to the protagonist, and he refuses, describing her ill treatment of several previous lovers. See Prichard (1958, 51–53) and Bottero (2001, 94).

Baldick (1965) is a history of dueling. Wilson (1988, 108) reports the decline of honor killings in Corsica. On the U.S. armed service honor codes, see http://www.navy.com/about/during/personaldevelopment/honor/.

City morals versus honor-bound pastoralists: the *Gilgamesh* epic contains this theme, as Gilgamesh, a city-dweller, fights but then becomes best friends with the barbarian Enkidu; see for example, Prichard (1958, 31–40). The Biblical story (I Samuel 17–31) of how David rose from shepherd to king also echoes some of these themes.

Moral codes evolve: examples include the very different Buddhist practices in Japan versus India, and the Protestant reformation, as discussed in Chapter 3. The Talmud documents a millennium of changes in Jewish religious law.

Morning-after pills: see, for instance, "Jesus and the FDA," by Karen Tumulty (*Time* Magazine, October 14, 2002).

Premotor mirror neuron areas of the human brain, previously thought to involve action recognition, turn out to be sensitive to context, as well as action, implying that they automatically encode perceived intentions: see Iacoboni et al. (2005).

"Darwin's God," by Robin Marantz Henig (*New York Times Magazine*, March 4, 2007) is a very nice overview of recent controversies.

On kivas and ceremonies: see, for example, Waters (1963). On kosher laws, note that the Biblical commands are quite simple (e.g., in Leviticus 11), but became increasingly elaborate in later teachings such as the Talmud and Shulchan Aruch.

A tangential remark: Dawkins and Dennett argue that the insights of evolutionary psychology give much better explanations of the human condition than do traditional religious beliefs, and that standard logical arguments for the existence of God are bogus. It seems to me, however, that believers need not worry about the new scientific findings. Suppose that there indeed is a benevolent God who wants humans to seek His presence. If He prefers to work through natural processes rather than to constantly re-jigger natural laws, then we—beings who see intentions everywhere and who seek meaning—represent an elegant solution to the very tricky problem He gave himself.

The population, per capita income, and life expectancy estimates come from the U.S. Census Web site http://www.census.gov/ipc/www/worldhis.html, from table 1-1a of Maddison (1995) and from the *Encyclopaedia Britannica* (1961).

See for example, "How Free is the Free Market?" by Noam Chomsky (LiP Magazine, May 15, 1997), http://www.lipmagazine.org/articles/featchomsky_63.htm.

One of the more eloquent criticisms of globalization is "The Idea of a Local Economy," in Berry (2001). For a classic treatment in a novel, see Callenbach (1982).

Wage Insurance: see Kletzer (2004).

Leamer (2007, 110) is the source of the quote.

Adam Smith's observation is encapsulated in the title of chapter 3 of Smith (1776): "That the division of labor is limited by the extent of the market." See also Anderson (2006) for a modern version of the point.

On inequality, see Levy and Temin (2007), Piketty and Saez (2003), and Goldberg and Pavcnik (2007). Alesina and Giavazzi (2006) argue that poorer people are among the major potential beneficiaries of freer international trade. See also "Larry Summers's Evolution," by David Leonhardt (*New York Times Magazine*, June 10, 2007).

On trade discouraging war, see John Stuart Mill (18xx, part 3, chap. 17); also, Bhagwati (2004, chap. 2) has a nice quote from section 14 of Mill.

On the Czech-Slovak breakup, see Innes (2001). On Belgium, see "Calls for a Breakup Grow Ever Louder in Belgium," by Elaine Sciolino (*New York Times*, September 21, 2007) and "Belgium Sets Interim Government," by Stephen Castle (*New York Times*, December 20, 2007). See also Arblaster (2005).

Defusing the crisis: see, for example, "India Success In Software Is Set Back By War Talk," by Saritha Rai (*New York Times*, June 6, 2002).

Moral clarion calls: recent masters include all the leaders in World War II, as well as symbiotic regional bullies like Milosevic in Serbia and Tudjman in Croatia in the 1990s. Recall Konrad Lorenz's view (*On Aggression* [1966], soon popularized in a host of books such as Morris [1967]) that aggression is a basic instinct. I argue that the willingness to wage war comes not from some primitive instinct, but rather from an essential part of the moral architecture. In the modern world, it can be amplified by media and exploited by opportunistic politicians.

German identity after World War II: this is an unscientific personal observation, gleaned mainly from chatting with young people on trains.

Roth (2006) persuasively argues that the boundary between categories 1 and 2 is neither fixed nor sharp. He is especially concerned with kidneys for transplant.

Some background on electric power deregulation: The industry was a natural monopoly when it came on line a century ago. One company could produce power and deliver it to a town or region at far lower cost per customer than two or more competing companies. To avoid monopoly's ill effects (price far above competitive equilibrium and inefficiently low usage), the government closely regulated the industry, in particular by setting prices. Newer textbooks (e.g., Baye, 2006, chap. 14) point out the ill effects of regulation: overly costly production, sluggish innovation, and costly political struggles over the regulated price—a variant of influence costs discussed in Chapter 8. But by the mid-twentieth century, the power grid spanned thousands of generating facilities, so supplying power could be competitive.

Recent popular accounts of deregulated power markets include: "Flaws Seen in Markets for Utilities," by David Cay Johnston (*New York Times*, November 21, 2006), and "Short-Circuited," by Jerry Taylor and Peter Van Doren (*Wall Street Journal*, August 30, 2007, A11).

The "anti-gaming" quotes come from FERC (2003).

The 2007 Nobel Prize in Economics went to three pioneers of mechanism design theory: Leonid Hurwicz, Eric S. Maskin, and Roger B. Myerson.

On early electronic stock exchanges, see Domowitz (1993).

On health care, the 16 percent figure is for 2005, and the 20 percent projection is standard: see for example Borger et al. (2006). Grol (2006) discusses Dutch health care.

Education cites include Tyack and Cuban (1995), Goldin (1999), and Card and Payne (2002). The case for vouchers is made on http://www.schoolchoices.org/index.html.

Bibliography

Acemoglu, D., S. Johnson, and J. Robinson. 2005. "The Rise of Europe: Atlantic Trade, Institutional Change, and Economic Growth." *American Economic Review* 95, no. 3: 546–79.

Aiello, L., and P. Wheeler. 1995. "The Expensive-Tissue Hypothesis: The Brain and the Digestive System in Human and Primate Evolution." *Current Anthropology* 36, no. 2: 199–221.

Aker, E. 2006. "Crime and Punishment." *Policy Today, California Edition* 3, no. 5: 4–17.

Akerlof, G. 1982. "Labor Contracts as Partial Gift Exchange." *The Quarterly Journal of Economics* 97, no. 4: 543–69.

Alesina, A., and F. Giavazzi. 2006. *The Future of Europe*. London: MIT Press.

Anderson, C. 2006. *The Long Tail: Why the Future of Business is Selling Less of More*. New York: Hyperion.

Aoki, M. 1988. *Information, Incentives, and Bargaining in the Japanese Economy*. New York: Cambridge University Press.

Arblaster, P. 2005. *A History of the Low Countries*. New York: Palgrave Essential Histories, Palgrave Macmillan.

Armstrong, D. 1984. "Why Don't Cellular Slime-Molds Cheat?" *Journal of Theoretical Biology* 109, no. 2: 271–83.

Aubet, M. E. 2001. *The Phoenicians and the West: Politics, Colonies, and Trade*. Translated by M. Turton. New York: Cambridge University Press.

Babcock, L., and G. Loewenstein. 1997. "Explaining Bargaining Impasse: The Role of Self-Serving Biases." *Journal of Economic Perspectives* 11, no. 1: 109–26.

Baldick, R. 1965. *The Duel: A History of Duelling*. London: Chapman & Hall.

Barrett, S. 1994. "Self-enforcing International Environmental Agreements." *Oxford Economic Papers* 46: 878–94.

Baumol, W. 2002. *The Free Market Innovation Machine*. Princeton: Princeton University Press.

Baye, 2006. *Managerial Economics and Business Strategy*, 5th ed. New York: McGraw-Hill.

Becker, G. 1974. "A Theory of Social Interactions." *Journal of Political Economy* 82: 1063–93.

Beecher, J. 1986. *Charles Fourier: The Visionary and His World*. Berkeley: University of California Press.

———. 2001. *Victor Considerant and the Rise and Fall of French Romantic Socialism*. Berkeley: University of California Press.

Beecher, J., and R. Bienvenu, ed. and trans. 1983. *The Utopian Vision of Charles Fourier: Selected Texts on Work, Love, and Passionate Attraction*. Columbia: University of Missouri Press.

Bennett, W. 1989. "Drug Use Degrades Human Character." In *National Drug Control Strategy*. Washington, DC: Office of National Drug Control Policy.

Ben-Sasson, H. H. 1976. *A History of the Jewish People.* Cambridge, MA: Harvard University Press.

Berman, E., and D. Laitin. 2005. "Hard Targets: Theory and Evidence on Suicide Attacks." *NBER working paper* 11740.

Bernhard, H., Fehr, E., and Fischbacher, U. 2006. "Group Affiliation and Altruistic Norm Enforcement." *American Economic Review* 96, no. 2: 217–21.

Bernstein, L. 1998. "Private Commercial Law." *New Palgrave Dictionary of Law and Economics.*

Berry, W. 2001. *In the Presence of Fear.* Great Barrington, MA: The Orion Society.

Besley, T. 1995. "Nonmarket Institutions for Credit and Risk Sharing in Low-Income Countries." *The Journal of Economic Perspectives* 9, no. 3: 115–27.

Besley, T., S. Coate, and G. Loury. 1993. "The Economics of Rotating Savings and Credit Associations." *The American Economic Review* 83, no. 4: 792–810.

Bezemer, D. J. 1999. "Post-Socialist Financial Fragility: The Case of Albania." *Tinbergen Institute Discussion Paper* #99045. http://www.tinbergen.nl/discussionpapers/99045.pdf.

Bhagwati, J. 2004. *In Defense of Globalization.* New York: Oxford University Press.

Blake, W. 1997. "Gnomic Verses viii." *The Complete Poetry & Prose of William Blake*, ed. Harold Bloom. New York: Anchor Books.

Bobe, R., and A. Behrensmeyer. 2004. "The Expansion of Grassland Ecosystems in Africa in Relation to Mammalian Evolution and the Origin of the Genus *Homo*." *Palaeogeography Palaeoclimatology Palaeoecology* 207, no. 3–4: 399–420.

Boehm, C. 1999. *Hierarchy in the Forest: The Evolution of Egalitarian Behavior.* Cambridge, MA: Harvard University Press.

Boone, J. L. 1992. "Competition, Conflict, and the Development of Social Hierarchies." In *Evolutionary Ecology and Human Behavior*, ed. E. A. Smith and B. Winterhalder. Hawthorne, NY: Walter de Gruyter.

Boorstin, D. 1983. *The Discoverers.* New York: Random House.

Borger, C., et al. 2006. "Health Spending Projections Through 2015: Changes on the Horizon." *Health Affairs Web Exclusive* W61.

Bottéro, J. 2001. *Everyday Life in Ancient Mesopotamia.* Translated by A. Nevill. Baltimore, MD: Johns Hopkins University Press.

Bowman, J. 2006. *Honor: A History.* New York: Encounter Books.

Boyd, R., and P. Richerson, 1985. *Culture and the Evolutionary Process.* Chicago: University of Chicago Press.

Bradford, D., R. Fender, S. Shore, and M. Wagner. 2005. "The Environmental Kuznets Curve: Exploring a Fresh Specification." *Contributions to Economic Analysis & Policy* 4, no. 1: 5.

Brandon, J. 2005. "Koranic duels ease terror." *The Christian Science Monitor*. February 4.

Bridgeman, B. 2003. *Psychology and Evolution: The Origins of Mind.* New York: Sage Publications.

Callenbach, E. 1982. *Ecotopia.* New York: Bantam Doubleday Dell.

Cameron, R., and L. Neal. 2003. *A Concise Economic History of the World*, 4th ed. New York: Oxford University Press.

Cannon, J. 2005. *Apostle Paul: A Novel of the Man Who Brought Christianity to Western World.* Hanover, NH: Steerforth.

Card, D., and A. Payne. 2002. "School Finance Reform, the Distribution of School Spending, and the Distribution of Student Test Scores." *Journal of Public Economics* 83: 49–82.

Cargill, T., M. Hutchison, and T. Ito. 1997. *The Political Economy of Japanese Monetary Policy.* London: MIT Press.

Carlyle, T. 1843. *Past and Present.* London: Chapman and Hall.

Carson, R. 1962. *Silent Spring.* Boston: Houghton Mifflin Co.

Cason, T., and D. Friedman. 1999. "Learning in a Laboratory Market with Random Supply and Demand." *Experimental Economics* 2, no. 1: 77–98.

Cason, T., D. Friedman, and G. H. Milam. 2003. "Bargaining versus Posted Price Competition in Customer Markets." *International Journal of Industrial Organization* 21, no. 2: 223–51.

Cawley, R. M. 1996. *Federal Land, Western Anger: The Sagebrush Rebellion and Environmental Politics.* University Press of Kansas Press.

Cervellati, M., and U. Sunde. 2005. "Human Capital Formation, Life Expectancy, and the Process of Development." *The American Economic Review* 95, no. 5: 1655–72.

Chandler, A. D. 1977. *The Visible Hand: The Managerial Revolution in American Business* Boston: Harvard University Press.

Charness, G., J. Kagel, and G. Frechette. 2004. "How Robust is Laboratory Gift Exchange?" *Experimental Economics* 7, no. 2: 189–205.

Choi, J., and S. Bowles. 2007. "The Coevolution of Parochial Altruism and War." *Science* 318, no. 5850: 636–40.

Christensen, C. 2003. *The Innovator's Dilemma: The Revolutionary Book that Will Change the Way You Do Business.* London: Collins.

Clark, G. 2007. *A Farewell to Alms: A Brief Economic History of the World.* Princeton: Princeton University Press.

Clotfelder, et al. 1999. "State Lotteries at the Turn of the Century." *National Gambling Impact Study Commission.* Washington, DC.

Coase, R. 1937. "The Nature of the Firm." *Economica* 4, no. 16: 386–405.

———. 1960. The Problem of Social Cost." *Journal of Law and Economics* 3, no. 1: 1–44.

Cohen, D., R. Nisbett, B. Bowdle, and N. Schwarz. 1996. "Insult, Aggression, and the Southern Culture of Honor: An 'Experimental Ethnography.'" *Journal of Personality and Social Psychology* 70, no. 5: 945–60.

Coller, M., G. Harrison, and M. McInnes. 2004. "Evaluating the Tobacco Settlement Damage Awards: Too Much or Not Enough?" *American Journal of Public Health* 92, no. 6: 984–89.

Committee to Review Northeast Fishery Stock Assessments. 1998. *Review of Northeast Fishery Stock Assessments.* Washington, DC: National Research Council.

Cooper, C., and M. A. Etnier. 2005. "Mathematical Modeling of Human and Marine Mammal Interaction in the Prehistoric Monterey Bay." Poster presented at 70th Annual Meeting, Society of American Archaeology, Salt Lake City, UT.

Copeland and Taylor. 2004. "Trade, Growth, and the Environment." *Journal of Economic Literature* 42, no. 1: 7–71.

Cosmides, L., and J. Tooby. 1992. *The Adapted Mind.* New York: Oxford University Press.

Crichton, M. 2004. *State of Fear.* New York: HarperCollins.

Dahlman, C. J. 1980. *The Open Field System and Beyond.* New York: Cambridge University Press.

Darwin, C. 1859. *On the Origin of Species by Means of Natural Selection or the Preservation of Favored Races in the Struggle for Life.* London: John Murray.

Dawkins, R., 1976. *The Selfish Gene.* New York: Oxford University Press.

———. 2006. *The God Delusion.* Boston: Houghton Mifflin Co.

De Mieroop, M. V. 2005. "The Invention of Interest." In *The Origins of Value: The Financial Innovations that Created Modern Capital Markets,* ed. W. N. Goetzmann and K. G. Rouwenhorst. New York: Oxford University Press.

de Waal, F. 2005. *Our Inner Ape.* New York: Penguin.

Deming, W. E. 2000. *The New Economics for Industry, Government, Education,* 2nd ed. London: MIT Press.

Demsetz, H. 1984. "Purchasing Monopoly." In *Neoclassical Political Economy: The Analysis of Rent-seeking and DUP Activities*, ed. D. C. Colander. Cambridge, MA: Ballinger.

Dennett, D. 2006. *Breaking the Spell: Religion as a Natural Phenomenon* New York: Viking.

Dessi, R., and S. Ogilvie. 2003. "Social Capital and Collusion: The Case of the Merchant Guilds." *CESifo working paper* 1037.

Diamond, J. 1992. *The Third Chimpanzee*. New York: HarperCollins.

———. 1999. *Guns, Germs and Steel*. New York: W. W. Norton & Company.

———. 2005. *Collapse: How Societies Choose to Fail or Succeed*. New York: Viking.

Dinwiddy, J. 1989. *Bentham*. New York: Oxford University Press.

Domowitz, I. 1993. "Automating the Continuous Double Auction in Practice: Automated Trade Execution Systems in Financial Markets." In *The Double Auction Market: Institutions, Theories and Evidence*, ed. D. Friedman and J. Rust. Reading, MA: Addison Wesley.

Dow, G. K., N. Olewiler, and C. G. Reed. 2006. "The Transition to Agriculture: Climate Reversals, Population Density, and Technical Change." *Economics Department manuscript*. Simon Fraser University.

Dugatkin, L., 1997. *Cooperation Among Animals: An Evolutionary Perspective*. New York: Oxford University Press.

Dunbar, R. 1996. *Grooming, Gossip and the Evolution of Language*. London: Faber and Faber.

Dureau, G. 1984. *1848*. Cambridge, MA: Harvard University Press.

Durham, D. 1991. *Coevolution: Genes, Culture, and Human Diversity*. Palo Alto, CA: Stanford University Press.

Egan, T. 2005. *The Worst Hard Time: The Untold Story of Those Who Survived The Great American Dust Bowl*. New York: Houghton Mifflin Company.

Ehrenreich, B. 2001. *Nickel and Dimed: On (Not) getting by in America*. New York: Holt.

Ellickson, R. C. 1991. *Order without Law: How Neighbors Settle Disputes*. Harvard University Press.

Ennis, H., D. Dao, S. Pukatzki, R. Kessin, and H. Richard. 2000. "Dictyostelium Amoebae Lacking an F-Box Protein Form Spores Rather than Stalk in Chimeras with Wild Type." *Proceedings of the National Academy of Sciences* 97, no. 7: 3292–97.

Ernst and Young. 1996. *Compilation of Gaming Data*.

Evans, P., and B. Wolf. 2005. "Collaboration Rules." *Harvard Business Review* 83, no. 7.

Ezell, J. 1960. *Fortune's Merry Wheel: The Lottery in America*. Harvard University Press.

Fabozzi and Modigliani. 2003. *Capital Markets: Institutions and Instruments*, 3rd ed. Prentice-Hall.

Fafchamps, M. forthcoming. "Spontaneous Markets, Networks and Social Capital: Lessons from Africa." In *The Microeconomics of Institutions*, ed. T. Besley and R. Jayaraman. London: MIT Press.

Fagan, B. 2003 *Before California*. Lantham, MD: Rowman & Littlefield.

Falk, A., and M. Kosfeld. 2006. "The Hidden Costs of Control." *American Economic Review* 96, no. 5: 1611–30.

Fama, E. F. 1971. "Risk, Return, and Equilibrium." *The Journal of Political Economy* 79, no. 1: 30–55.

Fehr, E., G. Kirchsteiger, and A. Riedl. 1993. "Does Fairness Prevent Market Clearing? An Experimental Investigation." *The Quarterly Journal of Economics* 108, no. 2: 437–59.

FERC. 2003. "Final Report on Price Manipulation in Western Markets." *Federal Energy Regulatory Commission*.

Fernandez-Armesto, F. 2006. *Pathfinders: A Global History of Exploration*. New York: W. W. Norton & Co.

Fiorina, C. 2006. *Tough Choices: A Memoir.* New York: Portfolio Trade.

Fishman, C. 2006. *The Wal-Mart Effect: How the World's Most Powerful Company Really Works—and How It's Transforming the American Economy.* Boston: Penguin.

Foucault, M. 1995. *Discipline & Punish: The Birth of the Prison.* New York: Vintage Books.

Friedman, B. M. 2006. *The Moral Consequences of Economic Growth.* Westminster: Alfred A Knopf, Inc.

Friedman, D. 1998. "On Economic Applications of Evolutionary Game Theory." *Journal of Evolutionary Economics* 8, no. 1: 15–43.

———. 2007. "Market Theories Evolve, and So Do Markets." *Journal of Economic Behavior & Organization* 63, no. 2: 247–55.

———. 2008. "Laboratory Financial Markets." In *New Palgrave Dictionary of Economics,* 2nd ed., ed. S. Durlauf and L. Blume. New York: Palgrave Macmillan.

Friedman, D., and N. Singh. 2004. "Vengefulness Evolves in Small Groups." In *Advances in Understanding Strategic Behavior,* ed. S. Huck. New York: Palgrave Macmillan.

Friedman, D., and Ostroy, J. 1995. "Competitivity in Auction Markets: An Experimental and Theoretical Investigation." *Economic Journal* 105, no. 428: 22–53.

Friedman, T. 1998. *From Beirut to Jerusalem* London: Harper-Collins.

Garber, P. M. 1989. "Tulipmania." *Journal of Political Economy* 97, no. 3: 535–60.

Gerstner Jr., L. V. 2002. *Who Says Elephants Can't Dance? Inside IBM's Historic Turnaround.* New York: Harper-Collins.

Gibbons, A. 2006. *The First Human: The Race to Discover Our Earliest Ancestors.*

Gibbons, E. 2003. *The Decline and Fall of the Roman Empire.* New York: Modern Library.

Gies, F., and J. Gies. 1981. *Life in a Medieval City.* New York: Harper.

Gilmore, R. 2007. *Golden Gulag.* Berkeley: University of California Press.

Glazer, E. L., B. Sacerdote, and J. A. Scheinkman. 1996. "Crime and Social Interactions." *Quarterly Journal of Economics* 111, no. 1: 507–48.

Gode, D., and S. Sunder. 1993. "Allocative Efficiency of Markets with Zero Intelligence Traders: Market as a Partial Substitute for Individual Rationality." *Journal of Political Economy* 101: 119–37.

Gödel, K. 1931. "Über formal unentscheidbare Sätze der Principia Mathematica und verwandter Systeme, I." *Monatshefte für Mathematik und Physik* 38: 173–98. Translated in van Heijenoort, J. 1967. *From Frege to Gödel: A Source Book on Mathematical Logic.* Harvard University Press: 596–616.

Goetzmann, W. N., and K. G. Rouwenhorst, eds. 2005. *The Origins of Value: The Financial Innovations that Created Modern Capital Markets.* Oxford University Press.

Goldberg, J. 2004. "Among the Settlers: Will They Destroy Israel?" *The New Yorker,* May 31.

Goldberg, P., and N. Pavcnik. 2007. "Distributional Effects of Globalization in Developing Countries." *Journal of Economic Literature* 45, no. 1: 39–82.

Goldin, C. 1999. "Egalitarianism and the Returns to Education during the Great Transformation of American Education." *Journal of Political Economy* 107: S65–S94.

Goldman, E. 1923. *My Disillusionment in Russia.* Garden City, NY: Doubleday, Page & Co.

Goldsmith, T. H., and W. F. Zimmerman. 2001. *Biology, Evolution and Human Nature.* New York: Wiley.

Goody, J. 1996. *The East in the West.* New York: Cambridge University Press.

Gordon, P., and J. Grotenstein. 2004. *Poker: The Real Deal.* New York: Simon Spotlight Entertainment.

Gould, S., and N. Eldridge. 1993. "Punctuated Equilibrium Comes of Age." *Nature* 366: 223–27.

Goulder, A., 1960. "The Norm of Reciprocity: A Preliminary Statement." *American Sociological Review* 25: 161–78.

Goulder, L. H. 2007. "California's Bold New Climate Policy." *The Economists' Voice* 4, no. 3: 5.

Grantham, G. 1999. "Contra Ricardo: On the Macroeconomics of Pre-industrial Economies." *European Review of Economic History* 3: 199–232.

Greif, A. 1993. "Contract Enforceability and Economic Institutions in Early Trade: The Maghribi Traders' Coalition." *American Economic Review* 83, no. 3: 525–47.

———. 2006. "History Lessons: The Birth of Impersonal Exchange: The Community Responsibility System and Impartial Justice." *Journal of Economic Perspectives* 20, no. 2: 221–36.

Greif, A., P. Milgrom, and B. Weingast. 1994. "Coordination, Commitment and Enforcement: The Case of the Merchant Guild." *Journal of Political Economy* 102, no. 4: 745–76.

Grigoriev, L. 1995. "Ownership and Control in Privatization: Consequences for Foreign Investors." In *Foreign Investment in Russia: Salient Features and Trend—Second Report*, ed. A. Z. Astapovich. Moscow: Joint Stock Bank Imperial.

Grinols, E. 2004. *Gambling in America: Costs and Benefits*. New York: Cambridge University Press.

Grinols, E., and D. Mustard. 2006. "Casinos, Crime, and Community Costs." *Review of Economics and Statistics* 88, no. 1: 28–45.

Grol, R. 2006. *Quality Development in Health Care in the Netherlands*. New York: The Commonwealth Fund.

Gunderson, L., and Holling, C. S., eds. 2001. *Panarchy: Understanding Transformations in Human and Natural Systems*. Washington, DC: Island.

Güth, W., R. Schmittberger, and B. Schwarze. 1982. "An Experimental Analysis of Ultimatum Bargaining." *Journal of Economic Behavior and Organization* 3: 367–88.

Haldane, J. 1955. "Population Genetics." *New Biology* 18: 34–51.

Hamilton, W. 1964. "Genetic Evolution of Social Behavior, I and II." *Journal of Theoretical Biology* 7: 1–16, 17–52.

Hammerstein, P., ed. 2003. *Genetic and Cultural Evolution of Cooperation*. London: MIT Press.

Hammes, T. X. 2006. "Countering Evolved Insurgent Networks." *Military Review*: 18–26.

Hancock, R., P. Korsten, and G. Pohle. 2005. *On Demand Business: The New Agenda for Value Creation*. IBM Institute for Business Value.

Hardin, G. 1968. "The Tragedy of the Commons." *Science* 162, no. 3859: 1243–48.

Harris, M. 1988. *Cholas: Latino Girls and Gangs*. London: AMS.

Hassan, F. A. 1981. *Demographic Archaeology*. New York: Academic.

Hauser, M. 2006. *Moral Minds*. New York: Harper-Collins.

Hawkes, K. 1992. "Sharing and Collective Action." In *Evolutionary Ecology and Human Behavior*, ed. E. A. Smith and B. Winterhalder. Hawthorne, NY: Walter de Gruyter.

———. 2004. "The Grandmother Effect." *Nature* 428: 128–29.

Hayek, F. A. 1945. "The Use of Knowledge in Society." *American Economic Review* 45, no. 4: 519–30.

Healy, P., and K. Palepu. 2003. "The Fall of Enron." *Journal of Economic Perspectives* 17, no. 2: 3–26.

Henrich, J., and R. McElreath. 2003. "The Evolution of Cultural Evolution." *Evolutionary Anthropology: Issues, News, and Reviews* 12: 123–35.

Henrich, J., R. Boyd, S. Bowles, C. Camerer, H. Gintis, R. McElreath, and E. Fehr. 2001. "In Search of Homo Economicus: Experiments in 15 Small-Scale Societies." *American Economic Review* 91, no. 2: 73–79.

Hicks, Sir J. R. 1969. *A Theory of Economic History*. London: Oxford University Press.

Hirshleifer, J. 1995. "Anarchy and its Breakdown." *Journal of Political Economy* 101, no. 3: 26–52.

Hofstadter, D. 1979. *Gödel, Escher, Bach: An Eternal Golden Braid*. New York: Vintage Books.

Holmes, C. 2005. *Basil II and the Governance of Empire*. New York: Oxford University Press.

Hoshi, T., and A. Kashyap. 2001. *Corporate Financing and Governance in Japan*. London: MIT Press.

———. 2004. "Japan's Financial Crisis and Economic Stagnation." *Journal of Economic Perspectives* 18, no. 1: 3–26.

Hugo, V. *Les Miserables*. Translated by Lee Fahnestock. 1896. Reprint, Signet Classic Edition, New York: Penguin, 1987.

Howitt, P., and R. Clower. 2000. "The Emergence of Economic Organization." *Journal of Economic Behavior and Organization* 41: 55–84.

Huxley, A. 1932. *Brave New World*. New York: HarperCollins.

Iacoboni M, I. Molnar-Szakacs, V. Gallese, G. Buccino, and J. C. Mazziotta. 2005. "Grasping the Intentions of Others with One's Own Mirror Neuron System." *Public Library of Science Biology* 3, no. 3: e79.

Iannocone, L. 1992. "Sacrifice and Stigma: Reducing Free Riding in Cults, Communes and Other Collectives." *Journal of Political Economy*, 271–91.

Innes, A. 2001. *Czechoslovakia: The Short Goodbye*. New Haven: Yale University Press.

Innis, H. A. 1999. *Fur Trade in Canada: An Introduction to Canadian Economic History*, rev. ed. Toronto: University of Toronto Press.

Jansen, M. B. 2002. *The Making of Modern Japan*. Cambridge: Belknap.

Jarvis, C. 2000. "The Rise and Fall of Albania's Pyramid Schemes." *Finance and Development* 37, no. 1. http://www.imf.org/external/pubs/ft/fandd/2000/03/jarvis.htm.

Johns, C. H. W., M.A. 1903. *The Oldest Code of Laws in the World: The Code of Laws Promulgated by Hammurabi, King of Babylon B.C. 2285–2242*. Edinburgh: T & T Clark.

Johnson, R., and S. Raphael. 2006. "How Much Crime Reduction Does the Marginal Prisoner Buy?" *UC Berkeley School of Public Policy manuscript*.

Joinville, J. de. *Histoire de Saint Louis* ed. Natalis de Wailly, Paris. 1868. Reprint, Lille, nd.

Jones, E. 1981. *The European Miracle*. New York: Cambridge University Press.

Jordan, M., and K. Sullivan. 1998. "Death of 3 Salesmen—Partners in Suicide." *Washington Post*, October 7: A1.

Junger, S. 1999. *The Perfect Storm: A True Story of Men Against the Sea*. New York: Harper.

Kahn, A. 2004. *Lessons from Deregulation: Telecommunications and Airlines After the Crunch*. Washington, DC: Brookings.

Kaplan, G., and M. Guitierrez. 2006. "How Long Does It Take To Become A Proficient Hunter? Implications On The Evolution Of Delayed Growth." *Journal of Human Evolution*.

Kelly, R. 1985. *The Nuer Conquest: The Structure and Development of an Expansionist System* Michigan: University of Michigan Press.

Keneally, T. 2006. *A Commonwealth of Thieves*. London: Vintage.

Keynes, J. M. 1936. *The General Theory of Employment, Interest and Money*. London: Macmillan.

Kindleberger, C. P. 2000 *Manias, Panics and Crashes: A History of Financial Crises*. New York: Basic Books.

Klebnikov, P. 2000. *Godfather of the Kremlin: Boris Berezovsky and the Looting of Russia*. New York: Harcourt.

Klein, B., R. Crawford, and A. Alchian. 1978. "Vertical Integration, Appropriable Rents, and the Competitive Contracting Process." *Journal of Law & Economics* 21, no. 2: 297–326.

Klein, R. 1999. *The Human Career: Human Biological and Cultural Origins*, 2nd ed. Chicago: University Of Chicago Press.

Kletzer, L. 2004. "Trade-related Job Loss and Wage Insurance: A Synthetic Review." *Review of International Economics* 12, no. 5: 724–48.

Kramer, S. 1998. *Sumerian Mythology*. Pennsylvania: University of Pennsylvania Press.

Kromm, D. E., and S. White, eds. 1992. *Groundwater Exploitation in the High Plains*. Lawrence: University Press of Kansas.

Krueger, A., and A. Mas. 2004. "Strikes, Scabs and Tread Separations: Labor Strife and the Production of Defective Bridgestone/Firestone Tires." *Journal of Political Economy* 112: 253–89.

Kugler, T., Z. Neeman, and N. Vulcan. 2006. "Markets versus Negotiations: An Experimental Investigation." *Games and Economic Behavior* 56, no. 1: 121–34.

Kurlansky, M. 1997. *Cod: A Biography of the Fish That Changed the World*. New York: Walker & Company.

Lamoreaux, N., D. Raff, and P. Temin. 2002. "Beyond Markets and Hierarchies: Towards a New Synthesis of American Business History." *NBER Working Paper* 9029: 14.

Landes, D. S. 1998. *The Wealth and Poverty of Nations*. New York: W. W. Norton.

———. 2006. "Why Europe and the West? Why not China?" *Journal of Economic Perspectives* 20, no. 2: 3–22.

Lansing, J. S. 1991. *Priests and Programmers: Technologies of Power and the Engineered Landscape of Bali*. Princeton: Princeton University Press.

———. 2006. *Perfect Order: Recognizing Complexity in Bali*. Princeton: Princeton University Press.

Larsen, M. T. 1976. *The Old Assyrian City-State and Its Colonies*. Vol. 4. Mesopotamia, Copenhagen Studies in Assyriology. Copenhagen: Akademisk Forlag.

Lasch, C. 1996. *Revolt of the Elites*. New York: Norton.

Leamer, E. 2007. "A Review of Thomas L Friedman's *The World is Flat*." *Journal of Economic Literature* 45, no. 1: 83–126.

LeBlanc, A. 2003. *Random Family: Love, Drugs, Trouble, and Coming of Age in the Bronx*. New York: Scribner.

Lee, R. 1979. *The Kung San: Men, Women and Work in a Foraging Society*. New York: Cambridge University Press.

———. 2003. "The Demographic Transition: Three Centuries of Fundamental Change." *Journal of Economic Perspectives* 17, no. 4: 167–90.

Leijonhufvud, A. 2007. "The Individual, the Market, and the Division of Labor in Society." *Capitalism and Society* 2, no. 2: Article 3.

Leijonhufvud, A., and E. Craver. 2001. "Reform and the fate of Russia." *Documents de Travail de l'OFCE 2001–03, Observatoire Francais des Conjonctures Economiques (OFCE)*.

Lenin, V. I. 1902. *What Is to be Done?* New York: International Publishers.

Levathes, L. 1996. *When China Ruled the Seas*. Oxford University Press.

Levitt, A. 2002. *Take On the Street: What Wall Street and Corporate America Don't Want You to Know*. New York: Random House.

Levitt, S., and S. Dubner. 2005. *Freakonomics*. New York: William Morrow.

Levy, F., and P. Temin. 2007. "Inequality and Institutions in 20th Century America." *NBER Working Paper* No. W13106.

Lewis, B. 1968. *The Assassins: A Radical Sect in Islam*. New York: Basic Books.

Lichtenstein, N., ed. 2006. *Wal-Mart: The Face of Twenty-First-Century Capitalism*. New York: New Press.

Ligon, D. 1991. "Cooperation and Reciprocity in Birds and Mammals." In *Kin Recognition*, ed. P. Hepper. New York: Cambridge University Press.

Lipton, D., and J. D. Sachs. 1992. "Prospects for Russia's Economic Reforms." *Brookings Papers on Economic Activity* 2: 213–83.

Lorenz, K. 1966. *On Aggression*. New York: Methuen.

MacArthur, R., and E. O. Wilson. 1967. *The Theory of Island Biogeography*, Princeton: Princeton University Press.

Maccoby, H. 1986. *The Mythmaker: Paul and the Invention of Christianity*. New York: Harper & Row.

MacCoun, R., and P. Reuter. 2001. *Drug War Heresies*, New York: Cambridge University Press.

Mackay, C. *Extraordinary Popular Delusions and the Madness of Crowds*. 1941. Reprint, New York: Wiley Investment Classics.

Maddison, A. 1995. *Monitoring the World Economy, 1820–1992*. Paris: OECD Development Center.

———. 2001. *The World Economy: A Millennial Perspective*. Paris: OECD.

Maestripieri, D., ed. 2005. *Primate Psychology*. Cambridge, MA: Harvard University Press.

Malkiel, B. 2003. *A Random Walk Down Wall Street*. New York: W. W. Norton.

Malmendier, U. 2005. "Roman Shares." In *The Origins of Value*, ed. W. Goetzmann and K. Rouwenhorst. New York: Oxford University Press.

Malone, T. W. 2004. *The Future of Work*. New York: Harvard Business School Press.

Marée, A., and P. Hogeweg. 2001. "How Amoeboids Self-organize into a Fruiting Body: Multicellular Coordination in Dictyostelium discoideum." *Proceedings of the National Academy of Sciences* 98, no. 7 (March 27): 3879–83.

Marx, K. 1844. "Alienated Labor." *Economic and Philosophic Manuscripts*.

Marx, K., and F. Engels. 2002. *The Communist Manifesto*. London: Penguin.

Mas, A. 2007 "Labor Unrest and the Quality of Production: Evidence from the Construction Equipment Resale Market." *NBER Working Paper* W13138.

Maslow, A. 1943. "A Theory of Human Motivation." *Psychological Review* 50: 394–95.

Masten, S. 1984. "The Organization of Production: Evidence from the Aerospace Industry." *Journal of Law and Economics* 27, no. 2: 403–17.

Maynard Smith, J. 1982. *Evolution and the Theory of Games*. New York: Cambridge University Press.

McAfee, R. P. 2000. "The Real Lesson of Enron's Implosion: Market Makers are in the Trust Business." *The Economists' Voice* 1, no. 4: 2.

McBrearty, S., and A. Brooks. 2000. "The Revolution That Wasn't: A New Interpretation of the Origin of Modern Human Behavior." *Journal of Human Evolution* 39: 453–563.

McGinty, M. 2007. "International Environmental Agreements Among Asymmetric Nations." *Oxford Economic Papers* 59, no. 1: 45–62.

McIntyre, D. 2000. "Learning to Let Go." *Time* 156, no. 4.

McLean, B., and P. Elkind. 2004. *Smartest Guys in the Room: The Amazing Rise and Scandalous Fall of Enron*. New York: Portfolio.

McLean, P., and J. Padgett. Forthcoming. "Economic Credit and Elite Transformation in Renaissance Florence." *American Journal of Sociology*.

McNeill, W. H. 1989. *The Age of Gunpowder Empires 1450–1800*. New York: American Historical Association.

Milgrom, P., and J. Roberts. 1990. "The Economics of Modern Manufacturing: Technology, Strategy and Organization." *American Economic Review* 80: 511–28.

———. 1992. *Economics, Organization and Management*. Englewood Cliffs, NJ: Prentice Hall.

Milius, S. 2006. "Naked and Not: Two Species of Mole Rats Run Complex Societies Underground." *Science News* 169, no. 25: 394.

Mill, J. S. 1848. *The Principles of Political Economy*. London: Longmans, Green, and Co.

Millett, P. 1991. *Lending and Borrowing in Ancient Athens*. New York: Cambridge University Press.

Minksy, H. P. 1982. "Can 'IT' Happen Again?" *Essays on Instability and Finance*. New York: M. E. Sharpe, Inc.

Mirande, A. 1985. *The Chicano Experience*. Notre Dame: University of Notre Dame Press.

Monteverde, K., and D. Teece. 1982. "Supplier Switching Costs and Vertical Integration." *Bell Journal of Economics* 13, no. 1: 206–13.

Morck, R., and M. Nakamura. 2007. "Business Groups and the Big Push: Meiji Japan's Mass Privatization and Subsequent Growth." *NBER Working Paper* No. W13171.

Morris, D. 1967. *Naked Ape*. New York: Dell.

Moynahan, B. 1994. *The Russian Century: A History of the Last Hundred Years*. New York: Random House.

Murphy, R., and Murphy, Y. 1986. "Northern Shoshone." In *Handbook of North American Indians* 11, ed. Warren L. D'Azevedo and William C. Sturtevant. Washington, DC: Smithsonian Institution.

National Opinion Research Center. 1999. *Gambling Impact and Behavior Study*. Chicago.

Nemet-Nejat, K. 1998. *Daily Life in Ancient Mesopotamia*. London: Greenwood.

Newman, P. C. 2000. *Empire of the Bay: The Company of Adventurers that Seized a Continent*. New York: Penguin Putnam.

Nisbett, R. E., and Cohen, D. 1996. *Culture of Honor: the Psychology of Violence in the South*. Boulder, CO: Westview.

North, D., J. Wallis, and B. Weingast. 2006. "A Conceptual Framework for Interpreting Recorded Human History." *George Mason University Mercatus Center Working Paper* 75.

Office of Juvenile Justice and Delinquency Prevention. 2006. *Highlights of the 2004 National Youth Gang Survey*. U.S. Department of Justice.

Ohno, T. 1988. *Toyota Production System: Beyond Large-Scale Production*. Portland: Productivity.

Okada, T. 2007. "A Comment on Nishimura, Nakajima, and Kiyota's 'Does the Natural Selection Mechanism Still Work in Severe Recessions?' Examination of the Japanese Economy in the 1990s." *NBER Working Paper* No. W13298.

Olson, M. 1984. *The Rise and Decline of Nations: Economic Growth, Stagflation, and Social Rigidities*. New Haven: Yale University Press.

———. 1993. "Dictatorship, Democracy, and Development." *The American Political Science Review* 87, no. 3: 567–76.

Orwell, G. 1945. *Animal Farm*. London: Secker and Warburg.

Packer, C., and A. Pusey "Divided We Fall: Cooperation Among Lions." *Scientific American*: 52–59.

Palmer, R. R, J. Colton, and L. Kramer. 2003. *History of the Modern World*, 9th ed. New York: Knopf.

Paltsev, S., J. M. Reilly, H. D. Jacoby, A. C. Gurgel, G. E. Metcalf, A. P. Sokolov, and J. F. Holak. 2007. "Assessment of U.S. Cap-and-Trade Proposals." NBER Working Paper No. W13176.

Parker, I. 2007. "Our Far-Flung Correspondents: Swingers: Bonobos are Celebrated as Peace-loving, Matriarchal, and Sexually Liberated. Are They?" *The New Yorker*.

Partnoy, F. 2004. *Infectious Greed: How Deceit and Risk Corrupted the Financial Markets*. New York: Holt Paperbacks.

Patterson, N., D. Richeter, S. Gnerre, E. Lander, and D. Reich. 2006. "Genetic Evidence for Complex Speciation of Humans and Chimpanzees." *Nature* 441: 1103–8.

Pautzke, C. G., and C. W. Oliver. 1997. "Development of the Individual Fishing Quota Program for Sablefish and Halibut Longline Fisheries off Alaska." *National Research Council's Committee to Review Individual Fishing Quotas.* Anchorage, Alaska. Presented to North Pacific Fishery Management Council, Anchorage, September 4. Document revised October 8, 1997.

Paxton, R. O. 2004. *The Anatomy of Fascism.* New York: Knopf.

Peek, J., and E. Rosengren. 2005. "Unnatural Selection: Perverse Incentives and the Misallocation of Credit in Japan." *American Economic Review,* 1144–66.

Penso de la Vega, J. *Confusion e confusions.* 1688. Reprint New York: Wiley Investment Classics, 1996.

Peters, E. 1992. *St. Peter's Fair: The Fourth Chronicle of Brother Cadfael.* New York: Mysterious.

Pettigrew, J. 1975. *Robber Noblemen: A Study of the Political System of the Sikh Jats.* London: Routledge & Kegan Paul.

Piketty, T., and E. Saez. 2003. "Income Inequality in the United States, 1913–1998." *Quarterly Journal of Economics* 118, no. 1: 1–39.

Plato. 1945. *Republic.* Translated and introduced by F. Cornford. NY: Oxford University Press.

Polanyi, K. 1944. *The Great Transformation.* Boston: Beacon.

Polanyi, K., and A. Conrad. 1957. *Trade and Market in the Early Empires: Economies in History and Theory.* Lawrence, KS: Free/Falcon's Wing.

Popp, D. 2005. "Uncertain R&D and the Porter Hypothesis." *Contributions to Economic Analysis & Policy* 4, no. 1: 6.

Posner, E. 2000. "Law and the Emotions." *University of Chicago Law and Economics Working Paper* 103.

Posner, R. 2006. "A Review of Steven Shavell's *Foundations of Economic Analysis of Law.*" *Journal of Economic Literature* 44, no. 2: 405–14.

Potts, R. 1996. "Evolution and Climate Variability." *Science* 271: 922.

Prichard, J. B., ed. 1958. *The Ancient Near East: An Anthology of Texts and Pictures.* Princeton University Press.

Provine, W. 1986. *Sewall Wright and Evolutionary Biology.* Chicago: University of Chicago Press.

Pryce-Jones, D. 2002. *The Closed Circle: An Interpretation of the Arabs.* Chicago: Ivan R. Dee.

Putnam, R. 2000. *Bowling Alone: The Collapse and Revival of American Community.* Simon & Schuster.

Pynchon, T. R. 1984. "Is it O.K. to be a Luddite?" *The New York Times Book Review,* 40–41.

Rance, R. 2006. "Hamas Wins Out Over PLO Corruption." *Socialist Outlook.*

Rawls, J. 2001 *Justice as Fairness.* Cambridge, MA: Harvard University Press.

Remnick, D. 1994. *Lenin's Tomb: The Last Days of the Soviet Empire.* New York: Vintage Books.

Reppetto, T. 2006. *Bringing Down the Mob: The War Against the American Mafia.* New York: Henry Holt and Co.

Ricardo, D. 1817. *On the Principles of Political Economy and Taxation.* London: John Murray.

Richard, K. 1999. *Human Career: Human Biological and Cultural Origins,* 2nd ed. Chicago: University Of Chicago Press.

Richardson, E. 1999. "The Struggle for Sobriety: Anti-Alcohol Campaigning Under Gorbachev and Yeltsin." *Research Papers in Russian and East European Studies* No. REES99/1.

Richerson, P. 2007. *Rethinking Paleoantropology: A World Queerer than We Supposed*. Draft manuscript.

Roberts, J. 2004. *The Modern Firm: Organizational Design for Performance and Growth*. New York: Oxford University Press.

Roemer, J. 1986. *Value, Exploitation and Class*. Washington, DC: Taylor & Francis.

Rolvaag, E. 1927. *Giants in the Earth*. New York: Harper.

Romotsky, G., and S. Romotsky. 1976. *Los Angeles Barrio Calligraphy*. Los Angeles: Dawson's Book Shop.

Rosen, J. 1997. "The Social Police." *New Yorker*, 170–81.

Rosen, W. 2007. *Justinian's Flea: Plague, Empire and the Birth of Europe*. New York: Viking.

Rosenberg, N., and L. E. Birdsell, Jr. 1986. *How the West Grew Rich: The Economic Transformation of the Industrial World*. New York: Basic Books.

Roth, A. E. 2006. "Repugnance as a Constraint on Markets." *NBER Working Paper* No. W12702.

Rozin, P., and T. A. Vollmecke. 1986. "Food Likes and Dislikes." *Ann Rev Nutr.* 6: 433–56.

Rubin, P. H., and C. W. Paul. 1979. "An Evolutionary Model of Tastes for Risk." *Economic Inquiry* 17: 585–96.

Sachs, S. E. 2006. "From St. Ives to Cyberspace: The Modern Distortion of the Medieval 'Law Merchant.'" *American University International Law Review* 21, no. 5: 685–812.

Sahlins, M. 1972. *Stone Age Economics*. Chicago: Aldine.

Sanfey, A. et al. 2003. "The Neural Basis of Economic Decision-Making in the Ultimatum Game." *Science* 300, no. 5626: 1755–58.

Schiller, R. 2002. "From Efficient Market Theory to Behavioral Finance." *Cowles Discussion Paper* 1385.

Schmidt, F. 2000. "Albania's Pharaoh and His Pyramids." *RFE/RL Balkan Report* 4, no. 42 http://www.nettime.org/Lists-Archives/nettime-l-0006/msg00030.html.

Schumpeter, J. 1942. *Capitalism, Socialism, and Democracy*. New York: Harper and Brothers.

Scranton, P. 1983. *Proprietary Capitalism: The Textile Manufacture at Philadelphia, 1800–1885*. New York: Cambridge University Press.

Segerstrale, U., 2001. *Defenders of the Truth: The Sociobiology Debate*. New York: Oxford University Press.

Serchuk, F. M., and S. E. Wigley. 1992. "Assessment and Management of the Georges Bank Cod Fishery: An Historical Review and Evaluation." *Journal of Northwest Atlantic Fishery Science* 13: 25–52.

Shimer, R. 2007. "Daron Acemoglu, 2005 John Bates Clark Medalist." *Journal of Economic Perspectives* 21, no. 1: 191–208.

Shiue, C., and W. Keller "Markets in China and Europe on the Eve of the Industrial Revolution." *American Economic Review* 97, no. 4: 1189–1216.

Shkolnikov, V., M. McKee, D. A. Leon. 2001. "Changes in Life Expectancy in Russia in the mid-1990s." *Lancet* 357, no. 9260: 917–21.

Sinn, H. W. 2007. "Public Policies Against Global Warming." *NBER Working Paper* No. W13454.

Smith, A. 1776. *The Wealth of Nations*. London: Methuen and Co., Ltd.

Smith, V. L. 1962. "An Experimental Study of Competitive Market Behavior." *The Journal of Political Economy* 70, no. 2: 111–37.

————. 1982. "Markets as Economizers of Information: Experimental Examination of the 'Hayek Hypothesis.'" *Economic Inquiry* 20, no. 2: 165–79.

Smith, V. L., G. L. Suchanek, and A. W. Williams. 1988. "Bubbles, Crashes, and Endogenous Expectations in Experimental Spot Asset Markets." *Econometrica* 56, no. 5: 1119–51.

Sobel, D. 2005. *Longitude: The True Story of a Lone Genius Who Solved the Greatest Scientific Problem of his Time*. New York: Walker & Company.

Sobel, R. 1974. *The Entrepreneurs: Explorations Within the American Business Tradition*. New York: Weybright & Talley.

Soffer, O., J. Adovasio, and D. Hyland. 2000. "The 'Venus' Figurines." *Current Anthropology* 41, no. 4: 511ff.

Soler, M., J. J. Soler, J. G. Martinez, and A. P. Moller. 1995. "Magpie Host Manipulation by Great Spotted Cuckoos: Evidence for an Avian Mafia?" *Evolution* 49: 770–75.

Specter, M. 2007. "Letter from Moscow: Kremlin, Inc.: Why are Vladimir Putin's opponents dying?" *The New Yorker* 50–63.

Spencer, H. 1896. *The Principles of Biology*, Vol. 2. New York: D. Appleton and Company.

Spillane, J. 2000. *Cocaine: From Modern Marvel to Modern Menace in the United States, 1884–1920*. New York: Johns Hopkins University Press.

Stephenson, D., ed. 2000. *The Maslow Business Reader*. New York: Wiley.

Szathmary, E., and J. Maynard Smith. 1995. "The Major Evolutionary Transitions." *Nature* 374: 227–32.

Tawney, R. H. 1926. *Religion and the Rise of Capitalism*. Harcourt, Brace & World, Inc.

Temin, P. 2001. "A Market Economy in the Early Roman Empire." *The Journal of Roman Studies* 91: 169–81.

Temin, P., and H. Voth. 2004. "Riding the South Sea Bubble." *American Economic Review* 94, no. 5: 1654–68.

Thomas, E. 1958. *The Harmless People*. New York: Random House Vintage Books.

Thomas, G. 2007. *Gideon's Spies, Third Edition: The Secret History of the Mossad*. St. Martin's Griffin.

Thomas, J. P., and T. Worrall. 2002. "Gift-giving, Quasi-credit and Reciprocity." *CESIfo Working Paper* 687.

Thomson, D. 2006. *The Whole Equation: A History of Hollywood*. London: Vintage.

Thurow, L. 1985. *The Zero-Sum Solution*. Simon and Schuster.

Travers, J., and S. Milgram. 1969. "An Experimental Study of the Small World Problem." *Sociometry* 32, no. 4: 425–43.

Trivers, R. 1971. "The Evolution of Reciprocal Altruism." *Quarterly Review of Biology* 46: 35–57.

Trivers, R. L. 1985. *Social Evolution*. Menlo Park, CA: Benjamin/Cummings.

Tyack, D., and L. Cuban. 1995. *Tinkering Toward Utopia: A Century of Public School Reform*. Cambridge, MA: Harvard University Press.

Unger, H. 2007. "Criminal Justice in America." *Policy Today, California Edition* 4, no. 3: 6–10.

United States Department of State. 2006. "Country Reports on Terrorism 2005." *Office of the Coordinator for Counterterrorism U.S. Dept. of State Publication* 11324.

U.S. Environmental Protection Agency. 2001. "The United States Experience with Economic Incentives for Protecting the Environment." *EPA-240-R-01-001 of the Office of Policy, Economics and Innovation*.

U.S. National Research Council. 1999. *Pathological Gambling: A Critical Review*.

Vayda, A. P. 1967. "Pomo Trade Feasts." In *Tribal and Peasant Economies*, ed. by G. Dalton. Austin: University of Texas Press.

Virgil, D. 1983. "Chicano Gangs: One Response to Mexican Urban Adaptation in the Los Angeles Area." *Urban Anthropology*, 45–75.

Vise, D., and M. Malseed. 2006. *The Google Story: Inside the Hottest Business, Media, and Technology Success of Our Time*. Delta.

Vogel, E. 1979. *Japan as Number One*. Boston: Harvard University Press.

von Glahn, R. 2005. "The Origins of Paper Money in China." In *The Origins of Value: The Financial Innovations that Created Modern Capital Markets*, ed. W. N. Goetzmann and K. G. Rouwenhorst. Oxford University Press.

Wade, N. 2006. *Before the Dawn*. New York: Penguin.

Waters, F. 1963. *The Book of the Hopi*. New York: Viking.

Watson, J. 2007. *Strategy: An Introduction to Game Theory*, 2nd ed. New York: W. W. Norton.

Watts, D., and S. Strogatz. 1998. "Collective Dynamics of 'Small-world' Networks." *Nature* 393: 440–42.

Weatherford, J. 2004. *Genghis Khan and the Making of the Modern World*. New York: Crown Publishers.

Weber, M. 1930. *The Protestant Ethic and the Spirit of Capitalism*. London: Allen and Unwin.

White, T., and G. Ganley. 1983. "The 'Death of a Princess' Controversy." *Research Report P-83-9, Program on Information Resources Policy*, Harvard University. http://pirp.harvard.edu/pdf-blurb.asp?id=129.

Wilder, L. I. 1935. *Little House on the Prairie*.

Wilkinson, G. 1984. "Reciprocal Food Sharing in the Vampire Bat." *Nature* 308, no. 8: 181–84.

Williams, G., 1966. *Adaptation and Natural Selection*. Princeton: Princeton University Press.

Williamson, O. E. 1975. *Markets and Hierarchies*. Simon and Schuster.

Wilson, E. O., 1975. *Sociobiology: The New Synthesis*. Cambridge: Harvard University Press.

Wilson, E. O., and B. Hölldobler. 2005. "Eusociality: Origin and Consequences." *Proc. Nat. Acad. Sci. USA* 102: 13367–71.

Wilson, J. Q. 1990. "Against the Legalization of Drugs." *Commentary* 89: 21–28.

Wilson, S. 1988. *Feuding, Conflict and Banditry in Nineteenth-century Corsica*. Cambridge, UK: Cambridge University Press.

Wittman, D. 2006. *Economic Foundations of Law and Organization*. Cambridge University Press.

Wolfers, J., and E. Zitzewitz. 2004. "Prediction Markets." *Journal of Economic Perspectives* 18, no. 2: 107–26.

Wood, C. 1992. *The Bubble Economy: Japan's Extraordinary Speculative Boom of the '80s and the Dramatic Bust of the '90s*. Atlantic Monthly.

Yunus, M. 1999. "The Grameen Bank." *Scientific American*, 114–19.

Zinn, H. 2005. *A People's History of the United States*, Vol. I. New York: Harper.

Index

LaVergne, TN USA
11 April 2011
223786LV00001B/2/P